THE OFFICIAL
Formula 1™
SEASON REVIEW 2008

FOREWORD BY BERNIE ECCLESTONE

F1 Formula 1 (and device), F1, Formula One, FIA Formula
One World Championship (and device) and Grand Prix are
trademarks of Formula One Licensing B.V., a Formula One
Group Company, and are used under licence from Formula
One Administration Limited, a Formula One Group Company.

Published in November 2008

A catalogue record for this book is available
from the British Library

ISBN 978 1 84425 566 5

Library of Congress control no. 2008926783

Editor Bruce Jones
Managing Editor Steve Rendle

Design Lee Parsons, Richard Parsons, James Robertson

Contributors Adam Cooper (season overview and race
reports), Tony Dodgins (round table, teams' technical review
and race report panels)

Photographs All by LAT (Steven Tee, Lorenzo Bellanca,
Charles Coates, Glenn Dunbar, Steve Etherington and
Andrew Ferraro)
Group Operations Manager LAT Tim Wright
Digital Technicians LAT Steve Carpenter, Matt Smith

Technical illustrations Paul Laguette
www.studiopdesign.com
Illustrations Alan Eldridge

Publishing Manager Nairn Miller
Publishing Directors Peter Higham, Mark Hughes

Published by Haynes Publishing
in association with Haymarket Consumer Media

Haynes Publishing, Sparkford, Yeovil,
Somerset BA22 7JJ, UK
Tel: +44 (0) 1963 442030
Fax: +44 (0) 1963 440001
E-mail: sales@haynes.co.uk
Website: www.haynes.co.uk

Haymarket Consumer Media, Teddington Studios,
Broom Road, Teddington, Middlesex TW11 9BE, UK
Tel: +44 (0) 208 267 5000
Fax: +44 (0) 208 267 5022
E-mail: F1Review@haymarket.com
Website: www.haymarket.com

Printed and bound by J. H. Haynes & Co. Ltd,
Sparkford, Yeovil, Somerset BA22 7JJ, UK

CONTENTS

THE TEAMS 44

The year started with 11 teams, but Super Aguri fell by the wayside. We bring you the inside story on how teams worked their way to the front, or not, according to their technical chiefs, with each entry illustrated with superb graphics

THE RACES 78

Each of the year's 18 grands prix brought to you with superb photography, and with the race reports augmented with added insight from the drivers and team personnel on what really went on

THE STATISTICS 260

The 2008 World Championship table, showing on a race-by-race basis who finished where. Two further pages packed with stats show how today's drivers compare with the stars of yesteryear in the all-time rankings, in terms of grand prix wins, race starts, pole positions, fastest laps and even points scored

FOREWORD

It's been a good season, and I don't think you could ask for more. I think it's been nice to be able to come to a race and not say 'that guy's definitely going to win'.

It was difficult to know who I would have liked to win the World Championship. I felt sorry for Lewis last year, because he should have won it. And basically the team was the reason he didn't win. This year I thought it would be terrible if Felipe didn't win, because it was the team that let him down. Neither of the drivers has done anything that didn't warrant being champion.

Lewis is a race driver, as simple as that. I think he's made a lot of people sit up and take notice of F1, people that maybe wouldn't have done so before. He's one of those guys that gets a lot of press, which is good for us. And Felipe is absolutely one of the top three drivers.

Kimi woke up at the end of the season! Without a doubt he's extremely talented and gets the job done when he's motivated. It's the same for Fernando. It was nothing to do with him, as it was his car that didn't perform earlier in the season. I was the one who pushed BMW to take Kubica, so I'm a big supporter of him. If he was in a consistently competitive car you might well have seen him World Champion this year.

Vettel is a superstar. When you think of the car he was in, he's done a magic job. He's going to be World Champion. He's very open, and I hope he stays that way. I hope he doesn't get too corporate! Toro Rosso have done a great job. I can't say that they're underfinanced, but they certainly don't enjoy the finance that a lot of the teams have, or the support.

David Coulthard has been fantastic for F1. He's loved worldwide, and I've never heard anybody say anything bad about him. He would have been an ideal World Champion, obviously, so I wish him well.

Valencia and Singapore were great. The latter was good for Singapore and good for F1. You don't want too many street races, but three or four is about right. Next year we'll have Abu Dhabi, which will be good too.

We're trying to get the teams to save the necessity to spend money to be competitive. I'm quite sure some of the board members are going to sit down and ask what are we spending this on? They're still getting more coverage than they would get whatever they spent anywhere else. Notwithstanding that, why do they need to spend? The answer is they don't.

I don't think anybody knows how things will end up next year. If you really want to drastically reduce costs and have really super competitive racing, you don't change the regulations for five years. By then everybody's caught up, but we don't seem to want to do that!

BERNIE ECCLESTONE

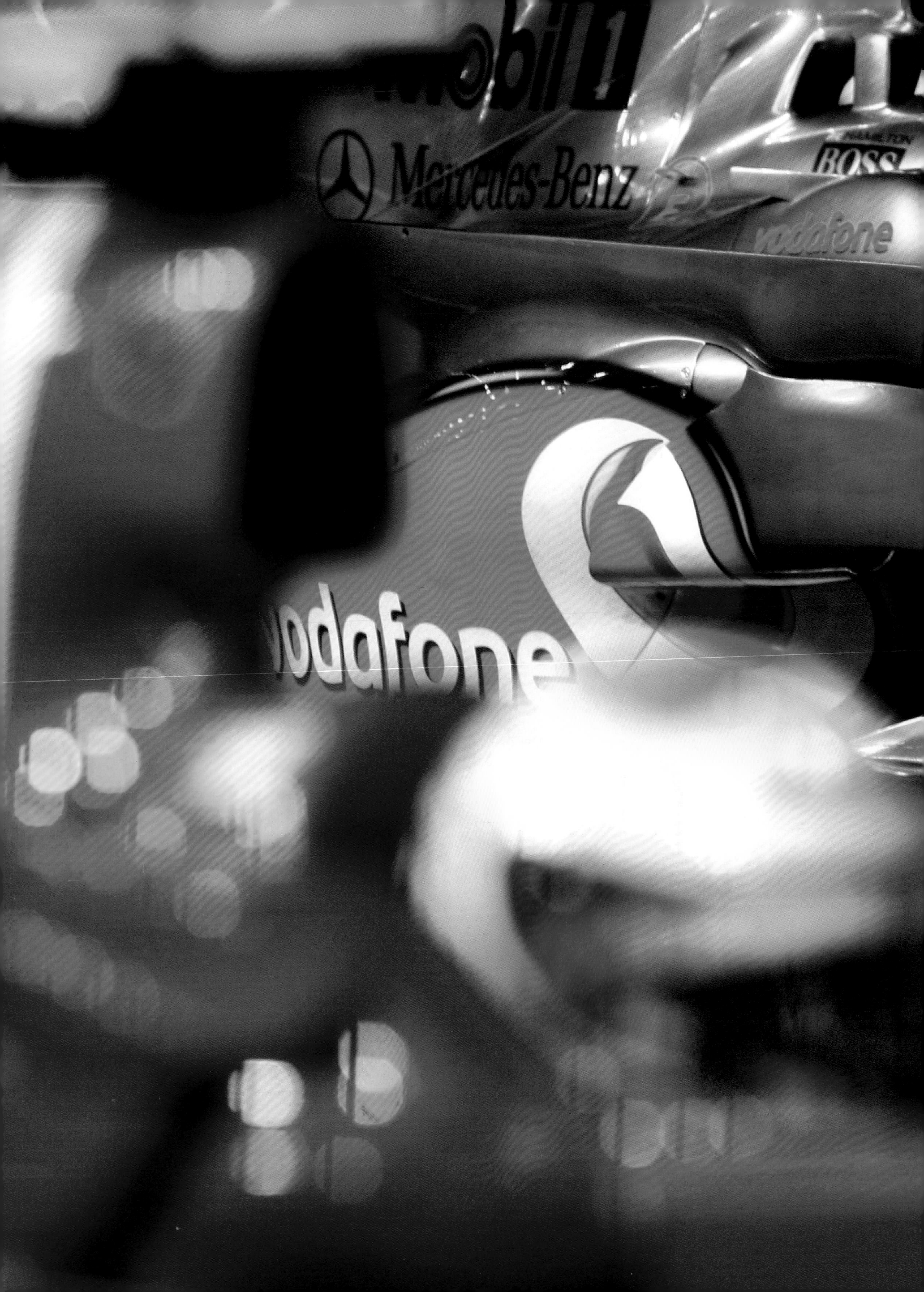
Mercedes-Benz
BOSS
vodafone
vodafone

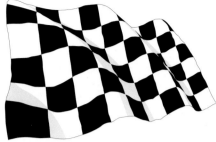

REFLECTING ON THE 2008
FORMULA ONE SEASON
A CLASSIC YEAR OF RACING

THE SEASON

Formula One is in rude health. There were some brilliant races in 2008, teams rising to the top and young guns proving their worth. And there was that stunning final grand prix

There have been many tense World Championship showdowns over the decades, but nothing has ever matched what we witnessed in the closing laps in Brazil this year. Will we ever see anything like it again? It would be nice to imagine that we might be thrilled by another last-corner title resolution, by just a single point, in the next year or two, but you wouldn't want to bet on it.

This 2008 season was simply sensational, marked by a string of entertaining races. An unusually large number of rain-struck events certainly helped, but the fact is that the racing was close and unpredictable throughout the year. McLaren and Ferrari generally led the way, but the other teams were so close that any slip-up would often drop a driver of one of the top cars right out of the points. Perhaps the most fascinating statistic is that in 18 attempts only three races saw only McLaren or Ferrari drivers on the podium.

Five of the 11 teams won grands prix in 2008, and four others earned podium finishes. The only team that went the distance to miss out was Force India – and even for them, a fourth place at Monaco went astray through no fault of Adrian Sutil.

ABOVE Everyone adored the new street circuit in Singapore, but none more so than Fernando Alonso who got his season and Renault's back on track with a surprise win there

The season included two new grands prix, and both proved to be huge successes. The European GP at Valencia was better than many had anticipated, but it was all too clear that the venue had been completed in a hurry and it will get better over time. On the down side, the race proved to be less than exciting, with virtually no passing and, against expectations, no safety-car periods to spice up the action.

By contrast, the Singapore GP was a wonderful event, with non-stop action ensuring that the sport's first-ever night race was a TV spectacular that brought extra attention to F1 around the world. The facilities were good, the organisers eager to please and everything ran like clockwork. And, most importantly, F1 cars looked sensational at night, spitting blue flames from their red-hot exhausts, and leaving showers of sparks in their wake as they bottomed out on the track's bumpy surface.

Thankfully, there were no major off-track controversies that had a direct impact on the racing, and there was no repeat of last year's spying scandals. In fact, with Jean Todt taking a step back and handing the reins of the Prancing Horse to Stefano Domenicali, there was a new spirit of co-operation between Ferrari

and the other teams, and notably a thawing in the frosty relationship with McLaren.

Indeed, Ferrari President Luca di Montezemolo was instrumental in setting up the Formula One Teams Association, becoming its first Chairman. Having Ferrari onside with all the other teams was essential as concerns over costs, exacerbated by the global economic crisis in the autumn, came into sharp focus. For the first time, everyone recognised that action had to be taken, although FIA President Max Mosley had his own ideas about which direction the sport should take.

Mosley made the global headlines in April for all the wrong reasons, after a British tabloid newspaper trapped him in a sex scandal. It seemed initially that there was no way that he would survive this personal crisis, and several manufacturers were quick to voice their concerns. Even Bernie Ecclestone, coming under pressure from all sides, distanced himself from his old friend. However, Mosley survived the difficult first few weeks, earned himself a vote of support from his FIA colleagues, and finally won a legal case against the newspaper concerned.

The FIA had been embroiled in a serious conflict

RULE CHANGES FOR 2008

For 2008, the FIA made some significant rule changes to which the teams and drivers had to adjust. And, as is so often the case, following much debate over the winter months there was very little change to the actual racing.

From this season, all teams had to use a standard electronic control unit, the 'brain' of the car that controls all of its functions. Put out to tender by the FIA, it was supplied by McLaren Electronic Systems. Some teams expressed reservations about the choice of a subsidiary company of a rival team, and there were some teething problems with the SECUs in testing. However, there were no complaints after the start of the season.

In conjunction with the introduction of the SECU, the FIA banned electronic driver aids. That meant no more traction control, launch control or engine-braking assistance. In effect, the SECU has allowed the FIA to properly police what the teams are doing. In the past, when such systems were outlawed, there was always some doubt about the effectiveness of the ban.

Against expectations, teams found that braking, rather than traction, was the key difference in 2008, although it's fair to say that while drivers got used to the lack of traction control there were more incidents in the early grands prix, and also in the later wet events.

From this season, teams had to use the same gearbox for four consecutive grand prix Saturdays and Sundays (Friday was regarded as testing, and therefore a different gearbox could be used). The only parts that the team could change between races were the actual gear ratios. If any other part was replaced, or the entire gearbox was changed, the driver concerned would be given a five-place grid penalty.

As previously, all teams had to use the same engine for two grand prix weekends (ie, Saturday and Sunday), and an engine change resulted in a 10-place grid penalty. However, for 2008 each driver was allowed to play a 'joker', and make his first change of the season without penalty, although the exemption did not apply for the final race of the year in Brazil.

In recent seasons, the fuel-burn period in the third qualifying session was difficult to explain to the public. However, the concept was consigned to history, and in 2008 the cars were no longer refuelled after Q3. Instead, the 10 drivers who made it through to Q3 took on the fuel they required for their planned race strategy, plus the fuel they used in qualifying.

BELOW Robert Kubica was a massive hit in 2008, featuring on the edges of the title battle, and even leading it after his win in Canada

with McLaren in 2007 and, while the spying affair had been consigned to history, there remains a certain degree of tension between the two. That was exacerbated by a series of penalties applied to both its drivers – Lewis Hamilton and Heikki Kovalainen – during the course of the season. There was always a good argument from the FIA side, and on occasions, as in the case of the Montréal pitlane accident, there was no defence. But even neutrals had to agree that sometimes it appeared that Hamilton in particular was subject to an extraordinary degree of scrutiny.

Thankfully, in the end, none of that mattered. Hamilton did just what he had to do in the Brazilian finale, earning fifth place and beating Felipe Massa by a single point. It was a superb second year from the Englishman, who bounced back from the bitter disappointment of the previous season and emerged as a stronger and more mature driver, better able to cope with the ups and downs of a long season.

The ups were many. He won the opening race in Australia and followed up with brilliant wet-weather successes at Monaco and Silverstone, then two further wins in Germany and China. Five wins out of 18 doesn't sound like a great strike rate, but it reflects just how competitive the season was, and also just how many hurdles he had to negotiate. Most frustrating of all, Hamilton lost a hard-earned Belgian GP win to a 25s time penalty after, once again, his wet-weather prowess had paid dividends.

There were mistakes of course, and his crash in the Montréal pitlane was the most blatant. It cost him not only a big haul of points in Canada, but also ruined the next race in France. A 10-place grid penalty was bad enough, but in trying to make up lost ground on the first lap at Magny-Cours, he ran off the road and was penalised again for gaining an advantage. In Japan, a penalty applied after a first-corner incident proved to be expensive.

However, it was made worse by the fact that having emerged from the Turn 1 mess in third place, Hamilton then skated off the road a few corners later while trying to pressure Fernando Alonso. That put him into a position where he was battling with Massa, which in turn led to a collision (for which Massa was penalised) that ultimately cost the British driver any chance of points.

We had seen that impatience before in Bahrain, where after a bad start Hamilton not once but twice hit the back of Alonso's car on the opening lap. In the Italian GP at Monza, he made a silly tyre decision in damp qualifying that ensured he took away only two points from a race that he could have won. Fortunately, Hamilton had no mechanical gremlins all year, and the only outside event that denied him points was a puncture in Hungary.

It was by no means a perfect season, but it was easy to forget that it was only his second on the sport's largest stage. He'd certainly done more than enough to be considered a worthy World Champion.

So too had Massa, though. Having become a contender for pole positions and race wins alongside Michael Schumacher in 2006, he matured further last year, and again this season. The Brazilian ended

OPPOSITE Sebastian Vettel served notice that Lewis Hamilton will have to look over his shoulder in 2008, by winning the Italian GP

ABOVE The other new addition to the calendar was the street circuit around the docks in Valencia. This is McLaren's Heikki Kovalainen

RIGHT Felipe Massa's grimace says it all, after he was comprehensively beaten by Hamilton in the penultimate race in China to leave him with a seven-point deficit

the year with six victories, although the Belgian GP was a gift from the FIA on a day when he was left trailing behind not only the McLaren driver, but also his own team-mate Kimi Räikkönen.

Elsewhere, they were solid successes, other than in France, where a mechanical problem for Räikkönen led to the two cars trading the lead. Massa also put in some brilliant pole laps, notably in Monaco where previously he had underperformed, and again under the most intense pressure in his home race, where his race performance was exemplary.

However, there were also bad days. Massa crashed on the first lap in Australia and later had an unnecessary collision with David Coulthard, then he spun off in Malaysia. He was hopeless at a wet Silverstone, although the team took the rap for some bad tyre decisions. His clumsy punt of Hamilton in Japan was also like something out of a Formula Ford race. Yet, overall, he showed signs of increasing maturity, on and off the track. His calm demeanour after that last-minute defeat in Brazil spoke volumes.

So, what of the team-mates of the title challengers? It was a bad year for Räikkönen, who had barely put a foot wrong on his way to the title in 2007. Like some other drivers, he found it hard to adapt to a new era of no traction control, and struggled all year to adjust the car to his liking. He also found it harder than Massa to get the most out of the tyres in qualifying.

Räikkönen scored early wins in Malaysia and Spain, and was well ahead of Massa in France when his exhaust broke. He was also leading at the pit exit in Montréal when Hamilton thumped him. Things began to go awry in the second half of the season as Räikkönen tried to adapt to changes made to the car. He made a silly mistake in Valencia, leaving the pits before the signal, but then his engine failed anyway. He was fast in Spa, but got caught out when it rained,

crashing spectacularly when he tried to keep up with Hamilton. He also went off in Singapore while running fifth. Most thought that by then he was going through the motions, but he outpaced Massa in China before handing him two vital points.

His countryman Heikki Kovalainen had a tough first year at McLaren. Mentally scarred after his difficult year under Flavio Briatore at Renault, he was quick straight away, but found it hard to deal with the steamroller that was Lewis Hamilton. He lost good points in Australia to a safety-car situation and then had a series of disasters, with a huge crash caused by a wheel failure in Spain, a first-lap puncture after a touch with Räikkönen in Turkey (where he could have won), and electronic gremlins on the grid at Monaco that stranded him at the back. It was hard to recover momentum after that, but Kovalainen took a fine pole at Silverstone and won in Hungary after Massa's engine failed. He also had a good run to second in difficult conditions at Monza. Kovalainen had his own engine failure in Japan, but his season was summed up by the Chinese GP, where in the first stint his incorrectly marked front tyres were fitted the wrong way round. It can only get better in 2009.

It was a wonderful year for BMW Sauber, and for much of it the team clearly had the third-fastest package in the field, and at times the white and blue cars could slip in among the Ferraris and McLarens. However, by the end of the year, others had caught up, notably Renault and Toro Rosso. Much to Robert Kubica's frustration, the team's development programme failed to match that of others, and the Pole's outside chance of stealing the title faded away.

Nevertheless, Kubica did himself a power of good with consistently strong performances, and his first win in Canada was well deserved. He also made no mistakes, other than at Silverstone when the car

BELOW Rubens Barrichello scored a third place for Honda at Silverstone, but ended the year unsure whether he'd remain in F1

OPPOSITE TOP Renault had every reason to be delighted in Japan, as Fernando Alonso had scored his second win and Nelson Piquet Jr had come home fourth

OPPOSITE BOTTOM Reigning World Champion Kimi Räikkönen found himself struggling through 2008 and will need to bounce back

swapped ends on the straight in fifth gear, something for which he can hardly be blamed. Nick Heidfeld struggled to match his team-mate's pace for much of the season, but proved adept at bringing the car home. Indeed, he finished every single race. He was particularly good at taking advantage on days when chaos reigned, earning four second places.

Renault got off to a poor start, and Alonso must have rued his decision to return to the team after his 'sabbatical' at McLaren. In the early races, his only satisfaction was the occasional good grid position earned with a low fuel load, but the car improved steadily as the year went on. Luck with the safety car propelled him to a shock win in Singapore, and he took advantage of the mistakes of others to score a well deserved victory in Japan. Over the last six races, he was clearly 'best of the rest', earning 43 points – more than anyone else. His team-mate Nelson Piquet Jr had a tough baptism.

The fifth team to register a win was Scuderia Toro Rosso. After delaying the introduction of its new car until the Monaco GP, the team rose steadily up the grid, propelled by the prodigious talent of Sebastian Vettel. His pole position and victory in the wet at

Monza was the stuff that dreams are made of, and elsewhere he was impressively quick, taking points on eight further occasions. His performance left rookie team-mate Sebastien Bourdais in the shade.

For the rest, it was a year of ups and downs. Toyota's form was erratic, but as usual Jarno Trulli was generally fast in qualifying, while Timo Glock proved to be good at bringing home points. Like Trulli, Mark Webber was usually in the top 10 in qualifying, and he scored some good points for Red Bull Racing earlier in the year, but later the team's fortunes faded as those of Toro Rosso rose. David Coulthard had the consolation of a third place in Canada before making a dignified exit from the sport.

Williams had a year of extremes. The car was quick on temporary and street tracks, and Nico Rosberg rode his luck to take a second-place finish in Singapore and third in Australia. But, elsewhere, the car was often hopelessly uncompetitive. Kazuki Nakajima couldn't match his team-mate's pace, but was good at picking up stray points.

It was a disastrous year for Honda and new team boss Ross Brawn, and eventually all efforts were focused towards 2009. Rubens Barrichello and Jenson Button were embarrassed by the hopeless RA108, although the Brazilian took third place in the wet at Silverstone. Force India showed clear signs of improvement, but the grid was so competitive that Giancarlo Fisichella and Adrian Sutil struggled to get off the back row. Both had some races where they humbled quicker cars, and Sutil was brilliant in the wet at Monaco until Räikkönen took him out. Unlike troubled Super Aguri, the team did at least survive the year in good health.

What a finale, what a season and what a champion. In fact, two top blokes who, all things considered, both deserved to win the title. This post-Schumacher era isn't too bad after all, is it?

OPPOSITE TOP Lewis Hamilton was at his very best when the tracks were slippery, with his drive to victory at Silverstone his best

OPPOSITE BOTTOM The Super Aguri team made it to the grid for the Australian opener, but managed only three more races before folding

BELOW Timo Glock came on strong through 2008 for Toyota. Here, he looks down on the spectacular Singapore street circuit

THE PANEL

STEFANO DOMENICALI
TEAM PRINCIPAL, FERRARI

JOHN HOWETT
PRESIDENT, TOYOTA

MARK HUGHES
JOURNALIST, *AUTOSPORT*

ADAM PARR
CHIEF EXECUTIVE OFFICER, WILLIAMS

MARIO THEISSEN
BMW MOTORSPORT DIRECTOR

MURRAY WALKER
BROADCASTER

MARTIN WHITMARSH
CHIEF OPERATING OFFICER, McLAREN

CHAIRED BY
TONY DODGINS
JOURNALIST, *AUTOSPORT*

ROUND TABLE

With an eye on the future, there was much meeting of minds in 2008. We gathered some of the key players to discuss the highs and lows of the Formula One scene

Everyone can see that Formula One is a fast-moving world, a sport and a multi-billion dollar business performing on a global stage. It's rare to find time to sit down and analyse all of its many pros and cons, but Tony Dodgins organised our second annual *Round Table* feature, held during F1's first visit to Singapore, and the hot topics included how grands prix should be refereed, the accessibility of F1 and how to make it more appealing to a new generation of fans, the rights and wrongs of customer cars, the likely impact of the economic downturn, freedom of speech and why celebrations should be more exuberant, plus, of course, whether the wholesale regulation changes will make the racing better in 2009.

Please note that the panelists are denoted by their initials, with Murray Walker being differentiated from Martin Whitmarsh by being listed as MWa.

TD: *How important are events like the Singapore GP? Also, as the American and European economies struggle, is it coincidence that Formula One is moving further east, or simply shrewd planning?*

AP: I don't think it's shrewd planning, but it's related, as the money in the world today, the liquidity, is in the Middle East and Asia. The cost of staging an F1 race is so phenomenal that without government support it is virtually impossible, and you can't really get that in Europe. So, I think it's inevitable that the races are migrating. It's also where the markets are, so it's good for everyone.

TD: *What about new circuits versus the traditional?*

JH: I think you need a mix. We need some of the classic racing circuits, and then a venue like Singapore is a total offer to the public and sponsors. Yes, it's phenomenal, but we need to maintain a balance.

SD: I totally agree. We need to have a balance between the historical grands prix at real tracks and these new sites.

TD: *With economists talking about the biggest downturn for 60 years, what are manufacturer sales figures like and what will the impact be for F1?*

MT: As car manufacturers, we are affected, but it impacts on the entire world. It's a situation we have to cope with and we have a good chance to get over it. Exploring new territories like the races in upcoming markets in Asia is a vital and substantial move for F1 in order not just to keep the business growing but also to foster it for the future.

TD: *What about the impact on your budgets?*

MT: It's definitely there. Fortunately, from a team

perspective, we were able to reduce our budget significantly in the past three or four years due to the regulations, especially on the engine side. And, so far it doesn't affect, and won't affect, the immediate future of our team. But it's important to maintain this commercial strength and it's definitely very difficult at the moment.

MW: Inevitably there is a delay, and I think F1 could be lulled into thinking that it's partially immune. The reality is that lots of teams have two-year or three-year contracts with partners and sponsors and so you do feel slightly isolated from it. The big world does affect us though, and when we get to renewals or replacements it's going to be incredibly difficult. That's going to take some time to wash through, but certainly the automotive manufacturers have committed to a battle in F1 that has contributed to the inflation of budgets. We all thought during the tobacco era that there was a tobacco premium that fuelled F1 and we were all expecting a budget contraction when it was over. Yet the fact is that the manufacturers have come in and driven budgets up. It's not a criticism, just an observation of the reality. They recognise the value of brand differentiation and the value of winning in F1, and were prepared to commit a lot of money and have given us an unprecedented era with the likes of Mercedes-Benz, BMW, Honda, Toyota, Ferrari and Renault all in F1 together. It's never happened before and there's not one of those manufacturers who isn't trying to win.

MT: And there is a second aspect, too, because with the manufacturers coming in to F1, big sponsors have also been brought in.

MW: That's true. The business-to-business funding wasn't present in the tobacco-sponsorship era.

MH: I think the interesting point, whether you accept that it will be in the short term, medium term or long term, is that there will be a contraction of sorts and it's always said that in racing you use whatever budget is available. That's fine, but what happens when it starts to impact on the structure and size of teams?

MW: It may well do, but it's like any business; you have to be flexible and cut costs. Everyone assumes that the automotive manufacturers, especially in their rosier times, just throw buckets of money at it, but that isn't the case. All those businesses are lean and pushing costs every day in all areas. Having said that, I'm not a pessimist and while I think it would be irresponsible not to expect tough times ahead, I also think that F1 has done a spectacularly bad job of developing its business. The fact that we attract this global audience is fairly amazing, and sometimes we don't deserve it because we don't do enough for the spectacle and the entertainment. There is not one dollar spent centrally on marketing the sport and not one sentence of marketing strategy written for our sport, so it's actually a miracle... The basic product must be fundamentally pretty damned good!

I think the recent Formula One Teams Association (FOTA) is one of the most exciting initiatives to happen in F1 in the past 20 years. It's the first time that all of the competitors have come together and said 'let's get real about this business and see how we can work together and improve

it'. It may fail, because other initiatives have. It may fail because of lack of harmony between the teams and the natural competition. It may fail because people pull us apart and there are a lot of people who have an interest in doing so, but if we've got good sense and come together now with a lot of trust and understanding, that will be very positive. We want to beat each other on the track on a Sunday afternoon, but the reality is that we all have common interests and actually want to make the sport better. We want to make it more inviting and create a new audience. The demographics of our audience are probably getting too old and so we've got to do something about that. We ought to be able to. We've got exciting young drivers, people like Sebastian Vettel, Felipe, Nico, Kubica. And we've got a couple of young exciting lads too! So, we've actually got the ingredients to do it and we have to come away from the turgid press conferences and press releases that we have at the circuit and actually do something that excites them. The drivers turn up at press conferences, the format of which hasn't changed for 25 years, and they look bored before they even get there.

MWa: Yes, I agree.

MW: Unfortunately, that comes across. Famously you look at someone like Kimi. People say he's got no personality, but the reality is that Kimi is a really engaging young man when you get him in the right environment and he doesn't feel that he's going to get the same question that he got at the last race and the race before that. We've got to do something about that. We team bosses sometimes denigrate the drivers, but on the whole they are pretty switched on, intelligent, motivated, interesting young people.

TD: *So how do we improve that?*

MW: We have to be creative. You probably need a studio environment on a Thursday evening when they haven't got their mind on other things, a few sexy girls who are going to get the best out of them, get them into a table tennis competition, put on some events. We've got to do all those things because there's a huge ingredient that we don't exploit. Our young drivers are positioned as young, bored automatons – answer some inane questions and go away. And it's not their fault. We, the teams, promoters, organisers, whatever, have got to look at it and say, that's our fault. Within FOTA now, we have the opportunity to start and be a bit more creative, change the show, change the weekends,

Whitmarsh puts his point across that
his team isn't totally against the
concept of customer cars...

save costs, work together and centrally market our sport.
We also have to make sure we don't walk away from the
Silverstones and Monacos.

JH: There is huge opportunity because the tough
companies will want to take a commanding position and
there will be more rationalisation of businesses, and so
rebranding or repositioning in certain markets. For example,
RBS is rebranding ABN AMRO, which means the RBS
master brand is more important. Television advertising is
dying. Everybody is switching off, so sports properties have
a higher emerging value in terms of advertising compared
to conventional advertising. So I think we can either be
pessimistic or say yes there are going to be tough times, but
there's huge opportunity.

TD: *Isn't the corporate environment often blamed for
this perceived lack of personality?*

MWa: I think from the point-of-view of somebody who
spends much of his time these days watching the races on
TV as opposed to being there, it is very important to make
the drivers be seen as individuals. Robert (Kubica) does not
come across well on the television, but when he's talking
to you he's an extremely nice bloke with a well-developed
sense of humour. The same may be true of Kimi, but it
certainly doesn't show. And it means that in that particular
instance we've got to break away from this post-race
thing when they put on clean clothes and sit in front of
the camera and answer boring questions with boring
replies. But that also means I would presume from the team
principals' point-of-view that they have got to be prepared
to allow their drivers more time to talk to the media and be
human beings. And they are really there to be racing drivers
and not cheerful charlies.

TD: *But what is the corporate reality?*

JH: The point for me is that F1 was positioned in the 1970s as
an exclusive brand. Everything is exclusive. If we want to get
a grid pass we have to beg for half a day sometimes and the
reality is that the world has moved on from exclusivity being
something that people actually aspire to, to a much more
level and more transparent and open environment in which
we live. The whole of F1 needs repositioning.

AP: I totally disagree, John. I think F1's kudos comes from
its exclusivity. I believe that the fans should get better access.
They pay a fortune and always will do because it costs a
fortune to put on an F1 race – and to build an F1 car. People
are astonished when I come to Singapore and explain that
Williams is spending five million Singapore dollars per week
to compete in F1. People just gasp. And then they go, 'wow,
that's amazing!' So, ironically, the fact that we are so exclusive
and spend so much money is, I think, what turns people on
about the sport. If we put the same drivers into GP2 cars and
the grid was open for 12 weeks a year, I think it would be as
dull as ditch water.

MW: It depends what you mean by exclusivity. I think we
have to differentiate. As John was saying, we really have to be
a bit more accessible.

JH: A bit more democratic I think, too, to be honest, and
more accessible. It's the way the world is moving, whether we
like it or not.

MT: What do you mean by democratic?

AP: Yes come on, take him on Mario, it's overrated.

JH: I think you have to be much more open and involving to
the public. We tend to be distancing ourselves and saying this
is unique and exclusive.

MWa: They do what John is suggesting in America.

AP: But America is a democracy. America has got this
people-power thing. All their sports are father-and-son stuff,
this is much more…

MWa: What I'm saying is if you went to a NASCAR meeting
or an Indycar meeting you could get much more involved
in what is happening than you can in F1, because the F1
paddock is a closed society.

AP: Quite right too.

TD: *But take a driver who swears, gets excited, has
an incident, makes headlines. What's the corporate
reaction? Are companies worried about that?*

AP: They love it. They love it. They love all the sex, scandals
and rock and roll.

MWa: Well, why don't we have more of it then?

SD: I'm a bit more cautious. They love it, I don't know. If it's
too excessive, no. We have to bear in mind that what we
are doing is in view of everyone. I would add one little point
to what has been said by Martin, John, Adam and Mario.

There is an example at Ferrari where we have a different level of positioning. We have the tifosi – supporters with a certain level of attitude. We have our top clients who are very rich and want to be differentiated from the others, and so I think F1 has to be something like that. Accessible to the people who are pushing with the flags and the caps as well as other areas where we need to keep the exclusivity to develop certain businesses. Martin's point relating to the old-fashioned media events is exactly what our sponsors are trying to do now. We are doing this because sponsors understand they have to be innovative. We don't do the classic media press conference because our new way is more involving clients or businessmen, like our ski event. This is something that we need to do. Not only team-by-team, but in a way that we can promote F1 as a brand.

TD: *Moving on to Monza and the Toro Rosso win, the constructor versus independent topic is a difficult one. How do you see that? Was it a great story for the sport or potentially a problem for those with billion-dollar investment and corporate boards to answer to?*

MW: Well it's both, isn't it. It should be a problem, but it was fantastic for the sport because Vettel is so young and it's a small team. It was fantastic.

MT: As long as he doesn't do it again…

MWa: It was an absolutely fantastic story for the sport. A young man, first time, small team. It was a breath of fresh air.

MH: It was, but where it leads is very dangerous though.

MWa: Most of the general public – and I'm sorry for what I'm about to say – don't want to see the same teams winning all the time, no matter what the sport is. So if you've got something different it's good.

AP: I agree there Murray, but I think…

SD: Maybe he's right, but in Italy I'm not so sure!

MT: Stefano, you can relax. You will not win all the time!

AP: I think there are two myths about this. What Toro Rosso did over that weekend was very impressive. They got the right strategy and we didn't. Then they got the right tyre call and we didn't. We had an opportunity to beat them on that weekend and we didn't, therefore they deserve credit, nothing to do with whether they are a constructor or not. The first myth is that they are a small team. They are not, as the budget of Red Bull Technology to make chassis is probably 70–80% more than Williams. And that chassis design, Adrian Newey's design, is the one they use. In fact, Toro Rosso's budget is more than Williams' budget. So it is simply not true to say that a small team won. A two-team group with a budget of 500 million Euros won a race.

The second thing is, the longer-term impact of customer teams in F1 would be pernicious, because, it just so happens it's Red Bull – stop smiling Martin! Let's just take the nightmare scenario, if Martin had done his deal with David Richards and this year we had two McLaren teams with the kind of performance they have got. Let's suppose that by

going light with two of them, they managed to block the front two rows of the grid. There would be total war. Ferrari would have to have a B team, they would have to go into qualifying tactically, the whole thing would be a nightmare and it would be a matter of time before F1 disintegrated, in my opinion, into A teams and B teams. It would be ruined.

TD: *You have people like Toyota and BMW who have recently made huge investments, with boards to report to, and someone has bought an Adrian Newey car with a Ferrari engine and won a race. How difficult is that for you Mario and John?*

MT: We are not opposed to truly small teams using a car which is not designed and manufactured by themselves, but there are implications on race strategy which we absolutely don't like. If one team effectively controls four cars on the grid, you can do strategic and technical things which separate the F1 grid into a two-class unit with some cars going for the victory and others supporting them. And that is something that is no good for us. We would not be interested in that.

MW: It would change the fundamental structure of F1. To be clear, if we were asked to vote if customer cars should

ABOVE **Mario Theissen explains a**
pertinent matter to Tony Dodgins,
as the rest await their turn to cut in
and put their points across

be allowed or not, we would vote against them. But, hypocritically, we are a business and so we went to the governing body and said, are you really sure this is what you want because we are against it. We were told categorically yes, so that's how that proposition grew. We've got mixed feelings about it. When you get involved, you think this would be an interesting thing to do, but we weren't heartbroken when it didn't happen either.

AP: You're darned lucky it didn't happen!

MW: We just talked earlier about how remarkable it is that F1 has survived such bad management for so long, and I think the reason it may have done is that there are one or two ingredients. To an extent exclusivity, the pinnacle of technology, some of the venues and the fact that there is the variety, because there are hundreds of one-make series and other categories that haven't achieved the prominence of F1. It's got the gladiatorial contest between Felipe and Lewis, the team competition, the technology competition, the tactical and strategic issues and then there's the glamour and the sex of it as well. F1 is multi-faceted and before we discard any of them we have to be very careful. If I was ruling the sport, I would maintain constructor status. But if those in power

decide that customer cars are admissible then you have to go and do it because we're in that business.

JH: I thought it had been clarified last year. There is a harmonisation period for Toro Rosso to become a full constructor and I'm surprised the issue keeps coming back on the table. Next year, we are faced with the entirely new challenge of a new car using KERS, so technically Red Bull could run four cars during testing and have a significant advantage. Also, I'm sure they would derive an advantage from having two cars during seasonal testing.

MT: Just to add one comment to that, we were approached by potential team owners when this first came on the cards and they basically said; 'give us the car free and we will do what you want all season'.

MWa: Enough said.

MW (grinning)**:** Why didn't you do it then?

AP: Because he's too clever…

TD: *Six months after the Max Mosley revelations, do*

you think it's acceptable that he is still FIA president? Did it damage F1 – long term, short term or not at all?

MWa: To me, what Max does in the privacy of someone else's home, among consenting adults, is indeed his business. And nobody else's. But the key word is privacy. And there isn't any privacy anymore because it all came out in public. And it came out in public about a man leading one of the major sports, a top politician who deals with royalty and extremely important people in business. I think Max's image has been damaged but, cynically, I have to say that I don't think it will affect F1 at all. It's all virtually gone away now. People have forgotten it. Some people won't want to meet him, other people won't care.

MH: I think regardless of how it came out, once it had come out it did damage F1. It lent it a seedy, unsavoury image and I'm surprised that he survived it.

TD: *Any comments from anyone involved with sponsors?*

MT: We didn't have any discussions with our sponsors.

TD: *Any other views?*

MW: Lots of views, but the reality is that we are not at liberty to discuss them, are we?

MH: That's part of the problem.

MW: There is not free speech in F1. No team is able to comment without fear of threats.

AP: Martin, it's so funny you should say that because to say there is no free speech in F1 is a demonstration that there is...

MW: If you move away from the Max Mosley affair, I think one of the things F1 lacks a little bit of is that it is so controlled – overtaking moves and so forth – that there ought to be an opportunity for drivers and team managers to remonstrate a bit more passionately in front of television than the current environment perhaps allows. The fear of bringing the sport into disrepute is such a powerfully overbearing tenet of our sport at the moment that it just doesn't happen.

AP: Martin I'll have to stop you there, because if you are a Premier League soccer manager and at the end of the game you say that the referee is an idiot, you will be hauled up in front of the governing body for the same reason. I don't agree that there is no free speech. I think people can say what they want. The truth is, a lot of people choose not to because they don't want to rock the boat or they feel they might be disadvantaged by doing that, but it's a choice that they make. If you feel something strongly enough, you can say it.

MW: Well of course you can, but there will be consequences for your team if you do.

MWa: You can't speak in the belief that there will be no consequences if you do say what you feel.

MW: Forget the teams, ask the professional journalists if they are allowed to say what they think, and they're not.

MH: We don't feel free to write what we want because of these passes round our neck. We earn our living from these and these can be switched off at their behest.

AP: That's true in your relationship with the teams. There are teams in this paddock who, if you make a story they don't appreciate, you will not get access to them or their drivers. That's true as well.

MW: I don't think it's the same. And I think if you do go to Premier League football you see managers, off the bench, remonstrating quite physically with linesmen and referees.

JH: There was an incident yesterday in the Premier League that I was watching, and the manager afterwards alluded very strongly towards the incompetence of the referee and said 'I'll probably be summoned before the board'. And the whole of the governing body was just ridiculed on television because of their behaviour. The commentators were saying it's a sad state that our sport has got to when a manager can't criticise what was a genuinely incompetent decision.

TD: *Didn't the Belgian GP highlight that our judicial process is far too complicated? How can we send everyone to Paris a week later just to say that an appeal is inadmissible?*

MWa: I think the tragedy of Spa is that millions of people watched what they thought was a bloody marvellous grand prix with a great result then, hours later, people who weren't basically interested in F1 but had been really switched on, found that the race result had been upturned because of politics. Clearly, that would adversely affect their attitude to the sport.

TD: *And do you think McLaren's appeal was upturned because of politics?*

BELOW Williams CEO Adam Parr had strong opinions on whether teams can and should say what they need to say on contentious issues

MWa: I would hesitate to say that, because that implies that the stewards were fixed and I like to believe that that was not true.

TD: *If you are a racing driver and you've been involved in an incident and have three people adjudicating it, with no experience of driving at that level, don't you think we should have a Derek Warwick type sitting in front of the FOM TV screens and making a binding decision within five minutes?*

MWa: Yes.

MH: Probably even more important than the fact that he's an ex-driver is that the decision would be his alone and binding. The stewards would have no access to him when the cars are on track and no authority over him.

TD: *So, by the time the guys climb out of the cars at the end of the race, that decision has been made, it's final, and the only thing that can be investigated later is a technical issue. Would that be better?*

MWa: Yes, certainly.

MW: In football, you can go to the referee, and the closest we've got to the referee in F1 is the race director. You can ask 'was it offside' and 'was it okay?' The referee says 'yes', you play on and then get nobbled at the end. That's what happened to us at the Belgian GP.

SD: I'm part involved in a way, so I don't really want to say but, honestly Martin, I don't think it was a political decision. But Martin's good point is both true and untrue. The real problem is that the race director is not the referee. To me, that's the key point. There is no sport at all where when you finish an event, that event is finished. There are appeal

procedures. It might be like that in a perfect world, but that is not the case in F1.

MWa: Is there a solution to this?

MT: Of course it can be fixed. I think the issue is not even if you have just one referee. It might still be three, but they should be experienced. They should give a decision after a maximum three minutes and it is not the race director being asked if it's okay, but the stewards.

AP: But there are sometimes more complex matters like the Brazilian fuel-temperature issue where you can't make a decision in three minutes because you have to weigh up quite complex technical evidence.

MW: There are technical-legality issues that you may have to delay, but if it's a sporting issue there should be a rule time because that's what people see. If you find out later that a pole vaulter's pole was too long, or a sprinter was on drugs, then you accept that. But if you determine three hours later that they planted their pole in the wrong place or their technique was wrong, I don't think that is acceptable.

TD: *Murray, you mentioned disillusioned people switching off after the Belgian GP, but is there such a thing as bad publicity? For every viewer who switches off, are there not another two who want to see the soap opera's next episode?*

MWa: I cynically have to say that I don't think that there is any such thing as bad publicity.

AP: It makes people more eager to see what happens next.

MWa: The more salacious and provocative, the better.

TD: *Some broadcasters thinks that drivers, faced with a microphone, are sometimes uncommunicative. The interviewer tells them he's just the messenger and that they are speaking to the fans. Does that aspect need to be improved?*

MWa: Ideally, yes, of course, but they are there as racing drivers and they are in the cockpit to win the race and you don't necessarily have to be a comedian to do that. There's one very well-known driver and I asked him years ago, 'when you get on the podium why don't you show a bit more enthusiasm about doing well?'. He said, 'look, if I haven't won the race there will be nothing to smile about, and if I have won the race that's what I'm paid for'.

SD: That's the perfect employee!

MWa: It's a question of what sort of person you are.

JH: But the drivers are not allowed to do a doughnut. We're not allowed to let the technicians jump the fences. We just squeeze the emotion out of the sport. It's clinical. Crazy.

MW: Remember that before you get to the podium the spontaneity is wrung out of it. You cross the line and you can't do anything like a doughnut or stop for a flag.

BELOW BMW Sauber chief Mario Theissen clearly enjoyed one of Stefano Domenicali's answers

SD: Did you see what Valentino Rossi did recently? He stopped and put a shirt on the top of his leathers, then went in front of a friend on a table to sign off the eighth title and then he came in. It was part of the show. But we can't do that. If we do something like that, we'll be crucified.

JH: That's what I'm talking about. We've got to be more involving, more democratic. We've lost the plot.

MWa: I would love to see more of the kind of thing that Valentino does. People absolutely love it.

MW: Yes, but he's allowed to do it.

MWa: Yes, and the reason we're not allowed to do it in F1 is because television rules and they have to be there to do the interviews.

MW: And there is a fear that a mechanic will put lead in his pocket or interfere with the car or the driver in some way.

TD: *Finally, for the second successive year we have had a really close championship, but for 2009 we have big aerodynamic changes and KERS. Do we actually risk having racing that is not so close and not so attractive?*

SD: That's a good question. I don't want to speak for others but today, 28 September, I don't know the answer. Theoretically, it's a great challenge and we have devoted a lot of technology and money, but we are not ready yet with a product that is reliable and with which we can make a judgement on the racing.

MH: What's implied in your question is that the closer the performance gap between the cars, the better the racing, and I don't think that's true.

JH: Next year there's a huge risk of it being much wider.

MWa: I'll tell you something that worries me about the changes, and that is that F1 is a terribly complicated sport to communicate to the great unwashed out there watching their televisions. KERS is going to make it even more complicated. I want there to be a light on the roll hoop that comes on when a driver presses his energy-release button, so that the public can see it and I can talk about it. Otherwise, it's absolutely pointless. We're not going to know if it's a brilliant bit of driving or an inspired strategic decision.

MT: That's a good idea.

MW: Yes, and it is under consideration.

AP: But you'll need extra current, extra electricity!

JH: And I'll have a higher-discharge bulb in my car than McLaren and use more of my stored energy!

AP: We've also got the adjustable wing, which will be quite good. It's just a little taster of what's going on with the set-up.

MW: I'm an optimist I suppose, but I think we are going to see more variety in the cars. For the first time ever, there

has been some thorough work done on trying to assist overtaking, so if the OWG group did a good job that bodes well. Also, if we take away some of the secrecy and are prepared to communicate much more it will be good, because for those involved it's phenomenally interesting, but we don't always give enough information or get that across. In fact, we're talking about giving much more strategy and technical information to the television viewers and even via telemetry so that it can be seen when we are harvesting energy and when we are releasing it.

MWa: In spite of it all, a hell of a lot of people still watch.

MW: Thank God for that!

MT: Whenever you throw all the balls into the air and open up the regulations, you will get a much broader spread of competitiveness. So, yes, we can't expect such a close finish at the end of the season but, on the other hand, we will see much more change during the season, with surprising results and moves, also on the technology side. So, in my view, it will be more interesting next year than the stable situation we have in 2008 with almost no change during the season between the individual teams.

ABOVE Toyota F1 president John Howett and journalist Mark Hughes listen in as Murray Walker expounds on a matter dear to his heart

THE PANEL

ALBERTO ANTONINI I/*AUTOSPRINT*
RAIMOND BLANCAFORT E/*MUNDO DEPORTIVO*
MATHIAS BRUNNER CH/*MOTORSPORT AKTUELL*
JEAN-MICHEL DESNOUES F/*AUTO HEBDO*
TONY DODGINS GB/*AUTOSPORT*
GERALD DONALDSON CDN
MARK FOGARTY AUS/*AUSTRALIAN AUTO ACTION*
ANDREW FRANKL H/HUNGARIAN TELEVISION
JEAN-FRANCOIS GALERON F/AGENCE GALERON
GERHARD KUNTSCHIK A/*SALZBURGER NACHRICHTEN*
ERKKI MUSTAKARI SF/STT FINNISH NEWS AGENCY
JONATHAN NOBLE GB/AUTOSPORT.COM
PETER NYGAARD DK/GRAND PRIX PHOTO
DECLAN QUIGLEY IRL/SETANTA SPORTS
DIETER RENCKEN ZA/*RACINGLINES*
ACHIM SCHLANG D/*F1SPEED*
INGA STRACKE D/POLE POSITION REPORTS
KARIN STURM D/ADRIVO SPORTPRESSE
MARC SURER CH/PREMIERE TV
STEVEN TEE GB/LAT PHOTOGRAPHIC
BYRON YOUNG GB/*DAILY MIRROR*

*Up and down arrows denote each driver's
position relative to his 2007 ranking*

THE DRIVERS

Lewis Hamilton topped our driver ranking
in 2007 as a rookie, and now he's done it
again, but our panel of leading journalists
has reshaped the order in his wake

In our quest to rank this year's drivers, taking into account
the level of competitiveness of the machinery at their
disposal, we asked leading journalists from around the
globe to place their votes. And here is their list.

This feature brings you the story of the drivers' years,
in their own words, but first here are a few selected
summaries from our panelists.

Hugely experienced Finnish journalist Erkki Mustakari
said of Hamilton: "A brilliant driver with aggressive and
effective style. Considering his lack of experience, he has a
champion's quality written all over his face."

Swiss journalist Mathias Brunner was hugely impressed
with Vettel, writing: "Arguably the best German racer
since Michael Schumacher – great natural talent combined
with a sharp mind."

Raimond Blancafort said of countryman Alonso "His
final sprint proves that he is the most complete driver to be
found on the grid." He also had time for Coulthard: "The
gentleman is retiring and his performances have always
been consistent, but luck hasn't been on his side."

Byron Young was less than impressed with Räkkönen:
"He should be ashamed of himself. Never has such a gifted
World Champion done so little to honour the crown he is
wearing or the exorbitant salary he is being paid."

1 LEWIS HAMILTON
◄ = ► **McLAREN**

"I don't think it has hit home yet. It keeps popping into my mind: wow, you are World Champion! Never in a million years would I have thought that I would be here. I had dreamed of having the title, which is why it probably does feel like having a dream. That is why it keeps popping back into my head, to show it is reality. So it is a great feeling.

I think this year was a lot different to the 2007 campaign. Last year we had considerably better consistency and perhaps made fewer mistakes. However, at the end of the year I was at a point in my life where I was thrown into the limelight. I was leading the World Championship and the pressure that I could be World Champion in Brazil was extremely tough to take on my young shoulders.

I think losing that World Championship last year probably made me stronger and that is why we pulled through at the end of this year's championship.

There were races this year that we won, including some of the best grands prix – at Silverstone, at Monaco and at Hockenheim – but there were races that we lost either through a mistake from myself, or a mistake made by the team. However, we win as a team and we lose as a team.

I think that going into next year's World Championship we are going to analyse absolutely everything that happened this year and just try and correct any mistakes that we made.

Just to get to one world title has been unbelievably difficult, so hopefully the next one will be rather easier – but the rules and regulations change every year. It is going to be just as competitive every year and there are some fantastic drivers like Felipe Massa and my team-mate Heikki Kovalainen. They are always going to be pushing me hard, and so to beat them every year is going to be tough.

Each year I am getting stronger. People say the second year in Formula One is always more difficult, but I don't believe that at all. I think you just get stronger with experience, you learn from mistakes and hopefully I will continue to grow as a driver with every year. If that means winning more World Championship titles, then so be it.

I think I am ready. Every year you have new experiences which just build your character and build you to do these things.

In my first year of Formula One, it took a lot of adjusting to all of the new situations and experiences. I think I have handled it alright this year, and towards the end of the championship I have just got stronger and stronger – and that is how I will keep moving forward from year to year. I will certainly do everything that I can to continue to improve.

We are working flat-out on next year's car, which is being built for a very different set of rules, and I want to be fitter when I get to the first grand prix of next season – which will be hard as I was really fit this year.

In almost every area, we are just focusing on trying not to make those mistakes that have cost us points and trying to be more consistent.

I don't know what to say about my father. He's a dad. He's been a true inspiration, he's been positive in many, many ways, but he's been a dad. He's been

a pain in the arse sometimes in my life as well! But he's been fantastic. He's done all the work to get me to where I am, and it's really him that's made all the sacrifices for me from the beginning. And still up until now he's doing that.

It's an incredible amount of dedication, not just to me but to the family. He's a huge family man, and I believe I've kind of followed in his footsteps. The man I am today is a reflection of him, I think.

Also, the World Championship title that we've achieved is a reflection of him, and his support, and my family. It means the world to me.

I am really, really happy in my life right now. It would be nice to have a house at some stage, but I don't know where or what I want in particular.

I've got a nice apartment, I've got a nice drum kit and some really nice guitars. I don't need anything more, actually.

There are some things that I might want to get in the future, but there'll be a time and a place when I get them. The reward here and now in Brazil is winning the World Championship. What else could I really need?

I wanted to celebrate in Brazil, but I didn't drink on the Sunday night after the grand prix. I only had a couple of glasses of champagne. Then I remember towards the end of the night that I just sat there at the side of it all and a song came on. It was 'We are the Champions', and I just watched all the team members, my mechanics, my engineers, the catering crew, the bosses, my dad, everyone and they were just so happy with the outcome of the championship and I was able to simply sit there and take all of that in. It was completely wonderful.

That was a feeling that you can't really put into words, to be able to see just how happy you've made everyone, and how much effort they've put in, and how satisfied they are with the outcome.

That was really my present for this season, just seeing all that."

NATIONALITY British
DATE OF BIRTH 7/1/85
PLACE OF BIRTH
Stevenage, England
GRANDS PRIX 35
WINS 9
POLES 13
FASTEST LAPS 3
POINTS 207
HONOURS F1 World
Champion 2008, GP2
Champion 2006, European
F3 Champion 2005, British
Formula Renault Champion
2003, World Kart Champion
2000

2 ROBERT KUBICA

↑+6   **BMW SAUBER**

NATIONALITY Polish
DATE OF BIRTH 7/12/84
PLACE OF BIRTH
Krakow, Poland
GRANDS PRIX 40
WINS 1
POLES 1
FASTEST LAPS 0
POINTS 120
HONOURS World Series
by Renault Champion 2005,
German & Italian Junior Kart
Champion 2000, Polish Junior
Kart Champion 1997

"In the winter, we knew that our car could be strong, as the team's evaluations, simulations and wind-tunnel data were saying it was a big improvement compared to last year. When we turned up at the first test, it wasn't the case, and we faced quite a lot of problems. But the response of the team was very good, although in Australia we were performing better than expected.

The engineers did a very good job. We tested quite a lot of new stuff, new solutions to help the car, and we did have a strong car. It was quite difficult to drive, quite difficult to set up, but it was performing well. I think we were in some ways surprised. As we were negatively surprised to see that the new car was not as quick as we thought, we were very surprised in a positive way when we saw in Australia that we were able to fight with Ferrari and McLaren.

We were very strong in the first three races, able to beat McLaren and Ferrari. When we came back to Europe, the gap slowly became bigger, and we lost a bit of ground. We kept that gap until the end of the season. Even when we won in Canada, we were not really the strongest. We were OK, we were in the front, but we were ahead because of circumstances. As this is racing it can happen, and on some occasions we were unlucky. All in all I think we started the season very strongly, stronger than we were later.

From a result point-of-view, Canada was a highlight for sure, but this year I think I have driven very good races on many occasions. Monaco was a difficult one! I think we were not the strongest ones in the wet, the car in my opinion is very difficult to drive – at least I don't feel it properly – with a very inconsistent balance. To finish second in Monaco and third in Monza in the wet was something special.

Another very good weekend was Valencia, where I think with a not very strong car I was able to finish third. OK, the gap to the winner was very big, but still in qualifying I did a very good lap, three laps heavier than Felipe and just three-tenths slower. It was an extremely good qualifying and a good race. In Spa we missed a podium due to a pit-stop problem, otherwise again it would have been a quite good race with a good podium finish. As always in a season there are ups and downs, but from a driving point of view I'm pretty happy with all the races I did.

It's true that the team was not really planning to fight for the World Championship this season, but in this sport you cannot plan everything. You have to just take the opportunity.

To be honest, I don't have any clue about how much work or how many people went towards next year's car, I just can see that we didn't improve as much as we were expecting. The guys were working hard to improve the car, but the parts that we tested were not giving us the expected results that we saw from simulation and the wind tunnel.

Mario mentioned many times that the goal of the team is to win races through hard work, and in some ways we have achieved the plan, because we won a grand prix. But I struggled to understand, as if you want to win races, it means that you are strong enough to fight for the championship. So, all in all, I don't see any reason why one thing should exclude the other. I was leading the drivers' championship after seven races, we also led the constructors' championship at some point, and I think we had to take the opportunity to fight.

I was taking this chance as if it was the only one I might ever have, because you never know in your life. It's very difficult to plan anything. Maybe the team has a big approach and they know a bit more and they have their own strategy of racing, but I'm a racer. I'm not a strategist, I'm not a businessman, I'm not planning my future. I think I have a different view.

It looks as though the team is confident that next year will be better, and they are putting quite a lot of effort into next year. They said in public that they will fight for the championship in 2009, and not this year. So, OK, let's see..."

3 FERNANDO ALONSO

◀ = ▶ **RENAULT**

NATIONALITY Spanish
DATE OF BIRTH 29/7/81
PLACE OF BIRTH
Oviedo, Spain
GRANDS PRIX 123
WINS 21
POLES 17
FASTEST LAPS 11
POINTS 551
HONOURS F1 World
Champion 2005, 2006,
Formula Nissan Champion
1999, Italian & Spanish Kart
Champion 1997, World Kart
Champion 1996

"I think the season has been rather difficult for us, because we didn't have the pace in any of the grands prix until the 15th round in Singapore. This was obviously a little bit of frustration for me, because I fought for the world title in 2005, 2006 and 2007, and then in 2008 you arrive to a grand prix knowing that you will not fight for the win or for the podium. So it was a little bit of frustration.

However, we didn't give up, we worked with the team as much as possible, and we recovered a lot of the gap that we had to Ferrari, McLaren and BMW Sauber at the beginning of the season, and we were more or less competitive by the end of the season. We were definitely better and better every race.

Obviously, it was a different approach, different motivation for me, taking the maximum of the car on every lap that I drove. And sometimes to get into the third qualifying session is extremely difficult, so you need to do some perfect laps in the first two qualifying sessions. So maybe I learned to maximise the car performance in single-lap qualifying, and I'm definitely a better driver in preparation for next year. I will definitely be more prepared for 2009.

I pushed the car to the limit this season. For sure, there was no time to relax or to play a little bit and understand the race. This year there was no race, it was more like 60 laps of qualifying, and you needed to push again and again all the way to the final lap. This made it very different compared to other seasons, and as I said before, it was a new thing for me. I learned a lot this season, to be able to push all through the races, practice, qualifying, no time to relax.

Every set-up change, everything you do in the car to improve by even half-a-tenth of a second, will be worth it. Because in qualifying maybe half-a-tenth puts you into the third qualifying session or not. I became more precise with decisions this year than any other year in my career, so I'm happy with the season.

The Italian GP, for example, was a very tough race. Monza was very difficult for us, we knew it would be, and we were not competitive in the dry. Then, with the wet conditions on Saturday and Sunday, we took fourth place, so it was a little bit unexpected, meaning that we enjoyed it very much.

In Singapore, we were hoping for rain. For us the best strategy was one-stop, but we had some concerns about the brakes with high fuel. So one-stop was not possible. So the team decided on a very short first stint, and it worked OK. Obviously with a normal race we were finishing maybe 10th or 11th, so it was a lucky race in a way.

In the fastest laps of the race I was third, two or three tenths quicker than Hamilton for example, so it was a little bit better than expected. Maybe with no problems in qualifying we would have been on the podium or close to the podium, so that was the good thing about the weekend. Obviously the win was fantastic, but apart from the win it was our best weekend up to that point.

In Singapore, there was a luck factor with the timing of the safety car that helped me a lot with the win, but the Japanese GP was just pure pace of the car. I think the title contenders were a little bit aggressive into Turn 1, so I took the benefit of that. Then I had the fight with Robert, and I was able to pull out a gap.

The speed of the car comes from hard work from the team. We identified our problems at the beginning of the season, or the middle of the season. It took a little bit longer to make the new parts and the new solutions for our specific problems and, by working hard in those areas, the car was much better, more comfortable to drive and more competitive. So a lot of the gains were thanks to the guys at the factory.

Motivation is always there, because I think for any sportsman you never like to lose, and to be worse than the others. You always want to win races and beat the others, but sometimes you know that it's impossible. We managed to win two grands prix, and we are extremely happy with that."

"To be honest, for the first time in the history of the team, we had a very strong winter's testing programme. We started off with the B-version from last year's car, but still we were hoping for more than what we got. We had four retirements straight away, and we never saw the chequered flag. So it was quite a big disaster in the beginning of the season. Except for the Malaysian GP where I had a hydraulic problem, I always had a collision with someone, or a collision that led to damage so we had to retire.

The Turkish GP was the first race that we finished, but Monaco was the turning point when we introduced the new car – the STR03 – and from then onwards I think we made quite a major step in the right direction.

The Monaco GP was a special race. It was so incredibly long. It was two hours. I think we ran out of time in that race. It was so difficult to keep up concentration, a street circuit, very tight, and in the beginning it was wet and very slippery as well. So it was all about staying on the track and not making mistakes. We were on a conservative one-stopper because we started from 19th. Things worked out perfectly, but it was mentally a very difficult race. The first thing I did after jumping out and shaking hands, after getting our first points of the season, was go to the toilet!

For the French GP at Magny-Cours, we introduced a completely new aerodynamic package, and it took us two or three races to understand that completely. You could simply see through the pace in qualifying and the races that we were in a stronger position, and for the first time we were able to fight for World Championship points. And we scored a lot of points from then onwards. Apart from all the track experience, I learned a lot. I made a huge step in comparison to the beginning of the season.

In the end, everybody made huge progress in the team, every single one, and then as a whole we made a huge step in the rankings in terms of how many points we scored and so on. At the Italian GP at Monza, alright it was raining, but nevertheless we were the fastest of all the teams in these conditions, we did the best job and we made no mistakes. I think that we fully deserved to win.

For sure it was the highlight of my year. Some of the photographs I will remember for all of my life. After the race, our Technical Director Giorgio Ascanelli came to me and said; "No matter what it is, nothing is ever better than the first time!" So for sure I will never forget my first win and also first pole position. It was a fantastic experience, just the emotions standing on the podium having won the race and listening to my national anthem and then the Italian anthem. I think it was quite special to win in Monza with an Italian team – and it wasn't Ferrari. I think it has been 50 years since the last time that happened, so it will be very difficult to repeat that one.

It was very, very special, and all the guys, no matter whether it was the mechanics or the engineers at home in the factory, the top management, everybody gave me so much and was pushing so hard to get success, and then if you can first say 'thank you', and

4 SEBASTIAN VETTEL

↑ +12 TORO ROSSO

second say thanks with your results and even with a win, there's nothing better than that.

In the last six or seven grands prix, we were nearly always in the points.

My other highlights? We set the fastest time in the second qualifying session in Valencia. We had a very strong car there and a very good race and very good qualifying. At my home race in Germany, I was able to score some points, which was very nice, even though the safety car penalised me, as I should have finished sixth, but finished eighth.

Belgium was special in the last two laps. I had a horrible start and first corner and lost a lot of positions. I was fighting back and pushing every lap so hard, and then in the last few laps there was the rain coming, and then I climbed up to fifth place."

NATIONALITY German
DATE OF BIRTH 3/7/87
PLACE OF BIRTH Heppenheim, Germany
GRANDS PRIX 26
WINS 1
POLES 1
FASTEST LAPS 0
POINTS 41
HONOURS German Formula BMW Champion 2004, European Junior Kart Champion 2001

5 FELIPE MASSA

⬆ +1 FERRARI

NATIONALITY Brazilian
DATE OF BIRTH 25/4/81
PLACE OF BIRTH
São Paulo, Brazil
GRANDS PRIX 106
WINS 11
POLES 14
FASTEST LAPS 12
POINTS 298
HONOURS Euro F3000
Champion 2001, European
Formula Renault Champion
2000

"I think we did a great championship. We had some up and downs through the year and we paid for that, and we are also paying now a little bit, but racing is like that. Sometimes you just have a perfect year, with so many victories, a very reliable car, and other times you have some ups and downs. From one year to the other, things always change.

This year, it should have been our championship, but even if we had some ups and downs, I think everybody did a great job. Everybody worked really hard to achieve our goals with all their hearts, and sometimes things don't happen in the way we want them to. That's motor racing. Sometimes it comes out a little bit different than we expect it to, but we really need to be happy with our constructors' championship this year. It is very important and I am

sure that our President [Luca di Montezemolo] and everybody inside the team is very, very proud and very happy like me, as we really need to be.

The second thing is that we need to congratulate Lewis, because he did a great championship and he scored more points than us through the campaign, so he deserves to be champion.

I know how to lose and I know how to win. I think it is part of our experience, part of our life.

I am sure everybody – me, Fernando, Kimi – knows how tough it is to be a driver. Sometimes things are very easy and something happens that you don't expect. Sometimes things are very difficult and you win without expecting to, so we know a lot about that.

I just do my job, try to do the best I can. I think last year Kimi did a better championship than me. This year, I did a better championship than him. So many things change from one year to the next. We just need to do our best, do what we can. I don't have to say anything, just do my job. People write things, and the day after they change their mind, so I think these people will change their minds a little bit. I don't care. But, to be honest, I hear much more good things about me than bad things, so I'm quite happy.

We've had some ups and downs. Sometimes we try to do everything perfectly and things go in the other direction. Some days things look very, very difficult, but then you win the race and you don't really know why. That's racing, and we need to learn from that, and it's not the first time that these things have happened to me. I had a lot of experience in other categories, even positive experiences as well.

We were very strong this season, we could have won even more races, but it shows that we did a great championship. At the end of the day, though, you need the points. I would easily exchange one win with an extra championship point in Brazil. But, anyway, I'm very proud of my victories.

In terms of emotion, I think Brazil was the most incredible race I ever had in my life. So many things happened. When I crossed the finish line, I was just waiting to hear the confirmation, then suddenly it changed, that was a big, crazy race.

I think it was a great day. We won the race, we did a perfect job. For a Brazilian to win the race in Brazil is already very special, so it was a day to remember. You always need to remember the difficult moments. Brazil was a great moment, but at the same time it was a difficult one, so it was a fantastic day to remember.

Nevertheless, I won at home and that's a great thing. We won the constructors' championship. As I said, now we need to think about the next step which is the beginning of the 2009 season and think about the next championship.

The drivers' title is a dream for everybody. It's not because of me having been a delivery boy. It's not because of anything. It's just because we are drivers and we love to do what we are doing. We race to win, we don't race to finish second, and if you can win, it's like a dream come true. My dream was always to become a Formula One driver and then to drive in a competitive car, to take my first win."

"I lost my world title this year, so well done to Lewis. He deserves it in the end. He got the most points from this year, so I don't feel bad.

Of course, my season was not what I wanted in the end, but that's racing.

At least we won the constructors' championship. In the end , it was unlucky for Felipe, but the constructors' title had been one of our aims for the season. I mean, we got that at least and it was what we wanted and we were able to do it.

It was not the easiest year for the team and for both of us, but we achieved good results for the team and we must be happy. It was Stefano's [Domenicali] first year as team boss and it has not been easy all the way through, so I am very happy for him.

In the end, the Brazilian GP wasn't the easiest race for us, but we got what we wanted for the team. It was a close call for Felipe, but Hamilton won in the end. He got the most points out of the races this year, so he deserves it. So congratulations.

For sure, I made too many mistakes this year, so we lost too many championship points at those times. And, when we have difficult times, it's always difficult to recover quickly enough. It's always easy to say 'if', but we lost it, and that's it.

I'm happy for the team that we won the constructors' championship for Stefano, for all the guys and for the sponsors. It was not an easy year for the team or for Felipe or I, but we still got something for everybody. We're going to be back next year and try to be on top.

It went alright at the start of the season, and then we had a couple of bad races. We changed something on the car, and it wasn't exactly what we wanted. We didn't really have the testing to try it, and then we went back to an earlier set-up for the Belgian GP, and the car was much better again. But it was a bit too late at that point, really.

It's not the first time it's been like that. Last year there was a similar thing at some point. The car is on the edge all the time, and if you get it right it's good, but if you're a little bit off, then it seems to make everything very difficult. I don't know whether it's the tyres or getting everything all together to get the tyres working to their best. It seems to be that once you get the tyres working the car seems to be good.

However, if the tyres are not working perfectly, it's very difficult. Everything seems to be much more difficult than it should be, and you lose time in one place, like three-tenths-of-a-second. Usually you lose a little bit, but you have this issue and it's hard to fix it.

We were getting more or less where we want to be, getting a little closer all the time, especially in the races when the car was usually good. But on one lap, sometimes it was good in the first qualifying session, but in the second qualifying session it was difficult. It was hard to get it consistently good.

Felipe and I have different driving styles for sure, and our cars were set up quite a bit differently. It's just a different way of driving. It was there last year, but we just haven't found a way to get everything for us exactly as we want it.

I crashed out of the Belgian GP because I wanted

6 KIMI RÄIKKÖNEN
↓ -4 FERRARI

to win. I made a lot of mistakes – probably more than for many, many years! But that's the price you pay. Sometimes you push hard and you want to do something, and you don't get anything.

For sure you feel worse when you make the mistakes yourself and you crash out of a race, like I did in the Singapore GP. It wasn't the fault of the car there, as the car was pretty good in the race, I just pushed a little bit too hard.

Sometimes you have bad moments during the season, and it cost too many points for me this year, but I will try to come back next year, and it will be a completely different story again.

I won the world title once and for sure I want to win it again, but this year it didn't happen, and we will come back stronger next year and try to get it back."

NATIONALITY Finnish
DATE OF BIRTH 17/10/79
PLACE OF BIRTH Espoo, Finland
GRANDS PRIX 140
WINS 17
POLES 16
FASTEST LAPS 35
POINTS 530
HONOURS F1 World Champion 2007, British Formula Renault Champion 2000, Finnish & Nordic Kart Champion 1998

7 NICO ROSBERG
↓-3 **WILLIAMS**

NATIONALITY German
DATE OF BIRTH 27/6/85
PLACE OF BIRTH Wiesbaden, Germany
GRANDS PRIX 53
WINS 0
POLES 0
FASTEST LAPS 1
POINTS 41
HONOURS GP2 Champion 2005,
German Formula BMW Champion 2002

"It's been a disappointing season, because our development through the year was not as good as it should have been, and the other teams just shot away from us – notably Renault, but also Toyota and Red Bull. Toro Rosso also put us back a bit more as well.

We just lacked performance in the car. We went the wrong way very early on, and it seemed to open up very quickly. By the time we got to Barcelona it was already clear that we had a problem. And that's why, in general, it's been quite a disappointing season.

The weakness was in the aerodynamics. On street tracks we were good, as we must have had a pretty good mechanical car. Our aerodynamics worked relatively well in short corners and slow corners, and I think that's the reason why we were relatively strong on street tracks. And mechanically it went over the bumps quite well.

We were third in Australia, but it was difficult as it gave us some false hopes. In qualifying there, we got beaten by Toyota, so already we were the fifth team. We were there where we wanted to be, but only just. It was very easy to quickly drop behind three teams who were there with us, and that's what happened. That really made it even more difficult, that we had such a positive boost initially, and then it just fell away.

Monaco and Montréal came at a difficult part of the season. We started to understand that at normal tracks it was going to be very difficult to have success, and we had a good car on those two street tracks, so the team had a lot of hopes on my shoulders to really get some big points. Unfortunately, especially in Monaco, I didn't do a good job, so the points got away.

Singapore was a break for us, because we'd been unlucky in many situations with the safety car. So, for once, I was on the right side of things – eventually, because in the first place the same thing happened as always, it went completely wrong. It was an important break for the whole team, it gave us a motivating, happy moment. I'd never done so many qualifying laps in one race!"

8 HEIKKI KOVALAINEN
↓-1 McLAREN

NATIONALITY Finnish
DATE OF BIRTH 19/10/81
PLACE OF BIRTH Suomussalmi, Finland
GRANDS PRIX 35
WINS 1
POLES 1
FASTEST LAPS 2
POINTS 83
HONOURS World Series by Nissan
Champion 2004

"It's disappointing not to have scored more points and not be near the fight for the championship. But, on a positive note, the pace has been generally very good. Qualifying has been strong, and even the race pace has been pretty positive, although the results were not what I was expecting. I think I've learned a lot, and I'm certainly in better shape starting preparation for next year than I was this year.

Initially, I got the hang of the car quite quickly, but to find the last bit, it was only really around Magny-Cours/Silverstone time that I felt we were really on top of everything and I should be able to fight for pole positions and victories every time.

The start of the season was better than I expected. In Australia, I was expecting to be in the top five, top six. I wasn't 100% sure exactly where I was yet. Despite a grid penalty, Malaysia went surprisingly well.

Then there was quite a difficult series of races. There was the crash in Spain, I didn't score any points in Turkey, and in Monaco we had an electrical problem with the gearbox and I couldn't get a gear and start the car for the formation lap. Canada was disappointing. To be honest the weekend was a little bit difficult, I never felt comfortable there, and my pace was not very good.

It was a heavy landing back to reality after a very good start to the season. Of course, I spent the next few races thinking I had to try to catch up. I needed to do something more, and maybe get myself back on track a little bit. But I recovered quite well, I finished fourth in France with a grid penalty, and at Silverstone I was on pole. But in the race, in the rain it didn't work out very well! Around that time, I thought we were getting back on track.

The whole Hungary weekend was good, we had good performance all the way through, and qualifying was good. Obviously, Felipe and Lewis were stronger in the first part of the race, but at the end I was catching Felipe on the softer tyres. I was hoping there would be a problem for him, and there was. Winning there was obviously the highlight of the season for me."

9 TIMO GLOCK

1st Yr TOYOTA

"I have to say that when you look back at the start of this year's World Championship, the first five or six grands prix were really quite tricky for us. This was up until we went to the Canadian GP in Montréal. From there on, though, we worked our way forwards in terms of bringing the car more in the direction that I wanted it to develop.

Also, by then, I grew accustomed to the team and adapted my driving style a little bit to the Toyota TF108.

It took a bit of time, but from the Canadian GP onwards I think it was a good second half of the season for me, and especially when you look back, because we lost quite a lot of points as well.

In the French GP at Magny-Cours, Jarno looked quite strong, but we made a mistake with the set-up there and the car was just not good enough in the race.

Then, in the German GP, my home race at Hockenheim, we had a really good race, but couldn't score any points after my accident. So we had a lot of grands prix in which we didn't score any points. But it was a good, solid first year.

The Hungarian GP was the highlight of the year for me. I knew already in the first two laps of free practice that when you can keep it in that window of performance, the car is really good. I had a lot of confidence already after just those two laps, and I knew that we could finish comfortably in the points at the Hungaroring.

With the high-downforce package, we looked quite strong. Maybe not super-efficient in terms of top speed, but in the end we had quite a lot of downforce, and this was really important in Hungary.

We were quickest in the final sector of the lap, and that made us really competitive at the Hungaroring. Everything came together and I was able to get it just right on that weekend, where everything was 100% perfect. The best thing was to cross the finish line in second place and see all the mechanics hanging over the pit wall. Everybody was really happy, and for me it was really good."

NATIONALITY German
DATE OF BIRTH 13/3/82
PLACE OF BIRTH Lindenfels, Germany
GRANDS PRIX 22
WINS 0
POLES 0
FASTEST LAPS 0
POINTS 27
HONOURS GP2 Champion 2007, German Formula BMW Champion 2001, German Formula BMW Junior Champion 2000

10 JARNO TRULLI

◄ = ► TOYOTA

"Apart from three races in a row where I had bad luck, in Spa, Monza and Singapore, the rest of the season wasn't too bad. I was consistently in the top 10, scoring points, with strong races and good qualifying performances. So I'm happy with myself, and I'm also very happy with the progress that the team has made. It makes me happy because it's my contribution as well.

The car's progress was clear, because both drivers scored some points and made some podiums. So I think it's a much better car, although it still had some ups and downs and was better in some race circuits than others.

Third place in France was the highlight. I lost an opportunity in Hungary because I had some problems. I was very unlucky in the race with the strategy, always falling behind slower cars, so I couldn't make any ground even if I was quick during the race.

In the beginning of the season I was always very strong, always very competitive. Fourth place in Malaysia was a good race, for example. Australia was another good one, but I had to retire with a battery problem when I should have finished third or fourth. My best qualifying was probably at Magny-Cours.

The biggest frustration, as I said, was those three races in a row where everything went wrong, Spa, Monza and especially Singapore. When I jumped out of the car there I was really, really down. It was 10 laps to go after a tough race battling with a heavy car. It was a good gamble, somehow calculated, and it should have worked out.

It's been good to have Timo in the team. Everyone is much more open now. We talk about everything, we talk about the car. He's a very good guy, very quick, very competitive, and as well, very fair. I think it's a very good atmosphere. I like working with him, and he's learning very quickly.

It's difficult to make any predictions for next year, because of the rule changes. As long as the car is competitive, I'm always happy to fight and take on a new challenge, but it's difficult to say if we're going to be better or not."

NATIONALITY Italian
DATE OF BIRTH 13/7/74
PLACE OF BIRTH Pescara, Italy
GRANDS PRIX 202
WINS 1
POLES 3
FASTEST LAPS 0
POINTS 214
HONOURS German F3 Champion 1996, World Kart Champion 1995, European Kart Champion 1994

11 MARK WEBBER
↓ -2 RED BULL

NATIONALITY Australian
DATE OF BIRTH 27/8/76
PLACE OF BIRTH Queanbeyan, Australia
GRANDS PRIX 122
WINS 0
POLES 0
FASTEST LAPS 0
POINTS 100
HONOURS Formula Ford Festival winner 1996

"The season started off very well. In Melbourne, a brake failure in qualifying put us out of position and we had a non-finish, but after that we scored points in six out of the next seven races, so we were looking good in the World Championship.

We took every result we could, really. We had a little bit of luck with Fernando blowing up in Barcelona, and also Fernando crashing with Lewis in Bahrain. We were there to capitalise on that, and we had some good first laps too, and everything went our way.

Monaco was a good race in terms of the extreme conditions. I had to put the dries on too early, and it was the first time I went to a two-hour race limit. So it was a very, very long race and mentally it was tough. It was very rewarding to get a fourth for the team.

At Hockenheim, I got debris from Glock's car in the radiator. We might have got a point, but that was the start of our struggle at hotter tracks, and also with softer tyres. In Valencia, we struggled all weekend.

Silverstone was disappointing, spinning on lap 1. Probably there and Monza, both wet races, we probably could have done a bit better. At Monza, we still got a point, but the difference between fourth and eighth was 12 seconds or something. Singapore was disappointing – the first time the car stopped – we were in good shape to get a chunk of points. I wouldn't have looked at it like my other podiums, but we would have taken it.

I'm very happy with my own consistency, from the middle part of last year through to the end. I've been very consistent with my opportunities to score points for the team and I delivered on most Saturdays, with the exception of Singapore. It's not that easy to nail it at every track around the world. Also, when you've got a car in the middle of the pack, it's very easy to be knocked out early. In qualifying, you've got to give yourself the best chance possible for the race, and that's why I scored a lot of points early in the season, because I was nailing qualifying. It's simple: if you don't nail qualifying, you're going to struggle on Sunday."

12 NICK HEIDFELD
↓ -7 BMW SAUBER

NATIONALITY German
DATE OF BIRTH 10/5/77
PLACE OF BIRTH Mönchengladbach, Germany
GRANDS PRIX 152
WINS 0
POLES 1
FASTEST LAPS 2
POINTS 200
HONOURS Formula 3000 Champion 1999,
German F3 Champion 1997

"It's not been a perfect season, but it's been positive for a couple of reasons. I had some problems in the middle of the year with the tyres, especially in qualifying. But on the other hand I've had several podium finishes, and I was fighting in the championship with Heikki and Kimi, who were not in the worst cars. The first couple of races were OK, so it's not all been negative, like I sometimes have the feeling it was looked at from the outside.

More importantly, what I'm happy about for myself personally is that during the time when I had problems with the tyres and in qualifying I still kept my cool and maximised the potential I had then. Alright, the potential was not good enough, but I still then drove strong races, I didn't throw the car away, I didn't crash, I didn't do anything stupid. I think that shows with my position in the championship that it was nowhere near as bad as one might think, looking at the problems I had. So I'm very happy about that.

Also, I seemed to find my way out of the problems. I changed a couple of things on the car and in my driving, and it was pretty clear that it was improving, and that's why I was reasonably happy with a season that, of course, should have gone better.

I had a good start, and after the first couple of races I was second in the championship! Australia was good. There was a safety-car phase, but even without that I would have finished third, so I only gained one position. In Malaysia, I did my first ever quickest lap, so everything looked alright.

Second place in Canada was nice, but it was the closest ever, and the only opportunity to date, where I could have won. So obviously I wasn't happy! I think I had the speed to win.

Spa was a special one. It was a bit of a gamble to go to wet tyres, and it was my own call to do it. It was a risky call, and it just paid off perfectly. After the stop, I lost positions, and then I just had two laps to go. In the middle of the last lap, I made up all the places. I think I would have finished sixth and instead in the end – with Hamilton's penalty – I finished second."

13 SEBASTIEN BOURDAIS

1st Yr TORO ROSSO

"It's been quite a difficult season. Pretty much every time that we've had a chance to score a good result, there's been something going in the way. The first race, Spa, Monza, Fuji – it's just never quite materialised.

It actually went a lot better to start with than I thought. We had a bit of a rough winter, mainly because we did some systematic changes and developed the car, and didn't worry too much about getting the car to my liking. So it was a bit difficult, as I was not too comfortable in the car.

Then the season started and we worked on set-up, found a few things, and it was very even with Sebastian. Then the STR03 came around. The first two races were about discovering the car. We had a good race in Monaco, but unluckily I got caught out by the aquaplaning, and it was a missed chance.

Then the new aero package came on the car, and it became harder. It made the car a lot quicker, there's no doubt about it, but it also made it a lot more pointy on entry, with a more nervous rear on entry to medium and slow corners, and quite a bit more understeer at high speed. It was one of those situations where you end up not being happy with the car at any point on the track, and it's difficult when you're not feeling good in the car to actually deliver.

There was no match any more with Sebastian, as he was very happy with the car and I was terribly uncomfortable, unable to do what I wanted to do in the car. And after that I was struggling massively.

The car potential went up quite dramatically in comparison with the others, and I looked quite decent in terms of position, but the gap with Sebastian was quite consistent. Only in rainy conditions and maybe in Spa was I a bit quicker. So it definitely proved to be quite a bit harder than I would have liked.

Then, with little changes and evolutions they found on the car, it went towards my direction in the last few races. It was a bit more stable on entry and that helped me to get closer to my window of operation."

NATIONALITY French
DATE OF BIRTH 28/2/79
PLACE OF BIRTH Le Mans, France
GRANDS PRIX 18
WINS 0
POLES 0
FASTEST LAPS 0
POINTS 4
HONOURS ChampCar Champion 2004–2007, Formula 3000 Champion 2002, French F3 Champion 1999, French FRenault Champion 1997

14 JENSON BUTTON

↓ –3 **HONDA**

"I didn't think this year would be quite as tough as this. After last season we expected to improve the car, and we have, but everyone made a step forward with their cars, and that's always the way it was going to be when we were so far back in 2007.

With this car, for some reason I found it very difficult to get a balance, which has been a bit of an issue for me. I really struggle when I've got rear movement towards the end of braking and on turn-in. With this car it caused understeer at the apex. It was just a very strange feeling. It was not direct enough for me: I like a car that I can turn in, with a tiny bit of understeer, but is very responsive.

There aren't many races where I feel that we had the perfect race. There probably were a couple – in Hungary I think we got the best out of the car, even though it wasn't a very good finishing position. The Turkish and German Grands Prix were reasonable as well. However, even when we got the best out of the car, we still finished 11th! There were a few races where we saw that we were quite competitive, and then we got to qualifying and we made mistakes and then struggled a little bit.

We qualified ninth in Bahrain, and that was a good feeling. But that was the third race – a long time ago! We improved the car, but not as much as we hoped. As soon as we started realising that points weren't feasible, even with some upgrades, we concentrated on next year's car. Which is tough for a driver, but then you've got to look further into the future than just tomorrow, which is exactly what I've been doing.

I think we've probably learned a lot this year about what not to do with the car, and strategy-wise as well. When you're that far back, strategy is so much more important than at the front. If you've got the quickest car, you can do what you want and still win. I think it's been a good team-building year, and a year when we've had to pull together and work closely, because there were a lot of new people in the team. I think we've got a good base now for heading into 2009."

NATIONALITY British
DATE OF BIRTH 19/1/80
PLACE OF BIRTH Frome, England
GRANDS PRIX 154
WINS 1
POLES 3
FASTEST LAPS 0
POINTS 232
HONOURS Formula Ford Festival winner 1998, European Super A Kart Champion 1997

15 NELSON PIQUET JR
1st Yr RENAULT

"It wasn't an ideal year for me, a lot of bad luck, a lot of silly mistakes, a lot of missed results. It's probably the year when I learned the most in my whole career. It was really interesting to see how different things are in F1, and how things work around here. And it was good to have Fernando as a team-mate.

I didn't really have a full year of testing in 2007, it wasn't like the year that Heikki had where he drove like crazy. It was a year of nearly no driving, and not racing, so it was tough for me to go straight back to racing.

In Germany, I was lucky with the safety car. OK, the second half of the race was really strong, really quick, but it was like Singapore for Fernando. When you're in front and you have clean air it's a completely different situation, you have nobody in front to bother you, and you're just pushing and pushing and there's nothing to stop you. It's just much easier. I realised that I was not made to fight for 17th. When I'm in the front, I drive much better! I definitely need to be in the top six to do a good race.

The most frustrating races were Spain and Monaco. They were two weekends when I had a good car. In Spain, we were really quick and I had a touch with Bourdais. At Monaco, I was lucky to be in the front because of all the mess, rain and dry, and people crashing, and I ended up also touching the wall. In those two races I could have had points easily, but didn't get them.

If you don't start well, the weekend is already not very good. At Monza, I was really quick, but starting from the back of the grid, it was nearly impossible. At Spa, I could have done much better if I hadn't touched the white line and spun.

Qualifying was often frustrating. Sometimes you're only two or three tenths off and you don't make it to Q3. The other car might go light and qualify top five, and you're 13th or something. People see a big difference and they don't understand it. It was like that in Monza, where I didn't make Q2, and Fernando only just made it, but then he got through to Q3."

NATIONALITY Brazilian
DATE OF BIRTH 25/7/85
PLACE OF BIRTH Heidelberg, Germany
GRANDS PRIX 18
WINS 0
POLES 0
FASTEST LAPS 0
POINTS 19
HONOURS British F3 Champion 2004, South American F3 Champion 2002

---

16 KAZUKI NAKAJIMA
+8 WILLIAMS

"Generally, I'm quite happy with my results in 2008. I was in the points several times, which is probably more than I expected. I'd done this already four times by Silverstone, so it was a little bit difficult after that, probably I would say similar to what I expected!

Initially, I struggled in some areas, like in qualifying, or sometimes in the race. The performance was not ideal, but I did still manage to score some points. The Australian GP was a little bit lucky, but some other grands prix were quite good.

I just had a good consistency in difficult conditions, and that was the key to scoring points. It was very good in terms of results for the first half of the season. In the second half, I think I had improved quite a lot, not only for the qualifying but for the race, especially improving my consistency

Fortunately, I have improved. But, as a team, we've struggled a little bit. We had quite a lot of difficult grands pix. But, for me, the important thing is to keep myself improving all the time.

The biggest things are experience of the track, and the conditions. That's the two big, big things. Even though I had a test drive and got some experience of the tracks in 2007, in the race weekend it's very different. Usually, the pressure is very big as well. Now I've got used to all of these things, and it's helping me to perform normally.

The thing is at the moment that I have a good feeling for the races and qualifying, so with more experience I am sure I can do better. Next year is totally different because everything will change. I think it's going to be a good chance for me.

It's difficult to choose one race, because every time when I scored points there were some bad moments in that race! But I would say Monaco was probably the highlight. It's a very difficult place to race, and it was raining. So it was probably one of the most difficult races ever. I managed to finish, and the race pace was pretty good. If we hadn't had a problem with the pit stop, I think that I could have finished even further up."

NATIONALITY Japanese
DATE OF BIRTH 11/1/85
PLACE OF BIRTH Aichi, Japan
GRANDS PRIX 19
WINS 0
POLES 0
FASTEST LAPS 0
POINTS 9
HONOURS Japanese Formula Toyota Champion 2003

17 RUBENS BARRICHELLO
↑ +2 HONDA

"In life, I understand that if you only enjoy it when you're actually winning, it's too bad, because at the end of the day you need to know that finishing 11th with a bad car is actually better than first with a good car. And that's how I see it.

If it wasn't for some minor problems – like the traffic lights in Australia, we should have scored in Barcelona, we should have scored in Singapore again – I should have 20 points with the second-to-last car on the grid.

Third at Silverstone was clearly the highlight. The decision on the tyres was obvious, as it was when I stayed on slicks in Hockenheim in 2000. I must have a small gift on that because luckily I put the right tyres on at the right time. And it was actually difficult not to crash into people, because they were going so slow! It felt great. It was a helluva race, and it was a great achievement because it was a bad car, and we know it was. Heavy rain helped us, and Silverstone is probably the best track I've ever driven – I love that one – so it really came together.

In Monaco, the situation was quite difficult on the first lap, and it was very hard not to get carried away and just crash. I took care and just raced to the end. Unfortunately, we misjudged Vettel, because we should have picked up another position. But it felt great to finish sixth, and it was my first points after no points last year. So it was a big deal for the press, I guess!

Singapore was the big disappointment. All weekend, we said that whatever the conditions, we needed to beat the safety car into the pitlane if this happened or that happened. And it happened exactly like we needed. We made it into the pits with a couple of seconds clear, and it looked great. We were going to be third on the road, and so it was really sad to see the car stopping.

Shanghai was also a helluva race. If we had a winning car we would have won the race by 20 seconds! I'm lacking a bit of modesty here, but it felt like that. It was a flat-out race from the beginning, but only for 11th place! There was no hope for better."

NATIONALITY Brazilian
DATE OF BIRTH 23/5/72
PLACE OF BIRTH São Paulo, Brazil
GRANDS PRIX 270
WINS 9
POLES 13
FASTEST LAPS 15
POINTS 530
HONOURS British F3 Champion 1991, European Formula Opel Champion 1990

18 ADRIAN SUTIL
↓ -6 FORCE INDIA

"We started quite well, as our car performance was a lot better than in 2007, but then we lost a little bit, as the development wasn't there anymore. We had a few updates for the first races and then we lost performance.

For the first six races it was quite tricky for me with the new regulations, without traction control. I had quite a big problem in using the tyres in the right way. Then, after Monaco, everything went better. I made good progress.

We had quite a lot of technical problems and some incidents in the races. There were plenty of races which could have been good, but the car broke down or something happened, which was very disappointing. I finished seven out of 18, a nightmare!

Monaco was my absolute highlight. When I look back, it's still a fantastic memory. It gives me motivation and makes me happy. I still have on my computer the picture of the timing screen when I was in fourth position, doing the fastest lap with a pink time!

I watch it and think that was a good day. Monaco in the rain is a very special circuit.

Other circuits have run-off areas, allowing you to make mistakes, and so everybody's pushing straight away. But in Monaco you have to go really easy. Some drivers risk more, while some of them are really scared. If you risk more, and you really put a good lap together, you'll be at the front at Monaco.

Kimi apologised straight after he'd hit me there, and when I see him he always comes up with this story. He's a good guy. It took me a while to get over it. After a week I thought, OK, you can't change it. But always when I look back like this I think I can't believe it. Why? Still now, when I really remember back, it's incredible the feeling that comes up, and I don't understand the words sometimes.

Half-a-year later, all the fans remember the situation very clearly. It was a good thing for my reputation. It was a very good race with a dramatic ending, and I think that was even better for reminding people. For sure, next year when I come back to Monaco, there will be lots of PR things to do and many questions about the incident with Kimi!"

NATIONALITY German
DATE OF BIRTH 11/1/83
PLACE OF BIRTH Graefeling, Germany
GRANDS PRIX 35
WINS 0
POLES 0
FASTEST LAPS 0
POINTS 1
HONOURS Swiss Formula Ford Champion 2002

19 DAVID COULTHARD
↓ -5 **RED BULL**

NATIONALITY British
DATE OF BIRTH 27/3/71
PLACE OF BIRTH Twynholm, Scotland
GRANDS PRIX 247
WINS 13
POLES 12
FASTEST LAPS 18
POINTS 535
HONOURS Macau F3 winner 1991, British Junior
Formula Ford Champion 1989, Scottish Kart
Champion 1988

"On balance, it's been a disappointing year, with only a couple of points-scoring finishes and a lot of incidents. I had a suspension failure in Malaysia and various other things which stopped running and affected your ability to get on and deliver. That's kind of the way these things go, and I've been around long enough to know that looking back is not going to change the results.

I was delighted to get a podium in Canada, and it came the race before the point at which I wanted to announce that I would be stopping in F1. There was a set of circumstances that enabled that to happen, but that's racing, and it was the best result the team had all year. I recognised that it could be my last podium in F1, and it was where I scored my first points in F1 in 1994, so there was a sort of symmetry to it.

It's fair to say that this year's car from a driveability point-of-view and rideability of kerbs didn't suit me as well, and I struggled with that situation. Through my career, some cars have suited me better than others.

Aerodynamically I think this was a better car than we had in the past, but perhaps not mechanically. In terms of driveability without traction control, I found it more difficult.

Qualifying is very close, very tight, and sometimes I've missed out on Q3 by fractions, but that's the bottom line: it's tight, and you've got to make sure that you get there. In his short F1 career, Mark has always done a good job in qualifying, and tends to be less strong in the races. I've always been stronger in the races through my career. But being in the wrong place on the grid makes it very difficult to do anything with that.

Retirement had been a growing thought since the beginning of the year, and it just crystallises in your mind one day that it's the right thing to do.

It takes a lot of energy and focus to compete at this level, and after 15 years, with no real chance of returning to my winning ways, it's better for all to acknowledge that and not fight it, and to go with it and be part of the future success of the team."

20 GIANCARLO FISICHELLA
↓ -7 **FORCE INDIA**

NATIONALITY Italian
DATE OF BIRTH 14/1/73
PLACE OF BIRTH Rome, Italy
GRANDS PRIX 214
WINS 3
POLES 3
FASTEST LAPS 2
POINTS 267
HONOURS Italian F3 Champion & Monaco
F3 GP winner 1994

"It was a difficult season, and we knew it would be. At the beginning of the season, we were very close to getting in the top 16 at some places, quite close to Honda, to others.

After three or four races our performance was static, as other people got better. Toro Rosso made a big step forward, they gained at least a second with their new car. So that was a bit of a shame.

We made a step forward mid-season, especially with the new gearbox in Valencia. In qualifying there, I was 1.3s slower than the quickest. It was a very good lap, but unfortunately I was only 18th. Four or five years ago, when you were 1.3s slower than the quickest, you were fourth or fifth!

We lost direction in the middle of the season, and the development wasn't as quick as expected. In the last four or five races they stopped development for the 2008 car. It was a bit frustrating.

The good thing was the good atmosphere in the team. Even in those conditions, the guys were really professional. They were always pushing, and that was good.

Sometimes, I kept cars that were much quicker than me behind me, like in Spain. The best position was 10th in Barcelona. It was a good race, actually. In Singapore I was third for a few laps, second, and even led for one lap, but there are no particularly good memories.

When you start at the back, it's not easy under braking for the first corner, as everyone wants to overtake, there isn't enough space and sometimes things happen. I was taken out by Glock or Piquet in Australia. It would have been good to have gone to the end of the race there.

It was tough mentally, but every time I sit in a car I do my best. I just hope that we have a better car for 2009.

With the new rules it could all change, especially with the slick tyres and different downforce levels. I think it's very important to build a good car for those rules, and to try to run as soon as possible with the new car with the slicks."

21 TAKUMA SATO
↓ -4
SUPER AGURI

"It's difficult to say much about the season! We faced so many difficulties, not just this year, but over the whole Super Aguri project. But we got over our problems, and we got stronger and better. The team was working well, and I really enjoyed being with them.

At the beginning of this year it was tough, because 2007 was very successful for us, and we had a lot of motivation. The environment was better this year, but from a performance point-of-view, we weren't as competitive. Then of course, we had financial difficulties from the beginning of the year, and the plan looked tougher as every race went by.

I tried to give 100% all the time, but we didn't get out what we wanted and it was a bit tough. A driver always wants to have a competitive package, but at the same time, as I was involved from Day One, I knew how hard people were trying to solve the problems. It was hard, but as we were both working together. I always thought there was something we could do to solve things.

The Australian GP was an eventful race,

and I was running in the top 10. It was a little miracle, as I was heading for a points-scoring position. Then we had a drivetrain problem, and I had to stop. It's a shame, because it would have made a huge difference. It was the only race I didn't finish this year!

Unfortunately, the last race for us was at Barcelona, where a year before it was a truly fantastic moment, when we first scored points for the team. In 2008, it was a relatively good race for us, I enjoyed having a little battle with the midfield pack and it was our best result of the year.

After that event, although it looked incredibly tough to continue, I was hoping we could move on. But, in the end, there was nothing I or the team could have done anymore, and unfortunately we had to stop.

I'll never forget the time I spent with this team. All the team members had done such an outstanding job all the time and they made the impossible possible. We had many happy days and fantastic memories. With my deepest respect, thank you Super Aguri."

NATIONALITY Japanese
DATE OF BIRTH 28/1/77
PLACE OF BIRTH Tokyo, Japan
GRANDS PRIX 91
WINS 0
POLES 0
FASTEST LAPS 0
POINTS 44
HONOURS British F3 Champion 2001

22 ANTHONY DAVIDSON
↓ -4
SUPER AGURI

"Overall, I was really happy with my race performances, especially compared with last year. I felt that I had grown a lot in terms of how to put a race together. I was working with a brand-new engineer as well, and we both managed to extract the most out of what we had, and we worked well as a team. It just really showed that you keep getting better the more races that you do, and it was a shame for it all to end so soon.

Australia was a really strange weekend. A few weeks beforehand none of us knew that we were going there at all. We hadn't had any time in the car since the Brazilian GP, and we were told to really watch ourselves and keep the car intact in practice. We had very limited running due to cost reasons as well as reliability problems, and it was a bit of a token effort. But the main thing was that we were there, and it was great to be back in the car after a long winter's break.

At the start of the race, the idea was to stay out of trouble. I avoided the chaos at Turn 1, and then I ended up side-by-side with

Webber at Turn 3. Nakajima, who had lost his front wing, understeered wide. I put my nose in to have a bit of a look and then he swooped back across and I got sandwiched between both cars. I backed out of it, but they both clipped my front wheels from either side, and broke the steering arm. So, not a very good start to the year!

In Malaysia, I really got into the swing of things, and drove a nice, consistent, quick race. Bahrain was a fantastic one for me where I got the maximum out of the car in qualifying and put a strong race together. Doing 14th-best lap time in the race in a clearly uncompetitive car was really good. I would say it was my best race weekend ever.

Unfortunately, after a good qualifying in Barcelona, Piquet Jr went off and swept gravel onto the track, which punctured my water radiator. But it was looking good, and with big questionmarks hanging over the weekend, I could still perform at my best. And that's where we left it as, after that, we heard the inevitable..."

NATIONALITY British
DATE OF BIRTH 18/4/79
PLACE OF BIRTH Hemel Hempstead, England
GRANDS PRIX 24
WINS 0
POLES 0
FASTEST LAPS 0
POINTS 0
HONOURS European F3 Champion 2001, Formula Ford Festival winner 2000, British Formula Ford Champion 1999

THE TEAMS

Two new circuits, one of them introducing racing after dark, were just a couple of the unknown factors for the technical directors of the 11 teams to cope with through 2008

FERRARI

BMW SAUBER

TOYOTA

RED BULL

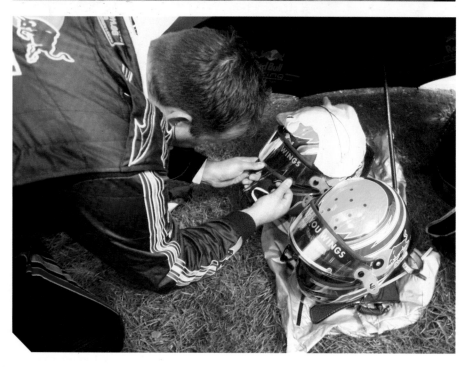

HONDA

FORCE INDIA

SUPER AGURI

FERRARI

THE TEAM

PERSONNEL

PRESIDENT Luca di Montezemolo
TEAM PRINCIPAL Stefano Domenicali
TECHNICAL DIRECTOR Aldo Costa (above)
TEAM MANAGER Luca Baldisserri
ENGINE DIRECTOR Gilles Simon
OPERATIONS DIRECTOR Mario Almondo
CAR DESIGN & DEVELOPMENT CONSULTANTS
Rory Byrne & Michael Schumacher
CHIEF DESIGNER Nikolas Tombazis
CHIEF AERODYNAMICIST John Iley
HEAD OF CAR PERFORMANCE Marco Fainello
HEAD OF STRUCTURES DEPARTMENT Davide Terletti
RACE ENGINE MANAGER Mattia Binotto
DRIVERS Felipe Massa, Kimi Räikkönen
RACE ENGINEER (Massa) Rob Smedley
RACE ENGINEER (Räikkönen) Chris Dyer
TEST DRIVERS Luca Badoer, Marc Gené
PERFORMANCE DEVELOPMENT Luigi Mazzola
CHIEF MECHANICS (Massa) Salvatore Vargetto
(Räikkönen) Giuseppe Rizzo
TOTAL NUMBER OF EMPLOYEES 900+
NUMBER IN RACE TEAM 90
TEAM BASE Maranello, Italy
TELEPHONE +39 0536 949450
WEBSITE www.ferrariworld.com

TEAM STATS

IN F1 SINCE 1950 **FIRST GRAND PRIX** Britain 1950
STARTS 776 **WINS** 209 **POLE POSITIONS** 203
FASTEST LAPS 217 **PODIUMS** 615 **POINTS** 4007.5
CONSTRUCTORS' TITLES 16 **DRIVERS' TITLES** 15

SPONSORS

FIAT, Marlboro, Shell, AMD, Bridgestone, Etihad Airways,
Martini, Acer, Alice

1 KIMI RÄIKKÖNEN   **2** FELIPE MASSA

AN EVOLUTION WITH IMPROVED RELIABILITY

By Aldo Costa
(Head of Chassis)

"The car was an evolution from 2007. It was important to concentrate on the new electronic system, and it was quite difficult to manage because we didn't have any experience of the features with a completely different philosophy to what we used in the past. It cost us a bit of development time that we could otherwise have used chasing performance. We dedicated a lot of resource because we needed it to be working at the beginning of the season and we did have a couple of worrying failures, including a problem for Kimi in qualifying at Melbourne.

A BIG IMPROVEMENT OVER KERBS

We went deeper and deeper into some of the 2007 car's concepts, but there were no big radical changes. We altered the wheelbase a little for the purposes of weight distribution. Last year, we suffered at circuits like Monaco. We were not as strong in low-speed corners or with traction, so there was a big strong evolution on this year's car chasing that aspect and I have to say the car responded pretty well. We demonstrated in Monaco that we were good in low-speed corners, and on bumps and kerbs. That was one of the main evolutions from last year to this.

We kept the characteristic of being less aggressive on the tyres and did not have any tyre-wear issues. On the contrary, we seemed to suffer more in cool conditions where there was no grip, and with the first-lap performance.

The chassis was already able to run with the slotted nose, it was just quite difficult to tune this from the crash-test point-of-view, so we required more time and delayed its introduction a bit, until the Spanish GP. We also wanted a conventional nose, which we used at some circuits and not at others. We gave the priority to the standard nose, as it was easier.

DEVELOPMENT BATTLE WITH McLAREN

The development battle with McLaren went up a level and we had new parts grand prix by grand prix at the same time as designing next year's car.

We did recruit a few more people, but were trying to be as efficient as possible. We had people dedicated to this year's car and others to next year's car. These days, if you don't increase the size of the team you suffer a bit. We have to admit there is a serious risk that we will be in a more difficult position in 2009. It is inevitable. I think CFD (computational fluid dynamics) is a field where we have always been strong and we were running 24/7 in the wind tunnel with three shifts.

CONTINUITY IN THE DESIGN TEAM

Although there have been some moves with our top personnel in recent times, I've been with Ferrari 12 years and don't feel that the people I collaborate with have changed. There is a strong group with good continuity and the turnover is quite small. There is a good feel, good environment and good spirit. It helps us to improve continuously. The changes over the past three years have been so progressive and smooth that we haven't experienced any trauma.

A FEW RELIABILITY PROBLEMS

Reliability wise, we had a few specific problems on the engine and electronic side and that is it. Other than that, the car has been good. Compared to last year, we had fewer problems.

Looking at all the little detail problems, and compared with last year, we made a few alterations in the methodology and dramatically reduced these problems, although we certainly did have some operational problems with Felipe's pit stop in Singapore.

After the conrod failures that hit Felipe in Hungary and then Kimi in Valencia, there was a very thorough analysis and we had a lot of help from our supplier and an evolution was found to make sure that it didn't happen again.

DIFFERENT WAYS OF DRIVING

The drivers did seem to have a different pattern of performance but, from the hardware point-of-view, their requirements were not too different. Most of what is good for Felipe is good for Kimi and vice versa. There are small differences from the set-up point of view, but not major things. Car development is easy in that respect.

We used two types of brakes to give us options and, circuit to circuit, we try to adapt looking at the wear and performance. It varies a bit between the two drivers in terms of choice and there are some circuits where you need a certain material, others where you need another and some where the characteristics are in between the two and the drivers can select different options.

CAPABILITIES IN LESS WET CONDITIONS

We did notice that McLaren's car seemed better suited to rain or low-grip conditions. There is a window where a car is at its optimum and that window shifted this year, so perhaps they had an advantage in these low-grip conditions. They know and we know and we are both trying to understand. It can be the opposite when we go from full wet to less wet conditions, like the first stint at Silverstone and at Monza, where they struggled and we went faster. Also, this year was pretty unusual in terms of the weather.

I think that when conditions were right for our window, we had the faster car. If you look at the races in normal conditions, I recollect maybe only two where the McLaren was faster, in Hockenheim and Shanghai, and it was already on the low side in terms of temperature for the summer in Germany. Normally it is a very hot place in July, so again that was quite strange. If you remember, there was one of our two drivers fast and the other not and it was the same with our competitor and also in other teams. It seemed that the tyres were definitely too hard and just on the edge of having enough operating range so that the driver could be an influence. And then there was the deployment of the safety car, which again created this mechanism. Generally though, we were fast everywhere and it was another strong year."

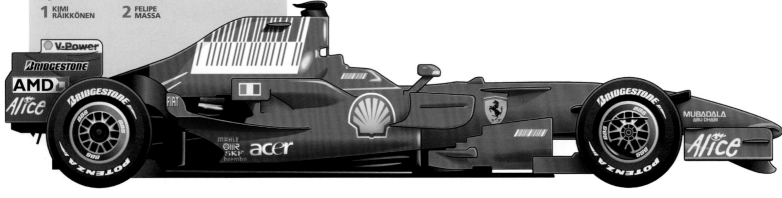

TECHNICAL SPECIFICATIONS

ENGINE
MAKE/MODEL Ferrari 056
CONFIGURATION 2398cc V8
(90 degree)
SPARK PLUGS NGK
ECU FIA standard issue
FUEL Shell
OIL Shell
BATTERY Magneti Marelli

TRANSMISSION
GEARBOX Ferrari
FORWARD GEARS Seven
CLUTCH ZF Sachs

CHASSIS
CHASSIS MODEL Ferrari F2008
FRONT SUSPENSION LAYOUT
Double wishbones with pushrod-activated torsion springs
REAR SUSPENSION LAYOUT
Double wishbones
with pushrod-activated
torsion springs
DAMPERS ZF Sachs
TYRES Bridgestone
WHEELS BBS
BRAKE DISCS Brembo
BRAKE PADS Brembo
BRAKE CALIPERS Brembo
FUEL TANK ATL
INSTRUMENTS
Ferrari/Magneti Marelli

DIMENSIONS
LENGTH Undisclosed
WIDTH Undisclosed
HEIGHT Undisclosed
WHEELBASE Undisclosed
TRACK front Undisclosed
rear Undisclosed
WEIGHT 605kg (including
driver and camera)

1 Ferrari unveiled its nose hole before the Spanish GP. It worked on the idea of taking air from the rear of the front wing and channelling it towards the rear wing
2 BMW Sauber led the way with this style of bargeboard extensions, and Ferrari followed suit at the German GP as the bargeboards fought to garner downforce

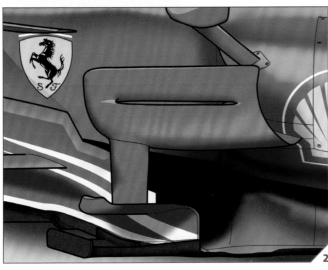

McLAREN

AN EXTRAORDINARY PACE OF DEVELOPMENT

By Paddy Lowe
(Engineering Director)

"Because the Bridgestone tyre stayed more or less the same as in 2007, we didn't depart a great deal from the package we knew. We pursued the normal themes of seeking more downforce, more efficient downforce, better downforce characteristics through a corner and, through ride height and then weight saving, better structural efficiency. And there was still the opportunity for more power, not least with gains being found through developments of fuel and oil.

As in 2007, our performance pattern relative to Ferrari has been neck and neck. The swings between the two teams were just tenths of a second and thus less extreme than last year when we seemed to be much stronger on the softer tyres than them and in the slower corners. This year, we seemed to be stronger on the harder tyres and at the faster circuits, with faster corners.

IMPROVEMENTS IN TYRE PRESERVATION
We were better this year at not over-using our tyres. We suffered a lot from heat degradation in 2007 and that largely disappeared. We worked them properly in order to warm them up for qualifying, but not to such an extent that the tyres went off. The rear tyres hung in better on long stints, although Heikki sometimes struggled to keep them intact, particularly early in the season. It may be that part of the improvement from last year to this is that Lewis became better at managing the tyres.

We again saw a right-front tyre problem at the Turkish GP. I think we are putting the most load through the tyres at the Istanbul circuit. If you go through the corner fastest, with the most downforce, it's going to be you that finds the limit of the tyre. We had to work hard with Bridgestone in Turkey to understand where that limit was and then protect it.

HAMILTON HELPS TAKE CAR TO LIMIT
Lewis is tremendously good at controlling an oversteering car. We saw that from the first moment he drove a McLaren. At every entry, we saw a massive correction on the data. Other drivers would have been bitching like hell that the car was undriveable, but he didn't even pass comment.

So, with a driver like that you're better equipped to push the boundaries to new levels. If the driver can't hang onto it, you have to introduce understeer in that zone, but if he can, you have a more oversteery car on the limit that is more balanced and has more total grip. The great drivers over the years – Ayrton Senna, Michael Schumacher and Nigel Mansell – have all had that ability and, compared to their contemporaries, want more front end.

KOVALAINEN WORE HIS TYRES TOO MUCH
The interesting thing about Heikki is that from the outset he was an outstanding qualifier. Some of the early part of the season he was faster than Lewis in qualifying. The trouble was, he was taking a lot out of the tyres in doing that and they weren't good for another 20 laps.

There has been an extraordinary rate of development this year. In Melbourne and Barcelona there were big gains, but it's been every race. The rate of development over the past couple of years has ramped to new levels – it's like a war. It's hard to pin down with real precision, but we've found more than a second during the season. We were still actively testing stuff for the last four races, doing a lot of aero work.

STRONGER DRIVERS HANDLE MORE BRAKING
We did quite a lot of brake work too, on materials and the braking system itelf. Last year, we did a lot of work with moving balance through the stop and that was still on the menu.

In the early 1990s, power braking was worth a lot of lap time, when there was more absolute downforce than today. Drivers are stronger now than they used to be and they achieve higher pressures with ease than used to be the case, while retaining the ability to modulate. The issue is not how hard can you press the pedal, but how hard can you press and modulate optimally. Lewis is incredibly strong on the brake.

The four-race gearbox was a challenge not unlike the longer-usage engines. It was a case of obtaining the right design detail to stretch to the necessary level without impacting on performance. These rules have forced us to do stuff we should have been doing for ourselves. We could have applied our own internal *parc fermé* 10 years ago. Instead, we messed about changing things and it usually happened that one time in five you'd introduce a problem.

STYLE AS WELL AS SPEED
Our first four-plane front wing was a great development, and while the nose wings were started by Honda, ours were more stylish!

We looked at a shark-fin engine cover, but actually found that it made the car worse when we tried it. It showed up alright in the wind tunnel but not on the car. It's very poorly modelled in the wind tunnel because you're behind the tunnel strut, so the detail is not great in that area.

SIMULATION GIVES A FOOT UP
Ferrari led the way with the static hub caps and we tried prototypes in late 2007 and then ran them in the first grand prix of the year in Melbourne. We're now on a type-two mounting system, which has a different mechanical arrangement and is more elegant and reliable. As with many things, it took up quite a lot of effort.

We were competitive everywhere with only one real blip, which was the Malaysian GP at Sepang, where we started eighth and ninth on the grid. We didn't hit the circuit on the front foot for that second meeting of the year, which is precisely one of the things we are normally good at. Kimi Räikkönen prided himself on not needing a simulator and could always hit the ground running, but it is actually really good for looking at new set-ups and saving a lot of time at the circuit. You need any little advantage you can get in a Formula 1 as competitive as we've seen these past two seasons."

THE TEAM

PERSONNEL
TEAM PRINCIPAL, CHAIRMAN & GROUP CEO
Ron Dennis
VICE-PRESIDENT MERCEDES-BENZ MOTORSPORT
Norbert Haug
CHIEF EXECUTIVE OFFICER, VODAFONE McLAREN MERCEDES Martin Whitmarsh
MANAGING DIRECTOR, McLAREN RACING
Jonathan Neale
MANAGING DIRECTOR, MERCEDES-BENZ HIGH- PERFORMANCE ENGINES Ola Kallenius
ENGINEERING DIRECTOR, McLAREN Paddy Lowe (above)
ENGINEERING DIRECTOR, MERCEDES Andy Cowell
DESIGN & DEVELOPMENT DIRECTOR Neil Oatley
HEAD OF AERODYNAMICS Simon Lacey
HEAD OF VEHICLE ENGINEERING Mark Williams
HEAD OF RACE OPERATIONS Steve Hallam
CHIEF ENGINEER MP4-23 Tim Goss
CHIEF ENGINEER MP4-24 Pat Fry
SPORTING DIRECTOR Dave Ryan
DRIVERS Lewis Hamilton, Heikki Kovalainen
RACE ENGINEER (Hamilton) Phil Prew
RACE ENGINEER (Kovalainen) Mark Slade
TEST TEAM MANAGER Indy Lall
TEST DRIVERS Pedro de la Rosa, Gary Paffett
CHIEF MECHANIC Pete Vale
TOTAL NUMBER OF EMPLOYEES 550 (McLaren Racing)
TEAM BASE Woking, England
TELEPHONE +44 (0)1483 261000
WEBSITE www.mclaren.com

TEAM STATS

IN F1 SINCE 1966 **FIRST GRAND PRIX** Monaco 1966
STARTS 648 **WINS** 161 **POLE POSITIONS** 140
FASTEST LAPS 136 **PODIUMS** 431 **POINTS** 3291.5
CONSTRUCTORS' TITLES 8 **DRIVERS' TITLES** 12

SPONSORS

Vodafone, Mobil 1, Johnnie Walker, Santander, Aigo, Henkel, Schuco, Hilton, Boss

22 LEWIS HAMILTON   **23** HEIKKI KOVALAINEN

TECHNICAL SPECIFICATIONS

ENGINE
MAKE/MODEL Mercedes-Ilmor
FO 108V
CONFIGURATION 2400cc V8
(90 degree)
SPARK PLUGS NGK
ECU FIA standard issue
FUEL Mobil 1
OIL Mobil 1
BATTERY GS Yuasa

TRANSMISSION
GEARBOX McLaren
FORWARD GEARS Seven
CLUTCH McLaren

CHASSIS
CHASSIS MODEL
McLaren MP4-23
FRONT SUSPENSION LAYOUT
Inboard torsion bar/damper system,
operated by pushrod and bellcrank with a
double-wishbone arrangement

REAR SUSPENSION LAYOUT
Inboard torsion bar/damper system,
operated by pushrod and bellcrank,
with a double-wishbone arrangement
DAMPERS Koni
TYRES Bridgestone
WHEELS Enkei
BRAKE DISCS Carbone Industrie
BRAKE PADS Carbone Industrie
BRAKE CALIPERS Akebono
FUEL TANK ATL
INSTRUMENTS
McLaren Electronic Systems

DIMENSIONS
LENGTH Undisclosed
WIDTH 1800mm
HEIGHT 950mm
WHEELBASE Undisclosed
TRACK front Undisclosed
rear Undisclosed
WEIGHT Undisclosed

Team McLaren Mercedes

1 McLaren made the MP4-23 less attractive but more efficient with the addition of these horn wings at the Hungarian GP to realign the air flow to the sidepods
2 The team also worked on developing its aerodynamic devices between the front wheels and the sidepod openings, adding turning vanes to the cockpit sides

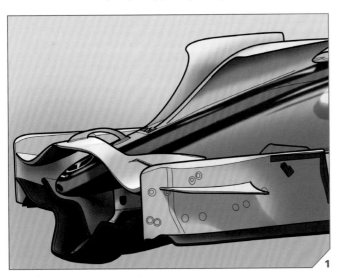

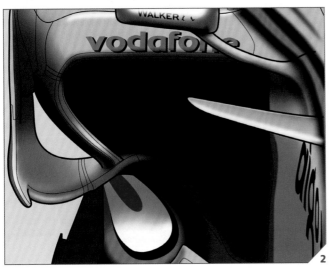

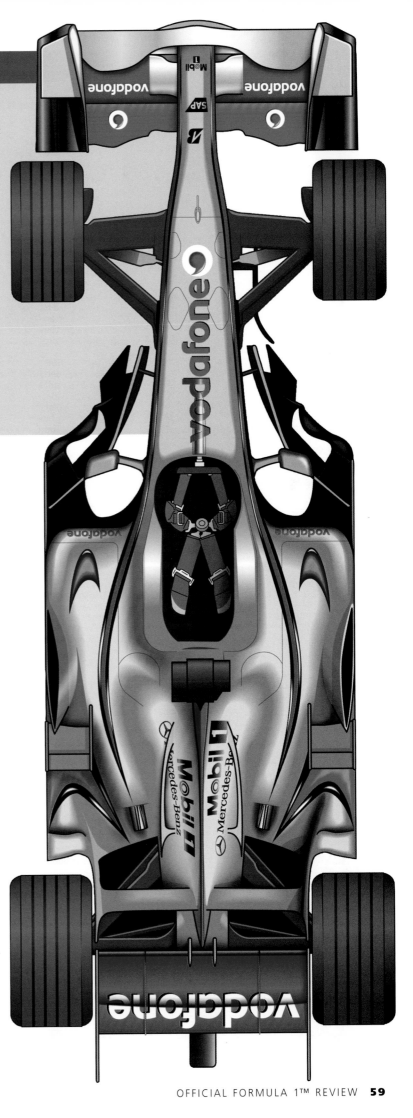

BMW SAUBER

AMBITIOUS STEP PURSUED TO RACE FOR WINS

By Willy Rampf
(Technical Director)

"Overall, the F1.08 was quite an aggressive development approach, because it was clear that if we'd just done a development of the F1.07, the step would not have been big enough to put us on course for our internal targets.

We tried some fairly drastic changes in the wind tunnel and came up with a slightly different concept of car. To improve the efficiency, it's not just wings and floors, it's much more complex. The F1.08 worked more with flow-control devices, strakes, barge boards and things not directly creating downforce on their own. This was one of the main targets for the F1.08. A lot of it was done with the aid of CFD (computational fluid dynamics). With conventional development, we would not have made such a big step, so we had to start with a different approach.

We tried different things in the beginning with CFD to investigate the areas which seemed to have the most potential. We then investigated these in the wind tunnel and tried to put them all together. It's difficult to describe what exactly was different.

LONG WHEELBASE FOR AERO PURPOSES
We were not immediately quick in testing. The chances of everything interacting perfectly at the very first test was small. But, by the third test, we had already got to where we thought we would get to when we first saw the numbers in the factory. We made good progress in the beginning, then the development curve was flat in the middle of the season, then we picked it up again. With the F1.07, the cycle was more continuous.

The car had a slightly longer wheelbase, which normally gives more stability, but that wasn't actually an issue. It was driven by aerodynamics and having more space available between the front wheels and sidepods. It gave us more aerodynamic freedom. Mechanically, it's not an advantage because a longer car is heavier and goes in the opposite direction in terms of weight distribution. But we still had more ballast available than with the old car.

BRAKING STABILITY WAS A STRENGTH
The car's braking stability was one of its best aspects. With the standard ECU, there was less variation to play with on the engine braking. This helped Robert a bit. He's quite aggressive in terms of braking and early downshifting, and it helped him more than Nick.

Nick has a different driving style. He's less aggressive on the tyres and finds it harder to heat them up. In mid-season, by tuning the set-up and Nick adapting, we achieved better tyre warm-up for him. It's not just temperature, but how to get the tyres loaded. That's the main thing.

With no traction control, we looked hard to see how we could help the tyres, and both our front and rear suspension was new. We continued the development during the year and we did continuous mechanical development too.

After Canada, Robert led the World Championship, but we made less progress than we hoped. With some developments that we brought to the track we didn't see the level of improvement we expected. Development also slowed during this time and not everything was correlating. The car is quite complex and a lot of the changes we did – like four different front wings, but with tiny radius changes or gaps between elements – were detail optimisation.

We closed the gap to Ferrari and McLaren this year, but there obviously is still a gap. I think it could be how to use the tyres on the mechanical side. There is scope and probably still potential locked in there that we've not been able to access. That's probably true on the aerodynamic side too. It's not pure downforce, but the right balance of downforce with the balance the drivers need.

TRYING MANY DIFFERENT WINGS
We used a pillar-mounted rear wing from the Spanish GP and this type of wing is lighter. We had a big variety of rear wings, some more efficient with pylons, some without. Even after Spain we ran without a pylon, such as at the European GP.

Our beam wing was lower than before. The main target is to work the diffuser, as it creates its own downforce, but it also helps the diffuser and is mounted on the rear crash structure.

We ran a front wing with quite an aggressive central section. Downforce levels have increased over the years as the regulations stayed stable, so we tried to have a powerful middle section. Everything around the tyres is very difficult to optimise, so we tried the powerful centre part and had the outer part with the endplates with which to balance the car. The T-wing we ran created some downforce, but the cockpit devices we used were to control flow and didn't produce downforce on their own.

The front wheel covers change the aerodynamics, not only the downforce but also the balance. You therefore have to put effort into optimising those and deciding which version to use for which track. Some of our developments were almost invisible, like foot plates and deflectors. The front wing ended the year looking almost the same as at the start, but there had been a considerable number of detail changes.

HARD TO COMPARE ENGINE PERFORMANCE
On the engine side, with the freeze, it was quite hard to know where you were. There was no real chance to have a proper comparison, but I think we had a good engine. Our four-race gearbox was new. Even though the internals, by regulation, were slightly heavier, we still managed to make a very slight overall weight reduction.

We started work on the 2009 car as soon as the regulations were finalised, and did some CFD and basic aero work, but the main development was still focused on 2008. The car performed well on tracks that placed a premium on braking stability and low-speed performance. The good braking stability was down to suspension kinematics. On tracks that didn't demand high downforce, we were quite good, but less so in high-downforce configuration."

THE TEAM

PERSONNEL
MOTORSPORT DIRECTOR Mario Theissen
TECHNICAL DIRECTOR Willy Rampf (above)
HEAD OF POWERTRAIN Markus Duesmann
PROJECT MANAGER Walter Riedl
CHIEF DESIGNER Christoph Zimmermann
HEAD OF AERODYNAMICS Willem Toet
TEAM MANAGER Beat Zehnder
CHIEF RACE ENGINEER Mike Krack
DRIVERS Nick Heidfeld, Robert Kubica
RACE ENGINEER (Heidfeld) Giampaolo Dall'Ara
RACE ENGINEER (Kubica) Antonio Cuquerella
CHIEF ENGINE ENGINEER Tomas Andor
TEST/THIRD DRIVERS Marko Asmer, Christian Klien
CHIEF MECHANIC Urs Kuratle
CHIEF ENGINEER TEST TEAM Ossi Oikarinen
TOTAL NUMBER OF EMPLOYEES 700
NUMBER IN RACE TEAM 80
TEAM BASE Hinwil, Switzerland & Munich, Germany
TELEPHONE +41 44 937 9000
WEBSITE www.bmw-sauber-f1.com

TEAM STATS
IN F1 SINCE 1993, as Sauber **FIRST GRAND PRIX** South Africa 1993 **STARTS** 270 **WINS** 1 **POLE POSITIONS** 1 **FASTEST LAPS** 2 **PODIUMS** 20 **POINTS** 461 **CONSTRUCTORS' TITLES** 0 **DRIVERS' TITLES** 0

SPONSORS
Petronas, Intel, Credit Suisse, Dell, Puma, T-Systems

3 NICK HEIDFELD   **4 ROBERT KUBICA**

TECHNICAL SPECIFICATIONS

ENGINE
MAKE/MODEL BMW P86/8
CONFIGURATION 2400cc V8
(90 degree)
SPARK PLUGS NGK
ECU FIA standard issue
FUEL Petronas
OIL Petronas
BATTERY Undisclosed

TRANSMISSION
GEARBOX BMW Sauber
FORWARD GEARS Seven
CLUTCH AP Racing

CHASSIS
CHASSIS MODEL
BMW Sauber F1.08
FRONT SUSPENSION LAYOUT
Upper and lower wishbones,
inboard springs and dampers activated
by pushrods

REAR SUSPENSION LAYOUT
Upper and lower wishbones,
inboard springs and dampers
activated by pushrods
DAMPERS Undisclosed
TYRES Bridgestone
WHEELS OZ Racing
BRAKE DISCS Brembo or
Carbone Industrie
BRAKE PADS Brembo or
Carbone Industrie
BRAKE CALIPERS Brembo
FUEL TANK ATL
INSTRUMENTS BMW Sauber
Electronics/MES

DIMENSIONS
LENGTH 4600mm
WIDTH 1800mm
HEIGHT 1000mm
WHEELBASE 3130mm
TRACK front 1470mm
rear 1410mm
WEIGHT 605kg (including
driver and camera)

BMW Sauber F1 Team

1 BMW Sauber set a trend from the outsest of the season with these nose wings that were later adopted by Honda and McLaren once the racing got underway
2 The BMW Sauber design crew worked hard on extracting the most from the F1.08's front wing endplates, adding little wings to their tops for the Monaco GP

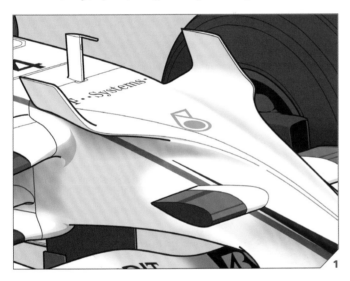

RENAULT

Pat Symonds (signature)

THE TEAM

PERSONNEL

PRESIDENT Bernard Rey
MANAGING DIRECTOR Flavio Briatore
DEPUTY MANAGING DIRECTOR (ENGINE) Rob White
DEPUTY MANAGING DIRECTOR (SUPPORT) Andre Laine
TECHNICAL DIRECTOR Bob Bell
EXECUTIVE DIRECTOR OF ENGINEERING Pat Symonds (above)
DEPUTY TECHNICAL DIRECTOR James Allison
HEAD OF VEHICLE TECHNOLOGY Tad Czapski
OPERATIONS DIRECTOR John Mardle
DIRECTOR AERODYNAMIC TECHNOLOGY Dirk de Veer
CHIEF DESIGNER Tim Densham
RS28 ENGINE PROJECT MANAGER Axel Plasse
HEAD OF TRACKSIDE ENGINE OPERATIONS Denis Chevrier
SPORTING MANAGER Steve Nielsen
CHIEF RACE ENGINEER Alan Permane
DRIVERS Fernando Alonso, Nelson Piquet Jr
RACE ENGINEER (Alonso) David Greenwood
RACE ENGINEER (Piquet Jr) Phil Charles
TEST TEAM MANAGER Carlos Nunes
TEST/THIRD DRIVERS Lucas di Grassi, Romain Grosjean
CHIEF MECHANIC Gavin Hudson
TOTAL NUMBER OF EMPLOYEES 790
NUMBER IN RACE TEAM 70
TEAM BASE Enstone, England
TELEPHONE +44 (0)1608 678000
WEBSITE www.ing-renaultf1.com

TEAM STATS

IN F1 SINCE 1977–1985 then from 2002 **FIRST GRAND PRIX**
Britain 1977, then Australia 2002 **STARTS** 246 **WINS** 35 **POLE
POSITIONS** 49 **FASTEST LAPS** 27 **PODIUMS** 92 **POINTS** 1120
CONSTRUCTORS' TITLES 2 **DRIVERS' TITLES** 2

SPONSORS

ING, Elf, Bridgestone, Pepe Jeans, Universia, Sanho-Human Service

5 **FERNANDO ALONSO**   6 **NELSON PIQUET JR**

THINGS COULD ONLY GET BETTER

By Pat Symonds
(Executive Director of Engineering)
"In 2007, we had found a modelling problem in the wind tunnel where we weren't representing the car well. It took a significant amount of time to sort out, and set us back. We tried to catch back up by going onto three shifts in the wind tunnel but, of course, everyone else is on three shifts too, so that didn't really help!

The knock-on effect was that we began this season down aerodynamically. For the first three flyaway races you're limited on what you can do for updates and so we concentrated on a big one for the Spanish GP. It wasn't just aerodynamic, as there were some mechanical elements too. It was probably one of the most significant upgrades I've ever been involved with on a car. And it showed.

In the first three grands prix, we were at the back end of the midfield. At Barcelona, we were top of the midfield and usually ran in the upper midfield from there onwards.

DEVELOPING THROUGH THE YEAR

I'd hoped to achieve for the opening race in Melbourne but we were too far behind. After that, the rate of progress was good. We out-developed most people during the year, which was quite gratifying because historically the development pace hasn't been our strongest point. We tended to start well and then fade a little. It's very, very difficult keeping up with the big teams, but this year we have. We certainly out-developed BMW Sauber and Red Bull.

The car concept was very much based on 2007, but we did a fundamental rethink on weight distribution – a percent or two forwards – to allow us to get our ballast into a different region. The real concentration went on understanding why our aero modelling wasn't as good as it could be and how to get that right. That was a combination of tunnel testing and straight-line testing.

NOT ALL ENGINES ARE EQUAL

There has been quite a lot of talk about engines, but I absolutely refute the idea of people, under the guise of a fair and equitable basis, getting performance gains. We see every bit of paper that goes to Charlie (Whiting, the FIA technical delegate) on that. They are completely innocent. But when it was known that the perimeter was going to extend, people did a lot of work before they had to re-present engines for 2007 and that gained them a lot.

We had effectively disbanded such a large part of our engine department that we weren't in a position to do that. There's no doubt we're behind. Competitor analysis these days is sophisticated and you have a reasonable idea where everyone else is. It's not just a question of peak power, but compared to Ferrari and Mercedes we lack torque from 15,000rpm. We're quite a bit down.

I don't know all the numbers, but I'm convinced we operate on a considerably smaller budget than some teams. It wasn't about internal politics as far as the engine is concerned, just a smaller purse.

We were all desperately sad about the loss of Dino Toso to cancer. Dino had done a great job and was responsible for all the aero on the title-winning 05/06 cars. He was getting more and more ill and we needed to do something. Dirk de Beer joined from BMW and is very good, very practical and began leading the aero dept.

CFD CENTRE SHOULD MAKE A DIFFERENCE

At the same time as we were investigating what had gone wrong in 2007, we weren't looking to place blame. There was a restructuring and planned-for expansion in 2008, which has now happened, and we have opened our CFD centre. That was a massive project and is quite a bit of kit. On the aerodynamic side, we now number 90–100 in total. We still operate just one tunnel, still at 50% and relatively low speed. We will be upgrading it at end of 2009. It's only 10 years old, but is already a bit of a pauper in F1 terms.

We ran an inerter as part of the Barcelona upgrade and it was a measurable lap time advantage. They are superb devices, lovely bits of engineering, but now that everyone's got them they're a bit of a waste of time! They are relatively simple but expensive. We fitted them at the front in Barcelona, and on the rear afterwards. It's an acceleration-sensitive damping device. A spring is sensitive to displacement, a hydraulic damper is sensitive to velocity and an inerter is sensitive to acceleration. There are some similarities to a tuned mass damper.

Initially, the R28 was a bit hard on the rear tyres and we had quite a programme to try to understand that. We found out how to tune it a bit, so we were able to take some advantage of poor conditions at Spa-Franchorchamps and Monza, and we made progress on how to understand the hotter temperatures.

ALONSO ROSE TO THE CHALLENGE

It's been good having Fernando back. The early part of the season was frustrating for him, particularly the first three races where he absolutely didn't have a car worthy of him. Even after that, it was hard because he's used to winning. As the season has worn on, he seems to have found the challenge in getting the best from what we've given him. He's back to the old Fernando we knew. He got stuck in and it was great that he had the back-to-back wins in Singapore and Fuji.

Nelson has struggled, no two ways about it. He hasn't found the season easy. Just like with Heikki [Kovalainen] at the beginning of the previous year, he began with a car that was very difficult to drive. It doesn't do anything for the confidence of a new driver. We didn't give him a car he could trust. As the car improved, so did his confidence. Some of his race performances have been pretty acceptable, the Japanese GP especially, but unfortunately the good races have been punctuated by mistakes.

In terms of focus, we had a new front wing quite late in the season for a component that has no relevance to next year, but for quite a while the only work on R28 was problem solving. Everyone was focused very much on next year."

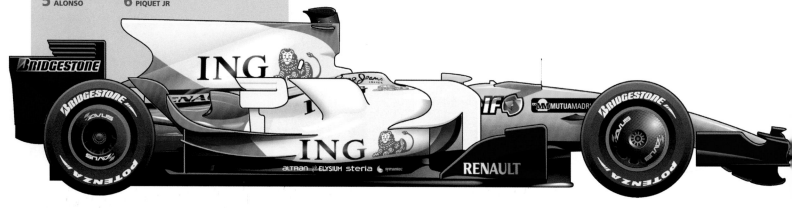

TECHNICAL SPECIFICATIONS

ENGINE
MAKE/MODEL Renault RS27
CONFIGURATION 2400cc V8 (90 degree)
SPARK PLUGS Champion
ECU FIA standard issue
FUEL Elf
OIL Elf
BATTERY Renault F1

TRANSMISSION
GEARBOX Renault F1
FORWARD GEARS Seven
CLUTCH Undisclosed

CHASSIS
CHASSIS MODEL Renault R28
FRONT SUSPENSION LAYOUT
Carbon-fibre top and bottom wishbones operating an inboard rocker via a pushrod system connected to a torsion bar and monocoque-mounted damper units

REAR SUSPENSION LAYOUT
Carbon-fibre wishbones operating vertically-mounted torsion bars and horizontally-mounted damper units
DAMPERS Undisclosed
TYRES Bridgestone
WHEELS AVUS Racing
BRAKE DISCS Brembo
BRAKE PADS Brembo
BRAKE CALIPERS AP Racing
FUEL TANK ATL
INSTRUMENTS Renault F1

DIMENSIONS
LENGTH 4800mm
WIDTH 1800mm
HEIGHT 950mm
WHEELBASE 3100mm
TRACK front 1450mm
rear 1400mm
WEIGHT 605kg (including driver and camera)

RENAULT F1 Team

1 This *de rigueur* bridge wing used on the R28 was developed through the year, with this graduated version replaced by one with outer flaps joined by a bar
2 Renault followed Red Bull and took a route that became increasingly popular in having a shark-fin on top of the engine cover in their quest for rear-end stability

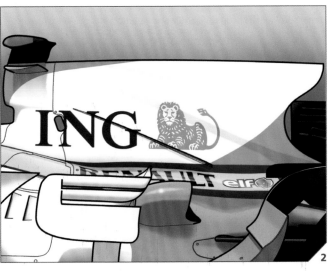

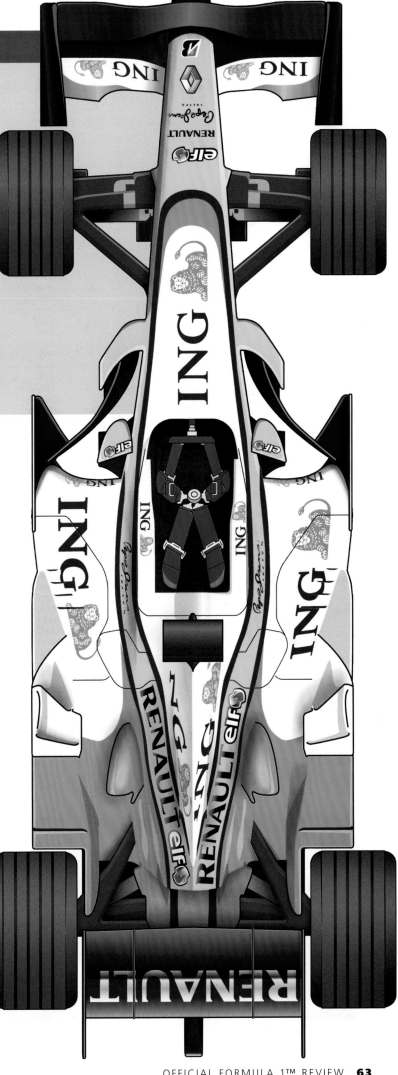

TOYOTA

EARLY PROMISE SETS THE SEASON ON ITS WAY

THE TEAM

PERSONNEL
CHAIRMAN & TEAM PRINCIPAL Tadashi Yamashina
PRESIDENT John Howett
EXECUTIVE VICE-PRESIDENT Yoshiaki Kinoshita
SENIOR GENERAL MANAGER, CHASSIS
Pascal Vasselon (above)
SENIOR GENERAL MANAGER, ENGINE
Luca Marmorini
DIRECTOR TECHNICAL CO-ORDINATION, CHASSIS
Noritosshi Akai
DIRECTOR TECHNICAL CO-ORDINATION, ENGINE
Kazuo Takeuchi
HEAD OF AERODYNAMICS Mark Gillan
TEAM MANAGER Richard Cregan
DRIVERS Timo Glock, Jarno Trulli
CHIEF RACE & TEST ENGINEER Dieter Gass
RACE ENGINEER (Glock) Francesco Nenci
RACE ENGINEER (Trulli) Gianluca Pisanello
TEST DRIVER Kamui Kobayashi
CHIEF MECHANIC Gerard Lecoq
TOTAL NUMBER OF EMPLOYEES 650
NUMBER IN RACE TEAM 80
TEAM BASE Cologne, Germany
TELEPHONE +49 (0)223 4182 3444
WEBSITE www.toyota-f1.com

TEAM STATS
IN F1 SINCE 2002 **FIRST GRAND PRIX** Australia 2002
STARTS 123 **WINS** 0 **POLE POSITIONS** 2
FASTEST LAPS 1 **PODIUMS** 8 **POINTS** 217
CONSTRUCTORS' TITLES 0 **DRIVERS' TITLES** 0

SPONSORS
Panasonic, Denso, Bridgestone, Dassault Systemes, Ebbon-Dacs, EMC Corporation, KDDI

11 JARNO TRULLI **12 TIMO GLOCK**

**By Pascal Vasselon
(Senior General Manager, Chassis)**

"We achieved most of our targets and it was a better season than 2006 and 2007. We saw quite early on that we were in a situation to meet our targets and it was a boost for the whole team. It started in the fifth pre-season test, at Barcelona, where we introduced our race-one package. We saw we were on a different level to 2007.

A FLYNG START THEN MID-SEASON UPGRADES
We had a reasonable start in Malaysia and Bahrain, then a down corresponding to the so-called Barcelona package. I wouldn't say that we got it wrong, but some teams had a better Barcelona package than us, as both Renault and Red Bull made a bigger step. As a consequence, we had a couple of difficult races where we were struggling to qualify in the top 10 and get into the points, such as Barcelona itself, and Turkey. Then we had a succession of upgrades that worked well. It started in Magny-Cours where we had a significant package including front wing, rear wing and other details, then it continued at Hockenheim. From Hungary – with a specific package – onwards, we operated at a higher level than before.

You could say that Monza and Spa were blips, but not in terms of our performance. It was a blip in terms of specific conditions with low downforce and hard tyres. In these two races, Bridgestone was massively conservative and came with tyres that were just not suited. Clearly in these conditions we suffer more than the others because our car concept is really down to managing the tyres, and we take more advantage than others from the soft tyres. Low downforce and hard tyres certainly did not suit us, but at Monza, as soon as we went to wet conditions, we were back at our normal level.

TWO PODIUM FINISHES ON MERIT
One target was to get back to the podium and we did it twice. Our two podiums were on merit with no safety-car interventions. Of course, some cars dropped out, but that happens all the time. With Jarno's podium at Magny-Cours he was third after the start and he finished there. In Hungary, Timo was in touch all race and was fast in qualifying, so that was on merit too.

Our second target was to finish fourth in the constructors' championship and we just lost out to Renault's strong finish to the season.

Timo was a bit like our car in that he developed strongly through the season. We saw immediately from his first test in the TF107 in Jerez that he had the potential. Usually we don't perform well there, but he was very competitive and showed he had the pace. Then he had a down towards the start of the season, where he was paying for his lack of experience, especially relative to someone like Jarno, who makes very few mistakes and is always there in both qualifying and race.

That had to affect Timo a little because he's not there to be second every time. But it didn't affect him to the point that it compromised his progress. He did a lot of work with his race engineer, Francesco Nenci, analysing what was

wrong. He was a little bit inconsistent. Sometimes he was in the top 10, like at the first race, and then a situation developed where he was showing the potential and then when it counted – the second outing in Q2 – he'd make a couple of mistakes. We worked on that with him and he began to put everything together. He was strong in Hungary and has been there almost every time since, consistent and able to do it in any conditions, especially when it's tricky, like a wet track. He's especially brilliant on a new track, like Valencia. If you look at the first laps of P1 in Valencia or Singapore, the driver that you see in front is Timo. He is on course for a strong season next year.

Jarno was as good as usual, strong in qualifying and race. I think the race he did in Magny-Cours was the perfect answer to anyone who suggests that his pace sometimes drops off through a race. He had fights with Alonso, Kubica and finally with Kovalainen and resisted them all. He is strong in races, without doubt.

A PROBLEM WARMING THE TYRES
We sometimes had a problem with tyre warm-up, but it varied and sometimes Timo had an issue, other times it was Jarno. When we had a genuine warming-up problem, like at Spa and Monza, both drivers were affected. I wouldn't say that there was a big difference between them. It's not as clear as with BMW Sauber for example, for whom Robert Kubica never had a problem and Nick Heidfeld did. In our case, it has been really balanced. For sure, it's more interesting when you can steer the tyres in a certain direction to maximise the benefits of your chassis concept, but we are all in the same situation and it's a case of teams and drivers simply having to adapt.

Overall, I was happy with the reliability, but still we had a few glitches at the wrong moments that cost us quite a few points. In Melbourne, Jarno was on for fifth place when we had a battery explosion, and he was running fifth again in Singapore when we had a stupid problem that was down to a quality problem on a hydraulic line. However, we can't say our reliability has been bad.

Mindful of the big changes for 2009, we knew we needed an early start and needed to push the development of the 2008 car, so we decided quite early to stagger the two cars and so we stopped developing the TF108 at the end of August.

NOT IN FAVOUR OF THE ENGINE FREEZE
From the engine side, Toyota was not in favour of the engine freeze: we're not in F1 to have frozen development. But we stopped all engine development concerned by the freeze and, now that some teams want to open the freeze, it all seems to be a bit inconsistent.

How much the changes for 2009 will alter the status quo is really an open question. You can always say that it will be the same ones in front, but it's a total reset. In our case, Toyota being new to F1, we were always playing catch-up to those teams that had been working within the existing regulations. So, for us, the rule changes are seen as a favourable opportunity."

TECHNICAL SPECIFICATIONS

ENGINE
MAKE/MODEL Toyota RVX-08
CONFIGURATION 2398cc V8 (90 degree)
SPARK PLUGS Denso
ECU FIA standard issue
FUEL Esso
OIL Esso
BATTERY Panasonic

TRANSMISSION
GEARBOX Toyota
FORWARD GEARS Seven
CLUTCH Sachs

CHASSIS
CHASSIS MODEL Toyota TF108
FRONT SUSPENSION LAYOUT
Carbon-fibre double wishbones with carbon-fibre trackrod and pushrod
REAR SUSPENSION LAYOUT
Carbon-fibre double wishbones with carbon-fibre toelink and pushrod

DAMPERS Penske
TYRES Bridgestone
WHEELS BBS
BRAKE DISCS Hitco
BRAKE PADS Hitco
BRAKE CALIPERS Brembo
FUEL TANK ATL
INSTRUMENTS
Toyota/Magneti Marelli

DIMENSIONS
LENGTH 4636mm
WIDTH 1800mm
HEIGHT 950mm
WHEELBASE Undisclosed
TRACK front Undisclosed
rear Undisclosed
WEIGHT 605kg (including driver and camera)

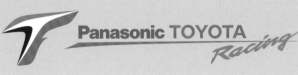

1 Rear wheel fairings were fitted for the Spanish GP and adopted thereafter for extracting air from the inside of the wheel to assist in the cooling of the brakes
2 The TF108 was fitted with chunky turning vanes on its nose for the first time in Bahrain to help tidy up the air flow off the front wing on its way to the rear wing

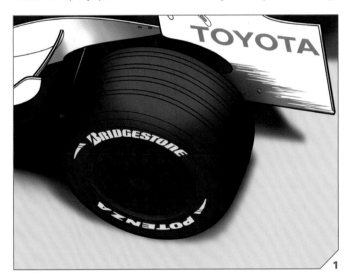

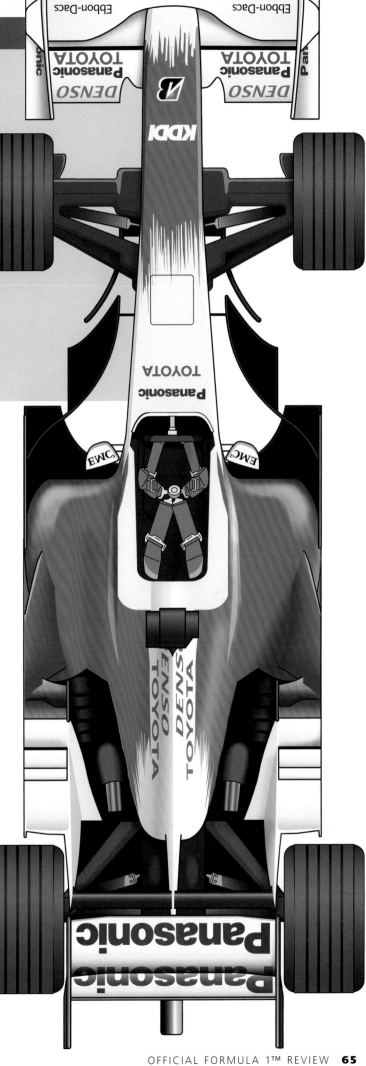

TORO ROSSO

THE TEAM

PERSONNEL

TEAM OWNERS Dietrich Mateschitz & Gerhard Berger
TEAM PRINCIPAL Franz Tost
TECHNICAL DIRECTOR Giorgio Ascanelli (above)
GENERAL MANAGER Gianfranco Fantuzzi
CHIEF DESIGNER Alex Hitzinger (Red Bull Technology)
CHIEF ENGINEER Laurent Mekies
TEAM MANAGER Massimo Rivola
DRIVERS Sebastien Bourdais, Sebastian Vettel
TECHNICAL CO-ORDINATOR Sandro Parrini
LOGISTICS MANAGER Domenico Sangiorgi
RACE ENGINEER (Bourdais) Claudio Balestri
RACE ENGINEER (Vettel) Riccardo Adami
CHIEF MECHANIC Paolo Piancastelli
ASSISTANT CHIEF MECHANIC Marco Campoduni
NO 1 MECHANIC (Bourdais) Alberto Gavarini
NO 1 MECHANIC (Vettel) Gabriele Vegnana
SENIOR TEST ENGINEER Gianvito Amico
SENIOR ENGINE ENGINEER Ernst Knoorst
RACE ENGINES MANAGER Mattia Binotto
TOTAL NUMBER OF EMPLOYEES 158
NUMBER IN RACE TEAM 62
TEAM BASE Faenza, Italy
TELEPHONE +39 (0)546 696111
WEBSITE www.tororosso.com

TEAM STATS

IN F1 SINCE 1985, as Minardi **FIRST GRAND PRIX** Brazil 1985 **STARTS** 394 **WINS** 1 **POLE POSITIONS** 1 **FASTEST LAPS** 0 **PODIUMS** 1 **POINTS** 86 **CONSTRUCTORS' TITLES** 0 **DRIVERS' TITLES** 0

SPONSORS

Red Bull, Hangar-7, Bridgestone, Magneti Marelli

 14 SEBASTIEN BOURDAIS   **15** SEBASTIAN VETTEL

A GIGANTIC STEP IN THE RIGHT DIRECTION

**By Giorgio Ascanelli
(Technical Director)**

"It has been a great season for us. The start was not so dramatic and we went to Melbourne with the old STR02. It was a good choice and we were in the battle for points, with Sebastien Bourdais running as high as fourth place before we had a hydraulic problem near the end and he was classified in seventh place.

The manufacturing constraints we had meant that it was impossible to get to the start of the season with a developed package. So we modified the old car for the new rules, which meant the head-protection matter.

Throughout the year, one clear element of our improvement was moving the weight around. We would shuffle it around in testing, making some lightweight parts and some heavyweight parts. Mechanically, we had also done quite a lot of work on the braking during the winter, and that paid off. So we went to Melbourne quite well prepared.

The drawback was, we started suffering a lack of reliability, as we had to count on different suppliers. Our standard suppliers were busy doing parts for the new car, which was late. That meant we had to find different sources and typically we had some early mortality failures if something in the process wasn't quite right. That's a normal difficulty with a team as small as Toro Rosso, which now stands at around 158 people.

SPLITTING THE WORKFORCE

Another challenge was starting the season without our best people to operate the car because they were busy working on the new one, which came later than planned. We took the STR03 to Monaco and suffered the five-place grid penalty because it meant using a different gearbox. Monaco was actually a bit of a lottery, we had some good fortune and a great fourth place with Sebastian Vettel. He benefited from Sutil and Räikkönen's accident near the end, but the car was very sound.

I was quite pleased with the general reliability of STR03. Bourdais had an accident in Barcelona testing, then in Monaco, and we had two accidents in Canada. And then after that the sun came out!

AERO UPGRADE IS A HIT

We received the car in the aerodynamic configuration Red Bull had at the beginning of the year, which wasn't anything special. Then at Magny-Cours we introduced the upgrade. It was clear at the pre-French GP Barcelona test that the character of the car was fundamentally changed. It was a clear step forward. We exploited the potential of the changes in the French GP and kept learning from there on.

In parallel, we started benefiting from our own work on braking systems. We had two failures, but now it's the best braking car in the pitlane and I give credit to the 150 souls working with me on getting the job done. It was purely a Toro Rosso programme.

As far as the aero development goes, however, we don't actually own a wind tunnel and we have no CFD (computational fluid dynamics). Red

Bull Technology does a lot of research in those directions. But if you look at the cars, they are different. They are generated by the same group of people, but you can pick what you want if you know what you're picking. The way I make the decision is 'how many races can we apply this to?' I have the duty to be efficient.

There are advantages and disadvantages to that approach. You become familiar with your material and what the car likes and doesn't. You start appreciating the impact of the mechanical set-up on the aero side. Aerodynamics is fundamental to modern-day F1, but mechanical grip, whatever that means, has a component and so you have to strike a balance.

TWO DIFFERENT DRIVING STYLES

The two Sebs do not have similar driving styles at all. You cannot impose a set-up on a driver and have to figure out what they need. They are normally not that precise at giving you feedback. It was probably a question of vocabulary. I'm not saying that they can't do the job, but it's difficult to visualise what they feel and what they want. They drive in a very different manner.

Both have the speed. Vettel is a rough diamond. Bourdais is more of a worker, but I think he also has the speed. Their competition helped, because mentally they had weak spots at different places and it led them to address them.

Both drivers have fundamentally helped the growth of the team tremendously. Drivers can teach you things that no-one else can. Bourdais was normally within a couple of tenths of Vettel – sometimes faster, sometimes slower – but in qualifying struggled a little. He came from ChampCar, which is a very different universe of heavier cars with less-efficient braking. You can't attack with those cars in the same way as in F1.

FERRARI OFFERS POWER BUT HEAT TOO

On the engine front, Ferrari did a tremendous job, but I don't think the advantage was as big as perceived. It does require different things. It was probably a bit more powerful than the Renault, but it's more difficult in terms of vibration and exhaust. It requires larger quantities of coolant, more radiator size and more installation space. Nothing comes from nothing!

I'd say that we eventually reached the completion of development, got more mature and our race pace improved. Our pattern of reliability improved. We had a terrible race in Hungary because of something in the system we didn't understand, but now we do. Valencia was a fantastic performance with everyone starting from scratch. Our analysis was quite well developed, then we walked the circuit, saw sand and said we should change what we we're planning for the cars. The guys were saying the computer says this, and I said, has your computer got sand in it? Twenty-five years experience helped!

Then, of course, the Monza win was the highlight. We got that absolutely right and Sebastian drove a great race. It was just a fantastic moment for everyone in the whole team."

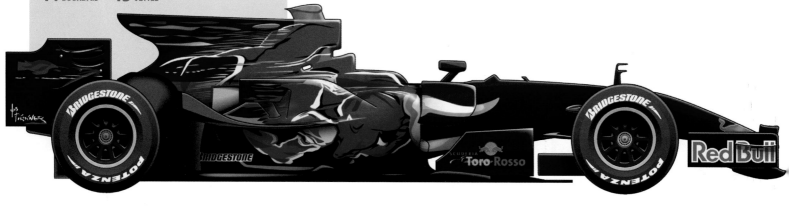

TECHNICAL SPECIFICATIONS

ENGINE
MAKE/MODEL Ferrari 056
CONFIGURATION 2398cc V8
(90 degree)
SPARK PLUGS Undisclosed
ECU FIA standard issue
FUEL Shell
OIL Shell
BATTERY Undisclosed

TRANSMISSION
GEARBOX Undisclosed
FORWARD GEARS Seven
CLUTCH AP Racing

CHASSIS
CHASSIS MODEL Toro Rosso STR03
FRONT SUSPENSION LAYOUT
Upper and lower carbon wishbones
and pushrods, torsion-bar springs and
anti-roll bars

REAR SUSPENSION LAYOUT
Upper and lower carbon wishbones
and pushrods, torsion-bar springs
and anti-roll bars
DAMPERS Multimatic
TYRES Bridgestone
WHEELS OZ Racing
BRAKE DISCS Hitco
BRAKE PADS Hitco
BRAKE CALIPERS Brembo
FUEL TANK ATL
INSTRUMENTS
Scuderia Toro Rosso

DIMENSIONS
LENGTH Undisclosed
WIDTH Undisclosed
HEIGHT Undisclosed
WHEELBASE
Undisclosed
TRACK front Undisclosed
rear Undisclosed
WEIGHT 605kg (including
driver and camera)

SCUDERIA Toro Rosso

1 Many teams worked particularly hard on tidying up the turbulent air coming off the front wheels, with Toro Rosso opting for these slotted sidepod boards
2 That same slotted sidepod board can be seen tucked behind the wheel on the right of this frontal view of the STR03's particularly sculpted sidepod opening

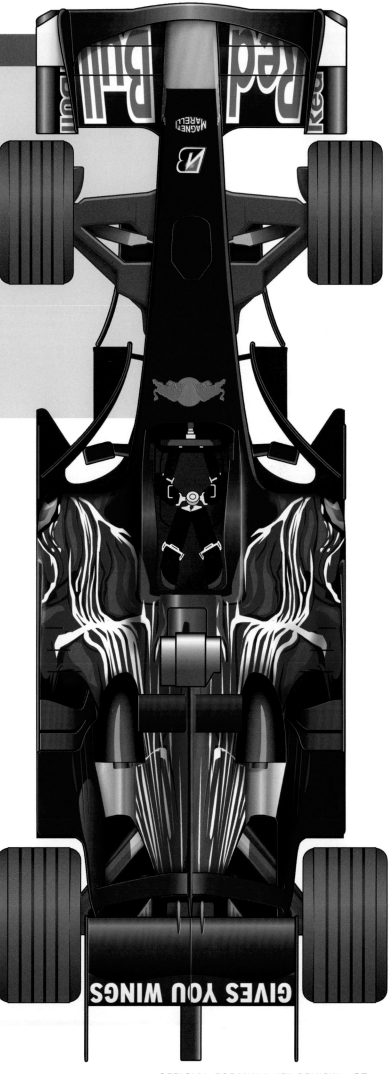

RED BULL

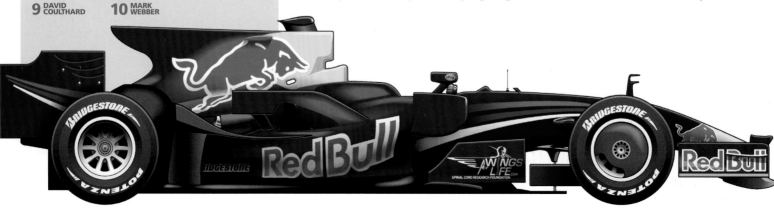

THE TEAM

PERSONNEL

CHAIRMAN Dietrich Mateschitz
TEAM PRINCIPAL Christian Horner
CHIEF TECHNICAL OFFICER Adrian Newey
TECHNICAL DIRECTOR Geoff Willis (above)
HEAD OF RACE & TEST ENGINEERING Paul Monaghan
CHIEF DESIGNER Rob Marshall
HEAD OF AERODYNAMICS Peter Prodromou
HEAD OF R&D Andrew Green
TEAM MANAGER Jonathan Wheatley
CHIEF ENGINEER ENGINES Fabrice Lom
DRIVERS David Coulthard, Mark Webber
RACE ENGINEER (Coulthard) Guillaume Rocquelin
RACE ENGINEER (Webber) Ciaron Pilbeam
TEST TEAM MANAGER Tony Burrows
TEST DRIVER Sébastien Buemi
CHIEF MECHANIC Kenny Handkammer
CHIEF TEST ENGINEER Ian Morgan
TOTAL NUMBER OF EMPLOYEES 540
NUMBER IN RACE TEAM 85
TEAM BASE Milton Keynes, England
TELEPHONE +44 (0)1908 279700
WEBSITE www.redbullracing.com

TEAM STATS

IN F1 SINCE 1997 as Stewart Grand Prix then Jaguar Racing
FIRST GRAND PRIX Australia 1997 **STARTS** 206
WINS 1 **POLE POSITIONS** 1 **FASTEST LAPS** 0
PODIUMS 8 **POINTS** 191 **CONSTRUCTORS' TITLES** 0
DRIVERS' TITLES 0

SPONSORS

Red Bull, Rauch, Quehenberger, Bridgestone. Renault, Wings
For Life

9 DAVID COULTHARD

10 MARK WEBBER

GREAT IN HIGH-SPEED CORNERS, BUT THWARTED

By Geoff Willis
(Technical Director)

"The RB4 was in a lot of ways a development of the RB3 with a number of aerodynamic subtleties. Adrian Newey and his group worked in quite different directions, even though from a structural point-of-view you could see the evolution. The focus, as well as the desire to improve performance, was to address the 2007 car's poor reliability. Indeed, until Mark Webber's retirement in the Singapore GP we'd had 100% reliability during the race on the chassis side with him.

We launched a number of developments prior to the opening grand prix, most obviously the big engine cover, which turned up at a late test, and then it was a busy season.

FOCUS ON THE FRONT END

We did a lot of work on front-wing development and characteristics of wings, barge boards, suspension and a number of rear wing developments. But probably most of our effort has gone into the front end of the car as we learned a lot more through our aero development.

We used just the Bedford wind tunnel which is not yet 24/7, but it now runs five and a half to six days a week. CFD is clearly an important tool and both the processing capacity and affordability of big processing has meant that you can take more and more realistic jobs and understand the car in a lot more complexity.

We focused on being able to get the weight distribution where we want so that we have more ballast to move and we put a lot of effort into understanding what the tyres need. You are refining your aero characteristics in light of that and what you can balance mechanically.

We had a couple of suspension issues with David in Melbourne and in practice in Malaysia. It was a poor design detail for the shim arrangement for the front pushrod. We couldn't understand the failure and so were slow in responding to it, but what effectively happened was that we had a buckling effect in something that shouldn't have failed and, as a result, the pushrod buckled.

COMING ON STRONG AT THE FINAL RACES

We had an aero package for the Spanish GP that improved the car and we delivered points in most races around mid-season. The second half of the season was harder. The competition caught us up, but in the last few races we had a good number of steps, the biggest one of which was for the Singapore GP. I think we identified what we thought the car issues were, then struggled for a while to add performance.

The primary driver for performance now is aerodynamics, but at the same time we were looking at behaviour in low-speed corners, low-speed traction, kerbing and considering if we had other issues in terms of suspension geometry.

On the engine side, we have a good relationship with Renault and it has always worked well. There are suggestions that as we went through the season some engine manufacturers found ways of – how can I put it sensibly? – getting advantages within the rules, and it's possible we've not done as good a job of that.

HOW THE RB4 DIFFERED TO THE TORO ROSSO

People ask about the way it works with Toro Rosso. Red Bull Technology designs cars for Red Bull Racing and Toro Rosso. They are to all intents and purposes the same car but, because one's a Ferrari installation and one's a Renault, there are quite a lot of differences. The chassis is different in arrangement of engine mounts and oil tank and in quite a lot of detail around the rear bulkhead. The gearboxes are slightly different because there are differences in crank heights between the two engines. The hydraulic systems and fuel systems are completely different.

There were small differences in set-up and I think when we got to Valencia we were concerned that we had missed something. We did quite a lot of experiments at Monza to replicate the two sets of set-ups but fundamentally the cars have been quite close all year. Certainly, the two distinguishing features are the different engines and two different sets of drivers. We have some estimates of where we think the differences in engine are, which is not just power but driveability and other characteristics. And, quite clearly, Sebastian Vettel has arrived and proved his mettle in Monza without any doubt.

BIZARRE GEARBOX PROBLEM IN SINGAPORE

Mark has always been strong in qualifying, and apart from no score at Melbourne he scored in every race bar Canada until Silverstone, and always raced well to get points. David has had a bit more of an inconsistent year and struggled a bit in qualifying. It's difficult when we are racing mid-grid as there are not many points out there to get.

Mark's Singapore problem, when he could have been second, was odd, and very frustrating. There was an uncommanded operation of one of the moog valves and it partly operated a gearshift and we ended up with a double engagement and broke the gearbox. We don't know why. We know other teams were having similar unrequested things. With some, it was happening to their clutch or throttle – all in more or less the same area of the track near Turn 13. We believe there is high-power cabling there for the tram or subway and we wondered about that. Perhaps now that the teams are mounting the hydraulic systems lower and lower, it might be that there was something in the road surface and we were picking it up.

Picking out the highs, Montréal was fortunate and we made the most of it with David's third place, and Singapore to a certain extent because we'd thought about that safety-car scenario and got it absolutely right. We stopped both cars just at the right point and after that it just didn't work out for us. The car was very impressive at Silverstone. It was one of the few cars that were flat through Copse and the next sequence and was clearly working very well. It was as strong in high-speed corners as any car this year and where we have struggled more is low-speed and how much of that was aero and how much was set-up."

TECHNICAL SPECIFICATIONS

ENGINE
MAKE/MODEL Renault RS27
CONFIGURATION 2400cc V8
(90 degree)
SPARK PLUGS Champion
ECU FIA standard issue
FUEL Elf
OIL Elf
BATTERY Panasonic

TRANSMISSION
GEARBOX Red Bull Racing
FORWARD GEARS Seven
CLUTCH AP Racing

CHASSIS
CHASSIS MODEL Red Bull RB4
FRONT SUSPENSION LAYOUT
Aluminium alloy uprights with upper and
lower wishbones and pushrods, torsion-
bar springs and anti-roll bars

REAR SUSPENSION LAYOUT
Aluminium alloy uprights with upper
and lower wishbones and pushrods,
torsion-bar springs and anti-roll bars
DAMPERS Multimatic
TYRES Bridgestone
WHEELS OZ Racing
BRAKE DISCS Hitco
BRAKE PADS Hitco
BRAKE CALIPERS Brembo
FUEL TANK ATL
INSTRUMENTS MES

DIMENSIONS
LENGTH 4600mm
WIDTH 1800mm
HEIGHT 950mm
WHEELBASE Undisclosed
TRACK front Undisclosed
rear Undisclosed
WEIGHT Undisclosed

1 The Red Bull RB4 appeared at the French GP with this style of narrower, slot-ended front wing, which meant that a wider endplate could be utilised
2 Like its sister team, Scuderia Toro Rosso, Red Bull fitted slotted boards ahead of the leading edge of its sidepods to help tidy up the turbulent air off the wheels

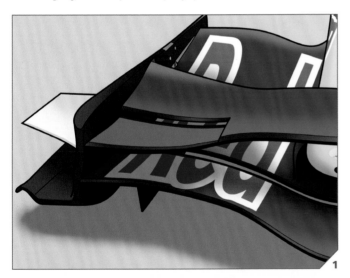

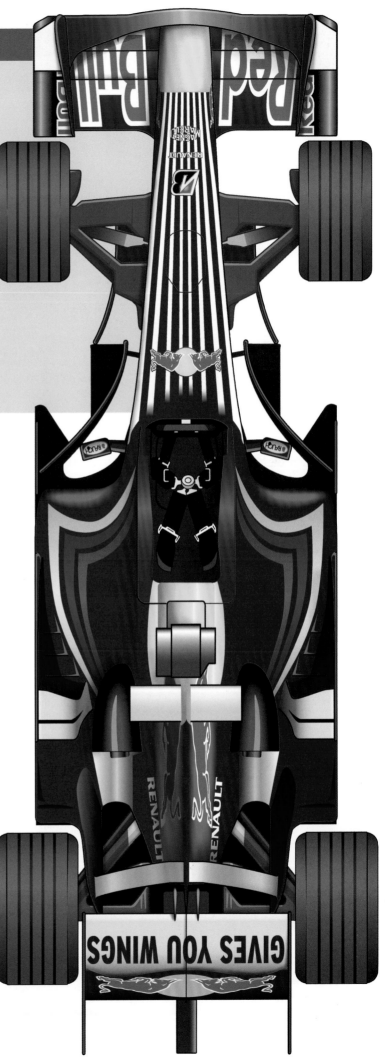

WILLIAMS

THE TEAM

PERSONNEL

TEAM PRINCIPAL Sir Frank Williams
DIRECTOR OF ENGINEERING Patrick Head
CHIEF EXECUTIVE OFFICER Adam Parr
TECHNICAL DIRECTOR Sam Michael (above)
CHIEF OPERATING OFFICER Alex Burns
CHIEF DESIGNER Ed Wood
HEAD OF AERODYNAMICS Jon Tomlinson
SENIOR SYSTEMS ENGINEER John Russell
CHIEF OPERATIONS ENGINEER Rod Nelson
TEAM MANAGER Tim Newton
DRIVERS Kazuki Nakajima, Nico Rosberg
RACE ENGINEER (Rosberg) Tony Ross
RACE ENGINEER (Nakajima) Xevi Pujolar
TEST TEAM MANAGER Dickie Stanford
TEST DRIVER Nico Hulkenberg
CHIEF MECHANIC Carl Gaden
SENIOR TEST ENGINEER Peter Harrison
TOTAL NUMBER OF EMPLOYEES 520
NUMBER IN RACE TEAM 70
TEAM BASE Grove, England
TELEPHONE +44 (0)1235 777700
WEBSITE www.attwilliamsf1.com

TEAM STATS

IN F1 SINCE 1973 **FIRST GRAND PRIX** Argentina
1973 **STARTS** 568 **WINS** 113 **POLE POSITIONS** 125
FASTEST LAPS 129 **PODIUMS** 296 **POINTS** 2571.5
CONSTRUCTORS' TITLES 9 **DRIVERS' TITLES** 7

SPONSORS

AT&T, RBS, Lenovo, Philips, Petrobras, Accenture, Allianz,
Battery, Randstand, Reuters, Air Asia, Hamleys, MAN Trucks

7 **NICO ROSBERG**   8 **KAZUKI NAKAJIMA**

CONSIDERABLE CHANGE, BUT FEW TOP RESULTS

By Sam Michael
(Technical Director)

"We changed a lot aerodynamically from the FW29, and the car was a good step when it launched and good in winter testing. It was straight away 0.8–0.9s quicker per lap than the FW29, so we knew we were doing the right thing. We had a more aggressive diffuser, a bigger front wing, a different engine cover and rear wing, and the sidepod area, barge boards and front-wing endplates all changed.

The Australian GP was good and then we had a couple of difficult races in Malaysia and Bahrain. The Spanish GP wasn't bad: Nico was running in seventh place and then we had a failure. Although we brought performance to the car there, we didn't bring it as strongly as other teams did.

The FW30 was quite strong at Monaco and Montréal, which have specific aero packages, and we'd done a lot of work on them.

BALANCING THIS YEAR AGAINST NEXT

I think the main thing we have struggled with, and hopefully it will pay off in 2009, is balancing working next year versus working on this year's car. That's a struggle that everyone had, but it probably affected us more than others. Plus the fact that everyone had up and down performances. The thing that penalised us the most through the year is that at the tracks at which we were strong, we didn't score any points. At places like Monaco or Montréal, we should have been taking away six or seven points, but we didn't and that hurt. We're not a lot different from some teams that scored 25 points more.

The FW30 was quite good in low-speed corners and when you were on soft tyres. We were on one end of the extreme in terms of being very good on low-speed tracks and Red Bull were pretty much the opposite.

It is quite interesting observing the cars, because we do see Red Bull as having a pretty similar lift-over-drag ratio to ours as well as similar power and drivers. Where we've been really strong, they have been massively weak and where they've been strong, we've been weak. We weren't good at Silverstone or Spa and it was in high-speed corners that we struggled most.

Throughout the season, I'd say we probably found half-a-second per lap, which is quite a lot considering how close the grid is. Often a couple of tenths of a second was the difference between fifth place or 15th. That's a number of things: control tyres, homologated engines and the rules being the same for four years.

We made a semi-shark-fin engine cover and tested it at Silverstone, but never really got anything out of it. It was neutral within the tunnel, slightly better, but it's about another kilo-and-a-half of mass up quite high.

SPEED AND DETERMINATION

Nico was quick, did well and will get even quicker when we give him a faster car. Kazuki scored nine points, which is not bad for a rookie year and just never gives up. In difficult conditions and those races where everything goes wrong, out of the smoke comes Kaz and picks up the points. If someone does that once or twice you think it's just lucky but, statistically, whenever there is a difficult race and he's there, you realise it's part of his driving character. He's very calm, doesn't get flustered very easily and I think that can be his strength as he gets more experienced. I think he came into this season wanting to make sure he didn't develop a reputation as a crasher and he has done well at that. Whether a guy is a world champion or a grade-two or grade-three driver, one thing I have seen is that rookies between their first and second year will always make a big step. Next year is a big one for Kaz. He's proven that he can be intelligent, and next year is going to be about how quick he is.

GOOD ENGINE, STRONG RELIABILITY

Engine-wise we were very happy. We have work to do on the chassis and hope to use the delta between 2008 and 2009 to catch up. Until we're there, the engine is definitely doing the job. For all we know, maybe the Toyota and Williams chassis are not good enough and the Toyota is a great engine. Unless you put all the engines on the same dyno, it's really difficult to tell.

Our reliability was solid. We only had one DNF due to poor reliability, which was the engine failure in Barcelona, and probably not entirely down to Toyota because there were places where we'd over-revved it. Apart from that, only a damper failure in qualifying for the British GP affected Nico's race.

We had a couple of close calls early on with the four-race gearbox as well. The 2007 gearbox was already four-race capable and this year's gearbox has been solid. Actually, the four-race rule has been fantastic for us. You hear people say it's more expensive or has made little difference, but that's just so wrong. Our spend on internals for gear ratios and things has come down by about 65% – it's massive. It has saved several million pounds rather than a hundred grand here and there. In fact, we're getting grief from Peter Digby at Xtrac for not buying enough ratios! I love rules like that, because doing long-life things doesn't detract from trying to do things stiffer and lighter and packaging them nicely.

A STRING OF HIU FAILURES

We had a few niggles with the standard ECU, but generally it's been alright There have been a few silly things like the HIUs (hub interface units) we have to put out on the uprights, so instead of having wires out there you have to buy these HIUs from McLaren and they are over a grand a pop. As soon as you overheat them once in the pitlane they're scrap, so they're making a fortune out of HIUs. When you talk to them they say, 'no, you guys seem to be the only ones with the problem'. Then you read Charlie's sheet which comes out on Sunday morning and everyone else has replaced HIUs! I think we've got about 35 grand's worth of dud HIUs sitting in a cardboard box. But apart from things like that, it's been alright!"

TECHNICAL SPECIFICATIONS

ENGINE
MAKE/MODEL Toyota RVX-08
CONFIGURATION 2398cc V8
(90 degree)
SPARK PLUGS Denso
ECU FIA standard issue
FUEL Petrobras
OIL Lubrax
BATTERY Panasonic

TRANSMISSION
GEARBOX WilliamsF1
FORWARD GEARS Seven
CLUTCH AP Racing

CHASSIS
CHASSIS MODEL Williams FW30
FRONT SUSPENSION LAYOUT
Carbon-fibre double wishbones with
composite toelink and pushrod-activated
torsion springs

REAR SUSPENSION LAYOUT
Double wishbones and pushrod-activated
torsion springs and rockers
DAMPERS WilliamsF1
TYRES Bridgestone
WHEELS RAYS
BRAKE DISCS Carbone Industrie
BRAKE PADS Carbone Industrie
BRAKE CALIPERS AP Racing
FUEL TANK ATL
INSTRUMENTS WilliamsF1

DIMENSIONS
LENGTH 4500mm
WIDTH 1800mm
HEIGHT 950mm
WHEELBASE 3100mm
TRACK front Undisclosed
rear Undisclosed
WEIGHT 605kg (including
driver and camera)

WILLIAMS F1

1 The FW30 turned up for the Monaco GP looking different, with its engine cover fitted with a winged tail to its rear, but it flexed too much to do the job asked of it
2 The Spanish GP was the scene for numerous new front wings, and Williams split its bridge wing into three, enabling the outer sections to be angled more

1

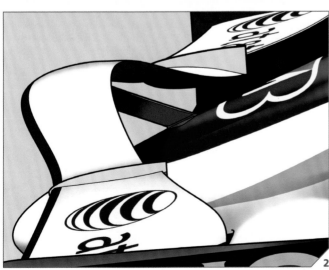

2

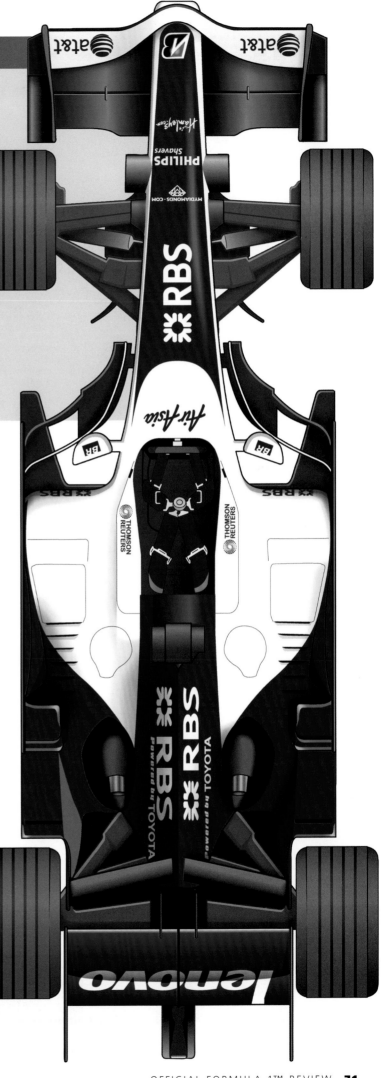

HONDA

THE TEAM

PERSONNEL

TEAM PRINCIPAL Ross Brawn (above)
CHIEF EXECUTIVE OFFICER Nick Fry
PRESIDENT HONDA RACING DEVELOPMENT
Hiroshi Abe
DEPUTY MANAGING DIRECTOR, TECHNICAL
Shuhei Nakamoto
DEPUTY TECHNICAL DIRECTOR Jorg Zander
DIRECTOR OF ADVANCED RESEARCH Jacky Eeckelaert
OPERATIONS DIRECTOR Gary Savage
HEAD OF AERODYNAMICS Loïc Bigois
HEAD OF RACE AND TEST ENGINEERING Steve Clark
HEAD OF VEHICLE ENGINEERING AND DYNAMICS
Craig Wilson
CHIEF TEST ENGINEER Simon Cole
SPORTING DIRECTOR Ron Meadows
DRIVERS Rubens Barrichello, Jenson Button
SENIOR RACE ENGINEER (Barrichello) Jock Clear
SENIOR RACE ENGINEER (Button) Andrew Shovlin
CHIEF MECHANIC Matt Deane
TEST TEAM MANAGER Andrew Alsworth
TEST/THIRD DRIVERS Alex Wurz, Mike Conway, Luca Filippi
TOTAL NUMBER OF EMPLOYEES 650
NUMBER IN RACE TEAM 100
TEAM BASE Brackley, England
TELEPHONE +44 (0)1280 844000
WEBSITE www.hondaracingf1.com

TEAM STATS

IN F1 SINCE 1999, as BAR **FIRST GRAND PRIX** Australia
1999 **STARTS** 171 **WINS** 1 **POLE POSITIONS** 3
FASTEST LAPS 0 **PODIUMS** 19 **POINTS** 326
CONSTRUCTORS' TITLES 0 **DRIVERS' TITLES** 0

SPONSORS

Bridgestone, Celerant, ENEOS, Fila, NGK, NTN, Ray-Ban, Seiko

16 JENSON BUTTON   **17** RUBENS BARRICHELLO

THE FRUITS OF REORGANISATION WILL COME

By Ross Brawn
(Team Principal)

"What we froze for testing was Loic Bigois and John's Owen's first stab at a car. It was an unusual circumstance as it hadn't evolved from the last one. There was very little wind-tunnel work and CFD is not our strongest area, but we have some very good people, although we haven't got the strength of organisation yet.

It was a funny set-up because up until about a year ago CFD was still a Reynard company and so was part-subcontracted. That wasn't the best solution. They were doing a variety of things, not just F1. It's an area where every team seems to be expanding, so it's quite hard to find good people.

A LACK OF AN ESTABLISHED CULTURE

I didn't have experience with the 2007 Honda, and Loic and John arrived quite late in the design cycle. So they had to drop in and do a basic, sensible job. They each had their ideas, but we didn't have a philosophy or culture established and had a lot of new people coming together, so it was a bit of a compendium of ideas.

They arrived in September, expected to do an aero concept and didn't like what was being planned, so scrapped it. It was all a bit traumatic. We kept the chassis and gearbox, but there were inevitable compromises there. That was really why I had to re-do the rear suspension because there were some wrong decisions made in terms of compromise between aero and structure.

Before that, there were limitations on the rear suspension and the ride quality was dreadful. It was encouraging to see that the suspension was such a step forward. In terms of magnitude of effect, I can see other areas on the car that would have far more influence, but we simply couldn't do it with this car.

IN SEARCH OF AERODYNAMIC GAIN

There was a feeling in 2007 that the car was aerodynamically weak and structurally good, and that the structure could be compromised to try to achieve better aero. That was a mistake. The stronger aero needed to come without compromising the structure. From my experience, I know that the top teams have very good structures – kinematics, low centre of gravity, the masses in the right places – and very good aero too.

But, one important aspect of team building was to make a success of the suspension project with our existing people. They'd been led down the wrong path a little. If it had been another pig's ear, it would have been clear what we had to do, but I think they did a great job considering the compromises around the existing gearbox.

The rear-damper velocity was very poor, which made it almost impossible to put some damping into the car. The compliance at the rear was poor too, so even if you tried to damp it out, you couldn't. So the ratio of tyre movement to suspension movement was way out – it was all happening on the tyres. It was a bit difficult to understand how some of the decisions had been made. That's why doing a new suspension was

important. I wanted to see how the team system there worked.

We had also moved from one CAD system to another, which was traumatic, but we've got through the heartache of all that now. We're still building systems and tools because we've never had great tools within the company in terms of rigs. By the end of this year, we are expecting a big improvement in capacity there.

A TALE OF TWO CENTRES

Integrating Honda's Tochigi facilities is a fascinating challenge. They have a history of engine and gearbox work and their gearbox work this year has been good. We're working at trying to make it more effective in the chassis area, where we have to find the areas that suit Tochigi and the areas that suit Brackley in order to avoid a competition between the two.

The relationship is not historically easy. BAR designed the car and Honda gave them the engine. However, as Honda became the owner, Tochigi became much more involved – but it wasn't very well structured. There was friction about who was doing what.

Tochigi can't operate frontline car design because decisions are made on an hour-by-hour basis in Brackley. So it's a question of finding the right balance. The trick is that when you have a problem you've got to make sure that the relevant people have a plan to deal with it, and the rest concentrate on their bit and keep their blinkers on.

I think what's happened with the last car or two is that everyone has poured into aero because that was the problem – and the rest gets left. The huge enthusiasm that people have can lead to loss of focus. It's a discipline, not a change of structure. I see Tochigi as a wonderful opportunity. But we have to make sure it's an asset, not a distraction.

DRIVERS SHOWED STOICISM

I already knew Rubens very well but Jenson was new to me. I'm very impressed with his speed and composure. One thing I really like is that when he makes a mistake he comes clean immediately. There's nothing worse than chasing your tail because the driver's keeping something from you!

I don't think we've seen the best of Jenson this year. I've seen some races that were very good and others where he hasn't got it together. I think if we gave him a really good car we'd see the good races every weekend. He went through a difficult spell where he had too many crashes, but I don't hold that against him.

We were almost so far away that the drivers were entitled to come to me and say that it was unacceptable. But they understood we had to knife-and-fork our way through this year without compromising what we're doing for 2009. They both kept a positive outlook and worked hard with the engineers, but it must have been galling.

The new regulations are great and give us a fresh starting point. The good teams will still be good because they have the tools, capacity and experience. We have a chance to get on that bandwagon if we're good."

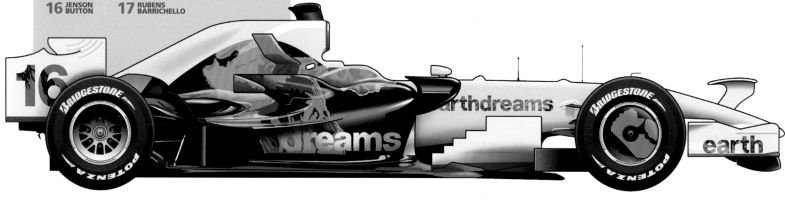

ENGINE
MAKE/MODEL Honda RA808E
CONFIGURATION 2400cc V8 (90 degree)
SPARK PLUGS NGK
ECU FIA standard issue
FUEL Elf
OIL ENEOS
BATTERY NGK

TRANSMISSION
GEARBOX Honda F1
FORWARD GEARS Seven
CLUTCH Undisclosed

CHASSIS
CHASSIS MODEL Honda RA108
FRONT SUSPENSION LAYOUT
Wishbones and pushrod-activated
torsion springs and rockers, with a
mechanical anti-roll bar
REAR SUSPENSION LAYOUT
Wishbones and pushrod-activated
torsion springs and rockers, with a
mechanical anti-roll bar

DAMPERS Showa
TYRES Bridgestone
WHEELS BBS
BRAKE DISCS
Carbon Industrie
BRAKE PADS
Carbon Industrie
BRAKE CALIPERS
Alcon
FUEL TANK ATL
INSTRUMENTS
Honda F1

DIMENSIONS
LENGTH 4700mm
WIDTH 1800mm
HEIGHT 950mm
WHEELBASE
Undisclosed
TRACK
front Undisclosed
rear Undisclosed
WEIGHT Undisclosed

1 The RA108's 'dumbo ear' nose wings were made bigger for the Monaco GP, with the addition of vertical end sections to help to realign the air flow to the rear
2 This lower graphic shows just how these 'dumbo ear' nose wings sit up from the car's nose above the front wing, with their role prinicpally to tidy the air flow

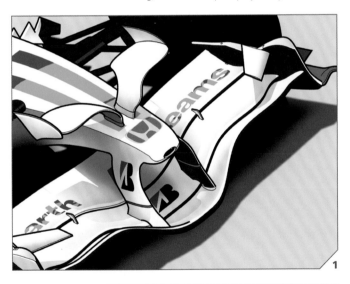

1

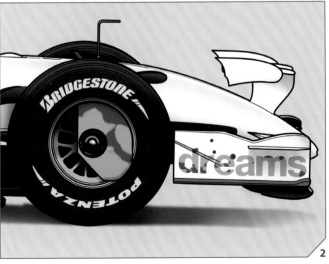

2

FORCE INDIA

THE TEAM

PERSONNEL

CHAIRMAN & MANAGING DIRECTOR Vijay Mallya
CO-OWNER Michiel Mol
TEAM PRINCIPAL Colin Kolles
CHIEF TECHNICAL OFFICER Mike Gascoyne (above)
DIRECTOR CORPORATE AFFAIRS Patrick Missling
TECHNICAL DIRECTOR James Key
DESIGN DIRECTOR Mark Smith
HEAD OF R&D Simon Gardner
HEAD OF AERODYNAMICS Simon Phillips
TEAM MANAGER Andy Stevenson
DRIVERS Giancarlo Fisichella, Adrian Sutil
CHIEF ENGINEER Dominic Harlow
RACE ENGINEER (Sutil) Jody Eggington
RACE ENGINEER (Fisichella) Brad Joyce
TEST/THIRD DRIVER Vitantonio Liuzzi
HEAD OF CAR BUILD Nick Burrows
CHIEF MECHANIC Andy Deeming
TEAM CO-ORDINATOR Franco Massano
TOTAL NUMBER OF EMPLOYEES 250
NUMBER IN RACE TEAM 60
TEAM BASE Silverstone, England
TELEPHONE +44 (0)1327 850800
WEBSITE www.forceindiaf1.com

TEAM STATS

IN F1 SINCE 1991, as Jordan then Midland **FIRST GRAND PRIX** USA 1991 **STARTS** 303 **WINS** 4 **POLE POSITIONS** 2 **FASTEST LAPS** 2 **PODIUMS** 20 **POINTS** 288 **CONSTRUCTORS' TITLES** 0 **DRIVERS' TITLES** 0

SPONSORS

Kingfisher, Medion, ICICI Bank, Kanyan Capital

20 ADRIAN SUTIL

21 GIANCARLO FISICHELLA

BUDGET BOOST CAME TOO LATE TO TRANSFORM

By Mike Gascoyne
(Chief Technical Officer)

"We introduced a new rear end on the B-spec version of our 2007 car and basically the 2008 car was a rebodied version of that.

Although we are now Force India and have a much better budget, that was only available as from January 1 of this year, so its impact on the VJM01 wasn't as great as it could have been. Mind you, at the end of last year when we were still Spyker, it wasn't clear whether we could continue or not, or even what budget we had, so there was no option but to carry over.

We put a programme in place to update the wind tunnel and that took a lot longer than planned because we couldn't pay the bills, so it didn't come on stream until September. We had the AeroLab tunnel running as well. The upshot was that we didn't have long in the tunnel to do as much as we would have liked.

QUICK-SHIFT GEARBOX WAS A MUST

From January 1, with a proper budget in place at last, we instigated the quick-shift gearbox programme and the benefits of that were fairly clear. Once the transition from Spyker to Force India had been made, we wanted to get better results.

In terms of performance, we have improved and the VJM01 was a good step. We moved closer to the rest of the field by around 1s per lap prior to the introduction of the quick-shift and we then found another 0.3–0.4s per lap after that. But we're still at the back, which is not surprising after the demise of Super Aguri and Scuderia Toro Rosso being given a car that's had a huge investment made in it by Red Bull Technologies.

HAMPERED BY A LIMITED STAFF COUNT

The quick-shift was actually a tricky project without a transient dynamometer. We have a gearbox department of just two people! They did the 2008 box, which was modified from last year's a little, then they started on the quick-shift. They did a tremendous job and we also had notably good input from Mark Smith via his experience at Red Bull Racing and from Ian Hall's experience at Toyota. This meant we were able to shortcut some of the issues.

The car wasn't a pure carry-over and we did do some upgrades. Mark joined in November and Ian in January, so they were able to provide input into the update. However, all the major mechanical components were carry-overs.

DIVISION OF LABOUR

The way we were organised was that Mark concentrates on all the cars, as the design director. We appointed Akio Haga, who took over as project leader for the 2008 car, with Ian on the 2009 car. In fact, the drawing office has almost doubled in size from a year ago and, from the European GP at Valencia onwards, we've been all but matching the works Hondas.

We do aero work in the AeroLab tunnel, which we've expanded and now run four weeks a month rather than two. We're 24/7 in our own tunnel and we have been using the Lola tunnel for continued development of the VJM01.

We had a very effective programme that correlates reasonably well. It is effectively the same model in each tunnel. At Lola's tunnel, we started doing yaw testing, which we can now also do in our tunnel.

The capability has really gone up a lot in a year. Including people in Italy, the aero department is nearly 90 people out of our 280 total, headed up by Simon Phillips. That is quite a high proportion.

LACK OF DRIVER AIDS HELPED TEAM'S PUSH

This year's car has a lot more downforce for the same drag level. We looked better at the start of the year by putting updates on that some of the other teams put on for the Spanish GP. Then we dropped back. Look at Williams and Honda, and we've joined that group. Even though we have had a better budget to work with, it is still only half of any other team and a third of the budgets that most of them have, or less.

We made some diffuser changes in a general push for efficiency. Some of the things were incorporated through being able to do the yaw testing. We caught up in a lot of areas that, before, we just couldn't test in. The lack of driver aids also maybe helped us a little bit by bringing some of the top teams back towards us.

We've used the Wurth simulator on a couple of occasions, for Valencia and Singapore, and will look at trying to instigate something like that for 2009 for ourselves. We introduced an updated airbox for the Singapore GP. Ferrari has comparison data to compare it to and they don't see a problem with ours.

The update we did for the British GP was worth about 0.4s per lap and, combined with the quick-shift gearbox, brought us from 1 second off the back of the field to being right there with Honda. We have matched or gained on all the teams in terms of a season-long gain.

INERTER MAKES A DIFFERENCE OVER KERBS

An inerter was part of the Silverstone update and it was very beneficial. The guys really noticed it at the Monza test, where you use the kerbs. Adrian, on his first run, said that the car was just so much better than last year's around there. That was down to the inerter and the fact that when the car landed it had more downforce.

Both drivers had too many shunts, which is something they need to address. Adrian struggled early on to match Fisi in qualifying but came good on that. Adrian's first couple of runs were good but, when everyone improved by three or four tenths on the last run, he'd over-drive. He identified that and worked on it. Generally, he's raised his game and kept Fisi honest in the second half of the season, which Fisi needed.

The relationship with Ferrari was always very good. They always tried to help and they appreciated that, for the money, we were doing a very good job. In Valencia, we were just 0.5s per lap off the World Champion in his Ferrari."

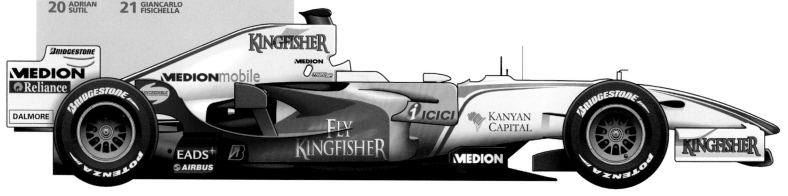

TECHNICAL SPECIFICATIONS

ENGINE
MAKE/MODEL Ferrari 056
CONFIGURATION 2398cc V8
(90 degree)
SPARK PLUGS NGK
ECU FIA standard issue
FUEL Mobil 1
OIL Mobil 1
BATTERY Magneti Marelli

TRANSMISSION
GEARBOX Force India
FORWARD GEARS Seven
CLUTCH AP Racing

CHASSIS
CHASSIS MODEL Force India VJM01
FRONT SUSPENSION LAYOUT
Composite pushrods activating
chassis-mounted in-line dampers
and torsion bars, unequal length
composite aerodynamic wishbones,
front anti-roll bar

REAR SUSPENSION LAYOUT
Composite pushrods activating
gearbox-mounted rotary dampers
and torsion bars, unequal length
composite aerodynamic wishbones,
DAMPERS Penske
TYRES Bridgestone
WHEELS BBS
BRAKE DISCS Hitco
BRAKE PADS Hitco
BRAKE CALIPERS
AP Racing/Brembo
FUEL TANK ATL
INSTRUMENTS Force India

DIMENSIONS
LENGTH Undisclosed
WIDTH Undisclosed
HEIGHT 950mm
WHEELBASE Undisclosed
TRACK front 1480mm
rear 1418mm
WEIGHT 605kg (including driver
and camera)

1 Putting a shroud over the inner half of the lower wishbone of the VJM01 is yet
another device tried by the teams to tidy up the air flowing off the front wing
2 When is a wing miror mount not a wing mirror mount? When it's a turning
vane... Force India made it even more efficient by linking it to the sidepod fence

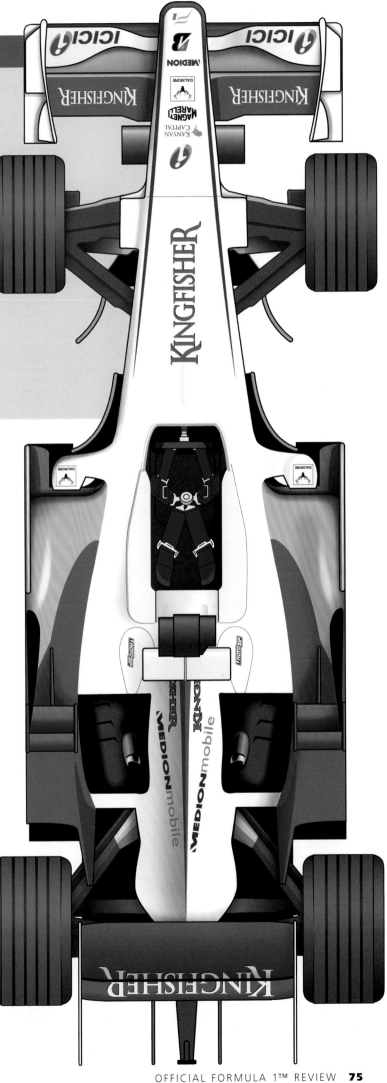

SUPER AGURI

LIVING IN HOPE FAILED TO LAST FOR VERY LONG

THE TEAM

PERSONNEL

TEAM PRINCIPAL Aguri Suzuki
MANAGING DIRECTOR Daniele Audetto
TECHNICAL DIRECTOR Mark Preston (above)
SPORTING DIRECTOR Graham Taylor
CHIEF DESIGNER Peter McCool
HEAD OF AERODYNAMICS Ben Wood
OPERATIONS DIRECTOR Kevin Lee
HEAD OF R&D & CHIEF RACE ENGINEER Gerry Hughes
TEAM MANAGER Mick Ainsley-Cowlishaw
DRIVERS Anthony Davidson, Takuma Sato
RACE ENGINEER (Sato) Richard Connell
RACE ENGINEER (Davidson) Richard Lane
TEST DRIVER James Rossiter
CHIEF MECHANIC Phill Spencer
TOTAL NUMBER OF EMPLOYEES 152
NUMBER IN RACE TEAM 43
TEAM BASE Witney, England
TELEPHONE +44 (0)1993 871600
WEBSITE www.saf1.co.jp

TEAM STATS

IN F1 SINCE 2006 **FIRST GRAND PRIX** Bahrain 2006
STARTS 39 **WINS** 0 **POLE POSITIONS** 0
FASTEST LAPS 0 **PODIUMS** 0 **POINTS** 4
CONSTRUCTORS' TITLES 0 **DRIVERS' TITLES** 0

SPONSORS

Honda, Bridgestone, Seiko, Smantha Kingz, NGK Spark Plugs, Autobacs, Takata Corporation

18 TAKUMA SATO　　**19 ANTHONY DAVIDSON**

By Mark Preston
(Technical Director)

"We had to have the four-race gearbox and already we had financial problems and couldn't really test before the start of the season. Our main target through the close-season was just to get to the Australian GP. At the time, Martin Leach's operation was trying to buy the place and everything was in a holding pattern until we found out what was going to happen, so understandably we were minimising our spend while the powers-that-be negotiated for the clinching of a sale.

We did a run to check the gearbox and then in Melbourne we were obviously behind the competition and the car was pretty slow. It wasn't like the year before when we'd arrived with quite a bit of testing, everything on song and surprised even ourselves by making it through to Q3.

COOLING WAS THE NUMBER ONE PROBLEM

Not having the right amount of preparation really showed in Melbourne. We had a lot of problems with cooling. Our aero guy, Ben Wood, had come out to that race and was busy trying to make the most unobtrusive cuts in the bodywork. I remember him sketching a few things and saying, 'here's your first level of cooling, here's your second and here's your absolute emergency level...' In the end, it didn't look too bad.

Melbourne hadn't been that hot for years and a lot of people had problems. I remember all our computing systems with fans turned on them, and drafting in air-conditioning units to keep everything going. My family lives in Melbourne and my Dad had to go off and buy some more fans for us!

The car was pretty much an SA07 with a four-race gearbox from Honda. We were allowed to have the engine/gearbox and that was good. I don't envy Force India if they do decide to change to running McLaren chassis for 2009, because it will be a lot of work depending upon what they get in the end, even if it's just an engine. So, that side of things made it slightly easier, or at least bearable.

SALVATION LOOKED TO BE A POSSIBILITY

We had to do a little modification to the headrest, but that was the only rule change and so we had minimal work to do. People wonder what the vibe was like at that time, but it was actually good because we thought it was going to be saved. Martin Leach came to Melbourne, they were getting quite involved and it all seemed as if Honda wanted it to happen as well and it was going to go ahead. Everyone was happy to go into cost-saving mode knowing, or hoping, that there was going to be a deal and then we could get on with life.

We had to just do what we could with what we had. It was frustrating but, at the same time, we were looking forward to a change and getting ready for 2009. All in all, everyone was really upbeat and trying to be entrepreneurial and spend no money! There were a couple of nice ideas in the garage to make things slicker, and guys making things back at the factory using whatever we had left in the freezer!

We were still working in the tunnel because our philosophy was that aero is king, so to keep our hands in we were running at a really low level. The nice thing about having a CAD system is that you can keep working, you just can't make any parts!

WE KEPT FOCUSING ON 2009

We were all trying to keep motivated by coming up with schemes and there was plenty to do looking ahead to 2009. Peter McCool, our chief designer, is now at McLaren with some of the design guys. Gerry Hughes was chief race engineer and head of R&D, a dual role as we waited to see what happened.

In Malaysia, Martin Leach and Honda were saying, look guys, let's just get through the flyaways, get back to Europe and hopefully the deal will happen with the investors and we'll have a sensible go at the second half of the year. We'd got the car slightly more optimised with a bit of input from Ben, but it was still slow and we were battling the Force Indias. We were quite happy that even they were in reach because we thought they were doing a pretty good job. Our only bit of excitement was trying to beat those guys.

The Bahrain GP was alright because it was another flyaway and we were on our way back to the UK. However, our participation in the Spanish GP was very 11th hour. That was the final knockings really and the negotiations fell down before we got to Turkey. They called everyone into the factory and we had maybe one more week of chances. When the last one didn't happen, that was it and we were put into administration.

The test is basically whether there is hope of a deal that can rescue the creditors and once they were sure that that wasn't going to happen, it was the end. It was quite quick, not like some of those in the past that were strung out for ages. The trucks had been sent to Turkey just in case, because it was only a couple of tanks of fuel to get them back and if you don't turn up for a race you get clobbered. We were actually all confident until the last minute, but after we'd missed a race it was almost impossible to continue.

SELLING OFF THE EQUIPMENT

I joined forces with a German company, Formtec, and we bought the assets and have set up a composites company at Leafield. We're actually busy selling off all the trucks and seeing all the pit stuff go out the door, which is quite sad. We're setting up and taking over the production area of Leafield. It's owned by John Menard and he's got an engine company here. Sadly, Martin Leach's company, Ultramotive, has also gone into administration and so the building is quite empty at the moment.

The nicest thing about Super Aguri is that we got a bit of respect from getting in there quickly and delivering. I'm pretty sure that almost everyone has a job in F1 or A1GP. Graham Taylor is running the Monaco A1GP team and has taken a lot of the mechanics with him. Many of the design guys went to Honda, McLaren and Renault. We're quite proud of that. In comparison to when Arrows went bankrupt, I think it's been quite alright."

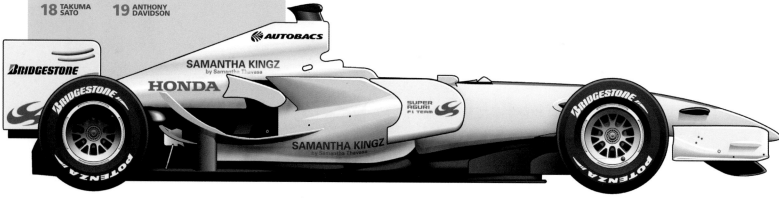

TECHNICAL SPECIFICATIONS

ENGINE
MAKE/MODEL Honda RA808E
CONFIGURATION 2400cc V8
(90 degree)
SPARK PLUGS NGK
ECU FIA standard issue
FUEL ENEOS
OIL ENEOS
BATTERY Undisclosed

TRANSMISSION
GEARBOX Super Aguri
FORWARD GEARS Seven
CLUTCH Sachs

CHASSIS
CHASSIS MODEL Super Aguri SA08
FRONT SUSPENSION LAYOUT
Upper and lower wishbones, pushrod-activated torsion springs and rockers, with mechanical anti-roll bars

REAR SUSPENSION LAYOUT
Upper and lower carbon-wrapped steel wishbones, pushrod-activated torsion springs and rockers, with mechanical anti-roll bars
DAMPERS Showa
TYRES Bridgestone
WHEELS BBS
BRAKE DISCS Hitco
BRAKE PADS Hitco
BRAKE CALIPERS Alcon
FUEL TANK ATL
INSTRUMENTS Super Aguri

DIMENSIONS
LENGTH 4685mm
WIDTH 1800mm
HEIGHT 950mm
WHEELBASE 3165mm
TRACK front 1450mm
rear 1400mm
WEIGHT 605kg (including driver and camera)

SUPER AGURI
F1 TEAM

1 There was little opportunity to change much on the SA08, as money was so tight. Here is some tidy detailing at the trailing edge of the exhaust chimneys
2 At the outset, the sidepod opening looked like this, but soaring temperatures in Australia made the team take drastic measures and cut the bodywork

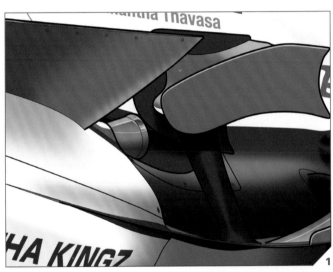

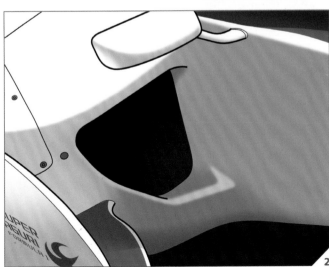

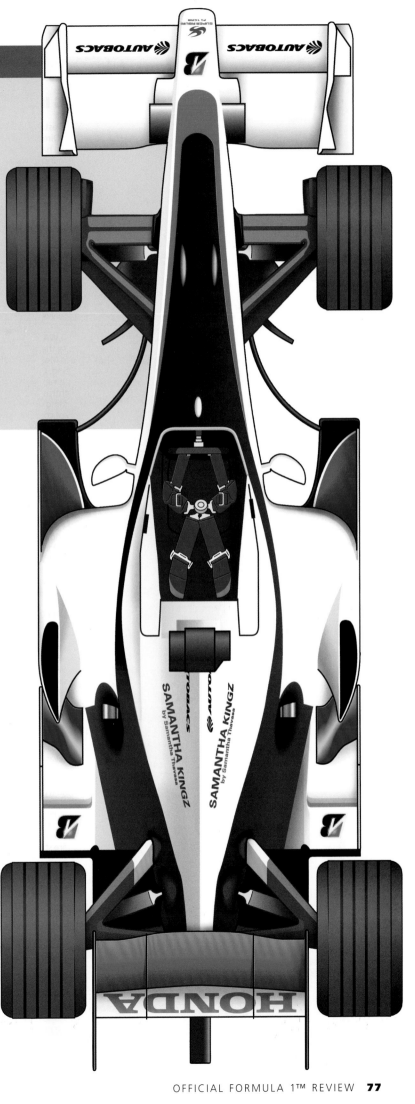

THE RACES

Two new circuits, F1's first night race and first victories for two teams offered a new taste for 2008, but the battle for honours remained between Ferrari and McLaren

2008 FORMULA 1 ING AUSTRALIAN GRAND PRIX
MELBOURNE

LEWIS AT A CANTER

It hadn't been an enjoyable close season for Ron Dennis and McLaren, so Lewis Hamilton's victory in Melbourne, combined with Ferrari's double failure, provided the perfect tonic

A year can be a long time both in politics and motor racing. Just 12 months after his first appearance as a wide-eyed rookie, Lewis Hamilton kicked off his sophomore season with a win achieved in the majestic style of a long-established champion.

It was the perfect response from a McLaren team that had tried very hard to put the nightmare that was the 2007 season behind it and start afresh. The fact that the cars carried numbers 22 and 23, though, was a constant and painful reminder that the beleaguered outfit had been dumped to the bottom of the constructors' championship table.

The Australian GP very often provides drama, and this race proved to be no exception, with a series of incidents and safety-car periods keeping the crowd on their toes. Remarkably, only seven of the 22 starters were still running when the flag fell, and when one of those was excluded for an infringement, two drivers who had retired several laps earlier actually earned championship points. It seemed that the new era of the standard ECU and lack of driver aids had made life harder for drivers and engineers alike.

Among those left pondering their bad luck was Kimi Räikkönen and, while his single point for eighth

place was better than nothing, it was a poor reward after a stressful weekend for a Ferrari team operating without Jean Todt at the helm for the first time since 1993. While the Frenchman's absence could in no way be blamed for any of the specific problems that arose, it was perhaps an unfortunate coincidence that the team had one of its worst races in many years on its first weekend under the stewardship of Stefano Domenicali.

The new qualifying regulations, which meant that the top 10 drivers started the race with the fuel load with which they finished qualifying, were in use for the first time. Hamilton secured his seventh career pole position for McLaren but, against expectations, his main opposition did not come from Ferrari. Instead, Robert Kubica qualified second, as BMW Sauber revealed its hand and showed that disappointing winter testing form was misleading. Indeed, had he not run wide on what was clearly an awesome lap, he would have taken pole.

Heikki Kovalainen qualified a respectable third on his debut for McLaren, while Felipe Massa was the better of the Ferrari drivers in fourth, having failed to get his tyres warm enough on his final run. There was even more disappointment for Räikkönen, who had a fuel pump problem that resulted from a wrong setting applied by the team, and stopped at the end of the first session. He just failed to coast into the pit entry, and a push from the marshals there meant that he was not eligible to take any further part in qualifying, so he had to start 15th.

Hamilton charged into the lead at the start, but there was chaos behind as Massa had his own accident when he changed down to first gear instead of second and didn't have traction control to help him out of trouble. Five drivers further down the field were eliminated in a series of incidents at Turn 1 and Turn 3, bringing out the safety car. Massa was able to continue after pitting for a new nose, but local hero Mark Webber, Jenson Button, Giancarlo Fisichella, Sebastian Vettel and Anthony Davidson were all out.

As soon as the race resumed, Hamilton pulled out a comfortable gap on the chasing Kubica. When the Pole pitted on lap 16, Hamilton had such an advantage that the team didn't even make full use of his fuel load. Instead, they brought him in two laps early on lap 18 to avoid any risk of being caught out by a closed pitlane should a safety car come out.

The wisdom of that decision was demonstrated a few laps later when Massa, trying desperately to make up ground, ran into David Coulthard under braking for Turn 1. Massa was able to continue on his way, but the Red Bull suspension's collapsed in spectacular fashion. Coulthard wasted little time in blaming Massa for the incident.

"He didn't see me," said the equally frustrated Brazilian. "Ask him, I don't know why he isn't very happy. Next time ask him to watch in the mirrors, because I was completely inside."

Inevitably, this triggered another safety-car period, and Hamilton lost a 12s advantage over his team-mate, who had Räikkönen – yet to make his single pit stop – sitting right on his tail.

When racing resumed for a second time, Hamilton simply set to work on rebuilding his lead. Meanwhile, Kubica lost ground in the shuffle when he made his second pit stop earlier than planned and was fuelled to the end. It could have worked well, but he then got caught behind a slower car.

Hamilton was 6s clear of Kovalainen when he made his second pit stop, again a couple of laps prematurely. This time it really was close, for soon

OPPOSITE TOP Hamilton leads from Kubica at Turn 1, with Massa already out of shape behind them

OPPOSITE BOTTOM Kovalainen, now a McLaren driver, qualified well, but being in the wrong place when the safety cars came out left him to settle for fifth

BELOW Turn 1 madness as Fisichella's Force India is forced skywards by a hit from Glock

TALKING POINT
LIFE WITHOUT DRIVER AIDS

There had been questions about it all winter: what difference to racing would standard electronic control units (ECUs) and a ban on driver aids make to the show?

Nobody had any doubts that things would be a lot trickier in the wet, but nobody was quite expecting the plethora of thrills,

spills and excursions we saw at a baking hot, dry Albert Park. It wasn't the rookies either. World Champion Kimi Räikkönen locked up and slid straight on trying to pass Heikki Kovalainen. And, if you put that down to over-exuberance in the heat of an all-Finnish tussle, he did it again while trying to pass Timo Glock's Toyota, which clearly pointed to something else.

In fact, as first encountered in the final few winter tests, it wasn't so much the absence of traction control that was causing problems as the absence of engine braking. Despite an ABS ban in F1, the teams had become adept at using sophisticated electronics to spread the front/rear braking loads and prevent lock-ups. Pushing hard on low-fuel qualifying run simulations,

a number of drivers had commented on the absence of engine braking but, largely running alone on the circuit in testing, it hadn't proved to be a major issue.

The Australian GP, of course, was the first time in more than four months that drivers had been called upon to run wheel-to-wheel. And so mistakes allied to a certain degree of ring-rustiness were predictable. Factor into the equation the heat in Australia and the fact that the 37 degrees on race day led to greater tyre degradation and thus reduced grip, and it all added up to the incident-packed season opener.

"We are trying to maximise the potential of the car and it makes it tricky on corner entry," explained winner McLaren's Lewis Hamilton.

"Carrying heavy fuel loads makes a big difference to your braking zones and it's a lot easier to slide off. But it's racing, it's the way it should be, so great..."

Renault's engineering chief Pat Symonds cautioned, though: "We certainly had safety-car periods and a large number of incidents, but don't forget that we always have incidents at Albert Park. It's tricky, slippery and the guys haven't raced for a while. How much was down to that and how much was lack of driver aids? I don't know. I'd say that the jury is still out."

Point taken, but if this was Melbourne, what might happen at low-grip venues with the barriers up close, like Monte Carlo? And what would happen if it rained in the Principality?

INSIDE LINE
LEWIS HAMILTON
McLAREN DRIVER

"What a really great way to start the new season! The team did a superb job all weekend and really we just had to keep our cool to come away with the win.

I said to Nico Rosberg on the podium that I think it was exactly eight years since we were on the podium together back in the days when we were in karting. It was great to be up there with him again.

Looking ahead, we obviously need to try and continue with the momentum we have. We could have gone quicker, so I am not particularly bothered about the Ferrari pace, although it may turn out that they had a substandard weekend here. BMW Sauber and Williams have clearly done a great job as well, so I need to keep on pushing and the team needs to keep on pushing.

We had a great car from the start and I found it easier here in Australia than I did in 2007. You could see that last year was pretty tough. Not as hot perhaps, but I think that my preparation was much better this time. I'm probably twice as fit this time around, but the car was also really fantastic to drive and it was quite an easy race. I was very comfortable driving at the pace I was going and I had more in hand if I'd needed it.

In testing and the build-up to the race, I found that the option tyre was graining quite heavily, but I seemed to be able to manage the tyres quite nicely and the performance on both types of tyre was pretty similar in the race. If anything, the option was quicker. The track had rubbered in quite well and the graining didn't affect us as much as I thought it might.

I wouldn't say that this start draws a line under all the baggage of last season but, for sure, coming into a new season, we really wanted to get off on the right foot.

Ron Dennis has been through a lot and so has the team, but we pulled through. I'm glad he's happy. It's an emotional feeling to win the first grand prix of the new season, especially with all the winter testing, the whole build-up and not really knowing whether you have the pace of everyone else. When you come out on top in the first big test it's a real relief and great satisfaction."

AUSTRALIA ROUND 1

afterwards Toyota rookie Timo Glock brought on a third safety-car period when he ran wide onto the grass and his car was literally shaken to bits by a rodeo ride over the bumps.

Hamilton had made his final stop and was safe, but Kovalainen – the temporary race leader – had not. He had to stay out while the cars joined the queue, and when the pitlane eventually opened he came in and dropped to the rear of a much depleted field. Once again, Hamilton pulled away after the restart and was out on his own when the chequered flag fell, to the very obvious delight of Ron Dennis. It all seemed so very easy.

"I was able to pull out a good gap on the exit of the first corner and just had to keep it cool and look after the tyres from then on," reported Hamilton. "I really just paced myself and didn't overdo it. I had plenty of time in me, so I just used that to my advantage and tried to look after the tyres, but there was a point in the second stint when I had to put my foot down due to the safety car.

"I guess it was a bit like my first win in Montréal last year when we had four safety-car periods. It was similar in that it was difficult to heat the tyres and the

brakes up. It was a good challenge, though, and I'd say that we've all done a great job."

His pursuer at the flag was Nick Heidfeld in the other BMW Sauber after a typically solid and unobtrusive run by the German.

Meanwhile, Williams underlined its winter promise as Nico Rosberg had a faultless drive to third place for his first top-three finish.

While the podium men all enjoyed faultless afternoons, there was much more fun behind as Fernando Alonso bagged fourth place on his return to Renault. After a difficult time in qualifying, luck came his way in the race, and the final safety-car period allowed him to close up. He chased down the battling Kovalainen and Räikkönen, and passed both when they tripped over each other. It was great stuff, and Kovalainen got Alonso back on the penultimate lap, only to hit his pit-limiter button when he went for a visor tear-off coming onto the pit straight to start the final lap. The engine died out of the corner, and Alonso nipped past, the Finn having to settle for fifth.

Kovalainen's former team boss Flavio Briatore was relieved to see Alonso bag some early points: "It was hard to know what kind of pace we had, because

Coulthard's Red Bull exited the race after a clash with Massa at Turn 1

OPPOSITE MIDDLE RIGHT
Trouble in the Honda pit after the refuelling hose got stuck during a Barrichello pit stop

OPPOSITE BOTTOM Alonso pushed hard to the finish, passing Kovalainen with just a lap to go

ABOVE Hamilton kept his cool through the safety-car periods and gave McLaren a much-needed boost

OFFICIAL FORMULA 1™ REVIEW **85**

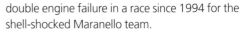

ABOVE Räikkönen ran his Ferrari off the track twice on his charge up the order, then retired, yet still was awarded the final point for eighth

BELOW Hamilton helps former karting team-mate Rosberg celebrate his first podium finish

you're always behind somebody when you start back there. Fernando's result was fantastic for us. It gives us motivation to push him very hard, and today it was important to finish."

From his lowly starting position, Räikkönen was strong in the early stages and gained numerous places, but he twice went off the road in his efforts to gain ground. His engine went off song in the closing laps and he dropped back. He stopped with five laps to go when it failed completely.

His team-mate Massa had experienced an identical breakage earlier in the race after making little progress up the order after his two incidents. It was the first double engine failure in a race since 1994 for the shell-shocked Maranello team.

Another late retirement was Kubica, hit in the rear by Williams rookie Kazuki Nakajima at the final safety-car restart as the field rounded the penultimate corner. The Pole came straight into the pits to retire. All the carnage meant that, despite twice changing noses, the Japanese driver brought his Williams home seventh. He then moved up a place when Honda's Rubens Barrichello was excluded for a pit exit infringement, the Brazilian having failed to spot a red light.

With no other cars finishing behind Nakajima in a race of extraordinary attrition, seventh place and two debut points went to Sebastien Bourdais, despite retiring his Toro Rosso with three laps to go. After struggling in qualifying, the Champ Car ace showed his race savvy by staying out of trouble and benefiting from a good pit call. When he stopped, he was running a solid fourth, ahead of the Alonso/Kovalainen battle. He seemed totally at home in such company until a hydraulic failure forced him to park up.

"It was a good performance, a very good performance," said a smiling Gerhard Berger afterwards. "It wasn't easy for him to keep Alonso on fresh tyres behind – and before that Kubica – and make no mistakes. He did a good job on this, and the team did a fantastic job with the pit stops."

That still left one point available for eighth place and, incredibly, it was gifted to Räikkönen, despite the Ferrari being out five laps before the chequered flag was flown. It had been many years since points were so freely available, and many who made early errors were kicking themselves after the race.

Without a doubt, it had been a great start to the season, and the sort of action-packed TV show that Bernie Ecclestone always loves. So, perhaps it was no coincidence that he'd added two street events to the 2008 championship schedule...

SNAPSHOT FROM
AUSTRALIA

CLOCKWISE FROM RIGHT A strange sight, with more people on the track than in the grandstand; Alonso was back with Renault, but the cockpit looked tight; Red Bull and an Australian flag, they must be cheering for Webber; Brazilian graffiti is always an art form, so Massa adds his mark; "no, it's my helmet, so I'll carry it"; this pre-race PR activity might have suggested that McLaren was all at sea, but its on-track form suggested quite the opposite; Bourdais scored points on his F1 debut

WEEKEND NEWS

- Shortly before the Australian GP, Super Aguri Racing revealed that it had been thrown a lifeline by investment group Magma. No details were forthcoming, but it seemed that the finance was from the Dubai government, while former Ford rally man Jost Capito was tipped to be the new boss.

- McLaren supremo Ron Dennis gathered his staff together a few days before the Australian GP and confirmed that he had no intention of stepping down from leading the team during the course of the season. However, he continued to quietly hand more of his duties to Martin Whitmarsh.

- Although he didn't attend the Australian GP, Bernie Ecclestone caused a stir by insisting that the event become a night race in the future, in order to appease European TV viewers. The Melbourne race promoters insisted, though, that they would go no later than 5pm in 2009. Inevitably, the discussion helped to inflame the traditional anti-F1 debate in the local media.

- Adrian Sutil became the first driver to be forced to start from the pitlane after a change of chassis under the new rules, following a crash in qualifying. He was also the first to play his joker by having a 'free' engine change. Since he was starting in the pits anyway, the associated 10-place penalty made no difference.

- Pedro de la Rosa was elected chairman of the GPDA as successor to Ralf Schumacher, who had left F1 to race in the DTM with Mercedes. Although not down to race in 2008, the Spaniard was present at all grands prix in his role as McLaren third driver. Lewis Hamilton and Kimi Räikkönen were among those who declined to join the organisation.

RACE RESULTS
AUSTRALIA
ALBERT PARK

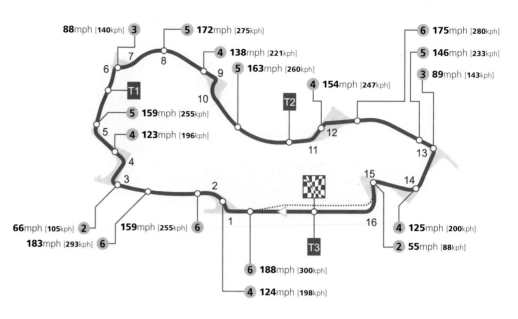

88mph [140kph] 3
5 172mph [275kph]
4 138mph [221kph]
6 175mph [280kph]
5 146mph [233kph]
5 163mph [260kph]
3 89mph [143kph]
4 154mph [247kph]
5 159mph [255kph]
4 123mph [196kph]
66mph [105kph] 2
159mph [255kph] 6
183mph [293kph] 6
4 125mph [200kph]
2 55mph [88kph]
6 188mph [300kph]
4 124mph [198kph]

Official Results © [2008]
Formula One Administration Limited,
6 Princes Gate, London, SW7 1QJ.
No reproduction without permission.
All copyright and database rights reserved.

RACE DATE March 16th
CIRCUIT LENGTH 3.295 miles
NO. OF LAPS 58
RACE DISTANCE 191.110 miles
WEATHER Dry and bright, 40°C
TRACK TEMP 51°C
RACE DAY ATTENDANCE 108,000
LAP RECORD Michael Schumacher
1m24.125s, 141.016mph, 2004

PRACTICE 1

	Driver	Time	Laps
1	K Räikkönen	1m26.461s	25
2	L Hamilton	1m26.948s	21
3	F Massa	1m26.958s	25
4	H Kovalainen	1m27.114s	19
5	M Webber	1m28.263s	18
6	F Alonso	1m28.360s	22
7	R Kubica	1m28.579s	12
8	T Glock	1m28.913s	16
9	S Vettel	1m28.957s	22
10	J Trulli	1m29.014s	23
11	J Button	1m29.124s	25
12	G Fisichella	1m29.230s	24
13	D Coulthard	1m29.301s	5
14	S Bourdais	1m29.363s	32
15	R Barrichello	1m29.533s	17
16	N Heidfeld	1m29.561s	7
17	A Sutil	1m30.155s	13
18	N Piquet Jr	1m30.357s	21
19	T Sato	1m31.048s	7
20	A Davidson	1m31.771s	7
21	K Nakajima	1m35.053s	3
22	N Rosberg	No time	3

PRACTICE 2

	Driver	Time	Laps
1	L Hamilton	1m26.559s	33
2	M Webber	1m27.473s	27
3	F Massa	1m27.640s	29
4	H Kovalainen	1m27.683s	29
5	D Coulthard	1m28.037s	26
6	K Räikkönen	1m28.208s	28
7	J Trulli	1m28.292s	22
8	N Rosberg	1m28.352s	31
9	G Fisichella	1m28.469s	32
10	T Glock	1m28.582s	28
11	J Button	1m28.632s	30
12	N Heidfeld	1m28.731s	33
13	F Alonso	1m28.779s	37
14	R Barrichello	1m28.849s	28
15	R Kubica	1m28.860s	35
16	K Nakajima	1m29.077s	23
17	A Sutil	1m29.161s	32
18	S Vettel	1m29.193s	40
19	N Piquet Jr	1m29.518s	14
20	S Bourdais	1m29.605s	11
21	T Sato	1m30.663s	16
22	A Davidson	1m31.527s	8

PRACTICE 3

	Driver	Time	Laps
1	R Kubica	1m25.613s	18
2	N Heidfeld	1m25.950s	16
3	F Alonso	1m26.082s	14
4	N Rosberg	1m26.171s	17
5	D Coulthard	1m26.385s	14
6	M Webber	1m26.407s	17
7	J Button	1m26.502s	18
8	S Vettel	1m26.663s	18
9	G Fisichella	1m26.682s	18
10	J Trulli	1m26.882s	11
11	F Massa	1m27.020s	19
12	L Hamilton	1m27.084s	14
13	T Glock	1m27.162s	15
14	K Räikkönen	1m27.163s	17
15	N Piquet Jr	1m27.284s	13
16	R Barrichello	1m27.333s	18
17	A Sutil	1m27.489s	18
18	S Bourdais	1m27.578s	17
19	K Nakajima	1m27.601s	15
20	H Kovalainen	1m27.992s	15
21	T Sato	1m28.363s	13
22	A Davidson	1m28.912s	15

QUALIFYING 1

	Driver	Time
1	H Kovalainen	1m25.664s
2	N Heidfeld	1m25.960s
3	F Massa	1m25.994s
4	R Kubica	1m26.103s
5	K Räikkönen	1m26.140s
6	N Rosberg	1m26.295s
7	R Barrichello	1m26.369s
8	D Coulthard	1m26.381s
9	J Trulli	1m26.427s
10	L Hamilton	1m26.572s
11	S Vettel	1m26.702s
12	J Button	1m26.712s
13	K Nakajima	1m26.891s
14	F Alonso	1m26.907s
15	M Webber	1m26.914s
16	T Glock	1m26.919s
17	G Fisichella	1m27.207s
18	S Bourdais	1m27.446s
19	A Sutil	1m27.859s
20	T Sato	1m28.208s
21	N Piquet Jr	1m28.330s
22	A Davidson	1m29.059s

QUALIFYING 2

	Driver	Time
1	L Hamilton	1m25.187s
2	R Kubica	1m25.315s
3	H Kovalainen	1m25.452s
4	N Heidfeld	1m25.518s
5	F Massa	1m25.691s
6	S Vettel	1m25.842s
7	N Rosberg	1m26.059s
8	D Coulthard	1m26.063s
9	J Trulli	1m26.101s
10	T Glock	1m26.164s
11	R Barrichello	1m26.173s
12	F Alonso	1m26.188s
13	J Button	1m26.259s
14	K Nakajima	1m26.413s
15	M Webber	no time
16	K Räikkönen	no time

Best sectors – Practice
Sec 1	R Kubica	28.404s
Sec 2	J Button	23.210s
Sec 3	R Kubica	34.073s

Speed trap – Practice
1	F Massa	191.071mph
2	K Räikkönen	190.947mph
3	D Coulthard	189.829mph

Best sectors – Qualifying
Sec 1	L Hamilton	28.342s
Sec 2	L Hamilton	22.934s
Sec 3	H Kovalainen	33.857s

Speed trap – Qualifying
1	H Kovalainen	190.326mph
2	L Hamilton	190.263mph
3	F Massa	190.015mph

Kimi Räikkönen
"I had an engine problem. I spun twice trying to pass those ahead of me. With Glock, I put a wheel on the grass and the second time, with Kovalainen, I was a bit optimistic."

Nick Heidfeld
"I had too much wheelspin and couldn't keep Rosberg back. I expected him to pit earlier than me, but we stopped on the same lap and our crew got me in front."

Fernando Alonso
"That was a very strange race with lots of overtaking, incidents and mechanical problems. We were able to make the most of all of the opportunities that came our way."

Nico Rosberg
"Being on the podium is a great feeling. The team has worked hard over the winter and I want to thank my father for all he has done to help me to get to this position."

David Coulthard
"I know that Massa was trying to pass, but you must be alongside to overtake. He took a lunge from too far back and Turn 1 is a corner where you have to turn in early."

Jarno Trulli
"The battery was too hot. When I pitted, it gave up. That is a pity as the car felt good. I was running in the points so it is unlucky to lose out on a scoring start to the year."

Felipe Massa
"We had engine problems. I lost control at Turn 1 while fighting Kovalainen and went off. The incident with Coulthard? I was on the inside and he closed the door."

Robert Kubica
"My strategy was changed, but this didn't pay off as I got stuck behind Bourdais. I still had a chance to score some points, but then Nakajima hit me."

Nelson Piquet Jr
"I was able to make up places on the first lap, which was pretty hectic. Unfortunately I was hit at the start, which damaged my car and so I did not manage to finish."

Kazuki Nakajima
"At the start, a car spun in front of me, turned side-on and damaged my nose. Then with the safety-car periods, the team did a great job to swap me to a one-stop strategy."

Mark Webber
"I was behind Kimi, on the outside, then someone hit Jenson and I took to the grass. At Turn 3, Nakajima came alongside with no wing. I tried to make room but got a clip."

Timo Glock
"I had contact with two cars at the start, but despite our heavy fuel load we made up ground. After the stop, it was hard work to drive and my race ended with the crash."

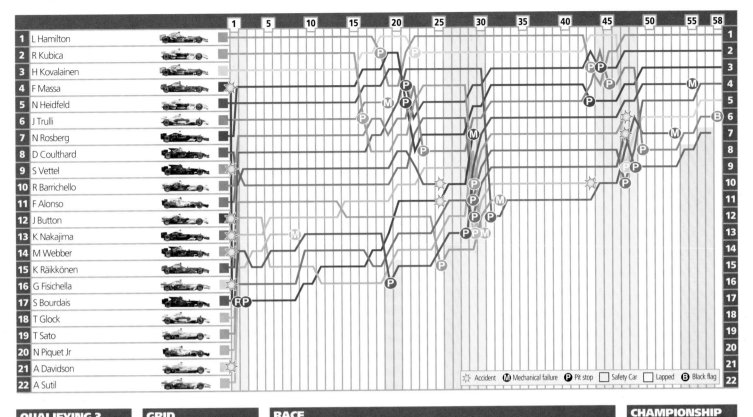

1	L Hamilton		1
2	R Kubica		2
3	H Kovalainen		3
4	F Massa		4
5	N Heidfeld		5
6	J Trulli		6
7	N Rosberg		7
8	D Coulthard		8
9	S Vettel		9
10	R Barrichello		10
11	F Alonso		11
12	J Button		12
13	K Nakajima		13
14	M Webber		14
15	K Räikkönen		15
16	G Fisichella		16
17	S Bourdais		17
18	T Glock		18
19	T Sato		19
20	N Piquet Jr		20
21	A Davidson		21
22	A Sutil		22

☆ Accident Ⓜ Mechanical failure Ⓟ Pit stop ☐ Safety Car ☐ Lapped Ⓑ Black flag

QUALIFYING 3

	Driver	Time
1	L Hamilton	1m26.714s
2	R Kubica	1m26.869s
3	H Kovalainen	1m27.079s
4	F Massa	1m27.178s
5	N Heidfeld	1m27.236s
6	J Trulli	1m28.527s
7	N Rosberg	1m28.687s
8	D Coulthard	1m29.041s
9	T Glock	1m29.593s
10	S Vettel	no time

GRID

	Driver	Time
1	L Hamilton	1m26.714s
2	R Kubica	1m26.869s
3	H Kovalainen	1m27.079s
4	F Massa	1m27.178s
5	N Heidfeld	1m27.236s
6	J Trulli	1m28.527s
7	N Rosberg	1m28.687s
8	D Coulthard	1m29.041s
9	S Vettel	no time
10	R Barrichello	1m26.173s
11	F Alonso	1m26.188s
12	J Button	1m26.259s
13	K Nakajima	1m26.413s
14	M Webber	no time
15	K Räikkönen	no time
16	G Fisichella	1m27.207s
17	S Bourdais	1m27.446s
18*	A Sutil	1m27.859s
19^	T Glock	1m29.593s
20	T Sato	1m28.208s
21	N Piquet Jr	1m28.330s
22	A Davidson	1m29.059s

* STARTED FROM PITLANE ^ 5-PLACE PENALTIES FOR GEARBOX CHANGE & FOR IMPEDING ANOTHER DRIVER

RACE

	Driver	Car	Laps	Time	Avg. mph	Fastest	Stops
1	L Hamilton	McLaren-Mercedes MP4-23	58	1h34m50.616s	120.930	1m27.452s	2
2	N Heidfeld	BMW Sauber F1.08	58	1h34m56.094s	120.813	1m27.739s	2
3	N Rosberg	Williams-Toyota FW30	58	1h34m58.779s	120.756	1m28.090s	2
4	F Alonso	Renault R28	58	1h35m07.797s	120.565	1m28.603s	2
5	H Kovalainen	McLaren-Mercedes MP4-23	58	1h35m08.630s	120.548	1m27.418s	2
D*	R Barrichello	Honda RA108	58	1h35m43.069s	119.805	1m28.736s	3
6	K Nakajima	Williams-Toyota FW30	57	1h35m04.685s	117.552	1m29.639s	3
7	S Bourdais	Toro Rosso-Ferrari STR02B	55	1h30m37.541s	120.821	1m29.534s	2
8	K Räikkönen	Ferrari F2008	53	Engine	-	1m27.903s	1
R	R Kubica	BMW Sauber F1.08	47	Collision	-	1m28.753s	2
R	T Glock	Toyota TF108	43	Spun off	-	1m29.558s	1
R	T Sato	Super Aguri-Honda SA08	32	Transmission	-	1m30.892s	1
R	N Piquet Jr	Renault R28	30	Collision	-	1m31.384s	1
R	F Massa	Ferrari F2008	29	Engine	-	1m28.175s	2
R	D Coulthard	Red Bull-Renault RB4	25	Collision	-	1m29.502s	1
R	J Trulli	Toyota TF108	19	Battery	-	1m29.310s	0
R	A Sutil	Force India-Ferrari VJM01	8	Hydraulics	-	1m32.021s	0
R	S Vettel	Toro Rosso-Ferrari STR02B	0	Collision	-	-	0
R	J Button	Honda RA108	0	Collision	-	-	0
R	M Webber	Red Bull-Renault RB4	0	Collision	-	-	0
R	G Fisichella	Force India-Ferrari VJM01	0	Collision	-	-	0
R	A Davidson	Super Aguri-Honda SA08	0	Collision	-	-	0

*DISQUALIFIED FOR PASSING RED LIGHT AT PIT EXIT

CHAMPIONSHIP

	Driver	Pts
1	L Hamilton	10
2	N Heidfeld	8
3	N Rosberg	6
4	F Alonso	5
5	H Kovalainen	4
6	K Nakajima	3
7	S Bourdais	2
8	K Räikkönen	1

Fastest lap
H Kovalainen 1m27.418s
(135.704mph) on lap 43

Fastest speed trap
H Kovalainen 191.58mph
Slowest speed trap
G Fisichella 139.63mph

Fastest pit stop
1	N Heidfeld	22.371s
2	R Barrichello	22.421s
3	N Piquet Jr	22.454s

	Constructor	Pts
1	McLaren-Mercedes	14
2	Williams-Toyota	9
3	BMW Sauber	8
4	Renault	5
5	Toro Rosso-Ferrari	2
6	Ferrari	1

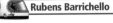

Sebastien Bourdais
"The team did well, getting me to pit after the second safety car. I was under pressure from a BMW and then Alonso and Kovalainen, but a hydraulic problem set in."

Jenson Button
"I got alongside Vettel into Turn 1, but I tapped him and he turned in and hit my rear wheel. I thought that I could reach the pit, but the rear left track-rod was broken."

Takuma Sato
"I didn't get off the start well, but I gained a few places in the first lap, and there was then some exciting battling. After the first stop, I had to stop with a gearbox problem."

Adrian Sutil
"It was good while it lasted. In the opening laps I stayed with the guys in front of me and got up to 13th, but then I had a hydraulic pressure problem and my race was over."

Lewis Hamilton
"What a dream start. I controlled things from the beginning. I was able to drive at a steady pace, but the three safety-car periods meant that there was never time to relax."

Sebastian Vettel
"Into Turn 1, I had Kimi on my left, Jenson my right. I tried to stay close to Kimi. Then, as I turned in, I felt that I had been hit on my rear right and that spun me around."

Rubens Barrichello
"Though the result is disappointing, I'm pleased that we were able to get the best out of the car. It was a crazy race and I lost control of the front damper after the first stop."

Anthony Davidson
"I was sandwiched between two cars, trying to avoid the inevitable. I tried to brake to get away and the cars rode over my front wheels, so there was nowhere for me to go."

Giancarlo Fisichella
"I lost the race at the first corner as another driver came like a kamikaze into my car and it was very frustrating, as it was a race in which there was a chance to get points."

Heikki Kovalainen
"The last safety-car phase stopped me from being second. I had a good battle with Kimi and managed to pass Fernando, but as I tore off a visor strip I hit the pitlane limiter."

2008 FORMULA 1 PETRONAS MALAYSIAN GRAND PRIX
KUALA LUMPUR

THE TRUE RÄIKKÖNEN

A single point from the opening grand prix was slim pickings, so Kimi Räikkönen was delighted that his Malaysian sortie yielded the full 10 points in a dominant display for Ferrari

After the miserable double engine failure in the Australian GP, Ferrari bounced back in style as Kimi Räikkönen took a dominant victory at a hot and humid Sepang. Indeed, it would have been an easy 1–2 for Ferrari had Felipe Massa not spun off while running second. Appropriately, Räikkönen's first win as reigning World Champion was the fifth anniversary of his first grand prix victory at the same venue, achieved of course with McLaren.

Conversely, the British outfit – so competitive in Australia just seven days earlier – struggled through a painful weekend. By the end of the race, third and fifth places were a valuable damage-limitation exercise, and the team headed to Bahrain still leading both the drivers' and constructors' championships.

The Ferraris appeared to be quicker from the start of the meeting, and it was Massa who had the upper hand in qualifying and duly secured pole position. Meanwhile, in only his second outing for McLaren, Heikki Kovalainen beat team-mate Lewis Hamilton to qualify third, despite being a little heavier on fuel, with the Briton clearly struggling for grip.

The second row was not a bad result, but McLaren's drivers were then charged with impeding

Robert Kubica, who lined up fourth. Convinced that he would have been third but for the obstruction, Heidfeld moved up from seventh to fifth.

"We did inform Lewis and Heikki that the drivers were on quick laps," said McLaren Chief Operating Officer Martin Whitmarsh, "but it's a team mistake, because everything's a team mistake, as we are a team, and we don't want to ascribe it to anyone. However, both drivers were told on the radio that there were guys on fast laps.

"You can complain about the regulations, which we were a part of, and you can complain about the circumstances. The reality is that we shouldn't get a situation that encourages drivers to be on track at the same time with closing speeds of over 200km/h, which the current regulations encourage you to do."

At the start of the race, the Ferrari drivers battled surprisingly hard into Turn 1, with Massa leaning on Räikkönen and ultimately emerging in front. Behind them, Kubica slotted into third, ahead of Red Bull's Mark Webber and the fast-starting Hamilton who had a productive first lap. Heidfeld and Trulli both lost places when they disputed the same piece of track.

The Ferraris soon left the rest of the field trailing, but this was no gentle run for either Ferrari driver. Indeed, when Massa stopped on lap 17 the Finn put in an ultra-quick final lap and, when he made his own first stop on lap 18, he emerged in front. Not for the first time, a frustrated Massa saw the strategy unfold in Räikkönen's favour. It was clear that the battle between the two was going to be even more intense than it had been in 2007.

Hamilton suffered with a stuck right front wheel at his first pit stop and, having lost 10 seconds, slipped down the order. He had to start gaining places all over again, but thereafter struggled to find the extra pace that required.

Any chance that Massa might have had of

ABOVE The Ferraris are to the fore, from Kubica, but the order is all the more competitive behind them

BELOW Rosberg leads Nakajima, but his race has already been ruined as the nose of his Williams is missing

OPPOSITE A study in team work as the Toyota crew go to work on Jarno Trulli's car on his run to fourth

Nick Heidfeld and Fernando Alonso at the end of final qualifying. It was not a deliberate act on their part, more a function of rules that led to drivers crawling back to the pits after their last runs, saving a little more fuel for the race.

In this case, most drivers had finished a little early because of the threat of rain, but Heidfeld and Alonso were on the traditional last-second schedule, and had to pass several cars that were virtually at a standstill. Both McLaren men were dropped five places, leaving them to line up eighth and ninth. The main beneficiaries were Jarno Trulli, who moved up to third on the grid for Toyota, and BMW Sauber's

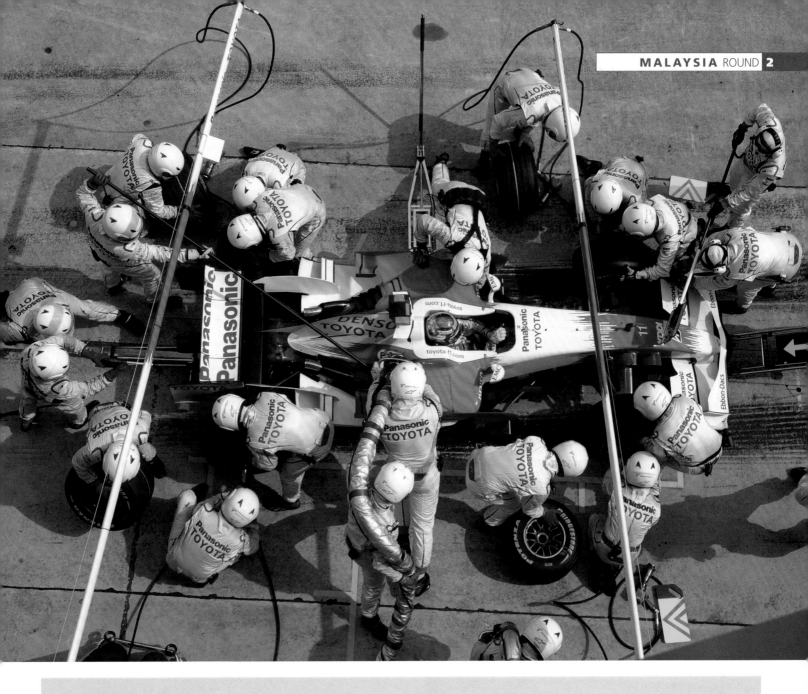

TALKING POINT
BOUNCING BACK

The Australian GP had not been a great start to Ferrari's title defences and hardly a first race for new Gestione Sportiva head Stefano Domenicali to remember with any fondness. World Champion Kimi Räikkönen was eliminated in the first session of qualifying after a fuel pump problem. Starting at the back, Kimi had little option but to fuel up for a one-stopper, but then had an error-strewn afternoon. There was a spin when he put a wheel on the grass challenging Timo Glock, then an off following an optimistic lunge down the inside of Heikki Kovalainen's McLaren after a safety-car period. He was out five laps before the end as Ferrari suffered its first double engine failure since Noah was a lad.

While the media were quick to start speculating about 'crisis' at Maranello, Domenicali remained philosophical: "We weren't a phenomenon before and we're not carthorses now..."

McLaren and Lewis Hamilton might have started on a high in Australia, but in Malaysia they came back down to earth with a bump. There was nothing imaginary about Ferrari's winter pace, and Malaysia proved that the Scuderia was a lot more phenomenon than carthorse after all. The red cars locked out the front row, Massa pipping Räikkönen to pole, but Kimi redressing the balance by dint of a longer first stint. This time it was left to McLaren to come up with the excuses as a locking wheelnut delayed Hamilton's pit stop and caused the Melbourne winner to miss out on a podium finish.

"Without that, we might have finished second and third," Hamilton said, while team boss Ron Dennis added: "Our race pace was largely dictated by backmarkers. We won't really know our true speed until we get to Barcelona."

Both Ferrari and McLaren also acknowledged the threat of BMW Sauber, for whom an unwell Robert Kubica finished second at Sepang, for his best ever F1 result.

The man who left Sepang feeling most dejected surely had to be Felipe Massa. Trying to stay in touch with his team-mate after the first round of pit stops, the Brazilian ran wide at Turn 6, damaged the underbody and ran out of downforce two turns later, finishing his afternoon in the gravel. Two races, two mistakes. Such is life under the spotlight that, immediately, the 'Massa under pressure' stories began. Felipe, of course, had been here before, precisely 12 months earlier. Just as he had then, he vowed to go and win the Bahrain GP.

reversing the positions at the front ended when he spun off on lap 31. He said that the aero balance had been changed after he struck a kerb a few seconds earlier but, either way, an element of driver error was clearly involved. After his messy race in Australia and, with mentor Jean Todt taking a back seat, the Brazilian was undoubtedly under the spotlight.

With his team-mate out, it was an easy run thereafter for Räikkönen, who drove only as fast as he needed to while preserving his engine and gearbox for another hot race in Bahrain.

"For sure, we had quite a difficult weekend in Australia," said the Finn. "We didn't really expect to have such difficulties and we were 100 per cent sure that it was going to be different here. Speed-wise, we knew that we were going to be fine once we were in the right place. Even in Australia, the speed should have been OK in the race.

"Everything worked perfectly here, and we took it quite easy in the race to make sure nothing went wrong. We still have a second race with the same engine, so we saved the engine quite well here. It was a perfect job by the team to come back like this after a difficult first race. Overall, we would have

been happier if Felipe had been second, but things go wrong sometimes. This is a good start now for the season for us and we are in a pretty good position."

This was Ferrari's first win under new team boss Stefano Domenicali, although Todt – out of uniform – was a high-profile guest in the garage.

"Of course we wanted to show the response of Ferrari," said Domenicali, who picked up the constructors' trophy on the podium. "After a very different weekend in Australia, which was not really our standard, or was something that was difficult to digest, I'm very happy because we showed that the team can do a great job."

Massa's demise promoted Kubica to second place, and the Pole had a relatively lonely race to the best result of his career to date, despite not feeling too well through the weekend. The result underlined the unexpected step that BMW Sauber had made since its disappointing form in winter testing, and showed that the Swiss-based team was now strong enough to upset the status quo.

"I didn't have a good start," reported Kubica. "There was some wheelspin at the start which compromised my acceleration, so it was quite close

BELOW LEFT Hamilton lost 10s when his right front wheel jammed at his first pit stop

BELOW RIGHT Button had a trouble-free run in the mid-field to finish 10th for Honda

BOTTOM Heidfeld, Alonso and Coulthard fight over position

INSIDE LINE
KIMI RÄIKKÖNEN
FERRARI DRIVER

"After the problems in Australia, it was good to get the 10 points. Sepang is more of a normal circuit than Melbourne and the car was fast all weekend. In qualifying, I did a very quick lap in Q2, the fastest overall, but I'm not sure what happened in Q3. The car felt fine, but I just couldn't get the grip. I didn't get the best out of it, but still managed to qualify second behind my team-mate.

Felipe and I were pretty similar speed-wise and I got a bit better start and got alongside him. I didn't push it though, because I knew that we would run one lap longer and so I didn't risk an incident between team-mates at the first corner! Maybe I could have made it past, but I decided that it was better to stay behind and make my move at the pit stop. It worked out perfectly.

Once Felipe went into the pits, my car was much faster because the handling characteristics improve a lot when you're not following someone closely. After the pit stop, it was quite easy to pull away from him in the clean air. It is always difficult to follow people closely and you need to be very close if you are going to make the extra lap count and pass them at the pit stops. Really, the car in front needs to be about six seconds ahead for you not to feel any aerodynamic effects. That made life a bit more difficult, but it was no real problem. After that, it was quite easy, the car felt really good in the second stint and I was able to pull away.

Although we had a difficult race in Australia, we never lost confidence. The car has worked really well during the whole of the winter test programme and it has always been quick. We had some mechanical issues in Melbourne, but hopefully we have got rid of them and we had no problems at all here. I think our speed in Australia would have been fine too, but when you start behind someone, as we did there, you are not in a position to use it.

Last year, we were much faster than everyone in Australia and then not so happy when we got to Sepang. This year, it's the opposite way round!"

with Trulli and Nick. I nearly lost the car under braking for the first corner as I was on the dirty inside line, but I think they touched, so I managed to overtake them. I was trying to keep a consistent pace.

"We know we cannot outrun Ferrari, but I was trying to make up time, as I thought McLaren would be a bit stronger. I saw after the second pit stop that Heikki was around 17 seconds behind me and didn't close the gap. We did the last pit stop and then just dropped the revs to keep the engine a bit fresh for the next grand prix, which is very important.

"With the heat, it was a tough race and I didn't feel well all weekend. I was a bit sick, and our new car is especially hot inside. The last 10 laps were pretty tough to keep concentration, as Kimi was 20 seconds in front and Heikki was 20 seconds behind, so I was just cruising to the end."

Kovalainen was only seventh on the first lap, but some quick times and good strategy helped him up to third, giving McLaren at least something to cheer as he registered his first podium finish for his new team. And, by beating Hamilton in qualifying, he had really made his point. The one real encouragement the team could draw from the race was the performance of the

ABOVE Räikkönen shows off his steering wheel as he celebrates the first win of his world title defence

man that outsiders at least had hitherto perceived as Hamilton's number two.

"In only his second race, Heikki really did a flawless job," said Martin Whitmarsh. "As you saw, he was heavier than Lewis in qualifying, and yet quicker, so he and his guys did a good job to get there. He made no mistakes and was flawless. In fact, Heikki would be leading the World Championship if he had a bit more luck, because he should have finished second in both races."

"The negatives frankly were that Ferrari looked quick, and we underperformed," Whitmarsh continued. "We didn't quite get to where we wanted

to be with balance and set-up and, once you do that, you're starting to damage the tyres and it gets away from you. We were disappointed by what happened in qualifying, but accept entirely what the stewards did, but it was just unfortunate circumstances that led us to that. And then we were disappointed by what happened at Hamilton's first pit stop."

Fourth place went to Trulli, after Toyota's best race in some time. So depressed for the past couple of seasons, the Italian was delighted to have a car in which he had total faith. After his troubled first lap, Trulli passed Webber at the first round of pit stops, and in the latter stages had to go quickly to keep Hamilton behind him, which he did successfully. The British driver charged hard, but had to settle for fifth place. Indeed, at flagfall, he was about to come under threat from Heidfeld, who set fastest lap right at the end on his way to sixth.

Seventh place was claimed by Webber, who had to carry extra fuel for much of the race due to a refuelling rig problem. After the grid penalties were applied to his former team, World Champion Alonso started seventh, but he struggled to get much speed out of the Renault, and eventually finished eighth, ahead of David Coulthard.

Like so many others, Jenson Button found it hard to make much progress, but he had a reliable run to 10th place for Honda. After his pit-exit infringement in the Australian GP, his frustrated team-mate Rubens Barrichello collected a pit speeding drive-through penalty, which cost him a position, and dropped him to an eventual 13th place.

Fortunes can change quickly in this game, however, as was demonstrated by Melbourne podium man Nico Rosberg, who started his Williams all the way back in 16th place on the grid and could finish only 14th after clashing with Toyota's Timo Glock on the opening lap.

SNAPSHOT FROM
MALAYSIA

CLOCKWISE FROM RIGHT Plenty of space for the national flag, as the fans stay in the shade; Coulthard stays cool; from Malaysia, with love; Massa knew he had to deliver; Hamilton – ever on camera; Wurz, Barrichello and Button pose with the retiring Alastair Gibson; don't ask...; Rosberg puts his name on an AirAsia plane

WEEKEND NEWS

■ Honda chief mechanic and long-time lollipop man Alastair Gibson had his last race for the team in Malaysia, having been in the job since the birth of BAR in 1999. The popular South African had long enjoyed a sideline of producing sculptures made from F1 cast-off materials, his favoured subject being sharks, and early retirement provided the opportunity to make it his fulltime career.

■ The future of the Brazilian GP was secured after São Paulo signed a deal with Bernie Ecclestone that took the Interlagos race into 2015. Meanwhile, there were strong suggestions that the United States GP would return to an already busy calendar in 2009, pending an agreement with a title sponsor.

■ Ongoing bad feeling between Eddie Jordan and the current boss of his former team, Colin Kolles, came into focus when EJ had some concrete blocks dumped on land he owned next to the team's Silverstone factory, making access difficult for the transporters. Jordan had bought the extra land when he owned the team, with the intention of using it for expansion.

■ The BBC announced that it was to become the British broadcaster for F1 from 2009, having ceded the deal to ITV back in 1997. The corporation insisted that it had some bold new ideas, and would integrate TV with its radio and internet coverage. Inevitably, the news led to much speculation as to which, if any, of the existing commentary team would be retained.

■ Having missed the Australian GP, Ferrari advisor and board member Jean Todt made his first appearance of the season. It was also his first appearance not in full team kit since he took the team principal job in 1993. Speculation continued to link the Frenchman with a future role at the FIA.

RACE RESULTS
MALAYSIA SEPANG

RACE DATE March 23rd
CIRCUIT LENGTH 3.444 miles
NO. OF LAPS 56
RACE DISTANCE 192.887 miles
WEATHER Sunny & humid, 30°C
TRACK TEMP 45°C
OVERALL ATTENDANCE 127,000
LAP RECORD Juan Pablo Montoya, 1m34.223s, 1131.995mph, 2004

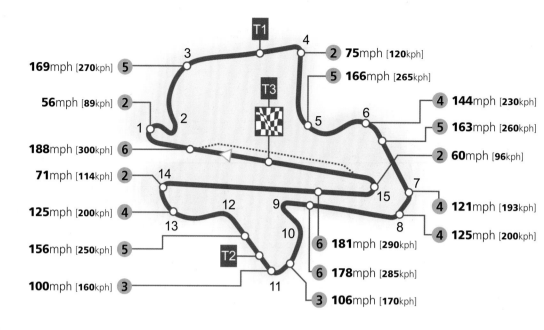

PRACTICE 1

	Driver	Time	Laps
1	F Massa	1m35.392s	20
2	K Räikkönen	1m36.459s	8
3	H Kovalainen	1m36.556s	21
4	N Rosberg	1m36.578s	23
5	L Hamilton	1m36.626s	17
6	F Alonso	1m37.022s	18
7	N Piquet Jr	1m37.034s	28
8	R Kubica	1m37.218s	9
9	J Button	1m37.282s	17
10	J Trulli	1m37.540s	24
11	N Heidfeld	1m37.649s	17
12	K Nakajima	1m37.649s	18
13	R Barrichello	1m37.776s	20
14	T Glock	1m37.782s	27
15	S Vettel	1m38.219s	26
16	D Coulthard	1m38.232s	7
17	M Webber	1m38.707s	12
18	S Bourdais	1m38.798s	25
19	G Fisichella	1m39.046s	21
20	T Sato	1m40.178s	11
21	A Davidson	1m40.351s	14
22	A Sutil	1m41.269s	5

PRACTICE 2

	Driver	Time	Laps
1	L Hamilton	1m35.055s	32
2	F Massa	1m35.206s	33
3	K Räikkönen	1m35.428s	36
4	J Button	1m36.037s	40
5	S Vettel	1m36.474s	35
6	J Trulli	1m36.493s	38
7	H Kovalainen	1m36.512s	30
8	R Kubica	1m36.671s	33
9	G Fisichella	1m36.756s	37
10	K Nakajima	1m36.838s	34
11	R Barrichello	1m36.879s	38
12	N Rosberg	1m36.908s	36
13	N Heidfeld	1m37.106s	35
14	F Alonso	1m37.328s	23
15	N Piquet Jr	1m37.331s	42
16	M Webber	1m37.346s	37
17	T Glock	1m37.512s	35
18	A Sutil	1m37.614s	35
19	T Sato	1m39.021s	27
20	A Davidson	1m39.361s	30
21	S Bourdais	no time	1
22	D Coulthard	no time	0

PRACTICE 3

	Driver	Time	Laps
1	N Heidfeld	1m35.019s	18
2	K Räikkönen	1m35.262s	17
3	F Massa	1m35.388s	17
4	J Trulli	1m35.389s	20
5	M Webber	1m35.437s	16
6	D Coulthard	1m35.653s	17
7	N Piquet Jr	1m35.768s	15
8	J Button	1m35.781s	19
9	S Vettel	1m35.827s	16
10	T Glock	1m35.911s	21
11	L Hamilton	1m35.927s	13
12	F Alonso	1m36.068s	14
13	K Nakajima	1m36.183s	14
14	G Fisichella	1m36.229s	21
15	N Rosberg	1m36.490s	7
16	H Kovalainen	1m36.529s	16
17	R Kubica	1m36.618s	19
18	S Bourdais	1m36.668s	15
19	T Sato	1m36.908s	14
20	A Sutil	1m36.939s	21
21	A Davidson	1m37.140s	12
22	R Barrichello	1m37.703s	6

QUALIFYING 1

	Driver	Time
1	J Trulli	1m35.205s
2	H Kovalainen	1m35.227s
3	F Massa	1m35.347s
4	L Hamilton	1m35.392s
5	M Webber	1m35.440s
6	K Räikkönen	1m35.645s
7	N Heidfeld	1m35.729s
8	R Kubica	1m35.794s
9	N Rosberg	1m35.843s
10	J Button	1m35.847s
11	T Glock	1m35.891s
12	F Alonso	1m35.983s
13	D Coulthard	1m36.058s
14	N Piquet Jr	1m36.074s
15	S Vettel	1m36.111s
16	R Barrichello	1m36.198s
17	G Fisichella	1m36.240s
18	K Nakajima	1m36.388s
19	S Bourdais	1m36.677s
20	T Sato	1m37.087s
21	A Sutil	1m37.101s
22	A Davidson	1m37.481s

QUALIFYING 2

	Driver	Time
1	K Räikkönen	1m34.188s
2	F Massa	1m34.412s
3	L Hamilton	1m34.627s
4	N Heidfeld	1m34.648s
5	H Kovalainen	1m34.759s
6	R Kubica	1m34.811s
7	J Trulli	1m34.825s
8	M Webber	1m34.967s
9	T Glock	1m35.000s
10	F Alonso	1m35.140s
11	J Button	1m35.208s
12	D Coulthard	1m35.408s
13	N Piquet Jr	1m35.562s
14	R Barrichello	1m35.622s
15	S Vettel	1m35.648s
16	N Rosberg	1m35.670s

Best sectors – Practice
Sec 1	N Piquet Jr	24.500s
Sec 2	L Hamilton	31.308s
Sec 3	N Heidfeld	38.822s

Speed trap – Practice
1	F Massa	188.337mph
2	K Räikkönen	188.213mph
3	L Hamilton	187.964mph

Best sectors – Qualifying
Sec 1	K Räikkönen	24.520s
Sec 2	F Massa	31.304s
Sec 3	K Räikkönen	38.293s

Speed trap – Qualifying
1	F Massa	191.133mph
2	L Hamilton	189.642mph
3	K Räikkönen	188.710mph

Kimi Räikkönen
"I came alongside Felipe, but didn't take a risk, knowing I was stopping a lap later than him. I managed to come out ahead and, from then on, on a clear track, the car was perfect."

Nick Heidfeld
"I tried to overtake on the outside of the first corner. Robert was on the inside and Trulli between us. I ran out of room, picked up some dirt and lost two more places."

Fernando Alonso
"I did the best that I could. We were able to see that in normal conditions we are a little off in terms of performance. Our goal is to try and score at each race."

Nico Rosberg
"Starting 16th, I knew I would have to take risks. When Glock left a gap, I went for it and I got alongside him. I guess he didn't see me as he turned in and I couldn't back out."

David Coulthard
"There was too much graining on my first set of tyres, so I lost 9s. It was very hot out there, but luckily it was also a little bit overcast, so that improved conditions."

Jarno Trulli
"It's nice to be in the points. I had a tricky first corner when I ran wide and touched Heidfeld. I was then able to match the McLarens, then made it past Webber at the stops."

Felipe Massa
"On lap 31, I clipped the kerb at the exit to Turn 6 and hit it quite hard and then lost the rear end going into Turn 7. We must now check for damage to the car."

Robert Kubica
"I was fighting with Nick and Trulli. I took the dirty inside line and all but lost the car, but passed them. The Ferraris were too quick, but I was able to drop the others."

Nelson Piquet Jr
"I am happy to have finished. I learned a lot and recognise that the group we are fighting with is competitive. I finished close to my team-mate which is encouraging."

Kazuki Nakajima
"I made up a few places from the start. On the second stint, I had a puncture and had to stop very early. I was struggling in the last stint and spun in a high-speed corner."

Mark Webber
"I got a good run through 1 and 2 and came out fourth. I struggled during the second stint and got stuck behind Sato when we should have stayed in front of Heidfeld."

Timo Glock
"I was hit by Rosberg at Turn 14. When I looked in the mirror he was further back, so I didn't expect him to try to pass. He hit me on the rear right, breaking my suspension."

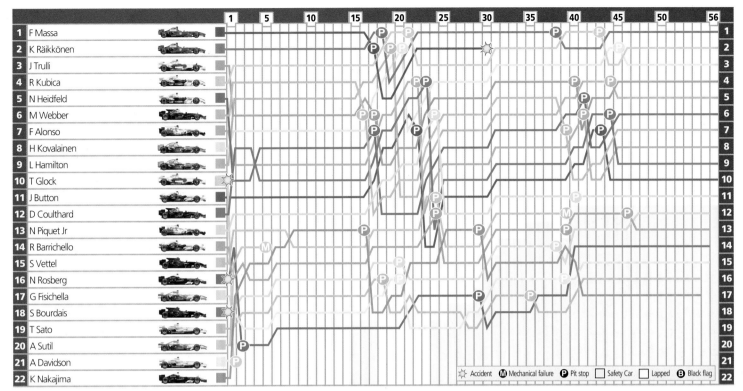

					1	5	10	15	20	25	30	35	40	45	50	56	
1	F Massa																1
2	K Räikkönen																2
3	J Trulli																3
4	R Kubica																4
5	N Heidfeld																5
6	M Webber																6
7	F Alonso																7
8	H Kovalainen																8
9	L Hamilton																9
10	T Glock																10
11	J Button																11
12	D Coulthard																12
13	N Piquet Jr																13
14	R Barrichello																14
15	S Vettel																15
16	N Rosberg																16
17	G Fisichella																17
18	S Bourdais																18
19	T Sato																19
20	A Sutil																20
21	A Davidson																21
22	K Nakajima																22

☆ Accident Ⓜ Mechanical failure Ⓟ Pit stop ☐ Safety Car ☐ Lapped Ⓑ Black flag

QUALIFYING 3

	Driver	Time
1	F Massa	1m35.748s
2	K Räikkönen	1m36.230s
3	H Kovalainen	1m36.613s
4	L Hamilton	1m36.709s
5	J Trulli	1m36.711s
6	R Kubica	1m36.727s
7	N Heidfeld	1m36.753s
8	M Webber	1m37.009s
9	F Alonso	1m38.450s
10	T Glock	1m39.656s

GRID

	Driver	Time
1	F Massa	1m35.748s
2	K Räikkönen	1m36.230s
3	J Trulli	1m36.711s
4	R Kubica	1m36.727s
5	N Heidfeld	1m36.753s
6	M Webber	1m37.009s
7	F Alonso	1m38.450s
8*	H Kovalainen	1m36.613s
9*	L Hamilton	1m36.709s
10	T Glock	1m39.656s
11	J Button	1m35.208s
12	D Coulthard	1m35.408s
13	N Piquet Jr	1m35.562s
14	R Barrichello	1m35.622s
15	S Vettel	1m35.648s
16	N Rosberg	1m35.670s
17	G Fisichella	1m36.240s
18	S Bourdais	1m36.677s
19	T Sato	1m37.087s
20	A Sutil	1m37.101s
21	A Davidson	1m37.481s
22^	K Nakajima	1m36.388s

* PENALISED 5 POSITIONS FOR BLOCKING ^ PENALISED 10 POSITIONS FOR CAUSING A COLLISION IN THE AUSTRALIAN GP

RACE

	Driver	Car	Laps	Time	Avg. mph	Fastest	Stops
1	K Räikkönen	Ferrari F2008	56	1h31m18.555s	126.768	1m35.405s	2
2	R Kubica	BMW Sauber F1.08	56	1h31m38.125s	126.317	1m35.921s	2
3	H Kovalainen	McLaren-Mercedes MP4-23	56	1h31m57.005s	125.884	1m35.922s	2
4	J Trulli	Toyota TF108	56	1h32m04.387s	125.716	1m36.068s	2
5	L Hamilton	McLaren-Mercedes MP4-23	56	1h32m05.103s	125.700	1m35.462s	2
6	N Heidfeld	BMW Sauber F1.08	56	1h32m08.388s	125.625	1m35.366s	2
7	M Webber	Red Bull-Renault RB4	56	1h32m26.685s	125.211	1m36.696s	2
8	F Alonso	Renault R28	56	1h32m28.596s	125.168	1m36.288s	2
9	D Coulthard	Red Bull-Renault RB4	56	1h32m34.775s	125.028	1m36.206s	2
10	J Button	Honda RA108	56	1h32m44.769s	124.804	1m35.715s	2
11	N Piquet Jr	Renault R28	56	1h32m50.757s	124.670	1m36.956s	2
12	G Fisichella	Force India-Ferrari VJM01	55	1h31m49.648s	123.802	1m36.962s	2
13	R Barrichello	Honda RA108	55	1h31m52.069s	123.747	1m36.693s	3
14	N Rosberg	Williams-Toyota FW30	55	1h32m01.227s	123.542	1m36.782s	2
15	A Davidson	Super Aguri-Honda SA08	55	1h32m49.328s	122.072	1m38.171s	2
16	T Sato	Super Aguri-Honda SA08	54	1h31m26.134s	122.072	1m38.504s	2
17	K Nakajima	Williams-Toyota FW30	54	1h31m37.131s	121.828	1m37.711s	2
R	S Vettel	Toro Rosso-Ferrari STR02B	39	Engine	-	1m36.870s	1
R	F Massa	Ferrari F2008	30	Spun off	-	1m35.914s	1
R	A Sutil	Force India-Ferrari VJM01	5	Engine	-	1m40.330s	0
R	T Glock	Toyota TF108	1	Collision	-	-	0
R	S Bourdais	Toro Rosso-Ferrari STR02B	0	Spun off	-	-	0

CHAMPIONSHIP

	Driver	Pts
1	L Hamilton	14
2	K Räikkönen	11
3	N Heidfeld	11
4	H Kovalainen	10
5	R Kubica	8
6	N Rosberg	6
7	F Alonso	6
8	J Trulli	5
9	K Nakajima	3
10	S Bourdais	3
11	M Webber	2

Fastest lap
N Heidfeld 1m35.366s
(130.045mph) on lap 55

Fastest speed trap
L Hamilton 192.128mph
Slowest speed trap
T Glock 50.704mph

Fastest pit stop
1 N Heidfeld 27.944s
2 R Kubica 28.121s
3 J Button 28.205s

	Constructor	Pts
1	McLaren-Mercedes	24
2	BMW Sauber	19
3	Ferrari	11
4	Williams-Toyota	9
5	Renault	6
6	Toyota	5
7	Red Bull-Renault	2
8	Toro Rosso-Ferrari	2

Sebastien Bourdais

"I was passed at Turn 4, found myself on the inside at Turn 5 with someone alongside me, and by Turn 6 I was on the outside and the car broke away and I spun off."

Jenson Button

"It was good to finish and get a lot of very useful data. I'm satisfied with 10th. With most of the cars ahead of us finishing, it's a good reflection of our overall position."

Takuma Sato

"The first two stints were good, but in the second stint I hit marbles, ran wide and lost time. We then had traffic, so it was a pity that I couldn't pick up the pace again."

Adrian Sutil

"Very early on, I developed a hydraulic problem and pulled off. I am disappointed with this start to the season, especially after I had to stop so soon in Australia too."

Lewis Hamilton

"I jumped four places to fifth. I was pushing Mark, but it's difficult to get past. We were set for a shot at third position, but then I had the problem in my first pit stop."

Sebastian Vettel

"I started to have difficulty shifting gear and with the power steering. And then the back end caught fire as I pulled over to stop. Up to that point, I was having a fair race."

Rubens Barrichello

"My weekend was compromised when we lost running on Saturday. I had a lot of understeer and the drive-through was unfortunate, even though I only lost one place."

Anthony Davidson

"It was great to do my first full-distance race since Brazil. The boys did an excellent job and the tyres worked well. I could push whenever I wanted to improve my lap time."

Giancarlo Fisichella

"I had wheelspin and lost a lot of positions. I suffered understeer with graining on the softs, but then in my stop I adjusted the front flap and went onto the harder tyres."

Heikki Kovalainen

"I am pretty happy with third, considering my penalty. I did have an issue with graining, but I stayed out until lap 20, which helped me pass Trulli during my first pit stop."

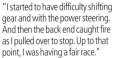

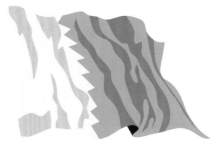

2008 FORMULA 1 GULF AIR BAHRAIN GRAND PRIX
BAHRAIN

MASSA MAKES UP

Although only the third race of the year, this was make-or-break for Ferrari's Felipe Massa, and he responded with a drive of measured excellence to put his campaign back on track

The way most of us saw it, Felipe Massa came to Bahrain looking like a rabbit caught in headlights. Following his disappointing outings in Australia and Malaysia, if he experienced a third disaster in a row then his hopes of winning the World Championship – and of challenging Kimi Räikkönen as the dominant force within Ferrari – would have evaporated.

Massa insisted that all was well, and that he had just been the victim of bad luck. In the end, that confidence proved to be justified, for the Brazilian repeated his 2007 win at the Middle Eastern venue, and put in a faultless performance that left Räikkönen trailing in his wake.

Conversely, the Bahrain GP was Lewis Hamilton's own worst nightmare come to life. A huge crash on Friday was followed by finger trouble on the grid that wasted his respectable qualifying position. And then an accident on the second lap led to suggestions that he tried too hard too soon to make up ground, when damage limitation – in the most literal sense – might have been more prudent. It seemed somehow appropriate that when he crossed the line after a hard afternoon's slog, he was in an unlucky 13th position.

This was by no means a classic encounter, which was a shame, as the sport sorely needed an entertaining

TALKING POINT
MOSLEY IN THE NEWS

Gossip in the Bahrain paddock was all about events in a Kensington basement. According to the previous Sunday's *News of the World*, FIA President Max Mosley had indulged in a five-hour sado-masochistic orgy involving five prostitutes with, it alleged, Nazi overtones.

There had been a deafening silence

in the intervening days before the teams congregated at Sakhir. Then came a joint statement from Mercedes and BMW, distancing themselves from Mosley's activities.

When Mosley's counter mentioned the Second World War, there was a degree of incredulity. "It's all a bit Basil Fawlty..." thought one hack. Toyota and Honda then chipped in, talking about standards of conduct and F1's image.

The Crown Prince of Bahrain had informed Mosley that his attendance, which was scheduled, would no longer be appropriate. The over-riding paddock view was that the FIA President had been fatally compromised and could not uphold his position with dignity and respect. He could no longer do his job effectively, therefore.

Yet Mosley was not about to go without a fight, as he announced that he would take his cue from an extraordinary meeting of the FIA general assembly on 3 June, thereby buying time.

Mosley soon announced that he would be taking legal action against the *News of the World*. He also tried and failed to get an injunction forcing the tabloid to remove a video of the events from its website.

Mosley refuted the Nazi element of the Kensington proceedings and contended that, while they were deeply embarrassing to himself and his family, they were carried out by adults, in private, and that no laws had been broken. His legal case would not focus on libel but, rather, on invasion of privacy.

It later emerged that Mosley had

been warned that he was being tailed before the revelations were published and he announced that he was hiring an investigation team headed by former Chief Police Commissioner Lord Stevens to discover who was behind the story.

In the paddock, leading figures claimed that the affair had brought the sport and the FIA into disrepute and that had Mosley been a major political figure or company head he would have been gone within 24 hours.

The question of whether Mosley could continue to do his job effectively became central to the issue. As a dignified figurehead commanding respect, it appeared that his position was compromised fatally. He could no longer go around pressing the flesh and that became more and more apparent by an increasingly long list of cancelled appearances.

race. The Bahrain weekend was inevitably dominated by talk of the scandal involving FIA President Max Mosley and the fallout that had resulted (see 'Talking Point'). The subject was the focus of every conversation to the extent that the race seemed like a sideshow...

Ferrari had been very strong in Bahrain in 2007, which made it surprising that only the Italian team and Toyota took up the option to test at Sakhir in early February, while their rivals stayed in Spain. That extra local knowledge gave the team a further edge, and Massa was the pacesetter all meeting.

It soon emerged from the BMW Sauber camp that the team was also very confident in its practice pace with a race fuel load on board, as used in final qualifying. That was fully backed up on Saturday afternoon when Robert Kubica put in a storming lap, generating the inevitable clichés about being the first Pole on pole. It was also the first for the team since its birth, as a privateer operation, back in 1993.

Second on the grid was clearly not in the game plan for Massa, and he looked worried, as clearly the general idea was that he would rush off into the distance. Also, right behind him he had Hamilton and Räikkönen. Unfortunately, things went wrong for Kubica when the lights went out, and he didn't get off the line cleanly, allowing Massa to charge into the lead.

Behind, it was even worse for Hamilton, who made a mistake with the settings for the starting procedure on his steering wheel. Before he even crossed the start/finish line, Räikkönen and his own team-mate, Heikki Kovalainen, had got past him and, as he straddled it, both Nick Heidfeld and Jarno Trulli were already coming alongside his McLaren and travelling with significantly more momentum. Nico Rosberg, Jenson Button, Fernando Alonso and Mark Webber also managed to sweep past before Turn 1.

After the race, Hamilton made no bones about it: he admitted that it was his mistake. "The anti-stall kicked in," he explained. "Basically, I hadn't hit the switch early enough, and therefore we weren't in the launch map, and I went straight into anti-stall. Everyone else was in their launch mode, and I wasn't."

There was a sense of desperation in the opening moments about Hamilton's driving as he fought to regain ground. He damaged his upper bridge wing on the back of Alonso's car when he outbraked Webber. Then, on the second lap, he ran into the back of the Spaniard again at much greater speed as the pair accelerated out of a high-speed corner. "I was very, very close and it looked like I could overtake," said Hamilton. "He went to defend his position and I went up the back of him somehow, but that's racing."

It was a strange accident, and the brief TV replays didn't give anybody – including personnel from the teams involved – much of a chance to assess what happened. Given the "previous" of the men involved, inevitably there were early suggestions that Alonso had, shall we say, indulged in a little gamesmanship. After the race, this was absolutely refuted by Renault's Executive Director of Engineering Pat Symonds, who had taken the trouble to print out the telemetry trace of Alonso's second lap by way of evidence.

OPPOSITE Massa leads away from Kubica and Räikkönen, as the slow-starting Hamilton is swallowed by the pack

BELOW Kubica messed up his start from pole, but was easily the quickest after the Ferrari drivers

BOTTOM Kovalainen locks up and comes close to collecting fellow Finn Räikkönen in their early scrap over fourth place

"I love the Sakhir circuit and I've always been very strong here. In my first year at Ferrari, alongside Michael in 2006, I almost made pole position but I got stuck in traffic in qualifying. Then I won last year and I came here really wanting to do that again.

After the problems in Australia and Malaysia I had not had easy weeks, but that's life. You have some bad days, it wasn't the first time and it won't be the last. Despite the problems in Melbourne and Sepang, I knew that we are quick, yet for sure there was some extra pressure because I really wanted to win the race, but I couldn't afford to make a mistake.

I was hoping to get pole position and it was a shame that Robert Kubica was 0.127s quicker. I suspected that we were heavier, but there were also concerns because it meant that I started on the dirty side of the grid and had to be aware that Lewis was third, on the clean side. It didn't change anything though, because we had a good start, Robert had too much wheelspin and I passed him.

The race was pretty difficult in the beginning because there was a lot of oil on the track. We almost went off, me and Robert. It was particularly bad in Turns 5, 6, 8 and 10, with a lot of oil on the line. After that, the car was really good throughout the race. I didn't push completely to the limit as I saw the gap increasing, Kimi was behind and I managed to maintain the gap over him.

It's great to get the 10 points but, although I've had difficult moments in my career, I don't consider that this was one. Maybe when I was fired by Sauber, or maybe when I had money to do one race in Formula Renault and if I didn't win I couldn't do the next one. They were difficult moments. So I don't really care what's happened over the past few weeks. It's just part of the job that journalists write things. That won't change and it's not important. What's important is what's going on in the team and inside Ferrari it's fantastic. I prefer to hear what my team thinks about me, so I'm fine, and for sure I'll get a lot of energy out of this race from Brazil!"

The flat-in-fifth impact could have had worse consequences, but Hamilton escaped with losing his front wing. A pit stop dropped him to the back of the field and, thanks to other aero damage, he didn't have the pace with which to stage any kind of comeback.

There had already been plenty of other activity round the first lap. Adrian Sutil, David Coulthard and Jenson Button all stopped for attention at the end of it, while Sebastian Vettel was out after an impact had ruptured an oil line, which made life tricky for everyone on lap 2, and caused a spin for Nelson Piquet Jr.

At the start of lap 3, Räikkönen demoted Kubica to third, and set about chasing leader Massa. The Brazilian has tended to win races by charging into the lead from pole and, while he'd actually started second, the outcome was the same. The gap grew to around 4 seconds and, as the first round of stops approached, it was clear that there would be no repeat of the Malaysian GP, where the two Ferrari drivers traded places when Massa stopped first. Indeed, to the surprise of many, Räikkönen came in a lap earlier than his team-mate, demonstrating that he had been lighter in qualifying, and that Felipe genuinely was the quicker man this weekend.

During the middle stint, the Ferraris traded fastest laps as Räikkönen kept the pressure on, hoping to be able to do something at the second stops. Massa always responded, though. However, only at the very end were they able to slacken their pace, as Kubica remained a threat. So, Massa had certainly made amends for his terrible start to the season.

"You have some bad days in your life," said the Brazilian. "I had two bad days in the first two races, but I know that we are quick. When you make a mistake and you are behind it means that something is wrong, but when you make a mistake and you are fighting for victory that's better.

"The race was pretty difficult because I didn't want to make any mistakes. I didn't push as much either, just tried to bring the car home, controlling the pace as well. But, for sure, I had a lot of time to think what's happened in the last race. That's pretty normal. I am sure now it's in the past and what is [also] in the past is one victory and that will help for the next race."

A first stop on lap 17 – four laps earlier than nearest qualifying rival Massa – gave some indication as to how Kubica secured pole position, but the BMW Sauber man also had genuine pace in the race. After the

OPPOSITE TOP Button qualified well, in ninth, but was out after a clash with Coulthard's Red Bull

OPPOSITE BOTTOM This is not the pitboard that Hamilton could have expected he'd be shown

BELOW Hamilton's stop for a new nose left him fighting with, and failing to pass, the likes of Fisichella

he achieved the fastest lap, which was some consolation. Switched to a one-stopper, on his way to 13th, Hamilton even made heavy-going of passing cars that should not normally trouble him, such as Giancarlo Fisichella's Force India. This time last year, it had all seemed so easy...

After the race, he was keen to shoulder the blame: "As a professional, if you start off bad you need to pick the pieces up and still deliver at least some points. I didn't do that for the team, I had the collision with Fernando, which lost us the race. I'm always the first to blame it on myself and, to be honest, I feel that's the right way to go."

That sort of response after one of the worst days of his career to date was pretty impressive, especially bearing in mind the sort of afternoon he'd endured. There were few retirements to help him move up the order and, more to the point, the car wasn't handling as it should.

"Further damage meant the car was understeering for the rest of the afternoon," said McLaren Chief Operating Officer Martin Whitmarsh. "The deflectors were taken out at the front, they were munched off in the collision." Despite running to the flag, Hamilton set only the 19th fastest lap, ahead of only Takuma Sato and retiree Button, with Vettel not completing a lap. His best was a full 2.327s behind Kovalainen's fastest lap.

Once again, Jarno Trulli showed that Toyota was a challenger for the best-of-the-rest award, the Italian driver taking a strong sixth place after an untroubled race. Mark Webber was again in the points for Red Bull in seventh, while Nico Rosberg completed the top eight, as Williams showed that its disastrous outing in the Malaysian GP was just a glitch. Timo Glock finished just outside the points in the other Toyota, while Alonso could not better 10th for Renault, hampered by rear wing damage from the Hamilton collision.

Having been delayed on the first lap, Coulthard and Button had a big collision while battling at the very back. This time, the Red Bull survived with all its wheels pointing in the right direction, but Button was out.

ABOVE Massa's relief is palpable as victory put his season back on track. Räikkönen applauds

BELOW Barrichello started mid-grid and ended up in pretty much the same position: 11th overall for Honda

final round of pit stops he was still within 12 seconds of the leader, which came down to 8 seconds by the flag. Meanwhile, his team-mate Nick Heidfeld, who led several laps late in the race thanks to a late final stop, was not far behind. This was truly an impressive performance, and indicated that BMW Sauber really was in the fight. Indeed, going back to Europe the team was leading the constructors' championship...

Kovalainen at least salvaged something from McLaren's bad day. The Finn made a good start, but then later in the opening lap flat-spotted his tyres. That compromised his pace, and he soon dropped back to his grid position of fifth, where he stayed. Late in the race,

SNAPSHOT FROM
BAHRAIN

CLOCKWISE FROM RIGHT Dust, men on horseback and a track in the middle of nowhere, it must be Bahrain; a message to neighbour Dubai which tries to be the home of every other sport...; Hamilton communicates with his crew; desert sunsets always inspire and bring welcome cool; BMW Sauber big-hitters Rampf and Theissen celebrate Kubica's first pole; as ever, Bernie Ecclestone keeps an eye on the action; ...and there's his daughter Tamara interviewing Eric Clapton on the grid.

WEEKEND NEWS

- The Sunday in between the Malaysian and Bahrain grands prix saw motor sport make unexpected headlines when British newspaper the *News of the World* printed revelations about Max Mosley's private life. On arrival in Bahrain, manufacturers Mercedes, BMW, Honda and Toyota all indicated their concern by issuing statements, while the FIA President confirmed that he would take legal action against the paper.

- Meanwhile, just two days before the Mosley scandal erupted, his predecessor Jean-Marie Balestre passed away in France, at the age of 86. Balestre had become the FIA's top sporting official in 1978, and remained in charge of the sport until challenged by Mosley in 1991.

- The FIA acted quickly in the light of the McLaren qualifying penalties at the Malaysian GP. In order to prevent cars from returning to the pits excessively slowly on in-laps while trying to save fuel for the race, drivers now had to run a minimum speed. A similar rule had already been imposed for laps to the grid.

- As usual, the Bahrain royal family entertained a number of high-profile guests during the weekend. Alongside jockey Frankie Dettori, comedian Rory Bremner and Pink Floyd drummer Nick Mason, the biggest name was undoubtedly long-time Ferrari enthusiast Eric Clapton, whose last visit to a race was some 16 years earlier at Suzuka.

- Having been allocated a garage halfway up the pitlane in the first two races, McLaren was moved to the 'poor' end for Bahrain, next to Force India. Made at the instigation of Max Mosley, the change reflected the team's position at the bottom of the 2007 championship table, rather than its true level of competitiveness.

RACE RESULTS
BAHRAIN
SAKHIR

Official Results © [2008]
Formula One Administration Limited,
6 Princes Gate, London, SW7 1QJ.
No reproduction without permission.
All copyright and database rights reserved.

RACE DATE April 6th
CIRCUIT LENGTH 3.363 miles
NO. OF LAPS 57
RACE DISTANCE 191.539 miles
WEATHER Sunny, 31°C
TRACK TEMP 35°C
RACE DAY ATTENDANCE 43,000
LAP RECORD Michael Schumacher,
1m30.252s, 134.262mph, 2004

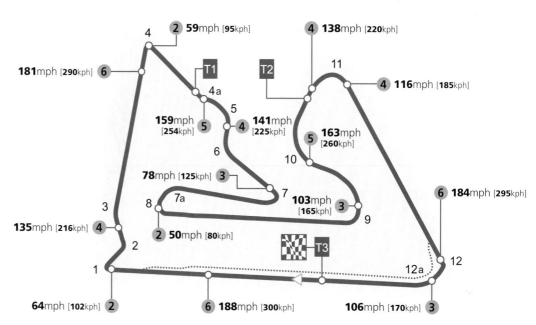

	PRACTICE 1		
	Driver	**Time**	**Laps**
1	F Massa	1m32.233s	20
2	K Räikkönen	1m32.350s	15
3	N Rosberg	1m32.415s	23
4	L Hamilton	1m32.705s	21
5	H Kovalainen	1m32.868s	20
6	K Nakajima	1m33.121s	24
7	R Kubica	1m33.333s	16
8	J Trulli	1m33.539s	27
9	D Coulthard	1m33.788s	20
10	F Alonso	1m33.815s	19
11	T Glock	1m33.929s	28
12	M Webber	1m33.950s	20
13	N Piquet Jr	1m33.981s	24
14	N Heidfeld	1m34.106s	17
15	S Bourdais	1m34.235s	27
16	S Vettel	1m34.321s	32
17	G Fisichella	1m34.892s	20
18	J Button	1m34.915s	16
19	R Barrichello	1m35.174s	12
20	A Sutil	1m35.429s	22
21	A Davidson	1m36.145s	6
22	T Sato	1m36.536s	6

	PRACTICE 2		
	Driver	**Time**	**Laps**
1	F Massa	1m31.420s	30
2	K Räikkönen	1m32.327s	30
3	H Kovalainen	1m32.752s	30
4	L Hamilton	1m32.847s	26
5	R Kubica	1m32.915s	29
6	N Rosberg	1m33.022s	34
7	D Coulthard	1m33.048s	27
8	K Nakajima	1m33.098s	33
9	S Bourdais	1m33.197s	37
10	N Piquet Jr	1m33.247s	37
11	J Button	1m33.710s	33
12	F Alonso	1m33.755s	26
13	M Webber	1m33.782s	34
14	J Trulli	1m33.822s	38
15	T Glock	1m33.856s	30
16	R Barrichello	1m33.966s	35
17	N Heidfeld	1m34.023s	36
18	G Fisichella	1m34.388s	35
19	A Sutil	1m34.405s	34
20	S Vettel	1m34.787s	30
21	T Sato	1m35.288s	24
22	A Davidson	1m35.712s	25

	PRACTICE 3		
	Driver	**Time**	**Laps**
1	N Rosberg	1m32.521s	17
2	F Massa	1m32.726s	10
3	M Webber	1m32.742s	16
4	J Trulli	1m32.901s	18
5	D Coulthard	1m32.918s	14
6	K Nakajima	1m33.020s	16
7	R Kubica	1m33.024s	18
8	N Piquet Jr	1m33.074s	16
9	K Räikkönen	1m33.237s	10
10	H Kovalainen	1m33.367s	15
11	S Bourdais	1m33.372s	17
12	G Fisichella	1m33.392s	20
13	F Alonso	1m33.445s	13
14	R Barrichello	1m33.551s	18
15	T Glock	1m33.595s	20
16	J Button	1m33.600s	17
17	S Vettel	1m33.651s	14
18	L Hamilton	1m33.659s	14
19	A Sutil	1m33.857s	16
20	N Heidfeld	1m34.074s	16
21	A Davidson	1m34.591s	18
22	T Sato	1m34.952s	16

	QUALIFYING 1	
	Driver	**Time**
1	F Massa	1m31.937s
2	J Trulli	1m32.493s
3	K Räikkönen	1m32.652s
4	L Hamilton	1m32.750s
5	J Button	1m32.793s
6	T Glock	1m32.800s
7	R Kubica	1m32.893s
8	N Rosberg	1m32.903s
9	R Barrichello	1m32.944s
10	F Alonso	1m32.947s
11	N Piquet Jr	1m32.975s
12	H Kovalainen	1m33.057s
13	N Heidfeld	1m33.137s
14	M Webber	1m33.194s
15	K Nakajima	1m33.386s
16	S Bourdais	1m33.415s
17	D Coulthard	1m33.433s
18	G Fisichella	1m33.501s
19	S Vettel	1m33.562s
20	A Sutil	1m33.845s
21	A Davidson	1m34.140s
22	T Sato	1m35.725s

	QUALIFYING 2	
	Driver	**Time**
1	F Massa	1m31.188s
2	H Kovalainen	1m31.718s
3	R Kubica	1m31.745s
4	N Heidfeld	1m31.909s
5	L Hamilton	1m31.922s
6	K Räikkönen	1m31.933s
7	J Trulli	1m32.159s
8	N Rosberg	1m32.185s
9	F Alonso	1m32.345s
10	J Button	1m32.362s
11	M Webber	1m32.371s
12	R Barrichello	1m32.508s
13	T Glock	1m32.528s
14	N Piquet Jr	1m32.790s
15	S Bourdais	1m32.915s
16	K Nakajima	1m32.943s

Best sectors – Practice		
Sec 1	F Massa	29.428s
Sec 2	F Massa	39.353s
Sec 3	F Massa	22.639s

Speed trap – Practice		
1	K Räikkönen	196.291mph
2	F Massa	196.229mph
3	N Piquet Jr	195.297mph

Best sectors – Qualifying		
Sec 1	F Massa	29.285s
Sec 2	F Massa	39.230s
Sec 3	H Kovalainen	22.663s

Speed trap – Qualifying		
1	F Massa	195.172mph
2	K Räikkönen	193.619mph
3	S Bourdais	192.625mph

Kimi Räikkönen
"Second was the best I could hope for. These eight points move me into the championship lead. My first stop was not very quick, as we had a problem with the lights."

Nick Heidfeld
"The car's balance was not right, but coming just one place behind Robert, who started from pole while I was sixth, is a good result. I enjoyed passing Jarno and Heikki."

Fernando Alonso
"The race was difficult. Our qualifying pace in Q3 had been a major surprise, but we knew that our race pace would not allow us to do much better in today's race."

Nico Rosberg
"I should go home happy, but we should have done better. It was very difficult, as tyre performance was changeable and the wind conditions were different to Friday."

David Coulthard
"I didn't make the best of starts, then became a pinball as cars bounced off me. I got a puncture. Later, I was fighting Jenson and we got too close in one corner."

Jarno Trulli
"I'm delighted with another top-six finish. I made a strong start and was able to gain two places into Turn 1. I came under pressure from Rosberg but then ran my own race."

Felipe Massa
"I can see sunshine again. We knew we had a great car. I made a good start, passing Robert. There were then a few tricky laps due to oil on track, but I was in control."

Robert Kubica
"This is my second consecutive podium finish. I had massive wheelspin at the start, then hit debris in Turn 1 on lap 2 and was sure I had a puncture, but I hadn't."

Nelson Piquet Jr
"I made a good start, but suffered a gearbox problem. I tried to go on but it became dangerous and my engineers asked me to retire to avoid a penalty in the next race."

Kazuki Nakajima
"I had a very bad start, then spun on the oil on lap 2. After that, I kept up a consistent pace, but it was difficult to make any more progress through the field than up to 14th."

Mark Webber
"I capitalised on a few incidents in the first few laps. You always have to be careful through the first few corners here. And then there was oil, which made things difficult."

Timo Glock
"That was good. We could have scored, but I lost speed when chasing Rosberg. It was quite hard to fend off Alonso after that, but I'm happy to have finished."

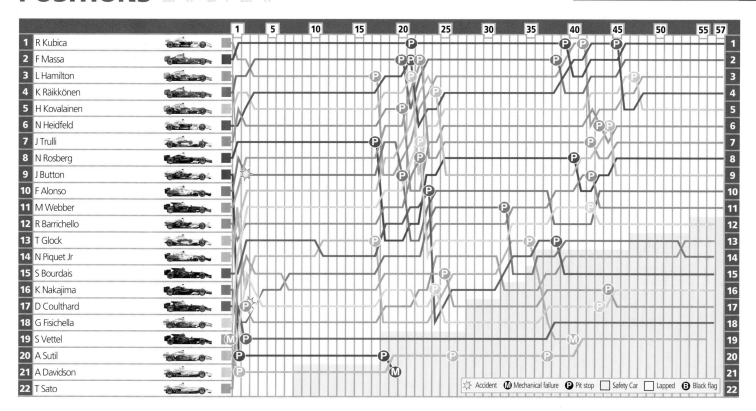

	Driver		1	5	10	15	20	25	30	35	40	45	50	55	57	
1	R Kubica															1
2	F Massa															2
3	L Hamilton															3
4	K Räikkönen															4
5	H Kovalainen															5
6	N Heidfeld															6
7	J Trulli															7
8	N Rosberg															8
9	J Button															9
10	F Alonso															10
11	M Webber															11
12	R Barrichello															12
13	T Glock															13
14	N Piquet Jr															14
15	S Bourdais															15
16	K Nakajima															16
17	D Coulthard															17
18	G Fisichella															18
19	S Vettel															19
20	A Sutil															20
21	A Davidson															21
22	T Sato															22

☆ Accident   Ⓜ Mechanical failure   Ⓟ Pit stop   ▢ Safety Car   ▢ Lapped   Ⓑ Black flag

QUALIFYING 3

	Driver	Time
1	R Kubica	1m33.096s
2	F Massa	1m33.123s
3	L Hamilton	1m33.292s
4	K Räikkönen	1m33.418s
5	H Kovalainen	1m33.488s
6	N Heidfeld	1m33.737s
7	J Trulli	1m33.994s
8	N Rosberg	1m34.015s
9	J Button	1m35.057s
10	F Alonso	1m35.115s

GRID

	Driver	Time
1	R Kubica	1m33.096s
2	F Massa	1m33.123s
3	L Hamilton	1m33.292s
4	K Räikkönen	1m33.418s
5	H Kovalainen	1m33.488s
6	N Heidfeld	1m33.737s
7	J Trulli	1m33.994s
8	N Rosberg	1m34.015s
9	J Button	1m35.057s
10	F Alonso	1m35.115s
11	M Webber	1m32.371s
12	R Barrichello	1m32.508s
13	T Glock	1m32.528s
14	N Piquet Jr	1m32.790s
15	S Bourdais	1m32.915s
16	K Nakajima	1m32.943s
17	D Coulthard	1m33.433s
18	G Fisichella	1m33.501s
19	S Vettel	1m33.562s
20	A Sutil	1m33.845s
21	A Davidson	1m34.140s
22	T Sato	1m35.725s

RACE

	Driver	Car	Laps	Time	Avg. mph	Fastest	Stops
1	F Massa	Ferrari F2008	57	1h31m06.970s	126.122	1m33.600s	2
2	K Räikkönen	Ferrari F2008	57	1h31m10.309s	126.045	1m33.709s	2
3	R Kubica	BMW Sauber F1.08	57	1h31m11.968s	126.007	1m33.775s	2
4	N Heidfeld	BMW Sauber F1.08	57	1h31m15.379s	125.928	1m33.565s	2
5	H Kovalainen	McLaren-Mercedes MP4-23	57	1h31m33.759s	125.507	1m33.193s	2
6	J Trulli	Toyota TF108	57	1h31m48.284s	125.176	1m34.204s	2
7	M Webber	Red Bull-Renault RB4	57	1h31m52.443s	125.082	1m34.305s	2
8	N Rosberg	Williams-Toyota FW30	57	1h32m02.859s	124.846	1m34.072s	2
9	T Glock	Toyota TF108	57	1h32m16.470s	124.539	1m34.807s	2
10	F Alonso	Renault R28	57	1h32m24.151s	124.367	1m35.194s	2
11	R Barrichello	Honda RA108	57	1h32m24.832s	124.351	1m34.855s	2
12	G Fisichella	Force India-Ferrari VJM01	56	1h31m08.446s	123.874	1m35.057s	2
13	L Hamilton	McLaren-Mercedes MP4-23	56	1h31m22.784s	123.550	1m35.520s	2
14	K Nakajima	Williams-Toyota FW30	56	1h31m24.437s	123.513	1m35.433s	1
15	S Bourdais	Toro Rosso-Ferrari STR02B	56	1h31m35.556s	123.263	1m35.333s	2
16	A Davidson	Super Aguri-Honda SA08	56	1h32m13.638s	122.415	1m35.324s	2
17	T Sato	Super Aguri-Honda SA08	56	1h32m22.074s	122.228	1m35.891s	2
18	D Coulthard	Red Bull-Renault RB4	56	1h32m31.666s	122.017	1m35.351s	3
19	A Sutil	Force India-Ferrari VJM01	55	1h31m41.547s	120.929	1m35.442s	3
R	N Piquet Jr	Renault R28	40	Gearbox	-	1m35.129s	2
R	J Button	Honda RA108	19	Collision	-	1m36.125s	2
R	S Vettel	Toro Rosso-Ferrari STR02B	0	Collision	-	-	0

CHAMPIONSHIP

	Driver	Pts
1	K Räikkönen	19
2	N Heidfeld	16
3	L Hamilton	14
4	R Kubica	14
5	H Kovalainen	14
6	F Massa	10
7	J Trulli	8
8	N Rosberg	7
9	F Alonso	6
10	M Webber	4
11	K Nakajima	3
12	S Bourdais	2

Fastest lap
H Kovalainen 1m33.193s
(129.905mph) on lap 49

Fastest speed trap
F Massa   196.360mph
Slowest speed trap
S Vettel   148.080mph

Fastest pit stop
1 N Heidfeld   27.678s
2 R Barrichello   28.183s
3 J Trulli   28.243s

	Constructor	Pts
1	BMW Sauber	30
2	Ferrari	29
3	McLaren-Mercedes	28
4	Williams-Toyota	10
5	Toyota	8
6	Renault	6
7	Red Bull-Renault	4
8	Toro Rosso-Ferrari	2

Sebastien Bourdais

"I had a problem with the brakes. On the plus side, I completed another race distance, which is satisfying. Maybe we did not make the best tyre choice for the start."

Jenson Button

"I was hit at Turn 5, got a puncture. I had a go at passing David into Turn 8. I committed as he hit the brakes. But he moved to the racing line and I had nowhere to go."

Takuma Sato

"I had eventful opening laps and enjoyed some good action but damaged the aero. I got up to 14th, but had a problem in the pits, which cost me a position."

Adrian Sutil

"I had an accident in Turn 1, losing my wing and puncturing my front left. After that, it was OK, but I had problems with the radio so I came in too early for my second stop."

Lewis Hamilton

"I messed up at the start, as I didn't hit the switch early enough. Then I had the incident with Fernando. I moved to the right, and he moved right and that was it"

Sebastian Vettel

"I was blocked into Turn 1. It was tight and I collided with a Force India. My wing was damaged, but the problem came in Turn 4 when someone hit me on the right rear."

Rubens Barrichello

"I avoided collisions on lap 1 but lost a few places. After that, I was stuck behind Fisichella until the team did a great job with my first stop to get me out ahead of him."

Anthony Davidson

"To score another two-car finish is great for the team. I hit a bit of traffic, but once that cleared I was able to get into a good rhythm. It was another strong race for me."

Giancarlo Fisichella

"I passed some cars in Turn 1 and some more when some cars spun in Turn 7. In the middle stint, there were problems with the soft tyres, but the hard tyres worked well."

Heikki Kovalainen

"I passed Kimi into Turn 2, but outbraked myself in Turn 4 and he got back. I went in too deep at Turn 8 and flat-spotted my front right, but fifth was the most I could do."

FORMULA 1 GRAN PREMIO
DE ESPANA TELEFÓNICA 2008
CATALUNYA

KIMI IN CONTROL

Räikkönen came, he saw and he conquered,
with not one of his rivals having an answer to
the Finnish Ferrari driver's pace in a race
remembered for Heikki Kovalainen's accident

Kimi Räikkönen scored his second victory of the
season with a dominant performance in the
Spanish GP at Barcelona, leading all the way and
leaving his team-mate – and likely title rival – Felipe
Massa trailing in his wake.

However, the big story of the afternoon was a
massive accident for McLaren's Heikki Kovalainen
(see 'Talking Point'). Just before his first pit stop,
the Finn suffered a right-front wheel failure at the
high-speed Turn 9. His McLaren speared across the
gravel trap and buried itself beneath the tyre wall, in
a similar fashion to Michael Schumacher's accident at
the British Grand Prix in 1999.

The car had to be pulled out by a tractor before
the driver could be extricated. Thankfully, a thumbs-
up to the TV cameras indicated that Kovalainen
was OK. It was confirmed later that he'd received
a bang on the head, and he was taken to hospital
for observation. The accident highlighted the safety
improvements that have been made over the years,
but nevertheless there was no doubt that Kovalainen
had had a lucky escape.

The Barcelona circuit rarely produces an exciting
race, and indeed this was the eighth time in

succession that the race had been won by the driver who started from pole. While there were few changes of position, it was at least close at the front, indicating that the latest updates introduced at the most recent test at the venue had not allowed Ferrari to pull away.

Räikkönen took pole, but there was something of a surprise package alongside him. Testing had suggested that Renault had made a step forward, and at his home track Fernando Alonso was regularly near the front during the weekend. Nobody expected him to qualify as high as second, though, and it was pretty obvious that he'd run with the minimum possible fuel level. Yet his performance added a little more interest, not least for the devoted home fans. Felipe Massa lined up third in the second Ferrari, ahead of Robert Kubica, Lewis Hamilton and Kovalainen.

Any thoughts that Alonso might enjoy a heroic afternoon were dispelled when he was beaten away by Massa, while Hamilton jumped past Kubica to claim fourth place. Further around the lap, Adrian Sutil spun when he tried to pass David Coulthard, and his Force India was collected by countryman Sebastian Vettel. A brief safety-car interlude followed before Räikkönen was able to set about building up a lead.

Massa was carrying a lap less of fuel, which put Räikkönen's qualifying performance in an even better light, added to which the Brazilian was unable to make much of an impression on his team-mate.

Alonso pitted from third as early as lap 16, while Massa came in on a more realistic lap 19, Räikkönen on lap 20, then Hamilton and Kubica on lap 21. All that activity was to the advantage of late-stopper Kovalainen but, just before he was due to come in, he speared across the gravel and hard into the tyre wall.

"I came past and saw there was a car in the wall," said Hamilton. "It just looked red, so I didn't know if it was one of us or one of the Ferraris. I did see a glimpse of the footage on the television and it looked very reminiscent of my incident last year at the Nürburgring. I was a bit terrified for whoever it was, as I saw the impact was quite heavy.

"The team told me it was Heikki, but they didn't know how he was immediately. Then Ron Dennis came onto the radio halfway through the race and said that he was OK, but slightly concussed."

It looked a lot nastier than it actually was, but a lengthy safety-car period followed. Unfortunately for Nick Heidfeld, that coincided with his planned fuel

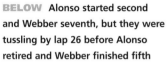

BELOW Alonso started second and Webber seventh, but they were tussling by lap 26 before Alonso retired and Webber finished fifth

ABOVE Kovalainen was all but buried under the tyre wall in this 140mph impact, but emerged OK

stop, so he had to pit and take a penalty. Although, had BMW Sauber reacted more quickly, they could have brought him in just before the pitlane was closed. A stop-and-go penalty dropped Heidfeld from his temporary lead to 16th, and he was faced with a hard slog through the field.

When the safety car withdrew at the end of lap 28, Räikkönen continued to run ahead of Massa and Hamilton, the three cars close enough to make it interesting should anyone encounter a problem. In fact, the only one who did was Alonso. Having dropped to fifth place after his early stop, his Renault suffered a rare engine failure on lap 35.

At the second round of pit stops, Massa again pitted a lap earlier than his team-mate, but Räikkönen had no dramas as he raced to the finish some 3.2s clear, with Hamilton less than a second behind the Brazilian, but never in a position to challenge.

"I didn't get the perfect start," said Räikkönen, "but it was good enough to stay in front. If we had wanted, we could have gone a bit faster, but there is no point to push it when you don't need to. I think it was closer than we expected, but there were many safety-car periods, so without them maybe it would have been looking a little bit different. It was a good day – everything was brilliant. I can't ask for anything

TALKING POINT
KOVALAINEN'S LUCKY ESCAPE

Early in the Barcelona weekend, Heikki Kovalainen was in top form. Easy-going and affable, he was already a popular man in the team and, as he acclimatised at McLaren, his pace was emerging.

He had qualified right behind team-mate Lewis Hamilton on the third row and, although not quite able to stay with Lewis, he was fuelled longer. He was on his in-lap, approaching the 140mph blind uphill right at Turn 9 when his left front tyre deflated through what McLaren later confirmed was a wheel-rim failure. The McLaren went deep into the tyre barrier and everyone briefly saw worrying TV pictures of piles of tyres on top of the Finn. As befits policy, there was no more coverage until it was known that Heikki was alright.

The bottom line is that the tyre barrier did its job and Heikki emerged unscathed. Indeed, he was racing again a fortnight later, but, in the 21st century, should F1 drivers be shunting into piles of tyres?

"Tyres are very economical and, in terms of bang for buck, they're pretty good," said GPDA man Mark Webber, "but you do wonder what we might have in 20 years time...".

At the 2006 Italian GP, the FIA introduced a new High Speed Barrier, developed by the FIA Institute following a programme of development with German automotive safety group, DEKRA, and French company Tekpro. It was installed at Monza's second chicane and Parabolica, both corners with high-speed approaches and limited run-off.

Although the FIA is rightly commended for its safety work, it's perhaps surprising that the barrier, still under development hasn't been introduced elsewhere, especially as it's an area where advances can be made, and not at exorbitant cost.

"You look at Luciano Burti's Spa accident (in 2001) and there has

to be a point where more tyres are maybe not the right thing to do," Webber added. "From what I heard about that, the pressure on his helmet was really intense. His head had nowhere to go and was pushed against the headrest.

"Then there was Gonzalo Rodriguez's (fatal) ChampCar shunt at Laguna Seca , where there were only a couple of rows of tyres and he went over the crash barrier. With Heikki, was it a blessing that he went in a bit deeper? It's a difficult one."

"It's not a simple subject," said Kovalainen. "If I'd hit something more solid head-on, maybe I would have come out without a head injury but with serious lower body damage. It's something we need to look at carefully."

INSIDE LINE
ANTHONY DAVIDSON
SUPER AGURI DRIVER

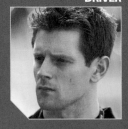

"The future all started looking negative at the end of last year. For a while, it looked alright again and then, literally a few weeks before the Australian GP, it all crumbled. Obviously that was devastating, but at that time there were still deals to be done elsewhere.

Then it was all back on again – it's been a roller-coaster ride. We had a great race in Bahrain and everyone was really pumped up. Then, the week before coming here to Spain, everyone heard the bad news again...

My head wasn't in a good place. I turned up on Friday morning and literally found out then that we were going to be driving. To be told it's all back on again... it's like being teased.

Driving is the easiest part of all of this. You're on auto pilot, in the zone and just doing your job. Then you get out of the car and it all hits home again, and it's everyone remember. The guys – they've got wives, mortgages and kids.

Always, in the back of your mind, is the question: is this the last one?

After qualifying I was thinking 'well, I've done a million laps around Barcelona, it would be very fitting if this was the last time I ever competed in qualifying in a Formula One car.'

I don't want to talk about contracts, but let's just say I fear for the rest of the year with the team not being here. I don't want to talk contracts, but you can pretty much catch my drift...

I've actually got to the stage where I really just feel that I don't deserve it. I'm not bitter and I thank everyone for giving me the chance to get to this stage of my career, but I think I've proved to everyone I'm good enough to be here and I'm proud of myself.

I think I've done a bloody good job in the circumstances. I think there are some more experienced drivers on the grid who would have cracked by now.

When this happens your first thought is obviously about your own security, just like any job in life. Obviously, by this time of year, every deal around the world in every class of racing is done and cemented. Not to have anything at this time of the year, for everyone in the team, was a diabolical situation."

more, as the guys did perfect work, apart from the second pit stop when I had two cars in traffic, so it took a little bit too long to get out and I had to wait a bit for them to pass me. Apart from that, it was OK."

Hamilton was happy to be back on the podium, after frustrating races in both Bahrain and Malaysia. "It's good to be back," he said. "Obviously, when we qualified fifth we knew that it would be very difficult to beat the Ferraris. The key was to get a good start and to make up as many places as possible, and fortunately I was able to do that. We sort of had a feeling that Fernando would be a bit lighter, and that didn't cause us any problems.

"Towards the middle stint, and less so towards the end, I had to try and keep up with Felipe, as I knew he was fuelled a lap shorter than I was, but the Ferraris seem to look after their rear tyres a little bit better than we did.

"It's amazing how close all the cars are. Even Robert Kubica was extremely close to me and I kept looking in the mirrors at a certain point and he was always in the exact same spot. It is very impressive that the top teams are so close."

Hamilton had made his life easier by getting past Kubica on the run to the first corner: "I know from past experiences in Formula 3 that Robert is one of the hardest to overtake. He is very aggressive on the first lap, but I was able to get up the inside of him. I was pretty much past him and I just had to make sure that I covered my ground. It was pretty smooth sailing from there."

Kubica had a relatively quiet afternoon but, once again, it was clear that BMW Sauber was right in the game, as shown by the way that he had Hamilton in his sights for most of the race. Kubica hadn't been entirely happy after qualifying fourth, and hadn't expected such a strong race performance.

"In Qualy 3," explained the Pole, "the balance

of the car changed quite a lot. It looks like when the rubber was laying down with the new tyres during qualifying and today we picked up understeer. I'm pretty sure that I know why, because on Friday we were a bit rushed with the set-up, as last week I didn't test for this race. Maybe we missed something, but I'm not worried. Anyway, five seconds to the winner, if someone had told me yesterday that I would manage this pace I would not have believed it, so that's good."

Behind Kubica, there was a long, long gap to Mark Webber. The Red Bull man lost a place to Heidfeld at the start, but moved up the order when

OPPOSITE Hamilton didn't expect much support, and was proved right as all eyes were for Alonso

ABOVE Piquet Jr continued to struggle and this accident took him out of the race after just six laps

BELOW Davidson leads Sato in the final battle of the Super Aguris, or that should read the final battle...

ABOVE Räikkönen sprays the bubbly, but Hamilton is the one looking happier on the podium

BELOW Webber qualified seventh and raced his Red Bull through to fifth for a third straight points score

Kovalainen crashed, Heidfeld was penalised and Alonso retired. Still trying to learn about Honda's new aero package, Jenson Button suffered with understeer and had to settle for 13th in qualifying. However, the Briton made a good start and moved steadily up to an eventual sixth place, taking full advantage of problems ahead.

It was a day of mixed fortunes for Williams. Kazuki Nakajima had his best qualifying result to date in 12th, and after a tidy race moved steadily up to seventh. Nico Rosberg struggled for grip on Saturday, lost time on his quick lap with a slide, and had to settle for a disappointing 15th on the grid,

but he made a good start and seemed destined to get into the points until he suffered a spectacular engine failure along the pit straight.

With Renault improving, Toyota seemed to have lost a little ground since it collected sixth place in Bahrain, and the TF108 didn't fare well in the windy conditions in Barcelona. Typically, Jarno Trulli dug out a quick lap, and earned himself eighth place on the grid and another shot at points. He was destined for sixth, but lost two places when he was accidentally called in for a wing change by his engineer. In fact, the wing was being readied for Timo Glock, who had nudged David Coulthard. The German had already changed his nose at his first stop after contact on the opening lap, and eventually finished 11th.

Trulli claimed the final point ahead of Heidfeld who spent several laps of his recovery drive stuck behind Force India's Giancarlo Fisichella. The Italian had made a good start and ran as high as eighth in the middle of the race. He finished a respectable 10th after surviving a pitlane brush with Rubens Barrichello. The Honda driver damaged his front wing, which in turn damaged the bargeboards, and led to his retirement.

It was not a great day for his countryman Nelson Piquet Jr. Starting 10th, he dropped back with an early off and, while trying to recover, he broke his front suspension when he tried an optimistic overtaking manoeuvre down the inside of Sebastien Bourdais that put both men out of the race.

We didn't know it at the time, but this was to be the final fling for Super Aguri Racing. Anthony Davidson ran into the back of the Vettel/Sutil collision on the first lap, damaging his nose, but his biggest problem was that a stone thrown up by Piquet Jr holed a radiator. Takuma Sato plugged away at the back of the field and finished 13th. It was an appropriately unlucky end to what had been a short but spectacular adventure.

SNAPSHOT FROM
SPAIN

CLOCKWISE FROM RIGHT Parasols were in evidence against the spring sunshine; beauty in the pits; Spanish fans had eyes only for Alonso...; ...although not one that looked like this dummy with his Hamilton counterpart; Coulthard was left regretting stopping for a bowl of soup on the Sunday morning, as it cost him 4000 Euros; the team chiefs met in private, but people could see through the windows; meet Nelson and Nelson Jr; Honda's extra nose wings weren't things of beauty

WEEKEND NEWS

■ Bernie Ecclestone chaired a meeting of team principals and technical chiefs in the Toyota motorhome on Saturday, and its windows allowed the media to get an unusual appreciation of the dynamics of the gathering. Key subjects included the future of troubled FIA President Max Mosley, but there was no unanimous agreement on a stance on this matter.

■ Also discussed at length in the team chiefs' meeting was the future of KERS (Kinetic Energy Recovery System). While some expressed doubts over its relevance and costs, it was accepted that the technology would be coming in 2009, as previously agreed. However, there were questions over how it should be rolled out in future years after Mosley had circulated a letter suggesting that the role of KERS would quickly become more significant.

■ David Coulthard was fined 4,000 Euros when he arrived too late to join the drivers' parade lorry on Sunday morning, the Scot having been enjoying what was probably the most expensive bowl of soup in history at the Red Bull motorhome. He failed to convince the stewards that the fine was compromising the future of his children...

■ Sebastien Bourdais had a heavy crash in pre-race testing at Barcelona at the wheel of Toro Rosso's new STR03. The team had always intended to give the car a late debut, but the Frenchman's accident and ongoing problems in readying replacement parts delayed the car's first appearance even further.

■ The Spanish GP hosted the official launch of the FIA's anti-racism campaign, prompted by problems suffered by Lewis Hamilton at the same venue earlier in the year. President Mosley did not attend the race to participate in the launch, but there was no repeat of the earlier crowd trouble.

RACE RESULTS
SPAIN
CATALUNYA

Official Results © [2008]
Formula One Administration Limited,
6 Princes Gate, London, SW7 1QJ.
No reproduction without permission.
All copyright and database rights reserved.

RACE DATE April 27th
CIRCUIT LENGTH 2.892 miles
NO. OF LAPS 65
RACE DISTANCE 187.980 miles
WEATHER Dry & bright, 24°C
TRACK TEMP 38°C
RACE DAY ATTENDANCE 132,000
LAP RECORD Kimi Räikkönen,
1m21.670s, 127.500mph, 2008

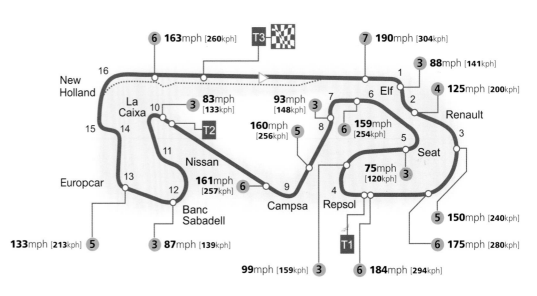

	PRACTICE 1				PRACTICE 2				PRACTICE 3				QUALIFYING 1			QUALIFYING 2	
	Driver	Time	Laps		Driver	Time	Laps		Driver	Time	Laps		Driver	Time		Driver	Time
1	K Räikkönen	1m20.649s	17	1	K Räikkönen	1m21.935s	38	1	N Heidfeld	1m21.269s	19	1	K Räikkönen	1m20.701s	1	F Massa	1m20.584s
2	F Massa	1m20.699s	9	2	N Piquet Jr	1m22.019s	38	2	D Coulthard	1m21.465s	16	2	J Trulli	1m21.158s	2	R Kubica	1m20.597s
3	L Hamilton	1m21.192s	20	3	F Alonso	1m22.032s	26	3	F Alonso	1m21.599s	16	3	F Alonso	1m21.347s	3	K Räikkönen	1m20.784s
4	R Kubica	1m21.568s	20	4	K Nakajima	1m22.172s	35	4	R Kubica	1m21.717s	23	4	L Hamilton	1m21.366s	4	F Alonso	1m20.804s
5	H Kovalainen	1m21.758s	10	5	F Massa	1m22.229s	32	5	J Trulli	1m21.771s	21	5	N Piquet Jr	1m21.409s	5	N Heidfeld	1m20.815s
6	F Alonso	1m21.933s	18	6	M Webber	1m22.238s	36	6	S Bourdais	1m21.942s	19	6	R Kubica	1m21.423s	6	H Kovalainen	1m20.817s
7	N Piquet Jr	1m21.936s	21	7	N Rosberg	1m22.266s	33	7	N Piquet Jr	1m21.992s	18	7	T Glock	1m21.427s	7	L Hamilton	1m20.825s
8	D Coulthard	1m22.118s	20	8	D Coulthard	1m22.289s	30	8	J Button	1m22.060s	17	8	H Kovalainen	1m21.430s	8	N Piquet Jr	1m20.894s
9	N Heidfeld	1m22.278s	24	9	G Fisichella	1m22.383s	38	9	F Massa	1m22.075s	16	9	N Heidfeld	1m21.466s	9	J Trulli	1m20.907s
10	J Button	1m22.632s	16	10	A Sutil	1m22.548s	38	10	T Glock	1m22.081s	23	10	N Rosberg	1m21.472s	10	M Webber	1m20.984s
11	T Glock	1m23.002s	21	11	L Hamilton	1m22.685s	33	11	L Hamilton	1m22.094s	15	11	M Webber	1m21.494s	11	R Barrichello	1m21.049s
12	N Rosberg	1m23.003s	25	12	R Kubica	1m22.788s	38	12	N Rosberg	1m22.174s	19	12	F Massa	1m21.528s	12	K Nakajima	1m21.117s
13	M Webber	1m23.015s	14	13	N Heidfeld	1m23.130s	40	13	K Räikkönen	1m22.176s	18	13	S Bourdais	1m21.540s	13	J Button	1m21.211s
14	J Trulli	1m23.141s	15	14	J Trulli	1m23.224s	34	14	K Nakajima	1m22.189s	16	14	R Barrichello	1m21.548s	14	T Glock	1m21.230s
15	K Nakajima	1m23.153s	24	15	J Button	1m23.263s	34	15	H Kovalainen	1m22.220s	16	15	K Nakajima	1m21.690s	15	N Rosberg	1m21.349s
16	A Sutil	1m23.156s	22	16	H Kovalainen	1m23.264s	8	16	S Vettel	1m22.292s	20	16	J Button	1m21.757s	16	S Bourdais	1m21.724s
17	G Fisichella	1m23.196s	20	17	R Barrichello	1m23.415s	31	17	R Barrichello	1m22.350s	17	17	D Coulthard	1m21.810s			
18	R Barrichello	1m23.353s	14	18	S Vettel	1m23.661s	35	18	G Fisichella	1m22.466s	22	18	S Vettel	1m22.108s			
19	S Bourdais	1m23.952s	15	19	S Bourdais	1m23.684s	37	19	A Sutil	1m22.689s	21	19	G Fisichella	1m22.516s			
20	S Vettel	1m24.082s	15	20	T Glock	1m23.883s	40	20	T Sato	1m23.726s	16	20	A Sutil	1m23.224s			
21	T Sato	1m24.278s	14	21	T Sato	1m25.110s	30	21	A Davidson	1m23.921s	15	21	A Davidson	1m23.318s			
22	A Davidson	1m25.068s	10	22	A Davidson	1m25.163s	31	22	M Webber	No time	2	22	T Sato	1m23.496s			

	Best sectors – Practice			Speed trap – Practice			Best sectors – Qualifying			Speed trap – Qualifying	
Sec 1	K Räikkönen	21.963s	1	K Räikkönen	195.172mph	Sec 1	H Kovalainen	27.044s	1	K Räikkönen	194.551mph
Sec 2	F Massa	30.394s	2	N Rosberg	194.178mph	Sec 2	L Hamilton	30.386s	2	H Kovalainen	193.060mph
Sec 3	K Räikkönen	27.997s	3	F Massa	193.992mph	Sec 3	R Kubica	27.749s	3	R Kubica	192.687mph

Kimi Räikkönen
"Yesterday pole, today the win. I did not get a perfect start, but it was enough to keep the lead. The two safety-car periods complicated things, but we never lost the lead."

Nick Heidfeld
"I was fifth when I had bad luck with the timing of the safety car and my stop. I had just passed the pits when I got the signal to come in. I couldn't and got a stop-go."

Fernando Alonso
"We were up there with the Ferraris and BMWs, so I am disappointed not to finish, but it was a nice surprise to see that we are more competitive than before."

Nico Rosberg
"We went the wrong way with our new aero package, but changed it for the race. I went from 15th to 11th on lap 1 and would have been on for at least seventh."

David Coulthard
"I got whacked by Sutil and picked up some damage. After my stop, I took a defensive line to show Glock that I knew he was there, but he hit me and punctured a tyre."

Jarno Trulli
"This race wasn't easy, but it was going well and we were heading for sixth. Then a communications error led to the team mistakenly calling me into the pits."

Felipe Massa
"I made a great start and passed Alonso, getting very close to Kimi. I knew I was stopping a lap before my team-mate and that it would have been difficult to get ahead."

Robert Kubica
"We had good pace. Sadly I lost a place at the start. At the end, our gap to the leader was only 5s. If you had told me that yesterday I would not have believed it."

Nelson Piquet Jr
"I made my first mistake early on and went off, but I was able to rejoin down the field and from then on I tried to attack, which meant I had to take a few risks."

Kazuki Nakajima
"It was a good race. After the start, I was caught behind Button so I lost position, but I'm happy with the end result and this race is another step forward for me."

Mark Webber
"The team worked really hard following the test to get all the parts ready and it paid off. We didn't have a great start, but we had good pace and were there at the end."

Timo Glock
"My front wing was damaged at the first corner, leaving me stuck in traffic. The car felt better after we changed the nose, but I hit Coulthard and destroyed it again."

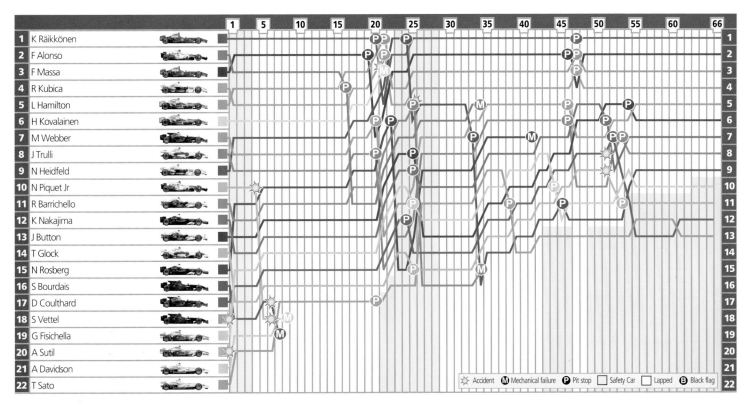

1	K Räikkönen	
2	F Alonso	
3	F Massa	
4	R Kubica	
5	L Hamilton	
6	H Kovalainen	
7	M Webber	
8	J Trulli	
9	N Heidfeld	
10	N Piquet Jr	
11	R Barrichello	
12	K Nakajima	
13	J Button	
14	T Glock	
15	N Rosberg	
16	S Bourdais	
17	D Coulthard	
18	S Vettel	
19	G Fisichella	
20	A Sutil	
21	A Davidson	
22	T Sato	

☆ Accident Ⓜ Mechanical failure Ⓟ Pit stop ☐ Safety Car ☐ Lapped Ⓑ Black flag

QUALIFYING 3

	Driver	Time
1	K Räikkönen	1m21.813s
2	F Alonso	1m21.904s
3	F Massa	1m22.058s
4	R Kubica	1m22.065s
5	L Hamilton	1m22.096s
6	H Kovalainen	1m22.231s
7	M Webber	1m22.429s
8	J Trulli	1m22.529s
9	N Heidfeld	1m22.542s
10	N Piquet Jr	1m22.699s

GRID

	Driver	Time
1	K Räikkönen	1m21.813s
2	F Alonso	1m21.904s
3	F Massa	1m22.058s
4	R Kubica	1m22.065s
5	L Hamilton	1m22.096s
6	H Kovalainen	1m22.231s
7	M Webber	1m22.429s
8	J Trulli	1m22.529s
9	N Heidfeld	1m22.542s
10	N Piquet Jr	1m22.699s
11	R Barrichello	1m21.049s
12	K Nakajima	1m21.117s
13	J Button	1m21.211s
14	T Glock	1m21.230s
15	N Rosberg	1m21.349s
16	S Bourdais	1m21.724s
17	D Coulthard	1m21.810s
18	S Vettel	1m22.108s
19	G Fisichella	1m22.516s
20	A Sutil	1m23.224s
21	A Davidson	1m23.318s
22	T Sato	1m23.496s

RACE

	Driver	Car	Laps	Time	Avg. mph	Fastest	Stops
1	K Räikkönen	Ferrari F2008	66	1h38m19.051s	116.454	1m21.670s	2
2	F Massa	Ferrari F2008	66	1h38m22.279s	116.391	1m21.801s	2
3	L Hamilton	McLaren-Mercedes MP4-23	66	1h38m23.238s	116.371	1m22.017s	2
4	R Kubica	BMW Sauber F1.08	66	1h38m24.745s	116.342	1m22.106s	2
5	M Webber	Red Bull-Renault RB4	66	1h38m54.989s	115.749	1m22.564s	2
6	J Button	Honda RA108	66	1h39m12.061s	115.417	1m22.353s	2
7	K Nakajima	Williams-Toyota FW30	66	1h39m17.295s	115.316	1m23.549s	2
8	J Trulli	Toyota TF108	66	1h39m18.486s	115.293	1m22.758s	2
9	N Heidfeld	BMW Sauber F1.08	66	1h39m22.124s	115.222	1m22.519s	3
10	G Fisichella	Force India-Ferrari VJM01	66	1h38m28.846s	114.499	1m23.439s	2
11	T Glock	Toyota TF108	65	1h38m33.054s	114.417	1m23.007s	3
12	D Coulthard	Red Bull-Renault RB4	65	1h39m09.241s	113.722	1m22.842s	3
13	T Sato	Super Aguri-Honda SA08	65	1h39m24.965s	113.422	1m24.617s	2
R	N Rosberg	Williams-Toyota FW30	41	Engine	-	1m23.319s	1
R	F Alonso	Renault R28	34	Engine	-	1m22.683s	1
R	R Barrichello	Honda RA108	34	Crash damage	-	1m23.858s	2
R	H Kovalainen	McLaren-Mercedes MP4-23	21	Spun off	-	1m22.453s	0
R	A Davidson	Super Aguri-Honda SA08	8	Radiator	-	1m26.864s	0
R	S Bourdais	Toro Rosso-Ferrari STR02B	7	Crash damage	-	1m25.999s	2
R	N Piquet Jr	Renault R28	6	Accident	-	1m25.444s	0
R	S Vettel	Toro Rosso-Ferrari STR02B	0	Accident	-	-	0
R	A Sutil	Force India-Ferrari VJM01	0	Accident	-	-	0

CHAMPIONSHIP

	Driver	Pts
1	K Räikkönen	29
2	L Hamilton	20
3	R Kubica	19
4	F Massa	18
5	N Heidfeld	16
6	H Kovalainen	14
7	J Trulli	9
8	M Webber	8
9	N Rosberg	7
10	F Alonso	6
11	K Nakajima	5
12	J Button	3
13	S Bourdais	2

	Fastest Lap
	K Räikkönen 1m21.670s
	(127.500mph) on lap 46

Fastest speed trap	
K Räikkönen	195.483mph
Slowest speed trap	
S Vettel	184.920mph

Fastest pit stop		
1	T Glock	25.324s
2	J Button	25.413s
3	R Kubica	26.156s

	Constructor	Pts
1	Ferrari	47
2	BMW Sauber	35
3	McLaren-Mercedes	34
4	Williams-Toyota	12
5	Toyota	9
6	Red Bull-Renault	8
7	Renault	6
8	Honda	3
9	Toro Rosso-Ferrari	2

Sebastien Bourdais

"I checked my mirrors and Nelson did not seem to be in a position to attack. I braked quite late for Turn 10, started to turn in and all of a sudden, he was alongside me."

Jenson Button

"I'm really pleased to finish sixth, but the safety car came out at the wrong time for us, as I was on a long first stint. This circuit is not the best for our car as it's bumpy."

Takuma Sato

"A few cars had a coming together in front of me and I lost part of the nose. The team said that the car looked OK, so we fought our way through the rest of the race."

Adrian Sutil

"Going into Turn 4 on lap 1, I was on the inside and tried to pass another car, but it was too close and I couldn't make the corner. I crashed into a car and my race was over."

Lewis Hamilton

"I made a good start and got lots of traction and went to the right alongside Robert. I managed to overtake him which is usually not easy as I recall from our F3 battles."

Sebastian Vettel

"Adrian (Sutil) clipped a car and spun in front of me. I tried to get through on the inside and might have managed it, but I had a Super Aguri also trying to get past it."

Rubens Barrichello

"The team released me and advised me of traffic, so I stayed out of the fast lane. Fisichella overtook me and cut into his box, clipping my front wing."

Anthony Davidson

"After Piquet ran wide at the beginning of the race, he dragged a lot of gravel on to the track and a stone from that damaged my water radiator, putting me out of the race."

Giancarlo Fisichella

"Tenth is our best result so far. Late in the race, I enjoyed my battle with Heidfeld – he was quicker than me, but I managed to keep him behind me for many laps."

Heikki Kovalainen

"The team told me that the left front wheel rim might have broken which would have led to the sudden deflation of the tyre, but we have to wait for other inspections."

2008 FORMULA 1 PETROL OFISI TURKISH GRAND PRIX
ISTANBUL

THREE IN A ROW

Felipe Massa clearly loves the Istanbul circuit, as he rediscovered his form and raced to his third win here in three years, putting his championship challenge right back on track

Felipe Massa has often been criticised for his occasionally erratic form, but for the second year running he put his season back on track here. In fact, his victory in Turkey marked his third straight win at the Istanbul circuit from pole position.

Consider that in 2006 he had to beat his Ferrari team-mate Michael Schumacher and you can appreciate that it's an impressive achievement. Indeed, the only drivers who have taken four successive wins from pole in the same grand prix are Jim Clark, Ayrton Senna and Schumacher himself. Also, Clark's British's GP successes were achieved at different tracks...

Massa's victory was also the fourth consecutive win for Ferrari since its humiliating performance in the season-opener in Australia. But, while the bare statistics suggested dominance, there were clear signs in Turkey that McLaren had closed the gap, and that this World Championship had a lot of life left in it yet.

Lewis Hamilton managed to split the Ferraris by finishing in second place in his McLaren, having put in a charging drive that the man himself felt was the best of his F1 career to date. At one stage, Hamilton even managed to pull off that extreme rarity: a genuine pass for the lead.

TALKING POINT
WOMEN IN F1?

Danica Patrick's victory in the IndyCar Japan 300 at Motegi – not to mention the *Sports Illustrated* swimsuit issue – had got the paddock talking. Women have driven in Formula One before, of course, with Lella Lombardi scoring half a point in the shortened, half-points 1975 Spanish Grand Prix for finishing sixth in her March, but the old question was being asked once more: is there anything stopping a woman from winning F1 races?

Patrick, admittedly, had better managed her fuel allocation to win tactically in Motegi, but has proven many times that she is capable of running with the men.

"We ran Sarah Fisher at Indianapolis once," said Mercedes motorsport chief Norbert Haug in reference to a publicity demonstration, "and we had a winner in DTM in 1992, with Ellen Lohr at Hockenheim beating Keke Rosberg, which was not very pleasing for my old friend Keke..."

At the time, Lohr's victory prompted a reworking of the lyrics to the well known Sonny Curtis and the Crickets and then the Bobby Fuller Four hit songs from the 1950s and 1960s. The new version became, 'Keke fought the Lohr and the Lohr won!'

Lohr's DTM win is still something that Nico Rosberg gently teases his father about every now and again...

"It is possible," Haug said, "and hopefully F1 will experience that in the future."

"Why not have a woman in F1 again?" said Toyota's John Howett. "I think it would probably be very good for the sport. We just need to see a driver with the capability to deliver top-level performance. I don't think there's any discrimination in our organisation. Unfortunately, though, most of those coming into karting and delivering top performances are male."

Honda's Technical Director Ross Brawn added: "We can all see the commercial attraction and how exciting it would be to have a female driver in F1, but it would be a shame if, purely because they were female, they got put in a car and couldn't compete properly, then hampering the progress of better female drivers in the future."

What about the physical side? Many leading F1 drivers have been small in stature and slight, but men tend to be naturally stronger than women. Would that become too significant on F1-style road courses?

"In sports like soccer, it's not possible for women to compete against men," said Haug, "but it should be basically possible in motorsport, as the IndyCar Series has proved."

Howett concluded: "I think Danica has proven that it's possible for an extremely talented lady to be competitive in what is historically seen as a male environment so, yes, it's probably opened people's eyes to the possibility."

Tyres have always been a key issue in Turkey, not least because of the demands of the glorious Turn 8, a never-ending lefthander in which driver and machine are subject to extreme g-loadings for an unusually long time. Hamilton suffered a major tyre failure immediately after the corner in 2007, and the points he lost ultimately contributed to his World Championship defeat.

This year, the added complication was that moving the race forward from August to May meant a significant drop in temperature, something that Bridgestone had not been able to factor in. Throw in a little Saturday morning rain that cleaned the track and cost dry practice running time, and everyone was struggling to get the best out of their tyres. The choice between the harder primes and softer options came into sharper focus than normal.

Indeed, the tyres determined the shape of Hamilton's weekend, as Friday practice revealed that the team discovered that once again they had a potentially worrying issue.

"The answer is very, very simple: Turn 8," said McLaren Chief Operating Officer Martin Whitmarsh. "We're very, very strong in high-speed corners: we generate a lot of front end. Last year, it was a chunking problem in the tyre, this was a delamination in the sidewall, so this was a different problem. We're generating high vertical loads through those corners, and I think Bridgestone acknowledge that."

The problem was examined overnight on Friday, and even before Saturday morning practice the team was looking at a potential three-stop strategy, simply because it would break the race up into four bite-size chunks and so minimise the mileage run on each set.

"It was decided on Saturday, before we were running in P3, as a consequence of durability concerns on the tyres," said Whitmarsh of the three-stopper. "So, from that point on, we knew that we had a

problem there. Obviously we didn't advertise the fact but, with Lewis in particular, we had a problem.

"We took a number of measures with Bridgestone. We came here running the pressures and camber that they specified. We then increased the pressures on Saturday morning, hoping that this would solve the problem, and in fact Bridgestone were very confident that it would do so, but it didn't sufficiently to give us the comfort that we needed. So we made some adjustments and limited the range for the race."

As far as McLaren was concerned, there was a clear explanation as to why Hamilton was affected and Kovalainen wasn't. "They've got a slightly different set-up, which puts a bit more load on the front tyres on Lewis's car," continued Whitmarsh. "Lewis was reasonably aggressive through Turn 8 – very, very quick incidentally – but he changed his style and driving line on Saturday. On a circuit like this, when you see there's a concern with tyres you've got to put safety first. We took a decision that I don't regret. What I do regret is the fact that we had to make a decision, but we made a decision based on 'how do we run this race safely for Lewis?'

OPPOSITE Massa leads from Hamilton, Kubica, Kovalainen and Alonso on the opening lap

BELOW Barrichello's livery indicated he was becoming F1's most experienced driver, with 257 starts

BOTTOM Nakajima and Fisichella clashed on the opening lap, ending both of their afternoon's sport

I think it was the right decision with the information that we had at the time."

The bottom line was that Hamilton went into qualifying knowing that he would have to make three stops, and that meant he absolutely had to be on pole to have any chance of converting that into a decent result. He had one advantage in that the chosen strategy meant he would be light – indeed he eventually came in on lap 16 compared with lap 19 for Massa and lap 21 for Kimi Räikkönen.

However, there were added complications. He had to adjust his line for Turn 8 and, more importantly, there was clearly some debate about which tyres to use. He felt more comfortable on the prime tyres, which was of course a highly unusual choice for qualifying. He didn't quite have the pace with it to secure top spot, instead earning only a frustrated third behind Massa and his own team-mate Kovalainen. Outpaced all weekend by Massa, Räikkönen had to settle for fourth on the grid.

At the start of the race, Hamilton was at least able to reduce the size of his problem by jumping ahead of Kovalainen. The Finn and his countryman Räikkönen both made bad starts from the dirty side of the track,

then contrived to collide at the first turn, although both were able to continue.

The safety car had to be scrambled for a more serious Turn 1 incident involving Giancarlo Fisichella and Kazuki Nakajima. Just as the race went green again, Kovalainen had to dive into the pits for new tyres, a legacy of his clash with Räikkönen, which had given him a slow puncture. That dropped him way off the rear of the field. Räikkönen meanwhile lost a few places, and fell out of contention.

This race was now all about Massa and Hamilton. The pair ran close together through the first stint, with the Brazilian on the softer tyre, and Hamilton on his preferred harder choice. As expected, Hamilton was the first of the duo to pit, on lap 16. Massa came in three laps later and resumed still ahead, but found his second set of softs slightly less comfortable than the first. Hamilton soon pounced. In a wonderful move on lap 24, he dived down the inside to take the lead and duly began to pull away.

It looked as though he had the race in the bag, but there was more to this than met the eye. His pit stop had been relatively short, and he had taken on a lot less fuel than his rival. His second stop thus

BELOW Piquet Jr and Button gave their all, but neither was able to finish in the top 10

OPPOSITE Hamilton had all manner of tyre concerns before the race but drove a great race to second

came unusually early, on lap 32, and McLaren gave Hamilton another set of hard tyres. This was the ultimate indication that he was going for a three-stop strategy, as he had yet to make a stint on the softs, as the rules demand.

The need for an extra pit stop swung the balance back in Massa's favour, but Hamilton continued to push. When his final stop played out, he was behind – but at least he was still ahead of Räikkönen, although only just.

Over that final stint, with the Ferraris now on the hard tyres and the McLaren man on his less-favoured softs, the three cars ran at exactly the same pace. Massa was some five seconds clear, while Hamilton and Räikkönen ran nose to tail, and it stayed that way to the chequered flag. It was good, close stuff, and suggested that we might see some great strategic battles as the year progressed.

"Today was a very difficult race and Lewis was pushing me hard for the whole race," said Massa. "Then, after my pit stop, he was there straight away, so I thought maybe he had put less fuel in or something. I then realised, and my team told me straight away, that he was on three stops. For sure,

INSIDE LINE
MARTIN WHITMARSH
McLAREN CHIEF OPERATING OFFICER

"Lewis thinks that second place here was his finest F1 drive, but my memory is so short that I don't make comparisons! His three-stop strategy was decided on Saturday and it was a consequence of a durability concern with tyres. Obviously we didn't advertise the fact but, with Lewis in particular, we had a problem. Bridgestone were very confident that increasing the tyre pressures, which we did on Saturday morning, would solve it, but it didn't give us the comfort zone we needed.

From a strategic point-of-view, Heikki was in the strongest position to win this race and I think he would have done so had it not been for the first lap racing incident with Kimi. I've never known him as disappointed. He knows he could have won and it eluded him.

With Lewis, we had no choice but to go to what was really a sub-optimal three-stop race. The problem was Turn 8. We're very strong in high-speed corners and generate a lot of front-end grip. Last year, when Lewis's tyre exploded,

it was a chunking problem. This time it was sidewall delamination, so a different issue.

The drivers had a slightly different set-up, which put a little bit more load on Lewis's front tyres. He was aggressive through Turn 8 and very quick and tried changing his style and line on Saturday. But, once you see that there's a concern with tyres you've got to put safety first, so we took a decision which we don't regret.

The difference between the optimum two-stop strategy and a three-stop race in simple time terms, was about 5s. It's more in reality because you don't always have the most cooperative traffic ahead of you. But we knew we had to do that and we knew that we had to put ourselves on pole position to be able to minimise any handicap. But the job we did in qualifying wasn't good enough. We were on the back foot, which made Lewis's race drive all the more extraordinary.

With Heikki, ordinarily we'd have reverted to a one-stop strategy after the early contact, but we couldn't do that either as we couldn't run any longer. Our safe range was circa 20–21 laps. That's all we felt we could do safely with the tyres. Heikki was unlucky and for Lewis to go and split the Ferraris was tremendous. He was just flat-out and his in- and out-laps were great. The team supported him superbly and he was able to take the race to Ferrari throughout."

that was a little bit of help as he was very strong and I couldn't hold him on the track and he passed me. But I knew that I still had a good chance to win the race, as three stops were a little bit optimistic. Anyway, I created a reasonable gap to be at the front after the pit stops. It was difficult, but we made it three times in Turkey which is just fantastic. I think I can get a passport here already..."

Hamilton had done enough to ensure that he stayed ahead of Räikkönen for second, an outcome that the team could not have predicted at the start.

"To be sub-optimal in your strategy and be so close to winning shows that we were really, really

quick," explained Whitmarsh. "Lewis did a fantastic job. I guess Lewis in Q3 was the slip of the weekend, the durability of the tyres has been a setback to us but, overall, the team has done a fantastic job. The reality is that we wouldn't have three-stopped on either car unless we had to, and I believe that both cars had a reasonable chance of winning had we been able to conventionally two-stop."

One question remained to be asked. Could Hamilton still have won if he'd taken pole and been able to escape from Massa in that first stint?

"I would have said from pole it would have been difficult," concluded Whitmarsh, "but, given the performance that he gave in the race, he possibly could have done..."

This time around, BMW Sauber didn't have the pace with which to worry the top two runners, which was a legacy of the team not making the best of the tyre equation. Nevertheless, Robert Kubica had a good run to fourth, and Nick Heidfeld rose from ninth on the grid to fifth, so nine points wasn't a bad haul on a less-than-perfect weekend.

The battle behind was intense as ever. Renault again signalled signs of improvement as Fernando Alonso emerged from the midfield pack to claim sixth place, running a light qualifying load and stopping early, while Mark Webber took seventh, earning valuable points for Red Bull for the fourth race in a row. The final point went to Nico Rosberg, with David Coulthard and Jarno Trulli completing the top 10. Kovalainen could recover only to 13th in a race that had but three retirements. Afterwards, McLaren chief Ron Dennis made it clear that without his early stop, the Finn had had the potential to win.

Monaco was next, a race in which McLaren had traditionally shone. The team urgently needed a win to swing the title balance back in its favour, the big question was, would it be Hamilton's turn?

SNAPSHOT FROM
TURKEY

CLOCKWISE FROM RIGHT The circuit's backdrop looked far greener in the spring; retaining modesty; walking the track, Renault-style; Barrichello took over from Riccardo Patrese as F1's most experienced driver; night-time in the paddock; caught snapping; it's "John Barrichello"; Senna's GP2 car after hitting a dog

WEEKEND NEWS

■ Super Aguri Racing's support vehicles made it to Turkey early in the week, but at a crunch meeting in Tokyo on Tuesday team principal Aguri Suzuki finally had to accept that Honda was no longer prepared to subsidise the team. The grand prix veteran had no choice but to announce the closure of the outfit, which had accumulated huge debts, most of which involved Honda.

■ In the absence of Super Aguri Racing, the FIA adjusted the rules of qualifying so that five rather than six cars were eliminated in the first qualifying session, and so 15 drivers instead of 16 went through to the second qualifying session. Ironically, the withdrawal of the team thus made it harder for the likes of Force India and Toro Rosso to progress through to the next stage.

■ Giancarlo Fisichella's chances of making it through to second qualifying were already ended on Friday morning when he failed to see the red light at the end of the pitlane at the start of the session. Although he passed through it only a few seconds early, he was docked three places on the grid.

■ The teams' divided positions on KERS were spotlighted when Ross Brawn revealed that Honda had already run a car on track with a prototype system, although he didn't say where or when. Other teams admitted that they were still some way from being able to test the system.

■ There was an alarming incident in Sunday's GP2 race when Bruno Senna had to retire after striking a stray dog at full speed. Bizarrely, a second dog also made it onto a different section of the track at the same time, prompting the deployment of a safety car. The FIA took extra security measures for the grand prix itself and launched an investigation.

RACE RESULTS

TURKEY
ISTANBUL

RACE DATE May 11th
CIRCUIT LENGTH 3.317 miles
NO. OF LAPS 58
RACE DISTANCE 192.388 miles
WEATHER Dry & cloudy, 18°C
TRACK TEMP 36°C
OVERALL ATTENDANCE 100,000
LAP RECORD Juan Pablo Montoya
1m24.770s, 138.056mph, 2005

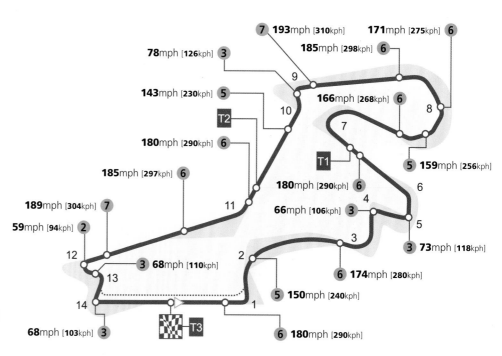

PRACTICE 1

	Driver	Time	Laps
1	F Massa	1m27.323s	16
2	H Kovalainen	1m27.456s	17
3	L Hamilton	1m27.752s	15
4	F Alonso	1m28.284s	16
5	J Button	1m28.919s	12
6	K Nakajima	1m29.002s	19
7	N Heidfeld	1m29.024s	21
8	R Barrichello	1m29.068s	11
9	N Piquet Jr	1m29.082s	23
10	T Glock	1m29.103s	19
11	J Trulli	1m29.329s	24
12	R Kubica	1m29.330s	7
13	N Rosberg	1m29.367s	20
14	A Sutil	1m29.756s	23
15	G Fisichella	1m29.811s	23
16	M Webber	1m30.088s	21
17	D Coulthard	1m30.340s	13
18	S Bourdais	1m30.388s	19
19	S Vettel	1m30.426s	21
20	K Räikkönen	1m30.732s	3

PRACTICE 2

	Driver	Time	Laps
1	K Räikkönen	1m27.543s	30
2	L Hamilton	1m27.579s	31
3	F Massa	1m27.682s	29
4	D Coulthard	1m27.763s	24
5	H Kovalainen	1m27.954s	27
6	R Kubica	1m28.431s	29
7	J Trulli	1m28.619s	29
8	K Nakajima	1m28.664s	27
9	F Alonso	1m28.681s	26
10	N Heidfeld	1m28.817s	31
11	J Button	1m28.826s	28
12	T Glock	1m28.849s	26
13	N Rosberg	1m28.907s	29
14	G Fisichella	1m29.008s	35
15	R Barrichello	1m29.024s	22
16	N Piquet Jr	1m29.212s	26
17	S Vettel	1m29.462s	30
18	S Bourdais	1m29.630s	32
19	M Webber	1m29.633s	4
20	A Sutil	1m30.832s	9

PRACTICE 3

	Driver	Time	Laps
1	M Webber	1m27.030s	16
2	F Alonso	1m27.172s	13
3	D Coulthard	1m27.193s	15
4	N Rosberg	1m27.365s	16
5	F Massa	1m27.530s	13
6	J Trulli	1m27.614s	15
7	L Hamilton	1m27.658s	18
8	T Glock	1m27.733s	22
9	J Button	1m27.766s	16
10	N Piquet Jr	1m27.781s	14
11	K Räikkönen	1m27.837s	15
12	H Kovalainen	1m27.849s	13
13	S Vettel	1m27.899s	18
14	R Barrichello	1m27.946s	14
15	S Bourdais	1m27.948s	17
16	R Kubica	1m27.971s	16
17	K Nakajima	1m28.301s	14
18	G Fisichella	1m28.573s	18
19	N Heidfeld	1m28.655s	19
20	A Sutil	1m29.131s	19

QUALIFYING 1

	Driver	Time
1	F Massa	1m25.994s
2	L Hamilton	1m26.192s
3	K Räikkönen	1m26.457s
4	T Glock	1m26.614s
5	J Trulli	1m26.695s
6	H Kovalainen	1m26.736s
7	R Kubica	1m26.761s
8	M Webber	1m26.773s
9	F Alonso	1m26.836s
10	D Coulthard	1m26.939s
11	N Heidfeld	1m27.107s
12	R Barrichello	1m27.355s
13	N Rosberg	1m27.367s
14	J Button	1m27.428s
15	S Vettel	1m27.442s
16	K Nakajima	1m27.547s
17	N Piquet Jr	1m27.568s
18	S Bourdais	1m27.621s
19	G Fisichella	1m27.807s
20	A Sutil	1m28.325s

QUALIFYING 2

	Driver	Time
1	K Räikkönen	1m26.050s
2	R Kubica	1m26.129s
3	F Massa	1m26.192s
4	H Kovalainen	1m26.290s
5	M Webber	1m26.466s
6	L Hamilton	1m26.477s
7	D Coulthard	1m26.520s
8	F Alonso	1m26.522s
9	N Heidfeld	1m26.607s
10	J Trulli	1m26.822s
11	N Rosberg	1m27.012s
12	R Barrichello	1m27.219s
13	J Button	1m27.298s
14	S Vettel	1m27.412s
15	T Glock	1m27.806s

Best sectors – Practice

Sec 1	F Alonso	32.311s
Sec 2	M Webber	30.381s
Sec 3	D Coulthard	24.040s

Speed trap – Practice

1	K Räikkönen	200.827mph
2	F Massa	198.901mph
3	L Hamilton	198.528mph

Best sectors – Qualifying

Sec 1	H Kovalainen	31.796s
Sec 2	R Kubica	30.049s
Sec 3	F Massa	23.855s

Speed trap – Qualifying

1	K Räikkönen	201.200mph
2	F Massa	201.137mph
3	L Hamilton	198.714mph

Kimi Räikkönen
"I was almost alongside Heikki at the start, but then he slowed and I had to brake too to avoid a crash. We touched just hard enough to damage my front wing endplate."

Nick Heidfeld
"This is what I hoped for from ninth. To finish fifth was the best I could do. I wanted to pass Trulli at the start and this worked, then I got by two more at the pit stops."

Fernando Alonso
"I made a good start, was on the pace and scored valuable points, which confirms the progress we have made and is thanks to the hard work of everyone in the team."

Nico Rosberg
"I had a fantastic first lap, though I nearly lost it all when Heidfeld went wide when I was alongside. When I came back on, I passed Coulthard and Trulli at Turn 3."

David Coulthard
"I've checked my car and there's no damage, so at least we finished without any collisions! I dropped 0.5s before my second pit stop and came out just behind Nico."

Jarno Trulli
"I think I was touched at Turn 1 and I lost three places. From the first lap to the last I tried to get past Coulthard, but as soon as you get within two lengths you lose grip."

Felipe Massa
"It's fantastic to have got the hat trick: it might be worth asking for a Turkish passport! When Hamilton came beneath me at an incredible pace, I preferred not to take risks."

Robert Kubica
"I made a very good start and managed to gain two positions at the start. I was then racing Räikkönen, but he pitted later and passed me at the pit stop."

Nelson Piquet Jr
"My race started badly as I had to avoid the accident. After that, we just stuck to our strategy. The most important thing is that I finished and gained more experience."

Kazuki Nakajima
"I went into Turn 1 and was hit from behind. I wanted to make it back to the garage as I thought there was a chance to get the problem fixed, but my car was too damaged."

Mark Webber
"I'm happy to get two points. It wasn't the most exciting race; I was just trying to hold on to Fernando. I was cruising in the last stint, as Rosberg wasn't a threat."

Timo Glock
"My race was destroyed by traffic. In the first stint I was behind Barrichello. After the stop Button was on soft tyres while we were on hards that were working well."

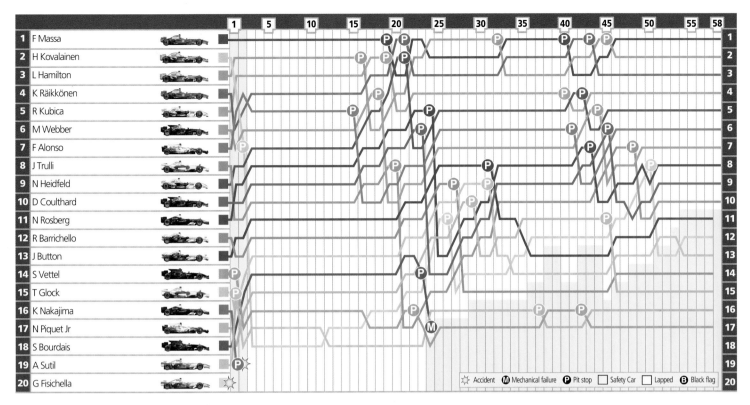

1	F Massa			
2	H Kovalainen			
3	L Hamilton			
4	K Räikkönen			
5	R Kubica			
6	M Webber			
7	F Alonso			
8	J Trulli			
9	N Heidfeld			
10	D Coulthard			
11	N Rosberg			
12	R Barrichello			
13	J Button			
14	S Vettel			
15	T Glock			
16	K Nakajima			
17	N Piquet Jr			
18	S Bourdais			
19	A Sutil			
20	G Fisichella			

☆ Accident　Ⓜ Mechanical failure　Ⓟ Pit stop　☐ Safety Car　☐ Lapped　Ⓑ Black flag

QUALIFYING 3

	Driver	Time
1	F Massa	1m27.617s
2	H Kovalainen	1m27.808s
3	L Hamilton	1m27.923s
4	K Räikkönen	1m27.936s
5	R Kubica	1m28.390s
6	M Webber	1m28.417s
7	F Alonso	1m28.422s
8	J Trulli	1m28.836s
9	N Heidfeld	1m28.882s
10	D Coulthard	1m29.959s

GRID

	Driver	Time
1	F Massa	1m27.617s
2	H Kovalainen	1m27.808s
3	L Hamilton	1m27.923s
4	K Räikkönen	1m27.936s
5	R Kubica	1m28.390s
6	M Webber	1m28.417s
7	F Alonso	1m28.422s
8	J Trulli	1m28.836s
9	N Heidfeld	1m28.882s
10	D Coulthard	1m29.959s
11	N Rosberg	1m27.012s
12	R Barrichello	1m27.219s
13	J Button	1m27.298s
14	S Vettel	1m27.412s
15	T Glock	1m27.806s
16	K Nakajima	1m27.547s
17	N Piquet Jr	1m27.568s
18	S Bourdais	1m27.621s
19	A Sutil	1m28.325s
20*	G Fisichella	1m27.807s

* 3-PLACE GRID PENALTY FOR PASSING RED LIGHT AT PIT EXIT

RACE

	Driver	Car	Laps	Time	Avg. mph	Fastest	Stops
1	F Massa	Ferrari F2008	58	1h26m49.451s	132.882	1m26.666s	2
2	L Hamilton	McLaren-Mercedes MP4-23	58	1h26m53.230s	132.785	1m26.529s	3
3	K Räikkönen	Ferrari F2008	58	1h26m53.722s	132.773	1m26.506s	2
4	R Kubica	BMW Sauber F1.08	58	1h27m11.396s	132.324	1m26.780s	2
5	N Heidfeld	BMW Sauber F1.08	58	1h27m28.192s	131.901	1m27.219s	2
6	F Alonso	Renault R28	58	1h27m43.175s	131.526	1m27.280s	2
7	M Webber	Red Bull-Renault RB4	58	1h27m53.680s	131.263	1m27.630s	2
8	N Rosberg	Williams-Toyota FW30	58	1h28m00.857s	131.085	1m27.795s	2
9	D Coulthard	Red Bull-Renault RB4	58	1h28m04.721s	130.989	1m27.966s	2
10	J Trulli	Toyota TF108	58	1h28m05.795s	130.962	1m27.926s	2
11	J Button	Honda RA108	57	1h26m50.629s	130.560	1m27.998s	1
12	H Kovalainen	McLaren-Mercedes MP4-23	57	1h26m51.412s	130.540	1m27.640s	3
13	T Glock	Toyota TF108	57	1h26m56.703s	130.407	1m28.303s	1
14	R Barrichello	Honda RA108	57	1h27m02.734s	130.257	1m28.017s	1
15	N Piquet Jr	Renault R28	57	1h27m03.906s	130.228	1m27.867s	2
16	A Sutil	Force India-Ferrari VJM01	57	1h27m51.473s	129.053	1m28.780s	3
17	S Vettel	Toro Rosso-Ferrari STR2B	57	1h27m52.085s	129.038	1m28.180s	4
R	S Bourdais	Toro Rosso-Ferrari STR2B	24	Spun off	-	1m28.745s	1
R	K Nakajima	Williams-Toyota FW30	1	Collision	-	-	0
R	G Fisichella	Force India-Ferrari VJM01	0	Collision	-	-	0

CHAMPIONSHIP

	Driver	Pts
1	K Räikkönen	35
2	F Massa	28
3	L Hamilton	28
4	R Kubica	24
5	N Heidfeld	20
6	H Kovalainen	14
7	M Webber	10
8	J Trulli	9
8	F Alonso	9
10	N Rosberg	8
11	K Nakajima	5
12	J Button	3
13	S Bourdais	2

Fastest Lap
K Räikkönen 1m26.506s
(138.034mph) on lap 20

Fastest speed trap
F Massa 201.262mph
Slowest speed trap
K Nakajima 115.202mph

Fastest pit stop
1 S Vettel 25.573s
2 J Trulli 25.642s
3 L Hamilton 25.763s

	Constructor	Pts
1	Ferrari	63
2	BMW Sauber	44
3	McLaren-Mercedes	42
4	Williams-Toyota	13
5	Red Bull-Renault	10
6	Toyota	9
7	Renault	9
8	Honda	3
9	Toro Rosso-Ferrari	2

Sebastien Bourdais
"Something broke at the back. Going into Turn 12, I braked as usual and the car went sideways, I felt the right rear corner of the car drop and it spun me around."

Jenson Button
"I had a pretty good first lap. I then had a problem with the front tyres, caused by the brakes overheating, so we changed our strategy to a one-stop which worked well."

Takuma Sato
TEAM WITHDREW

Adrian Sutil
"I saw Giancarlo fly over Nakajima, so by Turns 3 and 4 there were cars all over the place. I picked up some front wing damage through contact at Turn 5 so had to pit."

Lewis Hamilton
"This is the best race ever for me. Our prediction was that I would finish fifth, so second is a bonus. I passed Felipe at one point, so we have closed the gap to Ferrari."

Sebastian Vettel
"I had a good start, then realised I had a punctured left rear, so I had to pit immediately. My second problem came when no fuel went in, so I had to come in again."

Rubens Barrichello
"We didn't have the pace and I'm disappointed with our form. I suffered from understeer and traffic so we stopped early to try and get me out into some space."

Anthony Davidson
TEAM WITHDREW

Giancarlo Fisichella
"I made a good start but then under braking Bourdais changed direction twice and I couldn't brake in time and went into the back of the Williams."

Heikki Kovalainen
"I made a bad start and Kimi and I touched. I then realised that I had a slow puncture and, with my heavy fuel load and the traffic, it was hard to regain any places."

FORMULA 1 GRAND PRIX
DE MONACO 2008
MONTE CARLO

FLAT-OUT
TO VICTORY

This was one of the most exciting grands prix
for years. Rain spiced it up, but it's not every
day that the winner endures two punctures,
although this didn't stop Lewis Hamilton

Lewis Hamilton put his World Championship title
challenge back on track with a superb victory in an
exceedingly exciting Monaco GP. It was his first win
since the season-opener in Melbourne in March, and
it was also McLaren's 15th win in the principality since
the team made its debut at the event back in 1966, in
the days when Bruce McLaren was at the helm.

The grand prix began in soaking conditions and
was packed with drama from start to finish. Even
Hamilton survived a brush with a wall that left him
with a puncture and so forced him to pit for new
tyres, but which also fortuitously left him with a
perfect strategy.

McLaren had come to the Mediterranean
principality with high hopes of success, based upon
the team's form of previous years, and the fact that
Ferrari had not won on the streets of Monaco since
Michael Schumacher's last victory there in 2001.
However, the Maranello outfit had set out to improve
its slow-corner performance with the F2008, and from
the start of practice on Thursday it was evident that
the team had made good progress.

In an exciting qualifying session on Saturday
afternoon, Felipe Massa underlined his great

qualifying form by stealing pole position from team-mate Kimi Räikkönen. The Brazilian expressed his "surprise", which was his way of telling the world I'm heavier than the other guy. Although Sunday's rain would disguise the true facts, Massa was fuelled to lap 27 and Räikkönen to lap 25.

Hamilton claimed third spot on the grid, ahead of his McLaren team-mate Heikki Kovalainen, who lost track time with a crash at Ste Devote on Saturday morning. Robert Kubica and Nico Rosberg, the latter impressive throughout the meeting, filled the third row of the grid.

There had been much talk about the challenge of Monaco without traction control, but there were relatively few incidents. At least in the dry...

All meeting, though, weather forecasts had promised rain for Sunday. Saturday morning provided a modest taster with a brief shower, then Sunday's support events were drenched. Just minutes before the start, the rain came down in bucketloads. It wasn't quite enough to justify a start behind the safety car, and everyone headed off on intermediates, except for the ever-unlucky Kovalainen. He was pushed into the pitlane with a last-minute electronic glitch, and would

thus have to join the race at the rear of the field.

Against expectations, the leaders made it around Ste Devote intact on the opening lap, Hamilton once again making a good start and getting ahead of Räikkönen to slot into second place. Further back down the order, Rosberg lost his front wing on Fernando Alonso's Renault at the hairpin, sending the Williams man into the pits.

In the worsening conditions, Massa, Hamilton, Räikkönen and Kubica soon began to pull away from those behind, led by Mark Webber, at an astonishing rate. Then, on lap 5, Hamilton whacked the wall coming out of Tabac, breaking his car's right rear wheel. He dived into the pits and emerged still in fourth place, such was the margin that the leading group had pulled out. More importantly, the team had given him a heavy fuel load, enough to take him well into the race. With luck, he would be in the right place at the right time should the track eventually dry.

Hamilton knew that his car was handling well and was confident that he would be able to challenge Felipe at some point, even though at this point he couldn't see much in the spray.

Then he hit trouble at Tabac, hitting a river that

TALKING POINT
SCANDAL CASTS A LARGE SHADOW

As the cars took to the track for the first time on the Thursday morning, the usual plethora of long lenses focusing in on the action around every inch of track were somewhat depleted. The world's motorsport press was camped out in the paddock, outside the FIA hospitality unit. Every time the doors swished open, there was the FIA President eating his toast and marmalade. The morning's news picture was Max Mosley attending his first grand prix since the revelations about his private life published by the *News of the World*.

Mosley chose the opening moments of practice to walk the short distance to a paddock office, where he conducted business while maintaining a low profile. He was just days away from a vote of the FIA General Assembly which, by a comfortable margin, would allow him to continue in his role.

In the background, however, things were hotting up. Privately, team bosses were telling journalists that Mosley was damaging them. There were people on company boards who were not prepared to pledge budgets to F1 while Mosley was still in charge of the governing body, they said.

Then came a letter from Mosley to member clubs of the FIA claiming it was vital that he safeguard the governing body from marauding CRHs (commercial rights holders Bernie Ecclestone and CVC Capital Holdings), whom he alleged were trying to take over the whole F1 business.

Mosley's letter said: "We are in the middle of a renegotiation of the 100-year commercial agreement. In effect, this agreement governs Formula One... The CRH has also now asked for control over the F1 regulations and the right to sell the business to anyone – in effect to take over F1 completely. I do not believe that the FIA should agree to this."

Ecclestone issued his own response. The CRH supports the FIA, he said, which "should be led by a credible and respected President."

On the regulations, any changes having a material impact on the CRH and its interests should be discussed, Ecclestone said. Finally, he added, contradicting Mosley, there is no impending financial crisis in F1 and a new Concorde Agreement would provide financial and regulatory stability.

If there was still no Concorde Agreement and the manufacturers were unhappy with Mosley, what was there to stop a breakaway championship of the kind suggested by the manufacturers a few years ago?

was flowing across the track there. In an instant, his MP4-23 was sideways and slid into the barrier. He immediately radioed the team and they prepared a replacement tyre for an instant pit stop.

Hamilton wasn't the only one to err on the slippery track, as Jenson Button and Timo Glock were soon running at the back of the field after damaging their front wings and having to pit for replacements.

Then, on lap 7, David Coulthard and Sebastien Bourdais both went off at Massenet on the way into Casino Square, triggering a brief safety-car interlude.

Soon after that, things began to go awry for Ferrari, as Räikkönen was reported for having his tyres fitted too late on the grid after a wheelnut problem. In fact, he should have been forced to start the grand prix from the back of the grid, but he got away with a drive-though penalty that dropped him from second place to fourth, behind Hamilton.

Then leader Massa went off at Ste Devote on lap 16, recovering in second place with no damage done, but having handed the lead to Kubica.

Räikkönen had been struggling to get his tyres up to temperature, and then he too went off at Ste Devote on lap 27, damaging his front wing. He came

BELOW Coulthard crashed at Massenet on lap 8 and Bourdais was unable to avoid his spinning car. The pair of wrecks are winched clear

INSIDE LINE
LEWIS HAMILTON
McLAREN DRIVER

"I got a good start into second place and I felt comfortable from the beginning. I knew that I had a good car underneath me and that I would be able to challenge Felipe at some point in the race.

In the conditions, I couldn't really see anything and so I just stayed in second place because there was so much spray. But then, through Turn 12, Tabac, there was a sort of river on the surface. I hit it and the car just oversteered into the barrier.

I couldn't believe it, but I knew I had only just brushed it. I had a rear puncture and fortunately I was able to tell the team and they were able to react quickly enough and were ready.

I came in to the pits, didn't lose too much time, and when I came out I was still in fourth or fifth place and thinking, alright, I can still win it.

The safety car came out shortly afterwards, which helped me. It's difficult when the weather is like that. We thought it was going to start to dry out, but the important thing is to keep the car on the track. It was very difficult for all of us. There was aquaplaning, and at times you were almost tiptoeing.

Obviously, we had to change the strategy, but fortunately that played into my hands. The pace I had was ridiculous. I had one second on people for the majority of the race and it was quite easy, I was comfortable. I was asking the team, 'do I need to go quicker?' and they were saying 'slower'. There was a point where I was 40 seconds ahead, just maintaining the gap and then the safety car came out again. But I'm used to that – remember the Canadian Grand Prix last year! It was no sweat.

This has to be the highlight of my career and I'm sure it will continue to be the highlight for the rest of my life. For the last few laps I was just thinking about Ayrton Senna and how many times he won in Monaco.

To win here is just amazing, an incredible feeling, very emotional. I was just trying to keep the emotions in check and the car on the track. I was just driving round believing, 'I can do it, I can do it'!

This is my best win ever, for sure. Even if I was to win here again, which I plan on doing, this is the best one – the first one."

into the pits and, believing that it would stay wet throughout, the team gave him enough fuel to run to the end. He returned to the track with a heavy car that was tricky to handle.

An early pit stop on lap 26 had dropped Kubica back, so now Massa (still to pit) led from Hamilton, Kubica, Webber, Adrian Sutil and Räikkönen.

Adrian Sutil? Indeed, the Force India driver had made a great start and kept out of trouble, and he was pushing on with a heavy fuel load. He had gained several places when Alonso, already delayed after an early touch with the barrier, bumped into Nick Heidfeld at the hairpin. In the confusion, Sutil jumped past several stationary cars.

When Massa made his scheduled pit stop from the lead on lap 33, he was fuelled like Räikkönen to the flag. Hamilton moved into the lead, but he needed to pit once more for fuel. The British driver now had a lighter car than the Ferrari drivers, and his pace in the middle stint of the race effectively won him the day.

After the rain stopped, the track soon began to dry. Eventually, a few drivers, those with little to lose as they were running out of the points, switched to grooved tyres. Nelson Piquet Jr showed that the timing of this move from full-wet tyres was critical by going straight off at Ste Devote. McLaren still made the call, though, and when Hamilton came in on lap 54 he took on fuel and dry tyres and stayed in front.

Having lost out by running heavy, the Ferrari drivers had to make an extra stop to change to dries, thus having carried that extra weight for no benefit. When Massa eventually came in on lap 56, he emerged having lost second place to Kubica, who had made the switch three laps earlier.

A huge crash for Rosberg at the entry to Piscine brought out the safety car again shortly before the end, at which point Hamilton led from Kubica, Massa, the amazing Sutil and Räikkönen. A heavy load and a

perfect one-stop schedule had played into the young German's hands and, by coming in later than Webber – an early stopper for slicks – he gained another place.

Much of his good work was undone when the safety car came out and, with lapped traffic out of the way, Räikkönen and Webber were right on his tail for the restart. When the green flags flew, this had become a two-hour race rather than a 78-lapper, and there were just seven minutes left on the clock.

Then it all went wrong for Sutil. On the first flying lap, Räikkönen lost control under braking for the chicane and rammed the back of the Force India. Both men reported to the pits and, while Räikkönen

OPPOSITE Lewis Hamilton walked on water, but he had to survive two punctures to do so

ABOVE Trulli, Barrichello and Nakajima fight over seventh place at the Grand Hotel hairpin early on

BELOW Germany's rising stars Vettel and Sutil get up close and personal at Ste Devote

ABOVE The smiles were back at McLaren as Hamilton and Ron Dennis celebrate a welcome victory

was quite close to the pits, so we're quite happy that we switched so quickly. It worked out well. We were comfortable, and certainly in the latter part of the race we were just being very cautious to get off the rain tyres at the right time."

Kubica's second place was well deserved, and was the result of consistent driving and good strategy.

"After the first pit stop I was struggling with graining on the rear tyres, and Felipe managed to stay ahead of me after his first stop," Robert explained. "He was much heavier, even though he was pulling away, then suddenly the tyres started working again and I massively closed the gap to Felipe, in two laps something like five seconds. I was much quicker, but I couldn't overtake. I was lucky that Glock came out from the pits with grooved tyres, and as soon as I saw that he was lapping 2s quicker I told the team to put out grooved tyres, which we did, and that's why we overtook Felipe in the pit stops."

After a steady run, Webber moved up to take fourth place for Red Bull, scoring points for the fifth race in succession. One of the few drivers to keep his nose clean, Sebastian Vettel moved up the order in the latter stages of the race to claim fifth, and the first points for Toro Rosso's brand new STR03. Rubens Barrichello finished sixth, while Kazuki Nakajima did an impressive job to come home seventh for Williams, surviving a costly pit-stop delay and staying away from the walls on a day when his more experienced team-mate was involved in three separate incidents.

returned to the race with his second new nose of the afternoon, Sutil's day was done.

The top three remained unchanged to the finish, and Hamilton came home some three seconds ahead of Kubica, with Massa a little further back for the shell-shocked Ferrari team.

An ecstatic Hamilton said that his win was the outcome of remaining optimistic.

"I'm really pleased, it's one of the best race wins we've had," beamed McLaren supremo Ron Dennis. "Fifteen times we've won this race, which makes us proud. You never give up in Monte Carlo! Lewis made a mistake, but we switched the strategy. The accident

The final point went to Kovalainen, who charged hard from his pitlane start, and lost a lot of time when he was waved around the final safety car late. He crossed the line just ahead of Räikkönen, who set fastest lap, but crucially, failed to score. Funnily enough, he finished just ahead of another World Champion and past Monaco winner, Alonso, enduring a nightmare of a race.

BELOW Rosberg leaps out of his battered Williams after dropping it at Piscine on lap 60, scattering debris

SNAPSHOT FROM
MONACO

CLOCKWISE FROM RIGHT

Monaco with its harbour remains the jewel in F1's crown; Danni Minogue and Button share a joke; P Diddy and *Pussycat Dolls* singer Nicole Scherzinger lark around with Nicolas Hamilton; Steinmetz dressed the McLaren drivers' helmets with diamonds; "Calling all billionaire yacht owners…"; Cliff Richard looked as youthful as ever; Hamilton fans have a dig at their man, reminding him of his stumble in the 2007 Chinese GP, to keep him on his toes

WEEKEND NEWS

■ Max Mosley made his first appearance at a grand prix since his personal problems hit the press in early April. The FIA President made only a brief tour of the pitlane on the Thursday, preferring to meet selected F1 luminaries in private. He declined to talk to the media.

■ Force India's Giancarlo Fisichella started his 200th grand prix in Monaco, and the Italian wore special overalls and helmet design to mark the occasion. Unfortunately, his weekend was a disaster as he was outqualified by Adrian Sutil for the first time, and then had gearbox problems in the race.

■ Music legend Cliff Richard made a rare appearance at a grand prix, spending some time hanging around the Force India motorhome. When his first single 'Move It' was released in 1958, Juan Manuel Fangio was still a grand prix driver! Hollywood directors Quentin Tarantino and George Lucas were among the other luminaries to be spotted.

■ The social highlight of the week was the charity fashion show held at Sonia Irvine's Amber Lounge venue on Friday. Several drivers and their other halves became models for the evening, courtesy of Petra Ecclestone's new label. Proceeds from an auction went to the Elton John Aids Foundation.

■ A few days after Monaco, Felipe Massa's engineer Rob Smedley hosted a charity function in memory of his daughter Minnie, who sadly died in 2007. Michael Schumacher's 2007 Ferrari test overalls proved the highlight of an eBay auction that coincided with the event, realising over £7000.

RACE RESULTS
MONACO
MONTE CARLO

RACE DATE May 25th
CIRCUIT LENGTH 2.075 miles
NO. OF LAPS 76
RACE DISTANCE 157.700 miles
WEATHER Raining then damp, 21°C
TRACK TEMP 23°C
OVERALL ATTENDANCE 200,000
LAP RECORD Michael Schumacher
1m14.439s, 100.373mph, 2004

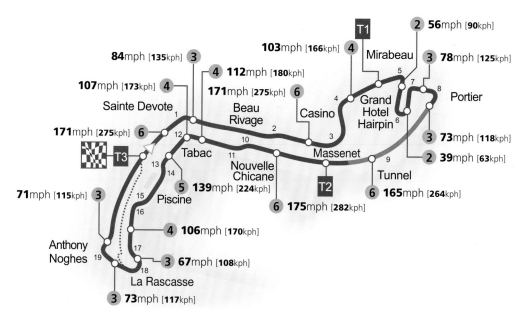

PRACTICE 1			
	Driver	Time	Laps
1	K Räikkönen	1m15.948s	26
2	L Hamilton	1m16.216s	27
3	H Kovalainen	1m16.248s	28
4	F Massa	1m16.292s	26
5	N Rosberg	1m16.653s	27
6	R Kubica	1m16.834s	23
7	F Alonso	1m17.498s	25
8	R Barrichello	1m17.511s	26
9	M Webber	1m17.798s	23
10	G Fisichella	1m17.835s	26
11	T Glock	1m17.942s	26
12	J Button	1m18.153s	26
13	S Bourdais	1m18.245s	30
14	N Heidfeld	1m18263s	13
15	K Nakajima	1m18.274s	28
16	J Trulli	1m18.360s	16
17	A Sutil	1m18.360s	25
18	N Piquet Jr	1m18.955s	32
19	S Vettel	1m19.176s	35
20	D Coulthard	No time	3

PRACTICE 2			
	Driver	Time	Laps
1	L Hamilton	1m15.140s	40
2	N Rosberg	1m15.533s	39
3	K Räikkönen	1m15.572s	42
4	F Massa	1m15.869s	37
5	H Kovalainen	1m15.881s	39
6	R Kubica	1m16.296s	34
7	F Alonso	1m16.310s	27
8	J Button	1m16.352s	45
9	K Nakajima	1m16.372s	40
10	R Barrichello	1m16.418s	32
11	N Heidfeld	1m16.426s	44
12	T Glock	1m16.688s	46
13	M Webber	1m17.094s	39
14	D Coulthard	1m17.131s	39
15	N Piquet Jr	1m17.246s	35
16	G Fisichella	1m17.251s	33
17	J Trulli	1m17.389s	28
18	S Bourdais	1m17.581s	38
19	A Sutil	1m18.176s	31
20	S Vettel	1m18.225s	38

PRACTICE 3			
	Driver	Time	Laps
1	H Kovalainen	1m16.567s	11
2	L Hamilton	1m17.084s	15
3	K Räikkönen	1m17.177s	21
4	N Rosberg	1m17.503s	26
5	R Kubica	1m17.687s	22
6	F Massa	1m17.691s	26
7	M Webber	1m17.856s	22
8	A Sutil	1m17.883s	23
9	K Nakajima	1m18.147s	26
10	J Button	1m18.225s	27
11	S Bourdais	1m18.367s	16
12	T Glock	1m18.424s	26
13	R Barrichello	1m18.455s	19
14	N Piquet Jr	1m18.615s	25
15	S Vettel	1m18.651s	29
16	F Alonso	1m18.795s	24
17	J Trulli	1m18.858s	25
18	N Heidfeld	1m19.024s	23
19	G Fisichella	1m19.131s	10
20	D Coulthard	1m20.805s	17

QUALIFYING 1		
	Driver	Time
1	F Massa	1m15.190s
2	H Kovalainen	1m15.295s
3	L Hamilton	1m15.582s
4	K Räikkönen	1m15.717s
5	N Rosberg	1m15.935s
6	R Kubica	1m15.977s
7	M Webber	1m16.074s
8	D Coulthard	1m16.086s
9	R Barrichello	1m16.208s
10	J Button	1m16.259s
11	T Glock	1m16.285s
12	J Trulli	1m16.306s
13	F Alonso	1m16.646s
14	N Heidfeld	1m16.650s
15	K Nakajima	1m16.756s
16	S Bourdais	1m16.806s
17	N Piquet Jr	1m16.933s
18	S Vettel	1m16.955s
19	A Sutil	1m17.225s
20	G Fisichella	1m17.823s

QUALIFYING 2		
	Driver	Time
1	F Massa	1m15.110s
2	N Rosberg	1m15.287s
3	L Hamilton	1m15.322s
4	H Kovalainen	1m15.389s
5	K Räikkönen	1m15.404s
6	R Kubica	1m15.483s
7	J Trulli	1m15.598s
8	M Webber	1m15.745s
9	F Alonso	1m15.827s
10	D Coulthard	1m15.839s
11	T Glock	1m15.907s
12	J Button	1m16.101s
13	N Heidfeld	1m16.455s
14	K Nakajima	1m16.479s
15	R Barrichello	1m16.537s

Best sectors – Practice		
Sec 1	L Hamilton	19.555s
Sec 2	L Hamilton	37.461s
Sec 3	H Kovalainen	17.988s

Speed trap – Practice		
1	L Hamilton	180.943mph
2	H Kovalainen	180.508mph
3	N Piquet Jr	179.079mph

Best sectors – Qualifying		
Sec 1	L Hamilton	19.493s
Sec 2	F Massa	37.085s
Sec 3	D Coulthard	18.025s

Speed trap – Qualifying		
1	H Kovalainen	181.067mph
2	L Hamilton	180.943mph
3	F Alonso	179.949mph

Kimi Räikkönen
"I had a wheel problem before the start and we broke the rules, so I got a drive-through. Twice I had to change the nose. I'm sorry for Sutil, who I hit with a few laps to go."

Nick Heidfeld
"The early laps went very well. I was up to fifth place, but Alonso crashed into my car. This damaged the left side of my car, and then due to a puncture I had to pit."

Fernando Alonso
"The track was always changing; the car was sensitive and I made some mistakes. After that, we tried to change our strategy, but it didn't pay off, which is a shame."

Nico Rosberg
"My crash at the Swimming Pool chicane was a big one. I was pushing really hard on dry tyres when the rear of the car flicked out, most probably on a patch of water."

David Coulthard
"We were always going to have to be careful early on. I was having difficulty with my downshifts and got caught out on the entry to Casino and ran out of road."

Jarno Trulli
"It was raining and we took the gamble to go on extreme wets. Then I did several good overtaking moves, but the rain stopped and I was struggling on a drying track."

Felipe Massa
"I was quick, but made a mistake at Ste Devote and lost a place to Robert. We switched strategies thinking the rain would return, but this turned out to be wrong."

Robert Kubica
"I am very happy with the result. It was a great race in very difficult conditions, and we didn't expect such heavy rain. I had visibility and tyre problems throughout."

Nelson Piquet Jr
"I am extremely disappointed. The conditions were changing, but we took the risk to switch to dry tyres when the track was still damp, which is when I damaged the car."

Kazuki Nakajima
"It was really difficult, especially at the start when the track was wet. I couldn't see anything. We then had some luck with the weather, as I was on a one-stop strategy."

Mark Webber
"It was very difficult in the wet and we were aquaplaning at Casino. It was too wet for the intermediates, but it started to dry and we had to think about changing tyres."

Timo Glock
"I passed Webber on the run to the first corner. I spun a few laps later and had to pit. We switched to extreme-wet tyres, but they became tricky as the track dried."

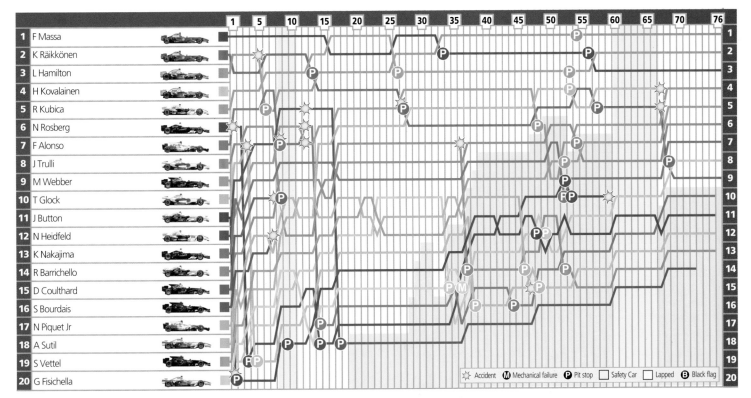

	Driver
1	F Massa
2	K Räikkönen
3	L Hamilton
4	H Kovalainen
5	R Kubica
6	N Rosberg
7	F Alonso
8	J Trulli
9	M Webber
10	T Glock
11	J Button
12	N Heidfeld
13	K Nakajima
14	R Barrichello
15	D Coulthard
16	S Bourdais
17	N Piquet Jr
18	A Sutil
19	S Vettel
20	G Fisichella

☆ Accident   Ⓜ Mechanical failure   Ⓟ Pit stop   ☐ Safety Car   ☐ Lapped   Ⓑ Black flag

QUALIFYING 3

	Driver	Time
1	F Massa	1m15.787s
2	K Räikkönen	1m15.815s
3	L Hamilton	1m15.839s
4	H Kovalainen	1m16.165s
5	R Kubica	1m16.171s
6	N Rosberg	1m16.548s
7	F Alonso	1m16.852s
8	J Trulli	1m17.203s
9	M Webber	1m17.343s
10	D Coulthard	No time

GRID

	Driver	Time
1	F Massa	1m15.787s
2	K Räikkönen	1m15.815s
3	L Hamilton	1m15.839s
4	H Kovalainen	1m16.165s
5	R Kubica	1m16.171s
6	N Rosberg	1m16.548s
7	F Alonso	1m16.852s
8	J Trulli	1m17.203s
9	M Webber	1m17.343s
10	T Glock	1m15.907s
11	J Button	1m16.101s
12	N Heidfeld	1m16.455s
13	K Nakajima	1m16.479s
14	R Barrichello	1m16.537s
15*	D Coulthard	No time
16	S Bourdais	1m16.806s
17	N Piquet Jr	1m16.933s
18*	S Vettel	1m17.225s
19	A Sutil	1m16.955s
20*	G Fisichella	1m17.823s

* 5-PLACE GRID PENALTY DUE TO GEARBOX CHANGE

RACE

	Driver	Car	Laps	Time	Avg. mph	Fastest	Stops
1	L Hamilton	McLaren-Mercedes MP4-23	76	2h00m42.742s	78.401	1m18.510s	2
2	R Kubica	BMW Sauber F1.08	76	2h00m45.806s	78.368	1m17.933s	2
3	F Massa	Ferrari F2008	76	2h00m47.553s	78.349	1m17.886s	2
4	M Webber	Red Bull-Renault RB4	76	2h01m02.037s	78.192	1m19.036s	1
5	S Vettel	Toro Rosso-Ferrari STR03	76	2h01m07.399s	78.145	1m18.787s	1
6	R Barrichello	Honda RA108	76	2h01m11.150s	78.094	1m19.574s	1
7	K Nakajima	Williams-Toyota FW30	76	2h01m12.922s	78.076	1m19.910s	1
8	H Kovalainen	McLaren-Mercedes MP4-23	76	2h01m15.933s	78.043	1m17.282s	2
9	K Räikkönen	Ferrari F2008	76	2h01m16.534s	78.037	1m16.689s	4
10	F Alonso	Renault R28	75	2h01m05.210s	77.130	1m17.869s	3
11	J Button	Honda RA108	75	2h01m12.175s	77.056	1m19.582s	3
12	T Glock	Toyota TF108	75	2h01m14.066s	77.035	1m19.618s	3
13	J Trulli	Toyota TF108	75	2h01m15.217s	77.024	1m19.830s	3
14	N Heidfeld	BMW Sauber F1.08	72	2h00m55.670s	74.142	1m20.251s	3
R	A Sutil	Force India-Ferrari VJM01	67	Collision	-	1m22.039s	1
R	N Rosberg	Williams-Toyota FW30	59	Spun off	-	1m21.270s	4
R	N Piquet Jr	Renault R28	47	Spun off	-	1m31.187s	1
R	G Fisichella	Force India-Ferrari VJM01	36	Gearbox	-	1m32.849s	0
R	D Coulthard	Red Bull-Renault RB4	7	Spun off	-	1m42.112s	0
R	S Bourdais	Toro Rosso-Ferrari STR03	7	Collision	-	1m41.150s	0

CHAMPIONSHIP

	Driver	Pts
1	L Hamilton	38
2	K Räikkönen	35
3	F Massa	34
4	R Kubica	32
5	N Heidfeld	20
6	H Kovalainen	15
7	M Webber	15
8	F Alonso	9
9	J Trulli	9
10	N Rosberg	8
11	K Nakajima	7
12	S Vettel	4
13	J Button	3
14	R Barrichello	3
15	S Bourdais	2

Fastest Lap
K Räikkönen 1m16.689s
(97.424mph) on lap 74

Fastest speed trap
H Kovalainen 181.067mph

Slowest speed trap
S Bourdais 144.841mph

Fastest pit stop
1 K Räikkönen 25.418s
2 J Trulli 25.767s
3 S Vettel 26.027s

	Constructor	Pts
1	Ferrari	69
2	McLaren-Mercedes	53
3	BMW Sauber	52
4	Williams-Toyota	15
5	Red Bull-Renault	15
6	Toyota	9
7	Renault	9
8	Toro Rosso-Ferrari	6
9	Honda	6

 **Sebastien Bourdais**

"David had gone off, but though it seemed to have stopped raining, there was more water on the track and when I saw the yellow flags, I backed off and lost control."

 Jenson Button

"I dropped two places, passed Rubens and Webber, was next to Heidfeld at Piscine when he overshot, but there wasn't enough space for me down the inside."

Adrian Sutil

"It's like a dream gone to a nightmare. It all looks fantastic, then you have to accept it is not going to happen. A few tears came as the adrenaline was high."

Lewis Hamilton

"I started well, but hit the barrier at Tabac and had to pit. The first safety car helped me to close the gap. We changed our strategy, and I had to make only one more stop."

 **Sebastian Vettel**

"The race was very difficult at the start when there was aquaplaning, but we were strong as it dried. It's great to score my first points of 2008, and with the new car."

 **Rubens Barrichello**

"It's great to be back in the points and I'm very happy for myself and for the team. We had a good race, but it was unlucky that I was held up by Trulli for so long early on."

 **Giancarlo Fisichella**

"I was just careful to stay out of trouble at the start, but then I lost first and second gear and I was left running in third gear. Then I lost fourth gear and the race was over."

Heikki Kovalainen

"Any chance of a top finish went when I couldn't engage a gear at the start of the formation lap. I had to change the steering wheel in the pits from where I had to start."

FORMULA 1 GRAND PRIX DU CANADA 2008
MONTREAL

KUBICA CASHES IN

The race belonged to Lewis Hamilton, but a safety-car period then an accident at pit exit removed him, leaving the way clear for Kubica to score both his, and BMW Sauber's, first wins

Just 12 months on from his potentially fatal accident at Montréal, Robert Kubica produced a flawless performance at the same venue, and came away with a well-earned first victory. For the BMW Sauber team that had arrived in Formula One as a privateer team in 1993, it was a double success, as Nick Heidfeld came home second, echoing Jordan's maiden win in Belgium in 1998 when it too got off the mark with a 1–2.

Kubica also took the lead in the drivers' championship thanks to his consistent good scoring while the title-chasing McLaren and Ferrari drivers continued to endure some unfortunate races. Indeed, the early stages of the Canadian GP were dominated by Lewis Hamilton, only for the Briton to make a silly error and ram into the back of rival Kimi Räikkönen at the pitlane exit when the Ferrari driver stopped for a red light.

After a damp and grey Friday, the sun came out for qualifying. Windy conditions made life tricky, though, while overnight rain meant that the track was still relatively 'green'. However, the real problem was that the track started to break up at the hairpin and several other spots around the lap.

Hamilton was quickest for most of the session, but his McLaren was demoted to second by Kubica right at the end. The McLaren man was on a quick lap of his own, though, and regained pole in the final seconds. Räikkönen, Fernando Alonso and Nico Rosberg were next up, while qualifying specialist Felipe Massa could manage only sixth in the difficult conditions.

Repair work continued on the track until the very last minute, and in the end the surface was not a major issue once the race got underway. The real concern was the prospect of a safety-car interlude, and just how it might shake things up.

Against expectations, it was an unusually clean first lap. Hamilton charged away from pole position and had opened up an advantage of nearly 7s over Kubica by lap 17, with Räikkönen third and Rosberg fourth. At that stage, a safety car was sent out to allow the retrieval of Adrian Sutil's Force India, which had stopped with a gearbox problem. All Hamilton's good work was undone as the field closed up.

The timing was just about right for those who had qualified with a light fuel load and, once the field had been bunched up and the pitlane opened, the frontrunners all charged into the pitlane. McLaren gave Hamilton a relatively high fuel load and that, combined with the team's position in the middle of the pitlane,

meant that when he pulled out of his pit box he saw that Kubica and Räikkönen had both beaten him away. Indeed, the pair indulged in a drag race down to the end of the pitlane, where a red light caused them to stop side by side.

The nature of the first two turns in Canada means that the red light stays on there longer than at other tracks, so as to stop those exiting their pit stops from charging straight out and barging into the queue behind the safety car. Juan Pablo Montoya did just that in 2005 and got black-flagged, while Massa and Giancarlo Fisichella made the same mistake in 2007.

And yet, despite the notoriety of the Montréal red light, Hamilton, perhaps distracted by the fact that he'd lost two places, failed to stop in time. At the last second, he swerved to the left and ran hard into the back of Räikkönen, just missing Kubica, taking off the Ferrari's rear wing and breaking his own front suspension. Rosberg made the same error, and ran into the back of Hamilton. He was able to continue with a broken nose, but Hamilton and Räikkönen were out on the spot, and the furious Ferrari driver pointed out the traffic light as he walked away from the scene. Hamilton and Rosberg were later given 10-place grid penalties for the next race in France.

McLaren folk did their best to defend Hamilton, but there was no question that they were extremely frustrated with him. They did admit that a reminder about the red light on the radio came a little late. Nevertheless, the onus is on the driver to always have his wits about him.

"I think Lewis knew the game, and knew the situation," said McLaren CEO Martin Whitmarsh. "In fairness, I can see how, in the adrenaline of the moment, he saw the two cars stopped, and thought; 'Is there a way I can pull alongside and out-jump them?' There was a moment of distraction there, and he didn't quite get it right, nor indeed did Nico a second later. He

BELOW Heikki Kovalainen's McLaren spent the race eating its tyres and he ended up ninth

BOTTOM David Coulthard kicks up gravel left in his path en route to a canny third position for Red Bull

OPPOSITE This pit stop appears to be running like clockwork, but Jenson Button had an off weekend

TALKING POINT
HEIDFELD HELPS OUT

Nick Heidfeld's body language spoke volumes after the Canadian Grand Prix. He'd finished second, equalling his best F1 result, and he was on the podium, but he wasn't smiling. His team, BMW Sauber, had just scored its first grand prix win and it was his team-mate Robert Kubica who had taken the 10 points.

More than that, it was a race in which Heidfeld and Kubica had been on different strategies, and Heidfeld had reason to suspect that he might have just driven a race for his team-mate's benefit.

There was a key point after Heidfeld had emerged from his only pit stop still ahead of the lighter Kubica, who needed to stop again, and Alonso caught the heavier Heidfeld. Kubica went by and Heidfeld held off Alonso, who posed a threat to Kubica at that point.

When Heidfeld was asked whether he let Kubica by voluntarily or whether he was 'advised' by the pit, he responded: "Well, as there are no team orders allowed, no (I wasn't advised) but, as I was on a one-stop strategy, a lot heavier than Robert, it's clear within the

team that I wouldn't make it too difficult for him..."

Having 'let' past the only man who would finish ahead of him, Heidfeld then had Alonso's lighter Renault ducking and diving in his mirrors, desperate for a way by. He obviously realised that any indiscretion by Alonso (who did eventually crash) could put him out of the race and so he radioed in to see if he could let the Renault go. The team, no doubt wanting to minimise the threat to Kubica, told him to keep Alonso behind. This clearly went on a lot longer than Heidfeld thought necessary.

Heidfeld gave the PR response to the question of whether he suspected he was helping Kubica win the race: "I was thinking about that, but I'm happy to help Robert

as long as it doesn't spoil my race..."

The debut win for Kubica and the team put the Pole four points clear at the head of the drivers' championship and 14 clear of Heidfeld. Kubica's assertion that he hoped the team would give him "100 per cent support" in defending his lead seemed like a thinly-veiled claim to number one status in the team. And, looking at the facts, there was every reason to suspect that he might get it. The car is not as quick as the Ferraris and McLarens, but it is not far away. At Ferrari, Räikkönen and Massa were proving evenly matched, and McLaren historically does not favour one driver over another until later in the season. Optimising strategy around Kubica might just prolong Munich's fight.

INSIDE LINE
ROBERT KUBICA
BMW SAUBER DRIVER

"I said before the race weekend started that I would talk about last year's accident just once, and it's nice to have something different to talk about now! It's a great atmosphere in Canada and there are so many Polish fans!

Qualifying was difficult with the track breaking up, but I did a good job to get on to the front row, even if everybody knows that the right-hand side of the grid is dirty. I thought Kimi would get me at the start, but I managed to defend my position. I was keeping a good pace for the first five or six laps, but we faced the same problem as in Australia: the car was sliding and there was a lot of tyre graining. The rear tyre temperature rocketed, so I just called into the pits for them to drop the pressures, and the car felt much better in the second stint. Lewis was still pulling away, but there was not as big a speed difference.

The pitlane incident was key. I heard a big shunt and then saw Lewis over Kimi's rear wing. I have to thank him for choosing Kimi and not me…

Then I was stuck behind slower cars and couldn't make overtaking moves with my heavy fuel load. The crucial point was when Glock went into the pits and I had eight laps to make a margin so that I could come back out after my second pit stop in front of Nick. That was seven laps of qualifying! I knew I had to make around a 21s gap and I managed 24s, so it was a great race.

It's fantastic to score my first win for BMW Sauber, who I have been with from the beginning. We have grown up together and thanks to the team for providing such a good car that we managed to finish first and second. Maybe the pace is still not the best, but at this race we were right there. I couldn't match Lewis's pace in the first stint, but it was a fantastic race and fantastic for me, for my country and for the fans.

Since Montréal last year, it has been an incredible year, but also a year of struggle. I'm happy I managed to fix some issues that were not working properly in 2007. The goal was to win a grand prix this season and we have done it. We are leading the drivers' championship, so I hope the team will give me 100 per cent support to try and maybe defend it until the last race."

saw the light, he was told about it, but I think he was conjuring a number of things in his mind at the time, and made a miscalculation..."

The collision wasn't the only drama going on at the stops. Massa's fuel rig suffered a major leak, and he was sent out and told to come in again a lap later to complete the job. That dropped him way down the field, to 17th place.

Many of the drivers had stayed out because they were running long and planned to stop only once, so the new leader was Heidfeld, who had a relatively high fuel load, and had the option to stop once or twice, thanks to the safety car stretching things out a bit. Behind him were Rubens Barrichello, Kazuki Nakajima, Mark Webber, David Coulthard, Timo Glock and Jarno Trulli. Kubica was the best placed of those who had stopped, way back in 10th, with Alonso just behind him.

Heidfeld had a clear track and was over 13s clear of Barrichello when he came in on lap 29. The team made the choice to fuel him to the end, and he emerged just in front of Kubica. With a heavy load and the less-favoured tyres, Heidfeld made no attempt to keep the Pole behind. We now had a fascinating race in prospect between the two BMW Saubers, with Kubica in 'sprint'

spec, with one stop still to make, and Heidfeld running to the flag in less than ideal circumstances.

Gradually, all the one-stoppers came in, and we had a succession of unexpected leaders – first Barrichello, then Coulthard, Trulli and finally Glock. When the German stopped, Kubica eased into the lead and it was now all about how much of a gap he could pull out on his team-mate. When he came in on lap 49, he had done just enough to emerge out still in front.

Thereafter, it was a demonstration run to the flag for the two BMW Sauber racers, with surprise third-place man Coulthard only a distant threat.

"It is fantastic to win my first race for BMW Sauber," said jubilant first-time winner Kubica. A scriptwriter would have been hard put to pen such a dramatic and successful comeback to the scene of the accident that could easily have claimed his life 12 months earlier.

In the post-race excitement, it was easy to overlook the fact that Heidfeld had brought the other car home in a strong second place. Under pressure thanks to his struggles in qualifying, lining up down in eighth, the German faced the difficult task of running to the flag.

"This wasn't planned," said BMW Sauber's Technical Director Willy Rampf. "We changed the strategy and

OPPOSITE Every photo tells a story as Lewis Hamilton arrives for his pit stop then, having hit Kimi Räikkönen's Ferrari, the pair climb out at pit exit and walk back in, having laid the way clear for Kubica to claim BMW Sauber's maiden win

ABOVE Nick Heidfeld drove a great race, but was forced to help team-mate Robert Kubica to victory

ABOVE Felipe Massa takes his fightback to the Toyota duo. He would split them to finish fifth behind Timo Glock, with Trulli sixth

BELOW The BMW Sauber crew revels in delight at its breakthrough victory, with the Swiss flag emphasising the team's roots

we were discussing it until the last lap, before Nick came in. Should we change it or not? One thing was that we had to fill the car, and we had to run with soft tyres, and there's not a lot of margin on the brakes. So it was a huge risk, but it paid off.

"Nick was setting a good pace, but this is also one of his strong sides, that he can manage this situation, because this was not planned at all. He handled a very heavy car, with the very soft tyres, and with the brakes being on the limit all the time, so he drove a very intelligent race."

Coulthard was delighted with his first score of the season: "Montréal is somewhere where there's always

incident and accident. I didn't expect it to happen in the pitlane! We did a one-stop run and kept out of trouble, and it all worked. I just went longer and all those guys pitted earlier. It was tricky of course on heavy fuel, because obviously you've got a lot of fuel off the line and, on a track that was breaking up, if you went off line it was terrible."

Like Coulthard, Glock benefited from a late one-stopper and earned his first Toyota points with fourth. Committed to an extra pit stop, Massa had fun passing people from the back, and managed to climb as high as fifth in the closing stages, salvaging some priceless points. Trulli, Barrichello and Vettel (from a pitlane start) completed the point scorers.

It was a terrible weekend for Heikki Kovalainen, who struggled to get his McLaren to work on this track. He had no particular dramas in the race, but was always in the wrong place at the wrong time, and could not better ninth. Of the rest, Alonso had been with Heidfeld in the middle of the race, but he was on a two-stopper and was destined to drop down the order. However, that became academic when brake problems contributed to a spin, and he nudged the wall.

It was an intriguing race, and the result was a refreshing one. But, without the pit accident, the prospect of Hamilton, Räikkönen and Kubica sitting side-by-side at the end of the pitlane was an enticing one. And after that it would have been a real fight to the flag. This was a case of the race we didn't see.

"What would have been great TV would have been the three of them dragging off the line," said one McLaren insider. "I think Lewis would have lined up alongside them, and you can overtake all the way to the safety-car line. It would have got very interesting, because the track isn't wide enough for three cars, and somebody would have had to give way, or all of them shunt! After that, there would have been a high risk of one of the cars being pushed over the white line..."

SNAPSHOT FROM
CANADA

CLOCKWISE FROM RIGHT

The geodesic dome built for Expo 1967 provides a distinctive backdrop to the Casino hairpin; a rare occasion for Lewis Hamilton to be on the other side of the lens; the Canadian GP provided the pretty face of F1; Germany-based Toyota F1 supported this team, but it was Spain that won the Euro 2008 football tournament; BMW motorsport chief Dr Mario Theissen's ambition was rewarded as Robert Kubica gave BMW Sauber its maiden win; Rubens Barrichello and friend try a different type of Honda for size; the track surface and its condition commanded considerable attention through the meeting as it broke up and had to be resurfaced on the Saturday evening

WEEKEND NEWS

■ Lewis Hamilton spent the week prior to the Canadian GP in Los Angeles with Adrian Sutil and another friend. They spent much of their time sampling borrowed supercars, but also made a visit to the MTV Awards. Lewis admitted that he enjoyed the relative anonymity he encountered in the USA.

■ Meanwhile, back home in England, Lewis's father Anthony found himself in the headlines after he managed to spin £330,000 worth of borrowed Porsche Carrera GT through a hedge. The incident happened as Anthony drove away from his house and apparently tried to prove to his neighbours that Lewis's talents are inherited…

■ Prior to the Canadian GP, Niki Lauda was chosen as the first guest on a new Austrian TV chat show hosted by former kidnap victim Natascha Kampusch. The F1 TV pundit and three-time World Champion said he'd been asked questions that "no-one has ever asked me before".

■ After years of complaints about the cramped facilities, the Canadian GP organisers had built a huge new media centre that sat on a platform floating on the lake behind the pits, replacing the cramped rooms in the control tower. The teams also had new hospitality and office buildings from which to work.

■ Courtesy of Red Bull, David Coulthard paid a visit to the NASCAR Sprint Cup event in Dover on the weekend before the Canadian GP. The Scottish driver admitted that, while he was impressed by the overall scene, the races did go on a bit. Meanwhile, Toyota took Jarno Trulli to the Michigan NASCAR race the weekend after the Canadian GP.

RACE RESULTS
CANADA
MONTREAL

RACE DATE June 8th
CIRCUIT LENGTH 2.710 miles
NO. OF LAPS 70
RACE DISTANCE 189.695 miles
WEATHER Sunny & dry, 26°C
TRACK TEMP 36°C
RACE DAY ATTENDANCE 121,000
LAP RECORD Rubens Barrichello
1m13.622s, 132.511mph, 2004

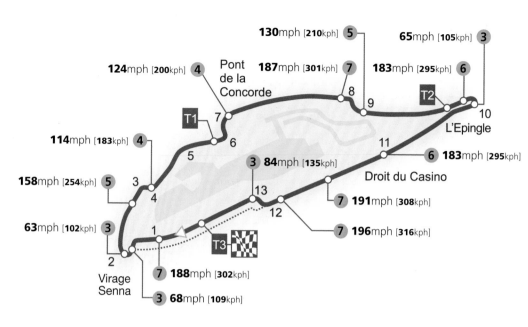

PRACTICE 1			
	Driver	Time	Laps
1	F Massa	1m17.553s	14
2	R Kubica	1m17.809s	12
3	H Kovalainen	1m18.133s	10
4	N Heidfeld	1m18.182s	13
5	K Räikkönen	1m18.292s	12
6	L Hamilton	1m18.303s	8
7	M Webber	1m18.712s	11
8	D Coulthard	1m18.809s	12
9	K Nakajima	1m18.971s	24
10	F Alonso	1m19.005s	13
11	N Rosberg	1m19.093s	20
12	S Vettel	1m19.228s	21
13	T Glock	1m19.346s	28
14	J Trulli	1m19.568s	31
15	G Fisichella	1m19.815s	16
16	A Sutil	1m19.888s	15
17	N Piquet Jr	1m20.091s	23
18	R Barrichello	1m20.173s	17
19	S Bourdais	1m20.541s	16
20	J Button	1m21.542s	17

PRACTICE 2			
	Driver	Time	Laps
1	L Hamilton	1m15.752s	42
2	R Kubica	1m16.023s	41
3	K Räikkönen	1m16.093s	39
4	H Kovalainen	1m16.331s	36
5	F Massa	1m16.413s	27
6	N Heidfeld	1m16.589s	43
7	M Webber	1m16.604s	39
8	N Rosberg	1m16.767s	37
9	S Vettel	1m17.019s	43
10	J Trulli	1m17.068s	46
11	K Nakajima	1m17.242s	37
12	D Coulthard	1m17.334s	31
13	R Barrichello	1m17.462s	39
14	G Fisichella	1m17.508s	39
15	T Glock	1m17.549s	31
16	S Bourdais	1m17.559s	38
17	F Alonso	1m17.644s	30
18	A Sutil	1m17.813s	37
19	J Button	1m17.842s	39
20	N Piquet Jr	1m18.076s	17

PRACTICE 3			
	Driver	Time	Laps
1	N Rosberg	1m16.555s	16
2	K Räikkönen	1m16.589s	22
3	L Hamilton	1m16.725s	17
4	F Massa	1m16.787s	19
5	K Nakajima	1m16.898s	16
6	J Trulli	1m16.946s	20
7	H Kovalainen	1m16.952s	16
8	N Piquet Jr	1m17.060s	19
9	M Webber	1m17.062s	16
10	S Vettel	1m17.085s	16
11	R Kubica	1m17.109s	17
12	S Bourdais	1m17.282s	17
13	D Coulthard	1m17.322s	20
14	R Barrichello	1m17.557s	19
15	T Glock	1m17.557s	20
16	G Fisichella	1m17.608s	24
17	F Alonso	1m17.683s	16
18	N Heidfeld	1m17.766s	17
19	J Button	1m18.178s	19
20	A Sutil	1m18.424s	21

QUALIFYING 1		
	Driver	Time
1	L Hamilton	1m16.909s
2	F Massa	1m17.231s
3	H Kovalainen	1m17.287s
4	K Räikkönen	1m17.301s
5	F Alonso	1m17.415s
6	R Kubica	1m17.471s
7	M Webber	1m17.582s
8	K Nakajima	1m17.638s
9	N Rosberg	1m17.991s
10	J Trulli	1m18.039s
11	N Heidfeld	1m18.082s
12	D Coulthard	1m18.168s
13	R Barrichello	1m18.256s
14	T Glock	1m18.321s
15	N Piquet Jr	1m18.505s
16	S Bourdais	1m18.916s
17	A Sutil	1m19.108s
18	G Fisichella	1m19.165s
19	J Button	1m23.565s
20	S Vettel	No time

QUALIFYING 2		
	Driver	Time
1	L Hamilton	1m17.034s
2	F Massa	1m17.353s
3	K Räikkönen	1m17.364s
4	F Alonso	1m17.488s
5	M Webber	1m17.523s
6	R Kubica	1m17.679s
7	H Kovalainen	1m17.684s
8	N Heidfeld	1m17.781s
9	N Rosberg	1m17.891s
10	R Barrichello	1m18.020s
11	T Glock	1m18.031s
12	K Nakajima	1m18.062s
13	D Coulthard	1m18.238s
14	J Trulli	1m18.327s
15	N Piquet Jr	1m18.393s

Best sectors – Practice
Sec 1	K Räikkönen	21.021s
Sec 2	L Hamilton	24.327s
Sec 3	L Hamilton	30.235s

Speed trap – Practice
1	H Kovalainen	199.336mph
2	L Hamilton	199.149mph
3	F Massa	198.963mph

Best sectors – Qualifying
Sec 1	F Massa	21.377s
Sec 2	M Webber	24.625s
Sec 3	L Hamilton	30.634s

Speed trap – Qualifying
1	L Hamilton	200.081mph
2	J Trulli	197.285mph
3	D Coulthard	197.161mph

Kimi Räikkönen
"My race was ruined by Hamilton. Anyone can make mistakes, as I did in Monaco, but it's one thing to make a mistake at 200mph, and another to hit a car at a red light."

Nick Heidfeld
"I made a poor start and lost a place to Barrichello. Luckily, I was able to pass him, and was one of the fastest cars on the track, so we switched to a one-stop strategy."

Fernando Alonso
"It's a missed opportunity. I am very disappointed, as is the team, but our strategy was not the best suited. We now have to work hard to challenge for big points."

Nico Rosberg
"I passed Alonso into Turn 1 and was getting away. Then there was the incident in the pitlane. Later, I tried to pass Vettel, but I went wide and Kovalainen got past me."

David Coulthard
"I'm delighted to get a podium. You expect unusual results here, so we fuelled it long. The strategy worked and all credit to Red Bull's engineers and mechanics."

Jarno Trulli
"This was a very good result, but near the end I had brake trouble. Unluckily, Timo made a small error, and when he came back on I had to lift and Massa got past."

Felipe Massa
"Once I found myself at the back, I tried to climb back up again, but I got stuck behind Glock and did not want to run the risk of ending up off the track after all my effort."

Robert Kubica
"I stopped as the light was red. Then Hamilton hit Kimi. I'm glad he missed me. I was then stuck behind the one-stoppers and had just eight laps to get 21s clear."

Nelson Piquet Jr
"It's a disappointing end, but I take some positives, as the car was good and our strategy looked promising. It was hectic early on, but then I had a brake problem."

Kazuki Nakajima
"When I was following Jenson, he got on the marbles in the hairpin and I couldn't avoid him. I damaged my front wing and when I came into the pits, it got stuck under the car."

Mark Webber
"I was on a two-stop strategy and David was on a one-stop. We were out of position after qualifying and it was hard to recover from there, but David's result brings a lot of points."

Timo Glock
"I lost three places at the start, leaving me behind Jarno. When I got close, I destroyed my rears. So I did my best to preserve them and was able to get by at the pit stop."

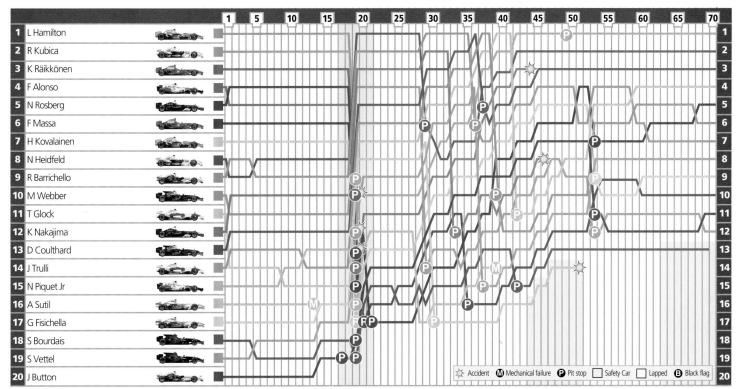

	Driver		
1	L Hamilton		
2	R Kubica		
3	K Räikkönen		
4	F Alonso		
5	N Rosberg		
6	F Massa		
7	H Kovalainen		
8	N Heidfeld		
9	R Barrichello		
10	M Webber		
11	T Glock		
12	K Nakajima		
13	D Coulthard		
14	J Trulli		
15	N Piquet Jr		
16	A Sutil		
17	G Fisichella		
18	S Bourdais		
19	S Vettel		
20	J Button		

☆ Accident Ⓜ Mechanical failure Ⓟ Pit stop ☐ Safety Car ☐ Lapped Ⓑ Black flag

QUALIFYING 3

	Driver	Time
1	L Hamilton	1m17.886s
2	R Kubica	1m18.498s
3	K Räikkönen	1m18.735s
4	F Alonso	1m18.746s
5	N Rosberg	1m18.844s
6	F Massa	1m19.048s
7	H Kovalainen	1m19.089s
8	N Heidfeld	1m19.633s
9	R Barrichello	1m20.848s
10	M Webber	No time

GRID

	Driver	Time
1	L Hamilton	1m17.886s
2	R Kubica	1m18.498s
3	K Räikkönen	1m18.735s
4	F Alonso	1m18.746s
5	N Rosberg	1m18.844s
6	F Massa	1m19.048s
7	H Kovalainen	1m19.089s
8	N Heidfeld	1m19.633s
9	R Barrichello	1m20.848s
10	M Webber	No time
11	T Glock	1m18.031s
12	K Nakajima	1m18.062s
13	D Coulthard	1m18.238s
14	J Trulli	1m18.327s
15	N Piquet Jr	1m18.393s
16	A Sutil	1m19.108s
17	G Fisichella	1m19.165s
18	S Vettel	No time
19*	S Bourdais	1m18.916s
20*	J Button	1m23.565s

*5-PLACE GRID PENALTY DUE TO GEARBOX CHANGE
BUTTON AND VETTEL STARTED FROM PITLANE

RACE

	Driver	Car	Laps	Time	Avg. mph	Fastest	Stops
1	R Kubica	BMW Sauber F1.08	70	1h36m24.447s	118.077	1m17.539s	2
2	N Heidfeld	BMW Sauber F1.08	70	1h36m40.942s	117.741	1m17.430s	1
3	D Coulthard	Red Bull-Renault RB4	70	1h36m47.799s	117.602	1m18.085s	1
4	T Glock	Toyota TF108	70	1h37m07.074s	117.213	1m19.087s	1
5	F Massa	Ferrari F2008	70	1h37m08.381s	117.187	1m18.006s	3
6	J Trulli	Toyota TF108	70	1h37m12.222s	117.110	1m18.870s	1
7	R Barrichello	Honda RA108	70	1h37m18.044s	116.993	1m18.301s	1
8	S Vettel	Toro Rosso-Ferrari STR03	70	1h37m18.567s	116.982	1m18.532s	1
9	H Kovalainen	McLaren-Mercedes MP4-23	70	1h37m18.880s	116.976	1m18.462s	2
10	N Rosberg	Williams-Toyota FW30	70	1h37m22.196s	116.910	1m17.977s	3
11	J Button	Honda RA108	70	1h37m31.987s	116.714	1m19.352s	3
12	M Webber	Red Bull-Renault RB4	70	1h37m35.676s	116.641	1m18.201s	2
13	S Bourdais	Toro Rosso-Ferrari STR03	69	1h36m43.167s	116.015	1m18.620s	2
R	G Fisichella	Force India-Ferrari VJM01	51	Spun off	-	1m19.066s	2
R	K Nakajima	Williams-Toyota FW30	46	Collision	-	1m18.784s	1
R	F Alonso	Renault R28	44	Spun off	-	1m18.225s	1
R	N Piquet Jr	Renault R28	39	Brakes	-	1m19.239s	1
R	K Räikkönen	Ferrari F2008	19	Collision	-	1m17.387s	1
R	L Hamilton	McLaren-Mercedes MP4-23	19	Collision	-	1m17.506s	1
R	A Sutil	Force India-Ferrari VJM01	13	Gearbox	-	1m20.666s	0

CHAMPIONSHIP

	Driver	Pts
1	R Kubica	42
2	L Hamilton	38
3	F Massa	38
4	K Räikkönen	35
5	N Heidfeld	28
6	H Kovalainen	15
7	M Webber	15
8	J Trulli	12
9	F Alonso	9
10	N Rosberg	8
11	K Nakajima	7
12	D Coulthard	6
13	T Glock	5
14	S Vettel	5
15	R Barrichello	5
16	J Button	3
17	S Bourdais	2

	Constructor	Pts
1	Ferrari	73
2	BMW Sauber	70
3	McLaren-Mercedes	53
4	Red Bull-Renault	21
5	Toyota	17
6	Williams-Toyota	15
7	Renault	9
8	Honda	8
9	Toro Rosso-Ferrari	7

Fastest Lap
K Räikkönen 1m17.387s
(126.058mph) on lap 14

Fastest speed trap
H Kovalainen 201.075mph
Slowest speed trap
J Button 193.122mph

Fastest pit stop
1 F Massa 27.197s
2 J Button 27.363s
3 M Webber 27.575s

Sebastien Bourdais
"In these conditions, I couldn't do anything with the car. I went only slightly off the line and hit the gravel, leaving me concerned that it could happen again. A disaster."

Jenson Button
"It's hard starting from the back and we were using an untried set-up. Things didn't go our way with the strategy and safety car, which meant I was unable to progress."

Adrian Sutil
"I couldn't shift into second or third gear and had to stop for 12 laps. The track wasn't too bad at the start, but I just couldn't find a way to get past the two Toyotas."

Lewis Hamilton
"I looked on course for the perfect result. But as I exited the box, I saw two cars jostling. I didn't want to be involved, then they stopped and it was too late for me to avoid them."

Sebastian Vettel
"Starting from pitlane, I made up two places. Then after the safety car came out, we ran a one-stop strategy. I think we had a fuel rig problem that cost us two places."

Rubens Barrichello
"I was suffering with a cold, but we were running well on the prime tyre and the safety car improved our position. But, when we switched to the option, I struggled for grip."

Giancarlo Fisichella
"The grip level was poor as the track broke up: it was like being in a four-wheel drive. Our pace was there, particularly in the second stint, but I stalled at the first stop."

Heikki Kovalainen
"I had the potential for a very good result, but I started to get graining. Changing tyres didn't help matters, and I was never able to push and left empty-handed."

FORMULA 1 GRAND PRIX DE FRANCE 2008
MAGNY-COURS

MASSA'S GAIN

Victory should have gone to pole starter Kimi Räikkönen, but a broken exhaust slowed him, letting Felipe Massa win as he pleased to take the championship lead from Robert Kubica

Felipe Massa led in France in 2007 and looked set for victory, only for Kimi Räikkönen to jump ahead by virtue of a later pit stop. This year, Räikkönen started from pole position and was in control from the start. However, Massa gained his revenge, but only after the Finn was slowed by a broken exhaust.

The victory moved Massa into the lead of the World Championship for the first time in his career. Indeed, no Brazilian had led since Ayrton Senna was on top after Monaco in 1993.

Not surprisingly, Lewis Hamilton's latest dramas occupied most of the headlines after the race, which was perhaps a little unfair on Ferrari. Clearly, grid penalties for both McLaren drivers – 10 places back for Hamilton for his Montréal pitlane misdemeanour, and five places back for Heikki Kovalainen for obstructing Mark Webber at the start of Q3 – gave the Italian team some breathing space come the race, but nevertheless their 1–2 finish was an impressive performance.

We'll never know how hard Hamilton and Kovalainen (who qualified heavy in an effort to make up for his penalty) would have pushed the Ferraris in a straight fight, but the likelihood is that the Italian team would have triumphed anyway, such was the

TALKING POINT
THE CHANGING FACE OF F1

Times change, and sport moves with them. A much-discussed subject in 2008 was the balancing of Grand Prix racing's 'traditional' events with a calendar that reflects more and more events in different parts of the globe.

In the past decade there have been new venues in Malaysia, Bahrain, Turkey and China, and 2008 saw pioneering races in Singapore and Valencia. However, with Magny-Cours followed by races at Silverstone and Hockenheim, we had three circuits all facing an uphill struggle to maintain their places.

Magny-Cours, first used for Formula 1 in 1991, was given the last rites at the 2007 French GP but was still on the calendar, although talk continued about the desirability of a site near Paris to safeguard the future of the French GP. There was mention of alternating the French and British GPs, although both races were on the provisional 2009 schedule released at the French GP.

Two weeks after the French GP, on the first day of action at Silverstone, the FIA announced that from 2010 the British GP would be at Donington Park. Commercial rights holder Bernie Ecclestone had wanted significant circuit upgrading pledged for 2010 as part of the negotiating around a new contract for Silverstone. The BRDC's President, Damon Hill, said that everything was progressing, but Ecclestone had run out of patience.

Donington's owners have pledged a £100 million investment programme, including improved access, and will attempt to generate the funding via the selling of debentures, in a similar manner to Wembley and Wimbledon.

The news permeated the Silverstone paddock just as the cars took to the track for first practice on Friday morning and there was a general sense of disbelief.

Hill intimated that there was a price at which it was sensible to do a deal and that if others had gone beyond that, then good luck to them. "The Donington owner has been quoted saying that he's bet the farm. Well, we haven't..." Hill said.

A fortnight later the rumours started about Hockenheim, one news source suggesting the circuit would go bankrupt the morning after the race. Managing Director Karl-Josef Schmidt explained that Hockenheim's balance sheet is in the black, even if the grand prix operates at a loss. "We have a contract for 2010 and both the will and the means to fulfil it," he said. Beyond that, he admitted, would depend on the circumstances and the deal offered.

Balancing the commercial realities of life against the traditional face of the sport is certainly no easy task.

pace of the red cars on a track where it has been so successful in the past.

Incredibly, since the place was opened in 1991, McLaren has won only once at Magny-Cours, with David Coulthard victorious in 2000, while Massa's victory was the *eighth* at the venue for Ferrari. Not bad when you consider how uncompetitive the team was over the first four or five years of that period...

Massa was quickest in the first two parts of qualifying, but when it really mattered Räikkönen found something extra, beating his team-mate by just 0.041s, as a brake-locking moment on his final hot lap proved expensive for the Brazilian.

Hamilton was third on lap time, but the Briton's 10-place penalty dropped him to 13th on the grid. Fernando Alonso showed improved form by taking fourth for Renault, and so inherited third, ahead of Jarno Trulli. McLaren's weekend was made worse by Kovalainen's penalty. Some considered it a marginal call and, aware that a penalty might be coming, McLaren gave him extra fuel for Q3 and he would ultimately start 10th.

The penalties moved a disappointed Robert Kubica up from seventh to fifth, while the biggest surprise of the day was the performance of Nick Heidfeld. The German just scraped into Q2 with a last-ditch effort, and ended up 12th before being promoted to 11th, although he was only 0.063s slower than Kubica.

Räikkönen slotted into the lead at the start, ahead of Massa, while Alonso made a poor getaway and was beaten into the first corner by Trulli. Of course, the big story was always going to be how much ground Hamilton could recover from 13th, and indeed on the first lap the McLaren man began slicing his way through the pack. But he tried just a little too hard, running off the track as he completed a move on Sebastian Vettel at the Nürburgring chicane to claim 10th. It was just the sort of thing that a title contender cannot afford to

tempt fate with and, sure enough, he was soon called in for a drive-through penalty for gaining an advantage. Any realistic chance he had of scoring points was gone.

"I had quite a good start, there were four people abreast in front of me, so I decided to take it easy," Hamilton said later. "I got a few in T5 and someone fairly going into T7. I was ahead, but I lost the back end and corrected it and went over the kerb, which I don't see as cheating. But rules are rules.

"I don't think I did anything. I went into the corner believing I was ahead on the outside and couldn't turn in on the guy otherwise we would have crashed, so I took a wider line. Then I lost the back, on the marbles I would have thought, and went over the kerb and continued. I don't believe I overtook him by going over the kerb. I overtook him before that and, as a result, I was forced wide."

Massa wasn't too upset about lining up second, because he knew he had a couple of laps of fuel in hand. He went into the race thinking that he might be able to turn the tables on Räikkönen, but the Finn made sure there was no chance of that by pulling away in that first stint. Despite stopping two laps later, Massa was not close enough to get ahead.

"Well, it was a little bit tough to be honest to follow him, as he was very quick at that stage," said Massa. "I was two or three tenths of a second slower than him, but I had two more laps of fuel, which is understandable. I think I would have liked to have been one tenth of a second slower per lap, and then it would have been possible to fight for the position in the pits.

"When I saw that the gap was already six seconds I said, 'OK, maybe it is better to concentrate on the driving and finish second', as that already was a great result for the championship. But then I saw that Kimi was slowing and I heard that he had a problem with the exhaust. Sometimes you need the luck…"

It was during the middle stint that Räikkönen suffered his broken exhaust, which could be seen flapping about at the rear of the car. The Ferrari crew did their best to minimise the damage to his lap times, although options were limited.

"You can make certain adjustments to the engine," said Rob Smedley, Massa's race engineer, "which we obviously also did with Felipe. And you can drive in a certain way to make sure that it doesn't happen on the other side, because we kind of understood why

OPPOSITE LEFT Bernie Ecclestone congratulates Kimi Räikkönen after he pipped Massa to pole position

OPPOSITE RIGHT Life remained a twisting road for Force India's Adrian Sutil (shown) and team-mate Giancarlo Fisichella

ABOVE Kimi Räikkönen leads Felipe Massa and Jarno Trulli on the first lap, but it wasn't to be his day

INSIDE LINE
JARNO TRULLI
TOYOTA DRIVER

"A podium was more than I expected, but we were competitive all weekend at Magny-Cours and I was delighted as much for the team as for myself, because everyone has been putting in a really big effort.

Timo got his fourth place finish in Canada and it was great to come back to Europe and build on that. The grid is so competitive at the moment and we had a good test at Barcelona before Magny-Cours, so I was optimistic.

In qualifying, there was just over a second covering the top 10. I did a good lap and I was pleased with fifth, even if you are never sure about who was carrying what fuel load. I had Alonso's Renault in front of me, for example, and Kovalainen and Kubica behind with the McLaren and BMW Sauber, so things were mixed up a bit and obviously the grid penalties for McLaren helped.

The Ferraris and McLarens have more performance, for sure, and I was under no illusions about racing them. Our opposition is Red Bull and Renault and possibly BMW Sauber, so that was what I was concentrating on. The team aim is to finish fourth in the constructors' championship and I felt from first thing Friday that our performance was good here, consistent on the long runs, and I had a chance to score good points.

I made a good start, passed Alonso, then defended into the hairpin. I couldn't stay with the Ferraris, but I managed to open up a 3s gap over Alonso, who stopped five laps before me, so we were in good shape. I made my first pit stop on lap 20, the same lap as Kubica. Robert jumped ahead of Alonso at the stop and now seemed pretty fast and started closing the gap to me. We had fuelled for a long second stint and it was good to see Robert go in for his second stop around four laps before me, so I could consolidate my position. My last stop was a good one and gave me 5s breathing space over him, but then I had Kovalainen to worry about. He ran a couple of laps longer than me and came out in front of Kubica.

It's difficult to pass at Magny-Cours and I was confident I could keep the McLaren behind but, with about 10 laps to go, it started to rain. It was only a shower, but the surface was slippery for a couple of laps and Heikki closed up. I had bad memories of losing a podium on the last lap here in 2004 and I wasn't going to let it happen again. We had a good fight, Heikki got alongside and we were wheel-to-wheel, but he wasn't coming through. That podium was mine!"

it happened. That's all you can do when you're in the middle of a race."

Räikkönen's times dropped by a second per lap, and he clearly lost power. But the guy is a World Champion, and true greats can adapt to difficult circumstances, as we saw so often with Michael Schumacher in the past.

"It wasn't particularly easy for Kimi," said Smedley, "and he had to get into a rhythm where he could drive the car as fast as it would go again, with the handicap that he had. And while he was doing that Felipe caught him, and eventually passed him. It was inevitable that he would do so, as he had a car that was a second a lap faster."

The margin over Massa shrank quickly, and the Brazilian took the lead on lap 39, then gradually edged from Räikkönen who focused on staying well clear of his main pursuer, Trulli.

In fact, the Toyota man was never a real threat, and the major concern in the closing laps was a light rain shower that made life difficult for everyone, although it wasn't heavy enough to justify a tyre change. The sighs of relief in the Ferrari camp afterwards were all too apparent. The heat-blast damage on the back of Räikkönen's car proved just how fortunate he was to

make it to the end without losing his second place.

Although obviously concerned that he too might suffer a breakage, Massa must have had a smile on his face when he inherited the lead, and he didn't exactly hide his pleasure afterwards. The same race last year had been a crucial tipping point in the balance of power between the two Ferrari drivers.

"It was fantastic, I did not expect that," he said. "Sometimes you need a little bit of luck and today I had a little bit of luck with what happened to Kimi and his exhaust. Fortunately he could finish the race, but it was, for sure, a good present. I was already quite comfortable in second position, as he had a very quick pace and I am sure it would have been very difficult for me to pass him. It was a great race and we showed our performance."

After failing to score in Monaco and Montréal, Räikkönen was relieved to take some points: "Yeah, it is disappointing in the end after having a good car all weekend, being on pole, leading it quite easily and then having a problem with the car. Unfortunately, that happens sometimes. In one way, we are still lucky to finish the race and get eight points, as in the last couple of laps the car almost stopped a few times.

FRANCE ROUND **8**

OPPOSITE TOP Jarno Trulli, his Toyota wearing a black band to mark Ove Andersson's death, raced to third place behind the Ferraris

OPPOSITE MIDDLE LEFT Heikki Kovalainen started with a five-place penalty, but climbed from 10th to fourth place for McLaren

OPPOSITE MIDDLE RIGHT Lewis Hamilton dives by Timo Glock

BELOW Mark Webber keeps Nelson Piquet behind him as he races to sixth place for Red Bull

ABOVE Fernando Alonso qualified well for Renault's home race, but pitted early and fell to eighth place

BELOW Jarno Trulli enjoyed the third place he collected for Toyota on a weekend when McLaren was pegged back by grid penalties

"I lost a lot of power. That was the biggest problem out there. Sometimes I just lost all the power and then it came back. It was slow in a straight line and it was especially difficult out of low-speed corners. Fortunately, the car was strong enough and it lasted, so even with the broken exhaust we were still fast enough and we had enough gap to the third-place car to be able to hold on to second place."

Toyota didn't arrive at Magny-Cours expecting to collect a podium finish, but third place went to Trulli, the Italian having made full use of his good grid position. He made a good start and, having got ahead of Alonso, pulled away from the Renault and built a useful advantage. He was caught by the flying Kovalainen in the closing stages, but Trulli showed admirable aggression as he kept the Finn back. The pair even made high-speed contact on the penultimate lap, but both survived the brush intact. It was a good effort by Kovalainen, who would surely have been pushing the Ferraris had it not been for his grid penalty.

Kubica ran in fifth place initially, but later managed to get ahead of Alonso for fourth. However, late in the race, he lost out to Kovalainen and dropped back to fifth, earning four more useful points for BMW Sauber. By contrast, Heidfeld lost a couple of places on lap 1 and had an undistinguished run to 13th, much to the bemusement of the Swiss-German team.

Mark Webber had a strong race for Red Bull Racing, apart from a moment when he lost it over the final chicane and nearly hit the pit wall. He lost the spot he had gained from Alonso, but later gained it back and took yet another good points finish in sixth place.

As noted, Alonso lost a spot to Trulli at the start, and his early stop (on lap 15) cost him ground. Team-mate Nelson Piquet Jr moved steadily up the order and was one of the last top runners to stop, coming in on lap 25. Their two strategies converged in the closing laps and Piquet Jr was close enough to steal seventh from Alonso when the Spaniard made a mistake. It was the first score for Nelsinho after a difficult start to his F1 career.

If Piquet Jr felt relieved, then his old GP2 sparring partner Hamilton was anything but. He'd clearly been under pressure since the Canadian GP, and really hadn't enjoyed the media coverage of his pitlane error. After finishing a frustrated 10th, he insisted he had not deserved the latest penalty.

"I did everything I needed to do. I stayed out of trouble, drove what I thought was a fair race, just missed out on points. That's three races without scoring points, but there are still 10 races to go…"

SNAPSHOT FROM
FRANCE

CLOCKWISE FROM RIGHT
Heikki Kovalainen parks in *parc ferme*; Rubens Barrichello is reflected in a fire marshal's mask; team chiefs Vijay Mallya and Flavio Briatore get up close in the pitlane; footballer Ronaldo dropped in to check out a very different sport; Toyota was delighted that it could honour Ove Andersson with Jarno Trulli's third place; Robert Kubica didn't look happy after qualifying, but he raced to fifth place; Nelson Piquet Jr relaxed, then came good to score his first points, for seventh; Keke Rosberg continues to look as charismatic as ever as he watches son Nico race for Williams

WEEKEND NEWS

■ The week before the French GP, former Toyota F1 boss Ove Andersson was killed while competing in a historic rally event in South Africa, where he had recently made his home. The 70-year-old Swede was sharing a 1957 Volvo when it was involved in a collision on a public road. As a mark of respect, Toyota team members wore black armbands during the Magny-Cours weekend.

■ Renault team boss Flavio Briatore took advantage of the gap between the Canadian and French grands prix to marry his girlfriend, Elisabetta Gregoraci. The ceremony took place in Rome in front of a VIP gathering that included the likes of Bernie Ecclestone and Fernando Alonso, the latter also performing chauffeuring duties. Duran Duran provided the evening entertainment.

■ ITV television colleagues Martin Brundle and Mark Blundell decided to go to the French GP by motorcycle, enjoying the challenge of country roads wherever they could. On one motorway stretch, Brundle tried a slalom run through some traffic cones, and was blissfully unaware when his pannier flicked one of the cones into the path of his travelling companion...

■ A dispute over the cost of the FIA Superlicence came to the fore at the French GP as drivers complained over how much they were being charged. An appreciable hike, related to points scored and apparently to cover the cost of safety improvements, meant that World Champion Kimi Räikkönen was 'priced' at $230,000. Fortunately, talk of a strike soon faded away.

■ The week before the French GP, Audi defeated Peugeot in one of the most exciting Le Mans 24 Hour races events in years. The French manufacturer's line-up included a trio of current F1 test drivers Alexander Wurz (Honda), Christian Klien (BMW) and Marc Gene (Ferrari), plus former F1 racers Jacques Villeneuve, Franck Montagny, Ricardo Zonta and Pedro Lamy.

RACE RESULTS
FRANCE
MAGNY-COURS

RACE DATE June 22nd
CIRCUIT LENGTH 2.741 miles
NO. OF LAPS 70
RACE DISTANCE 191.870 miles
WEATHER Damp then rain later, 25°C
TRACK TEMP 31°C
RACE DAY ATTENDANCE 78,000
LAP RECORD Michael Schumacher,
1m15.377s, 130.910mph, 2004

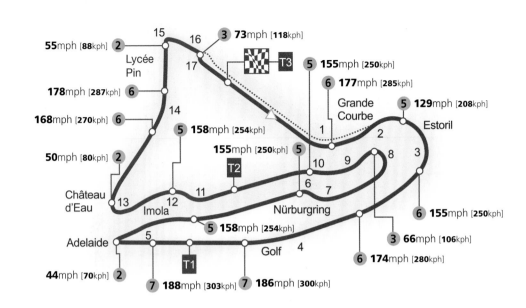

PRACTICE 1

	Driver	Time	Laps
1	F Massa	1m15.306s	22
2	L Hamilton	1m16.002s	22
3	H Kovalainen	1m16.055s	20
4	K Räikkönen	1m16.073s	21
5	R Kubica	1m16.377s	19
6	F Alonso	1m16.400s	23
7	J Trulli	1m16.758s	32
8	S Vettel	1m16.838s	27
9	H Neidfeld	1m16.870s	21
10	T Glock	1m16.886s	31
11	N Piquet Jr	1m17.063s	31
12	D Coulthard	1m17.234s	21
13	M Webber	1m17.269s	22
14	N Rosberg	1m17.394s	30
15	R Barrichello	1m17.491s	25
16	S Bourdais	1m17.683s	27
17	K Nakajima	1m17.696s	25
18	J Button	1m17.928s	21
19	G Fisichella	1m18.072s	27
20	A Sutil	1m18.673s	13

PRACTICE 2

	Driver	Time	Laps
1	F Alonso	1m15.778s	37
2	F Massa	1m15.854s	24
3	K Räikkönen	1m15.999s	42
4	L Hamilton	1m16.232s	29
5	S Vettel	1m16.298s	42
6	R Kubica	1m16.317s	35
7	H Kovalainen	1m16.340s	36
8	N Heidfeld	1m16.458s	43
9	N Piquet Jr	1m16.543s	39
10	D Coulthard	1m16.572s	36
11	N Rosberg	1m16.682s	42
12	J Trulli	1m16.743s	43
13	S Bourdais	1m16.758s	42
14	K Nakajima	1m17.002s	32
15	T Glock	1m17.092s	39
16	M Webber	1m17.106s	38
17	J Button	1m17.244s	37
18	G Fisichella	1m17.394s	42
19	R Barrichello	1m17.591s	27
20	A Sutil	1m17.868s	33

PRACTICE 3

	Driver	Time	Laps
1	N Piquet Jr	1m15.750s	19
2	M Webber	1m15.759s	14
3	S Vettel	1m15.827s	21
4	N Rosberg	1m15.974s	17
5	K Räikkönen	1m16.003s	18
6	J Trulli	1m16.147s	20
7	L Hamilton	1m16.182s	16
8	S Bourdais	1m16.235s	18
9	F Massa	1m16.256s	17
10	D Coulthard	1m16.282s	18
11	T Glock	1m16.344s	20
12	F Alonso	1m16.437s	20
13	H Kovalainen	1m16.545s	16
14	R Kubica	1m16.617s	20
15	K Nakajima	1m16.644s	16
16	J Button	1m16.651s	20
17	R Barrichello	1m16.658s	17
18	N Heidfeld	1m16.687s	19
19	G Fisichella	1m17.365s	23
20	A Sutil	1m17.612s	21

QUALIFYING 1

	Driver	Time
1	F Massa	1m15.024s
2	K Räikkönen	1m15.133s
3	J Trulli	1m15.521s
4	L Hamilton	1m15.634s
5	R Kubica	1m15.687s
6	T Glock	1m15.727s
7	F Alonso	1m15.754s
8	D Coulthard	1m15.802s
9	N Piquet Jr	1m15.848s
10	S Vettel	1m15.918s
11	H Kovalainen	1m15.965s
12	N Heidfeld	1m16.006s
13	M Webber	1m16.020s
14	S Bourdais	1m16.072s
15	N Rosberg	1m16.085s
16	K Nakajima	1m16.243s
17	J Button	1m16.306s
18	R Barrichello	1m16.330s
19	G Fisichella	1m16.971s
20	A Sutil	1m17.053s

QUALIFYING 2

	Driver	Time
1	F Massa	1m15.041s
2	K Räikkönen	1m15.161s
3	L Hamilton	1m15.293s
4	J Trulli	1m15.362s
5	F Alonso	1m15.483s
6	M Webber	1m15.488s
7	T Glock	1m15.558s
8	H Kovalainen	1m15.639s
9	D Coulthard	1m15.654s
10	R Kubica	1m15.723s
11	N Piquet Jr	1m15.770s
12	N Heidfeld	1m15.786s
13	S Vettel	1m15.816s
14	S Bourdais	1m16.045s
15	N Rosberg	1m16.235s

Best sectors – Practice

Sec 1	L Hamilton	21.933s
Sec 2	F Massa	28.945s
Sec 3	M Webber	24.217s

Speed trap – Practice

1	K Räikkönen	192.563mph
2	F Massa	191.631mph
3	L Hamilton	191.568mph

Best sectors – Qualifying

Sec 1	L Hamilton	21.472s
Sec 2	F Massa	28.818s
Sec 3	F Massa	24.198s

Speed trap – Qualifying

1	F Massa	191.133mph
2	N Piquet Jr	191.133mph
3	F Alonso	190.698mph

Kimi Räikkönen
"The right exhaust pipe broke and the engine lost power, especially on the straight after the slow corners. The situation seemed to improve, but it was a worry to the end."

Nick Heidfeld
"Having finished 13th is certainly a disappointing result. I lost two places right at the start and could not get them back. Now we will concentrate on next week's test."

Fernando Alonso
"I am sure we could have fought for the podium, but I lost too many places at the start. The car was fast in a straight line, but I still couldn't make any progress up the field."

Nico Rosberg
"In Canada, I was fighting Ferraris and BMWs, and here I was fighting at the back of the pack. It's not a very nice feeling. I thought I would be able to fight a bit more."

David Coulthard
"I lost three places at the start, two off the line and one when Kovalainen went around the outside into Turn 5. Balance on the prime tyres wasn't that good."

Jarno Trulli
"I want to dedicate this result to Ove Andersson. It was a great race, hard and tough. After the rain, I got back into a rhythm and had a wheel-to-wheel fight with Heikki."

Felipe Massa
"A great race, a fantastic result. It came my way as Kimi had a problem with his car. I would have been happy with second but of course, the win makes me even happier."

Robert Kubica
"We tried to minimise the problems we had and I tried to overtake Trulli, but did not manage it. I tried again in Turn 5 on the outside, but it did not work out."

Nelson Piquet Jr
"It's the first time that everything has gone without any problems for me. The car and the strategy worked well and I was able to score my first couple of points."

Kazuki Nakajima
"We decided to go for a two-stop strategy, which was the best way to go under the circumstances. We've been suffering with a lack of pace and that hurt us during the race."

Mark Webber
"My start wasn't great, but my first stint wasn't too bad. I was trying to keep up with Fernando, as he was [fuelled] short and I put in some laps that were right on the edge."

Timo Glock
"I made a good start, the car felt good and I was able to push hard. But after the pit stop I struggled to maintain the same pace, as I had graining then major understeer."

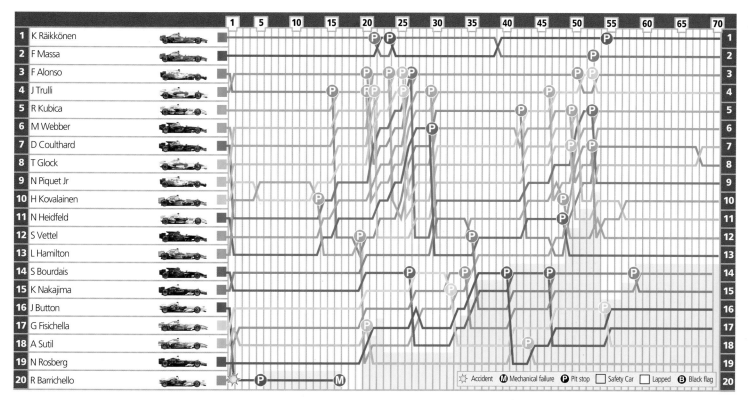

1	K Räikkönen		
2	F Massa		
3	F Alonso		
4	J Trulli		
5	R Kubica		
6	M Webber		
7	D Coulthard		
8	T Glock		
9	N Piquet Jr		
10	H Kovalainen		
11	N Heidfeld		
12	S Vettel		
13	L Hamilton		
14	S Bourdais		
15	K Nakajima		
16	J Button		
17	G Fisichella		
18	A Sutil		
19	N Rosberg		
20	R Barrichello		

☆ Accident Ⓜ Mechanical failure Ⓟ Pit stop ☐ Safety Car ☐ Lapped Ⓑ Black flag

QUALIFYING 3

	Driver	Time
1	K Räikkönen	1m16.449s
2	F Massa	1m16.490s
3	L Hamilton	1m16.693s
4	F Alonso	1m16.840s
5	J Trulli	1m16.920s
6	H Kovalainen	1m16.944s
7	R Kubica	1m17.037s
8	M Webber	1m17.233s
9	D Coulthard	1m17.426s
10	T Glock	1m17.596s

GRID

	Driver	Time
1	K Räikkönen	1m16.449s
2	F Massa	1m16.490s
3	F Alonso	1m16.840s
4	J Trulli	1m16.920s
5	R Kubica	1m17.037s
6	M Webber	1m17.233s
7	D Coulthard	1m17.426s
8	T Glock	1m17.596s
9	N Piquet Jr	1m15.770s
10*	H Kovalainen	1m16.944s
11	N Heidfeld	1m15.786s
12	S Vettel	1m15.816s
13^	L Hamilton	1m16.693s
14	S Bourdais	1m16.045s
15	K Nakajima	1m16.243s
16	J Button	1m16.306s
17	G Fisichella	1m16.971s
18	A Sutil	1m17.053s
19^	N Rosberg	1m16.235s
20'	R Barrichello	1m16.330s

* 5-PLACE PENALTY FOR OBSTRUCTION IN QUALIFYING
^ 10-PLACE PENALTY FOR PITLANE ACCIDENT IN CANADA
' 5-PLACE PENALTY FOR GEARBOX CHANGE

RACE

	Driver	Car	Laps	Time	Avg. mph	Fastest	Stops
1	F Massa	Ferrari F2008	70	1h31m50.245s	125.299	1m16.729s	2
2	K Räikkönen	Ferrari F2008	70	1h32m08.229	124.892	1m16.630s	2
3	J Trulli	Toyota TF108	70	1h32m18.495s	124.660	1m17.567s	2
4	H Kovalainen	McLaren-Mercedes MP4-23	70	1h32m19.174s	124.625	1m17.134s	2
5	R Kubica	BMW Sauber F1.08	70	1h32m20.757s	124.609	1m17.172s	2
6	M Webber	Red Bull-Renault RB4	70	1h32m30.549s	124.389	1m17.507s	2
7	N Piquet Jr	Renault R28	70	1h32m31.278s	124.373	1m17.758s	2
8	F Alonso	Renault R28	70	1h32m33.617s	124.321	1m17.641s	2
9	D Coulthard	Red Bull-Renault RB4	70	1h32m41.317s	124.148	1m17.818s	2
10	L Hamilton	McLaren-Mercedes MP4-23	70	1h32m44.766s	124.071	1m17.453s	3
11	T Glock	Toyota TF108	70	1h32m47.983s	124.000	1m17.836s	2
12	S Vettel	Toro Rosso-Ferrari STR03	70	1h32m48.310s	123.992	1m17.760s	2
13	N Heidfeld	BMW Sauber F1.08	70	1h32m52.324s	123.903	1m17.716s	2
14	R Barrichello	Honda RA108	69	1h32m05.471s	123.168	1m17.969s	2
15	K Nakajima	Williams-Toyota FW30	69	1h32m08.926s	123.091	1m18.054s	2
16	N Rosberg	Williams-Toyota FW30	69	1h32m09.617s	123.075	1m18.311s	1
17	S Bourdais	Toro Rosso-Ferrari STR03	69	1h32m10.274s	123.061	1m18.216s	2
18	G Fisichella	Force India-Ferrari VJM01	69	1h32m37.032s	122.469	1m18.557s	2
19	A Sutil	Force India-Ferrari VJM01	69	1h32m57.001s	122.030	1m18.462s	2
R	J Button	Honda RA108	16	Collision damage	-	1m20.876s	1

CHAMPIONSHIP

	Driver	Pts
1	F Massa	48
2	R Kubica	46
3	K Räikkönen	43
4	L Hamilton	38
5	N Heidfeld	28
6	H Kovalainen	20
7	J Trulli	18
8	M Webber	18
9	F Alonso	10
10	N Rosberg	8
11	K Nakajima	7
12	D Coulthard	6
13	T Glock	5
14	S Vettel	5
15	R Barrichello	5
16	J Button	2
17	N Piquet Jr	2
18	S Bourdais	2

	Constructor	Pts
1	Ferrari	91
2	BMW Sauber	74
3	McLaren-Mercedes	58
4	Red Bull-Renault	24
5	Toyota	23
6	Williams-Toyota	15
7	Renault	12
8	Honda	8
9	Toro Rosso-Ferrari	7

Fastest Lap
K Räikkönen 1m16.630s
(128.763mph) on lap 16

Fastest speed trap
F Massa 191.133mph
Slowest speed trap
J Button 180.632mph

Fastest pit stop
1 N Heidfeld 22.988s
2 H Kovlainen 23.304s
3 N Piquet Jr 23.540s

 **Sebastien Bourdais**

"Nakajima, on a one-stop, got ahead of me at the start after my engine bogged down, and it compromised my race as I lost touch with the pack ahead."

 Jenson Button

"After I hit Bourdais, the car was driveable, but the front wing came off and got stuck under the front of the car. We replaced it, but the bargeboards had been pulled off."

 Adrian Sutil

"We ran an aggressive strategy, but nothing happened to other people, so I had lots of times when I had to move over to let cars on the lead lap go past and got out of the rhythm."

Lewis Hamilton

"My drive-through was a close call: I felt I'd got past Vettel but was on the outside and could not turn-in in case we hit, then I lost the back end and drove over the kerb."

 **Sebastian Vettel**

"We had a very strong race in a pack that included McLaren and BMW. We were not so lucky in terms of traffic and I would have liked the rain to come earlier."

Rubens Barrichello

"It was a great race, with a difficult car. At least we were able to make a fight of it. As we expected, the car was slightly better in race trim and we had a good strategy."

Giancarlo Fisichella

"Our target was to get to the end. We had more reliability but the pace was not as good as we wanted. It was better than yesterday, but we really need a step forward."

Heikki Kovalainen

"Given my grid penalty, this was a good result, coming from 10th to fourth. In the first stint I lost time trying to get past slower cars, but after that the car felt fantastic."

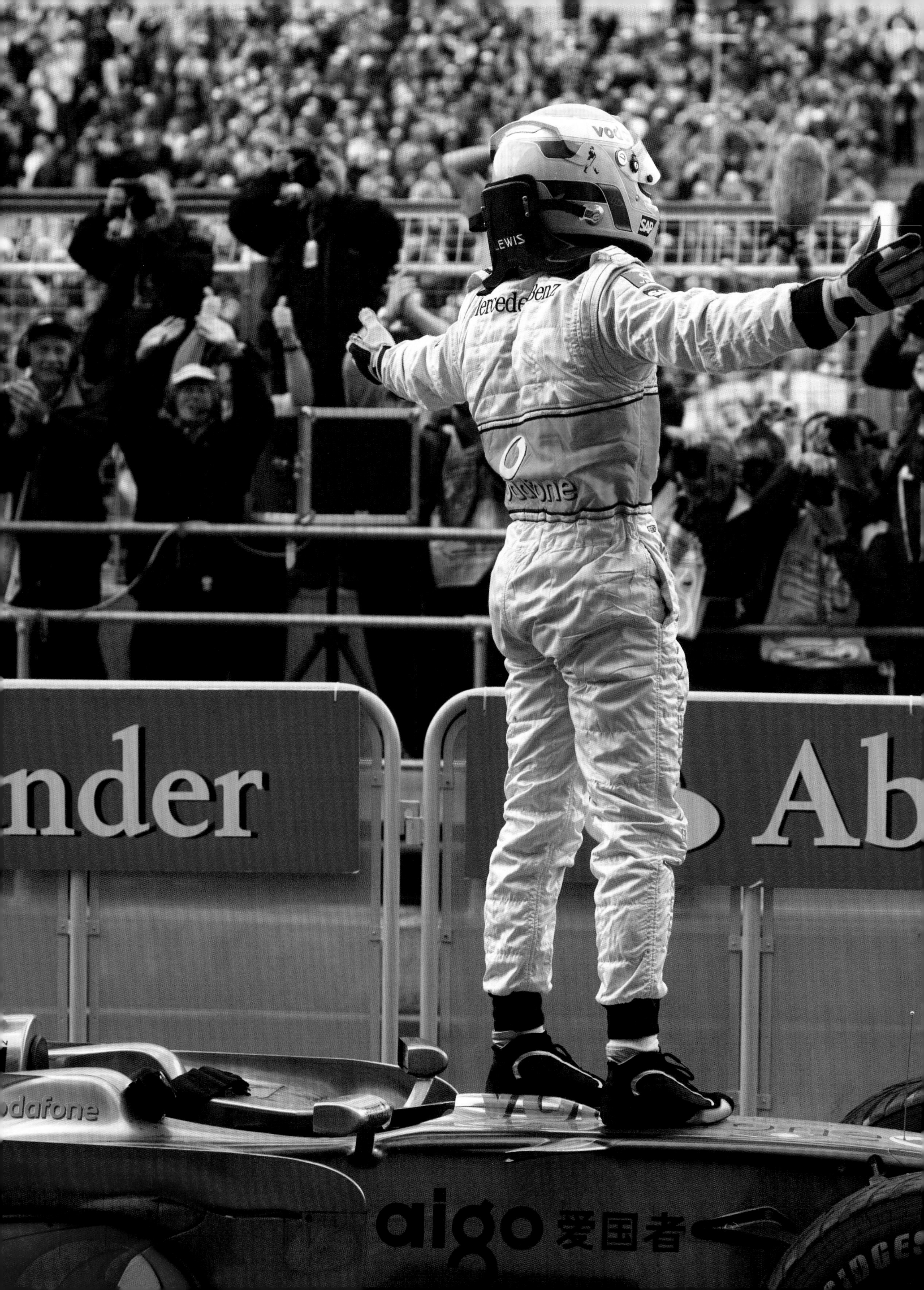
LEWIS
SAP
nder
Ab
odafone
aigo
爱国者

2008 FORMULA 1 SANTANDER BRITISH GRAND PRIX
SILVERSTONE

LEWIS ATONES

Lewis Hamilton countered press criticism to move back into title contention with a stunning victory in the wet on a day when Ferrari lost its gamble not to change its cars' tyres

Silverstone was the scene of a truly astonishing wet-weather performance from Lewis Hamilton, who made amends for his recent misfortunes in the best way possible. He not only finished 68 seconds ahead of his closest rival, Nick Heidfeld, but he lapped everyone up to third place. Both of those statistics are extremely unusual in the modern era, when the cars are so evenly matched and safety-car periods often serve to close up the field. And yet this was a strange race. Heidfeld actually set a quicker fastest lap than Hamilton, and Kimi Räikkönen's best was a full 0.677s faster than that achieved by the McLaren man. What's more, when he set that time Räikkönen was closing in and seemed destined to take the lead. But then a poor strategic call by Ferrari turned the Finn's race upside down.

Had it been dry on Sunday, the outcome could have been very different. From the start of the weekend, Hamilton had been outpaced by his team-mate, who really found the Silverstone groove. Beaten in all three practice sessions and Q1, Lewis only got ahead of Heikki Kovalainen in Q2, and then only by a tiny margin.

In Q3, Hamilton made his life difficult by running wide on his first hot lap. Without a banker time, he had to really make it count second time around, but his follow-up lap was good only for fourth, and it would surely have been sixth had both Felipe Massa and Robert Kubica not had problems that prevented them from running a full session. Hamilton ended up 0.786s behind Kovalainen who claimed his first pole position. The race was to prove that Hamilton had been two laps heavier on fuel load, but that didn't come close to accounting for the difference.

Rain fell throughout Sunday morning, and by the race start the track was still soaking. Hamilton got ahead of Räikkönen and second qualifier Mark Webber on the run to Copse, and had a look down the inside of Kovalainen as they swept into the first turn. The pair actually touched and, when he ran out to the damp kerb on the outside, Kovalainen got sideways. He held it all together but, if he had lost it, Hamilton would have had nowhere to go, and the day might not have been such a joyous one for McLaren.

"Just a little tap," said Kovalainen of the contact. "It reminded me of the Turkish GP, and I was feeling whether I'd got a puncture or not, because it was a similar kind of thing I got in Turkey, [when] half a lap later the team told me I'm losing air from the tyre. Apart from that it was no problem, it was no danger to any of us."

Concerned that he'd broken his wing, Hamilton wasn't about to sit back and wait for his chance. For four-and-a-half laps, he pressured Kovalainen, until finally getting past at Stowe.

"The first lap was very tough," said Hamilton. "I got a great start. I was on the inside and had no grip, so I sort of slid into Heikki. I just managed to stay behind him. I was quite a lot quicker than him, but managing it and making sure we didn't make any stupid mistakes was key. Fortunately I managed this, so I got past."

In fact, almost from the start, Kovalainen found himself struggling. Keeping your tyres in ideal condition in wet races is absolutely paramount, and it's a complicated equation that involves temperature, pressure and grip levels.

"I just struggled with my rear tyres all the way through the race, to be honest," said Kovalainen. "They were going away and I was damaging them excessively, and car control became difficult, so I had to slow down. This was the reason why I couldn't keep up.

"It looks like in low-grip conditions I put more load on the tyres. We saw that a little bit in Canada, I had more tyre wear than Lewis. And again in the rain when the grip is lower I put more load on them, especially the rear tyres."

Kovalainen slipped back and lost second place to Räikkönen on lap 10. At that stage, the reigning World Champion was 6.0s behind. The quickest man on the track at this stage, he then began to reel Hamilton in.

Hamilton suddenly realised that Räikkönen was getting too close for comfort, and he responded on laps 15 and 16 before the gap shrank again, to the point when it seemed that the Ferrari driver would try to find a way by. His advantage was in the second and third sectors, rather than the fast stuff at the start of the lap. In fact, like Kovalainen, the race leader was in tyre trouble, so a pit stop couldn't come too soon.

"I don't know if it was my line or what," said

BELOW Nick Heidfeld drove a sensible race and was rewarded with second place

BOTTOM Lewis Hamilton takes the lead from Heikki Kovalainen on lap 5 at Stowe and it was all Hamilton thereafter

OPPOSITE Rubens Barrichello profited from starting with a car set up for the wet, and might have come second if he hadn't been delayed by a fuel-rig problem

TALKING POINT
A COMEDY OF ERRORS

Lewis Hamilton's Silverstone win was fantastic, but...

In qualifying, Hamilton had been forced to give best to Heikki Kovalainen. His message to his crew on the race's slowdown lap was revealing: "It's been a tough weekend, guys, but we've done it!" The relief was almost palpable.

"I can't emphasise enough just how cool and collected Lewis stayed," McLaren CEO Martin Whitmarsh said. "He was under immense pressure, not only to get a result, but also not to make a mistake, in some of the trickiest conditions he has ever driven in."

Practically everyone else – driver, team or both – got it wrong somewhere. Rubens Barrichello and Honda were the exceptions and even they had a fuel-rig problem which prevented the Brazilian from finishing in second position.

Hamilton took the lead on lap 5, and by the time Kimi Räikkönen passed Kovalainen for second place was 6s in front. When they pitted together 11 laps later, though, the Finn was on the McLaren's gearbox. Ferrari opted not to change Räikkönen's intermediate Bridgestones and when

the rain started to fall again he was 5s off the pace, his challenge over.

Honda got the tyre calls absolutely right with Barrichello and Button, as did Williams with Rosberg and Nakajima, and Toro Rosso with Bourdais, who all stopped on lap 35. On lap 37, Hamilton's final lap before his second stop for fresh intermediates, he lapped in 1m54.6s and Barrichello did 1m41.2s on his extreme wets!

Hamilton, at that point, had a 26.5s lead over Nick Heidfeld's BMW, which also pitted on lap 38. The safe play may have been to put him on extremes to protect him from Barrichello and minimise the chances of him making a mistake but, had the track dried quicker, he would have needed to pit again for normal wets and would have been vulnerable to

Heidfeld. Barrichello took 15s out of Lewis over the next six laps and the call was undoubtedly the right one for Honda. It would probably have worked for Lewis too, but you can never second-guess the weather.

Hamilton's drive was talked of in similar terms to Ayrton Senna's at Donington Park in 1993. It's true that many of the potential threats were removed. Alonso, like Ferrari, didn't change tyres at the first stop. Webber, having put the Red Bull on the front row, spun on lap 1 and was then also left on worn intermediates after a superb recovery drive. One straight-on moment at Brooklands appeared to be the sole flaw in Hamilton's great drive. He finished 68s – better than a second per lap – ahead of Heidfeld, the only other error-free front-runner. That's how good Hamilton was.

ABOVE Reading the clouds was difficult, but keeping their cars on the island was harder still. Here are Räikkönen and Button mid-race

OPPOSITE TOP Jarno Trulli climbed from 14th to third, then fell back to seventh by the finish

OPPOSITE MIDDLE David Coulthard wanted to sign out in style, but his race didn't last a lap

OPPOSITE BOTTOM Fernando Alonso and Renault team-mate Nelson Piquet Jr lined up sixth and seventh, but only Alonso finished

Hamilton. "As soon as I got out of Turn 8 (Vale), I was really struggling. I don't know if my rear tyres were worse than his, they probably were because I was pushing quite hard at the beginning. Also, I was in such a good position, I didn't want to go off, so I was taking it easy in the last two sectors. I didn't know that he was catching me at the beginning, so I began to take it a little bit easy. I was comfortably quicker, and then he began to pick up pace."

Then they pitted together on lap 21. Hamilton managed to re-emerge still in the lead but, while they were on identical fuel strategies, McLaren and Ferrari had made very different calls on tyres. Hamilton had been given a fresh set of standard wets (intermediates), while Ferrari left Räikkönen on a set that had done 21 laps, more than a third of the race distance.

Ferrari must have known within half a lap that it had made the wrong call. Then, instead of coming around next time still on Hamilton's tail, Räikkönen dropped back. Over the next few laps, it was as if they were driving in different formulae, as in nine laps Kimi dropped more than 50s behind before he stopped for fresher tyres.

There was a reasonably heavy shower around laps 22–23, and that was enough to make Räikkönen's

worn inters utterly useless. The tyres would also have lost temperature while sitting on the car in the pits, and on the way in and out. On lap 20 they'd been good enough to allow him to outpace Hamilton, but by lap 22 they were well past their sell-by date. In contrast, the previously struggling Hamilton had a nice fresh set with full tread that proved just right for the conditions.

Ferrari wasn't the only team to get it wrong, but the others had a lot less to lose. Like everyone else, Ferrari relies on the FIA's weather information, and the team was convinced that it would not rain again. At Monaco, the team came to the opposite conclusion, fuelling its cars up on the premise that it *would* rain. On that occasion, it didn't. This time around, it did. Sometimes you can rely a little too much on science...

Ferrari then spent too much time calculating the pros and cons of stopping again instead of getting on and actually doing it. Räikkönen finally came in for fresh intermediate tyres on lap 30, and the team gave him enough fuel to get to the flag.

So, Hamilton's main rival was now out of the picture and, having survived the strongest possible pressure immediately before the pit stops, he now had to focus on Nick Heidfeld, who had taken new inters a lap after

INSIDE LINE
DAVID COULTHARD
RED BULL RACING DRIVER

"Retirement all sounds a bit final. I'm not looking at it like that. I will still have an involvement with Red Bull Racing and will probably also get involved with the team's testing programme.

If you look at sport, it's littered with people who didn't find the right time to stop. I've seen some people get to the point where they feel that they just can't do it anymore, or don't want to. That's not me. I still love my racing, I still really enjoy it, and I'm competitive. But you can't go on forever.

Other people retire from F1 with the regret that they never got an opportunity to perform in a competitive front-running car. That's not me. I've been runner-up in the championship, I've won 13 grands prix and I've been on pole a dozen times. I've had the pleasure of working with some great people in F1, like Frank Williams and Ron Dennis and all the staff at Williams and McLaren, and I'd like to thank people like David Leslie Senior and Junior and Jackie and Paul Stewart for all the help and support they gave me in the junior categories. And now, finishing my F1 racing career with Christian Horner, Adrian Newey and everyone at Red Bull has been a privilege too.

I'm just grateful for the opportunity to take the decision the way I have and to be able to race on until Brazil. I haven't got any concrete plans for the future as yet. Obviously I've seen the stories about a media role, but there's no hurry and I'm quite looking forward to the opportunity to take stock and see what the opportunities are. My fiancée Karen and I are also expecting a baby at the end of the year and I'm looking forward to becoming a father. There's no shortage of things happening!

Silverstone, of course, has got some great memories for me and it seemed as appropriate a place as any to announce my decision. I won the race here in 2000 and 2002, and I always have good support and a lot of family and friends at the race. I was hoping that my last British GP could be another memorable one, but that obviously wasn't in the stars! I wasn't expecting to win, but it would have been nice to last longer than three-quarters of a lap... Still, when you see a gap like that you have to go for it. I might be 37, but I'm still a racer!"

ABOVE Felipe Massa really struggled with the conditions, spinning his Ferrari five times...

BELOW Starting 16th but finishing third was the result of a superb drive from Rubens Barrichello and a great tyre call from Honda

he had. The gap to the BMW Sauber stayed within the 23–27s range for the next few laps as Hamilton consolidated his position.

Hamilton's serene progress was very nearly derailed when the heavy rains came on laps 35–36. This gave he and McLaren a serious headache, because it happened just before his second stop was due. Others changed on to extremes, but McLaren gave Hamilton another set of inters and fuel to go to the end. It was a difficult call.

The astonishing subsequent progress of Rubens Barrichello (and the pace of both Williams drivers) on extreme wets provided plenty of food for thought. But, when you're leading, choices aren't always so clear-cut.

"We didn't think it was going to rain that much," said Kovalainen, who really struggled when the track was at its wettest. "We just thought it was going to be a shower, and clear skies were going to come, and the extreme tyres were going to be a worse option. Perhaps we could have done it differently."

Hamilton did an impressive job with his inters. Significantly slower than the guys on extremes, he was also miles quicker than anyone else on inters. It was at this stage of the race that he secured his win, if nothing else simply by staying out of trouble, apart from one grassy trip at Abbey on lap 36, right at the start of the heavy rain. It says a lot that after his second stop his advantage over Heidfeld grew from 36s to 68s in the final third of the race, at a point when he was clearly pacing himself, at least by his standards.

"I couldn't see much, as my visor was a big problem," said Lewis. "I was just trying to stay calm with no mistakes, and that's why I kept building and building the gap."

It was an incredible performance, one that – after Fuji 2007 and Monaco 2008 – confirmed Hamilton as one of the greatest wet weather specialists we've seen. The chassis/tyre/strategy package has to be right, but you still need to get the job done.

"Lewis was very much in the sweet spot of performance during the race," said McLaren Chief Operating Officer Martin Whitmarsh. "His tyres stayed in good condition. We felt we had it covered and the team made all the right tactical and strategic decisions during the grand prix.

"I think Lewis had really found the grip today that others weren't finding. For most of the race we were trying to slow him down, and he could have driven the race a lot quicker than he was going..."

Heidfeld did a great job to retain second place to the flag, while there was a surprise behind as Barrichello used his stint on extreme wet tyres to work his way up to claim a popular third place for Honda, despite a delay in the pits caused by a fuel-rig problem. His team-mate Jenson Button had the same chance, but blew it with a spin.

Räikkönen survived a couple of rotations to take fourth place, while Kovalainen had several moments of his own on the way to a disappointed fifth. Fernando Alonso took sixth for Renault, delayed like Räikkönen by staying on old intermediates, while the final points went to Jarno Trulli and Kazuki Nakajima.

Many other drivers had tales of woe. Aside from Button, those whose races ended up in gravel traps included Robert Kubica, Timo Glock, David Coulthard, Giancarlo Fisichella, Nelson Piquet Jr, Adrian Sutil and Sebastian Vettel. But the biggest loser on the day was Felipe Massa, who spun to the back of the field on the opening lap and then had an astonishing series of mishaps, including four more spins, before bringing his car home 13th, two laps down on winner Hamilton.

The most amazing outcome of a race that marked the half-way point of the season was that it left Hamilton, Massa and Räikkönen level at the top on 48 points apiece, with Kubica still in the game on 46. This was shaping up to be some contest.

SNAPSHOT FROM
BRITAIN

CLOCKWISE FROM RIGHT Jenson Button sported an extra-patriotic helmet design for his home grand prix; will Donington Park also offer a camp site and golf course in 2010?; Jenson and Lewis Hamilton cosy up to David Coulthard after he announced that he would stop racing in F1 at the end of the season, but Lewis was later made to decline Jenson's offer of a triathlon shoot-out; Lewis was the centre of attraction wherever he went at Silverstone; thankfully the new technical regulations for 2009 won't change the cars into this, the latest Batmobile; considerable care and attention was put into the making of this banner to show a unilateral support for all drivers, as long as they were British...; the weather was mixed, but this smile was welcoming

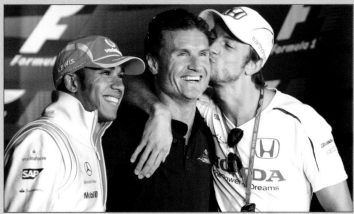

WEEKEND NEWS

■ The biggest story of the Silverstone weekend was the FIA's announcement on Friday that the British GP would be hosted by Donington Park from 2010. The 10-year deal was agreed with Bernie Ecclestone the previous day after the FOM boss decided that he'd waited long enough for a firm commitment from Silverstone owners the British Racing Drivers Club.

■ David Coulthard took the opportunity of his home race to announce that he would be retiring from driving at the end of the season, but would remain with Red Bull Racing as an advisor and test driver. DC had made the decision some months earlier, and had told RBR's management at the Canadian GP.

■ After all his problems with the media since the Canadian GP, Lewis Hamilton was dragged into another fine mess in a press conference on Thursday. Having suggested earlier in the week that he was fitter than Jenson Button, Lewis found himself agreeing to take on the aggrieved Honda racer in a triathlon. When Lewis's father Anthony reversed the decision, Lewis was portrayed as a wimp in Friday's papers...

■ As ever, the Silverstone paddock was chock-full with celebrities and VIPs who were keen to get some media coverage. However, one of the more unusual names went virtually unnoticed. Legendary pop artist Peter Blake was a guest of the Renault team, and he turned up on the grid to take a look at Fernando Alonso's car. His thoughts on its yellow, white, orange and blue livery went unrecorded...

■ A few days after the British GP, BMW Sauber became the second team (after Honda) to try a KERS system on track when Christian Klien did a shakedown test at the Miramas test track. Meanwhile, there was excitement at the Red Bull Racing factory when a KERS battery failed and led to a call out of the local fire brigade.

RACE RESULTS
GREAT BRITAIN
SILVERSTONE

Official Results © [2008]
Formula One Administration Limited,
6 Princes Gate, London, SW7 1QJ.
No reproduction without permission.
All copyright and database rights reserved.

RACE DATE July 6th
CIRCUIT LENGTH 3.194 miles
NO. OF LAPS 60
RACE DISTANCE 191.640 miles
WEATHER Overcast, then rain, 15°C
TRACK TEMP 16°C
RACE DAY ATTENDANCE 90,000
LAP RECORD Michael Schumacher
1m18.739s, 146.059mph, 2004

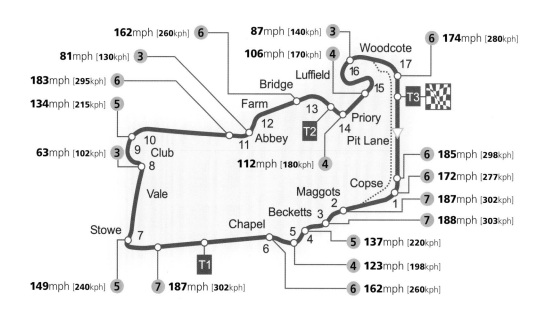

162mph [260kph] 6 — 87mph [140kph] 3 — Woodcote — 6 174mph [280kph]
81mph [130kph] 3 — 106mph [170kph] 4 — 16 — 17
183mph [295kph] 6 — Luffield — 15 — T3
134mph [215kph] 5 — Bridge — Farm — Priory
13 — 12 — 14 — Pit Lane
10 — 11 — Abbey — T2
63mph [102kph] 3 — 9 — Club — 6 185mph [298kph]
8 — 112mph [180kph] 4 — 6 172mph [277kph]
Vale — Copse — 7 187mph [302kph]
Maggots — 2 — 1 — 7 188mph [303kph]
Becketts — 3 — 5 137mph [220kph]
Chapel — 5 — 4 123mph [198kph]
Stowe — 7 — 4 — 6
149mph [240kph] 5 — T1 — 7 187mph [302kph] — 6 162mph [260kph]

PRACTICE 1

	Driver	Time	Laps
1	F Massa	1m19.575s	8
2	H Kovalainen	1m19.587s	15
3	L Hamilton	1m19.623s	13
4	K Räikkönen	1m19.948s	16
5	R Kubica	1m20.367s	11
6	F Alonso	1m20.436s	7
7	S Vettel	1m20.588s	18
8	N Piquet Jr	1m20.653s	16
9	D Coulthard	1m20.698s	16
10	N Rosberg	1m20.744s	27
11	M Webber	1m20.892s	10
12	T Glock	1m21.102s	22
13	N Heidfeld	1m21.107s	18
14	S Bourdais	1m21.166s	17
15	J Trulli	1m21.265s	22
16	K Nakajima	1m21.282s	21
17	J Button	1m21.901s	7
18	A Sutil	1m22.169s	16
19	G Fisichella	1m22.219s	19
20	R Barrichello	1m24.123s	4

PRACTICE 2

	Driver	Time	Laps
1	H Kovalainen	1m19.989s	35
2	M Webber	1m20.520s	32
3	L Hamilton	1m20.543s	31
4	D Coulthard	1m20.589s	36
5	N Rosberg	1m20.748s	43
6	S Vettel	1m20.805s	43
7	J Button	1m20.929s	39
8	F Massa	1m20.943s	18
9	K Nakajima	1m20.985s	18
10	R Barrichello	1m21.002s	34
11	R Kubica	1m21.023s	33
12	K Räikkönen	1m21.275s	31
13	N Heidfeld	1m21.453s	36
14	T Glock	1m21.472s	18
15	F Alonso	1m21.511s	27
16	G Fisichella	1m21.520s	42
17	S Bourdais	1m21.634s	39
18	N Piquet Jr	1m21.642s	45
19	A Sutil	1m21.756s	30
20	J Trulli	1m22.196s	23

PRACTICE 3

	Driver	Time	Laps
1	F Alonso	1m20.740s	16
2	M Webber	1m20.988s	18
3	H Kovalainen	1m21.266s	14
4	S Vettel	1m21.277s	19
5	L Hamilton	1m21.668s	14
6	N Piquet Jr	1m21.786s	14
7	S Bourdais	1m22.059s	21
8	T Glock	1m22.183s	21
9	K Räikkönen	1m22.355s	20
10	R Barrichello	1m22.387s	17
11	J Button	1m22.440s	19
12	F Massa	1m22.461s	20
13	N Rosberg	1m22.544s	18
14	J Trulli	1m22.556s	20
15	N Heidfeld	1m22.916s	22
16	K Nakajima	1m23.028s	17
17	A Sutil	1m23.049s	22
18	G Fisichella	1m23.112s	21
19	R Kubica	1m23.282s	20
20	D Coulthard	1m32.119s	6

QUALIFYING 1

	Driver	Time
1	H Kovalainen	1m19.957s
2	L Hamilton	1m20.288s
3	S Vettel	1m20.318s
4	K Räikkönen	1m20.370s
5	R Kubica	1m20.444s
6	S Bourdais	1m20.584s
7	F Massa	1m20.676s
8	N Piquet Jr	1m20.818s
9	T Glock	1m20.893s
10	M Webber	1m20.982s
11	F Alonso	1m20.998s
12	N Heidfeld	1m21.022s
13	J Trulli	1m21.145s
14	D Coulthard	1m21.224s
15	K Nakajima	1m21.407s
16	R Barrichello	1m21.512s
17	J Button	1m21.631s
18	N Rosberg	1m21.668s
19	A Sutil	1m21.786s
20	G Fisichella	1m21.885s

QUALIFYING 2

	Driver	Time
1	L Hamilton	1m19.537s
2	H Kovalainen	1m19.597s
3	M Webber	1m19.710s
4	R Kubica	1m19.788s
5	N Heidfeld	1m19.802s
6	K Räikkönen	1m19.971s
7	F Alonso	1m19.992s
8	F Massa	1m20.086s
9	S Vettel	1m20.109s
10	N Piquet Jr	1m20.115s
11	D Coulthard	1m20.174s
12	T Glock	1m20.274s
13	S Bourdais	1m20.531s
14	J Trulli	1m20.601s
15	K Nakajima	1m21.112s

Best sectors – Practice
Sec 1	K Räikkönen	25.076s
Sec 2	L Hamilton	34.202s
Sec 3	F Massa	19.886s

Speed trap – Practice
1	H Kovalainen	185.914mph
2	L Hamilton	185.790mph
3	K Räikkönen	185.293mph

Best sectors – Qualifying
Sec 1	L Hamilton	25.200s
Sec 2	R Kubica	34.259s
Sec 3	H Kovalainen	19.735s

Speed trap – Qualifying
1	K Räikkönen	187.095mph
2	L Hamilton	186.100mph
3	F Alonso	185.541mph

Kimi Räikkönen
"I am disappointed, but know that things could have been much worse. We had a chance to win, but made a mistake at the first stop, keeping on the same set of tyres."

Nick Heidfeld
"We were wondering if we should stay with used inters, but decided on new tyres. There was so much water and I couldn't see where it was. I almost spun before Abbey."

Fernando Alonso
"I had said that when it rains, anything can happen. I used up my tyres very quickly and finished the race virtually with slicks, which meant I lost a lot of time in places."

Nico Rosberg
"We came in for extreme wets at the right moment. Then, it was going well until I hit Timo. He was going much slower than me and I had planned to pass on the inside."

David Coulthard
"I was close to Sebastian after Abbey, as he had a wobble. There was a gap down the inside, but it closed as I made the move. I'm sorry for him that we collided."

Jarno Trulli
"I'd made it to third when heavy rain fell. At that point, I was aquaplaning. We should have gambled on the extreme wet. It's a pity as I could have made the podium."

Felipe Massa
"I had an accident, there was the problem in qualifying and today a series of mistakes. I could hardly keep the car straight. Only after the last stop did things improve."

Robert Kubica
"I was aquaplaning, then I lost it. Everything was going well and I was gaining places, but there was a lot of water and I couldn't even keep the car in a straight line."

Nelson Piquet Jr
"The car was good, our strategy was perfect and we were set for a great result. However, the track was flooded, even on the straights. It was impossible to control."

Kazuki Nakajima
"It was good to score a point, but it was a shame to lose seventh to Jarno on the last lap. His tyres were in a better condition than mine, and he was just a bit quicker than me."

Mark Webber
"I dropped it on the entrance to Becketts on lap 1. I was close to Kimi and got on the white line. I lost the car and had to let the field go past, so it was clear to spin round."

Timo Glock
"I focused on looking after my tyres during the first stint. When the rain came, I had no traction. There was aquaplaning and I had no chance to stay on the track."

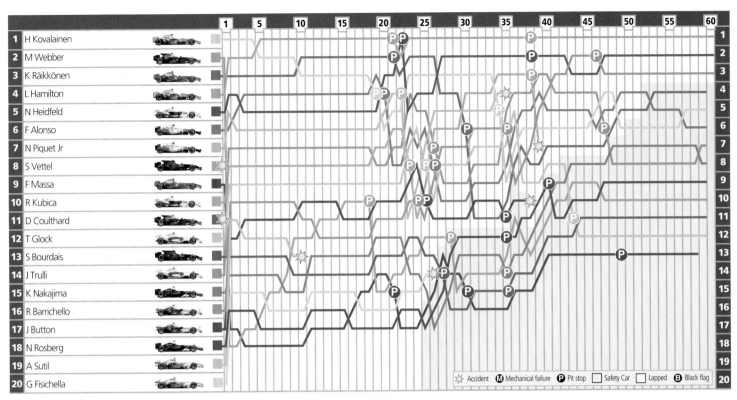

1	H Kovalainen	
2	M Webber	
3	K Räikkönen	
4	L Hamilton	
5	N Heidfeld	
6	F Alonso	
7	N Piquet Jr	
8	S Vettel	
9	F Massa	
10	R Kubica	
11	D Coulthard	
12	T Glock	
13	S Bourdais	
14	J Trulli	
15	K Nakajima	
16	R Barrichello	
17	J Button	
18	N Rosberg	
19	A Sutil	
20	G Fisichella	

Legend: ☆ Accident　Ⓜ Mechanical failure　Ⓟ Pit stop　☐ Safety Car　☐ Lapped　Ⓑ Black flag

QUALIFYING 3

	Driver	Time
1	H Kovalainen	1m21.049s
2	M Webber	1m21.554s
3	K Räikkönen	1m21.706s
4	L Hamilton	1m21.835s
5	N Heidfeld	1m21.873s
6	F Alonso	1m22.029s
7	N Piquet Jr	1m22.491s
8	S Vettel	1m23.251s
9	F Massa	1m23.305s
10	R Kubica	No time

GRID

	Driver	Time
1	H Kovalainen	1m21.049s
2	M Webber	1m21.554s
3	K Räikkönen	1m21.706s
4	L Hamilton	1m21.835s
5	N Heidfeld	1m21.873s
6	F Alonso	1m22.029s
7	N Piquet Jr	1m22.491s
8	S Vettel	1m23.251s
9	F Massa	1m23.305s
10	R Kubica	No time
11	D Coulthard	1m20.174s
12	T Glock	1m20.274s
13	S Bourdais	1m20.531s
14	J Trulli	1m20.601s
15	K Nakajima	1m21.112s
16	R Barrichello	1m21.512s
17	J Button	1m21.631s
18	A Sutil	1m21.786s
19	G Fisichella	1m21.885s
20*	N Rosberg	1m21.668s

* STARTED FROM THE PITLANE

RACE

	Driver	Car	Laps	Time	Avg. mph	Fastest	Stops
1	L Hamilton	McLaren-Mercedes MP4-23	60	1h39m09.440s	115.938	1m32.817s	2
2	N Heidfeld	BMW Sauber F1.08	60	1h40m18.017s	114.617	1m32.719s	2
3	R Barrichello	Honda RA108	60	1h40m31.713s	114.357	1m33.386s	3
4	K Räikkönen	Ferrari F2008	59	1h39m15.496s	113.889	1m32.150s	2
5	H Kovalainen	McLaren-Mercedes MP4-23	59	1h39m22.910s	113.747	1m33.130s	2
6	F Alonso	Renault R28	59	1h39m25.831s	113.692	1m33.133s	2
7	J Trulli	Toyota TF108	59	1h39m26.912s	113.672	1m33.808s	2
8	K Nakajima	Williams-Toyota FW30	59	1h39m28.098s	113.649	1m34.277s	2
9	N Rosberg	Williams-Toyota FW30	59	1h39m28.990s	113.632	1m34.797s	3
10	M Webber	Red Bull-Renault RB4	59	1h39m42.269s	113.380	1m32.952s	2
11	S Bourdais	Toro Rosso-Ferrari STR03	59	1h39m53.350s	113.170	1m33.367s	2
12	T Glock	Toyota TF108	59	1h40m19.115s	112.685	1m34.610s	2
13	F Massa	Ferrari F2008	58	1h39m45.994s	111.388	1m33.257s	3
R	R Kubica	BMW Sauber F1.08	39	Spun off	-	1m33.257s	2
R	J Button	Honda RA108	38	Spun off	-	1m33.376s	2
R	N Piquet Jr	Renault R28	35	Spun off	-	1m33.203s	1
R	G Fisichella	Force India-Ferrari VJM01	26	Spun off	-	1m34.930s	0
R	A Sutil	Force India-Ferrari VJM01	10	Spun off	-	1m38.160s	0
R	S Vettel	Toro Rosso-Ferrari STR03	0	Spun off	-	-	0
R	D Coulthard	Red Bull-Renault RB4	0	Spun off	-	-	0

CHAMPIONSHIP

	Driver	Pts
1	L Hamilton	48
2	F Massa	48
3	K Räikkönen	48
4	R Kubica	46
5	N Heidfeld	36
6	H Kovalainen	24
7	J Trulli	20
8	M Webber	18
9	F Alonso	13
10	R Barrichello	11
11	N Rosberg	8
12	K Nakajima	8
13	D Coulthard	6
14	T Glock	5
15	S Vettel	5
16	J Button	3
17	S Bourdais	2
18	N Piquet Jr	2

Fastest Lap
K Räikkönen 1m32.150s
(124.797mph) on lap 18

Fastest speed trap
T Glock　170.380mph

Slowest speed trap
S Vettel　122.286mph

Fastest pit stop
1	J Trulli	24.088s
2	F Massa	24.643s
3	T Glock	24.726s

	Constructor	Pts
1	Ferrari	96
2	BMW Sauber	82
3	McLaren-Mercedes	72
4	Toyota	25
5	Red Bull-Renault	24
6	Williams-Toyota	16
7	Renault	15
8	Honda	14
9	Toro Rosso-Ferrari	7

Sebastien Bourdais

"I couldn't see at the start as the water wasn't clearing off my visor. Putting the extreme wets on was a good call and the car was quick, but it was too late to do much."

Jenson Button

"We had good pace before the heavy rain that brought us into the pits for extreme wets. Shortly after that, I hit standing water at Bridge which caused the car to go off."

Adrian Sutil

"At the time of my spin, the track was starting to dry and it was tricky to tell where the wet patches were. I hit on one of these puddles and aquaplaned off. It was a shame."

Lewis Hamilton

"This was one of my best races. It was so slippery. I had troubles with my visor. When I came round the last time, I saw the crowd and I prayed: 'Just finish, just finish'."

Sebastian Vettel

"Massa spun into Bridge which caused a lot of confusion behind. Then at Priory, I got hit on the rear left and it spun me around. I tried to save it, but I stuck in the gravel."

Rubens Barrichello

"It's great to be back on the podium after the conditions helped us get the best out of the car. After fitting extreme wets, I was able to overtake the cars in front easily."

Giancarlo Fisichella

"I lost control going through the complex, as there was graining due to the fuel load I was carrying to be as flexible as possible. The grip level was zero and I spun."

Heikki Kovalainen

"Congratulations to Lewis on his win. I had a good start and, for a few laps, Lewis was pushing, passing me on lap 5 when I ran wide. I spun twice but I wasn't alone."

FORMULA 1 GROSSER PREIS VON DEUTSCHLAND 2008
HOCKENHEIM

LEWIS ON A CHARGE

Lewis Hamilton built a big lead, but the arrival of the safety car after Timo Glock shunted his Toyota left him with it all to do, with Nelson Piquet Jr lucking into a surprise second place

Lewis Hamilton followed his Silverstone success with another memorable win in the German GP at Hockenheim, a result that moved him four points clear in the title battle as the World Championship entered its second half. The victory was much tougher than it should have been for Hamilton, though, after a safety-car period cost him his hard-earned lead and McLaren took a strategy gamble that nearly backfired and left him to put on a stunning recovery drive to regain the lead.

After the race, Ron Dennis made it clear that the decision to leave Hamilton out while others pitted had been generated by his strategists back in the UK. Clearly there are many sound reasons for having this extra support, but there are times when those guys simply don't have all the information to be able to make the right call, and perhaps, this was one of those occasions.

The threatened rain stayed away in qualifying, but overcast and windy conditions made life difficult for all the drivers. Hamilton's pole was the perfect present for Mercedes at the company's home track, while third place for Heikki Kovalainen added to the team's joy. The Finn ran wide onto the gravel on his first run, so he could not afford any errors on his second outing.

TALKING POINT
VETTEL IS BIG NEWS

With a quarter of the F1 grid hailing from Germany, it was no surprise that Red Bull chose Hockenheim to announce that 21-year-old Sebastian Vettel would be promoted from Scuderia Toro Rosso to the Red Bull Racing senior team alongside Mark Webber in 2009.

After David Coulthard announced his decision to quit F1 at the end of the year at the British GP, it was logical that Vettel, the stand-out among those on the Red Bull development programme, would be the man to fill the void.

"It's a coup for the team," Webber said. "Sebastian is the first real Red Bull-backed driver to come through who has the talent to back the cash." He'd obviously had a little time since their tangle at Fuji last year to reconsider his opinion about the young German…

Almost immediately, there was healthy paddock speculation about which one would come out on top. Since Webber came into F1, he has always outpaced the man on the other side of his garage. Team-mates he has got the better of include many who were/are highly rated – Antonio Pizzonia, Justin Wilson, Nick Heidfeld, Nico Rosberg and Coulthard. Vettel, meanwhile, is viewed by some as the next Michael Schumacher. The only thing that makes you wonder – if he was that quick, why did BMW ever let him out of their clutches? Because Kubica was the yardstick and Heidfeld was already contracted?

Webber said with a wry smile: "If he blows me away, people will say Webber's past it, but if I blow him away then people will say Vettel's not quick. That's normal: I had that with Rosberg…"

The rivalry started sooner than expected when Webber and Vettel qualified eighth and ninth, split by just a quarter of a second, and then Vettel beat Webber off the line and ran ahead until the first round of pit stops. Webber then suffered his first mechanical failure of the year when debris from Timo Glock's accident punctured an oil cooler. Vettel delighted Toro Rosso with a point on merit.

"My target is to move up the field and keep getting better," said Vettel about his graduation to the senior team. "If you look at Red Bull's results, you can see a clear tendency that they are going in the right direction, so I'm pleased."

Since the arrival of the STR03, Scuderia Toro Rosso has taken a quantum step. "Hmmm," someone said on Sunday night, "The STR03 is basically a Red Bull with a Ferrari engine. When Vettel gets a Renault behind his shoulders instead, I wonder if he's still going to think of it as a promotion…"

The McLaren pair were split by Felipe Massa, who once again was the quicker of the Ferrari drivers. Struggling to find a balance, Kimi Räikkönen had a disappointing day and found himself bumped down to sixth. A surprise fourth on the grid went to Toyota's Jarno Trulli, while Fernando Alonso jumped up to fifth for Renault. BMW Sauber had a poor day, and Robert Kubica qualified only seventh.

Hamilton got away at the start and soon began pulling away from Massa. He was 11s clear when he came in for his first pit stop – a little prematurely to avoid the risk of a safety-car deployment – on lap 19. He took on a relatively large fuel load for a long middle stint. Massa ran a couple of laps further and that, combined with the fact that Hamilton spent longer at rest, helped him to close the gap to 8s. Lewis then edged it back out to 11s, where it stabilised for a few laps.

Then, on lap 35, Timo Glock had a huge accident on the pit straight, after his right rear suspension failed as he ran wide over the kerbs. The Toyota spun hard into the pit wall and sailed down the straight, giving Mark Webber and others in close pursuit a fright. Inevitably a safety car was called for, and instantly Hamilton's lead was cut to nothing. As the cars toured around awaiting the opening of the pitlane, the teams had plenty of time to do their sums. There were some 30 laps remaining, and logic suggested that it was the perfect time to come in and refuel for a run to the end.

And that's what all but three drivers did. To the astonishment of most observers, Hamilton stayed out. The pitlane was briefly full of traffic as some teams – such as Ferrari – had to double-shuffle their cars, keeping Räikkönen waiting behind Massa.

When the dust settled and the pitted cars rejoined the queue, Hamilton was still at the front, ahead of Nick Heidfeld (who had jumped up the order by

not pitting) and Nelson Piquet Jr. In fact, the Renault man had run an extra-long first stint and was due to make his single stop on the lap of the accident. He managed to duck into the pitlane before the safety car was officially dispatched and the pitlane closed, and thus filled up for the run to the end. Having started 17th and passed only one car (a spinning Kazuki Nakajima's Williams), he was third. And the two guys in front were both due a pit stop…

The remaining laps run during the safety-car deployment gave Hamilton plenty of time to think things through. What was going on here?

"There was no worry about the tyres, but they

INSIDE LINE
NELSON PIQUET JR
RENAULT DRIVER

"A podium is a really great result for me. Obviously, I had a bit of luck with the safety car coming out, but I was strong in the second stint and handled the pressure. I'm not saying that one second place is going to change a lot, but it was a really great feeling!

The car felt good in Friday practice and again on Saturday morning. Our set-up was working well and Fernando [Alonso] even took a bit of it because I think they'd gone in the wrong direction a little on his set-up.

In Q1, though, I didn't have a very good first run, had traffic on my second attempt and that was it: I was starting 17th and figured it was the end of my weekend.

However, with these safety-car rules you can get lucky, and we started with the flexibility to go for one stop or two. If we'd gone with an aggressive short first stint to try to overtake people, there is no way I'd have made the podium. As it was, I struggled a bit at the start, had a lock-up, was sliding everywhere and got mixed up at the

back. But the team brought me in at exactly the right moment and after the safety car, on the soft tyres, the car felt really good.

The safety car gave me the opportunity to bring the soft tyres in well. I knew I had to get to the end – 32 laps away – and so I didn't push them too much at first. When I was leading, I knew that Lewis [Hamilton] was catching up quickly, but I knew also that Felipe [Massa] wasn't that much quicker than me. I didn't want to have a big battle with Lewis, lose time and possibly have an incident, and allow Felipe to take advantage. Lewis was so much quicker than us that if I'd fought him there would have been a big risk.

I decided that a safe second place was better than finishing third

or fourth and being unhappy. So I just maintained pace, made sure I didn't make a mistake and kept the rear tyres alive.

I didn't know it was the last lap, as I was concentrating so much, but when I saw Lewis back off and then the chequered flag it felt amazing! I've had difficulty getting the best out of the tyres in qualifying sometimes, and getting a podium is good for the confidence. It also pushed the team up a bit in the championship. The car needs to improve, I need to improve, but the team is doing a great job."

strongly felt it was easy enough for us to pull out the gap!," he said later. "They clearly had so much confidence in me, but this sort of thing happens..."

Clearly, the team considered that everyone else would be heavier, and while they were all on newer tyres, chances are they would be the less favourable tyre types of that particular team or driver. The one thing that nobody knew, and which the guys in Woking had less chance of ascertaining than those on the pit wall, was how long the safety-car period would last. In fact, it stretched out to six laps.

When they did the sums, they thought Hamilton would have more laps in which to rebuild his lead.

So, every lap of safety-car running reduced that window (but in effect only by around half a lap, thanks to fuel saving while running slowly allowing him to stop later than scheduled). When the race finally went green at the start of lap 42, Hamilton had just nine laps with which to play before he would have to pit.

Even allowing for everyone else bar Heidfeld carrying the extra payload of 17 laps' worth of fuel, opening up 23s – on whoever was the next driver without a pit stop to make – was an impossible ask. It certainly didn't help that his tyres had been on the car since the start of lap 19, and had gone through that cycle of cooling off behind the safety car.

BELOW The tension is clear as the Renault crew waits to see if Piquet Jr can hang on

"As I started to extend my gap, I could see the people behind. It was hard for the first couple of laps, because the tyres were cold as the safety car was so slow. I was pulling out a good gap, but it was 13s, 13 and a bit, and it wasn't enough. I needed 23s. It was 'how am I going to get it?' So I made sure I got my pit entry and pit exit right, the pit stop was great, and I was on it. This is business time!"

In fact, when the time to stop came on lap 50, Hamilton had managed to open out only 4.8s on Heidfeld and 13.8s on Piquet Jr who, to most people's surprise, had stayed in front of Massa. Hamilton came out of the pits having dropped to fifth, right on the tail of his own team-mate. Had it been anybody else, he might have had a little more trouble, but after a lap the Finn prudently ran wide and invited him through.

Heidfeld ran three more laps before stopping, and wasn't too far off getting out in front of Hamilton. But he was out of the picture now, and with 13 laps to go Hamilton was 2.5s off Massa who was compromised by brake problems. He soon closed him down and aggressively barged past.

"I clearly had much better pace than him. I managed to get a good exit from the last corner, following him though Turn 1 and Turn 2, got a good exit and slipstreamed him. But I couldn't pull alongside him as they were very quick at the end of the straight.

"So I just pulled to the inside and had to outbrake him. In doing so, he braked very late as well. We both locked up and went a bit straight. I just had to cover my ground and got a good exit. He came back at the next exit, which was good of him. He was very fair..."

It took another three laps to catch and pass Piquet Jr who, to his great credit, was driving superbly on the softer tyres. On lap 60, Hamilton dived inside the Renault, and that was it, job done with seven laps to go.

"Nelsinho is very hard to overtake, but it was pretty straightforward. It didn't have to be do-or-die, I had easily got the pace. I positioned my car perfectly, and it was 'I'm coming past', full stop. It was a really good battle, they were very fair, and I enjoy that. But I had thought the job was done once I'd got past Felipe, I was like are you kidding me?"

Hamilton made it look easy, and given that of the three cars he had to pass one was his team-mate, one

TOP Hamilton pulls off the move of the race as he dives inside Felipe Massa at the hairpin

ABOVE LEFT Robert Kubica's title charge lost momentum here

ABOVE RIGHT Timo Glock's battered Toyota is winched clear after its clash with the pit wall

with them, and I knew I would have to keep them to the end, so I kept them cool. Obviously I was pushing, but I was making sure I wasn't locking the fronts. I put the brake bias a bit to the rear just not to lock the fronts and have a flat spot. I just kept it safe on the track."

Not stopping during the safety-car deployment allowed Heidfeld to jump up to fourth, ahead of Kovalainen. By not bringing in both McLarens together, the team may have ensured that Kovalainen ended up better off by a position or two.

Double-stacked behind Massa, Räikkönen lost five places after the safety car, to Trulli, Vettel, Alonso, Webber and Rosberg. Webber retired before the restart with an oil leak caused by Glock's debris, and Räikkönen managed to get past all of them – plus Kubica – to claim sixth. Had he been forced to wait behind Hamilton, Kovalainen would have been in a similar situation, and there was certainly no guarantee that he would have made it back to the fifth place he eventually claimed.

Kubica took a frustrated seventh place after struggling with his tyres in the last stint, while the final point went to Vettel, who had aggressively edged Alonso out of the way during the mass exodus from the pitlane. In fact, the Spaniard tumbled down to a mediocre 11th, behind Trulli and Rosberg.

It had been a close call for Hamilton, and he was aware that to win the title he was going to need some days when it all just fell into place, and he was not teetering on the brink of disaster.

"I was left to do an almost impossible job, but I managed to pull it off," he said. "We will go back and have a chat. But, at the end of the day, we won and without the superb job they did preparing the car, we wouldn't have been able to win. There's no blaming anyone, we all still did a solid job."

ABOVE Hamilton is both exhilarated and relieved, Piquet Jr delighted and Massa stunned

BELOW Not pitting under the safety car helped Nick Heidfeld to claim an eventual fourth place

was struggling with brake problems, and the other had qualified 17th, perhaps it was. It could all have gone horribly wrong, though. Far more risks were introduced by not stopping when the others did, and contact with Massa could have ended it all. Still, it worked, he won, and the 10 points were in the bank.

Piquet Jr took second, an amazing result considering that he was running only 18th in the first part of the race! He even managed to stay ahead of Massa.

"When I put the soft tyres on, I knew I had to push to the end, and I knew I was in a good position," said the delighted Brazilian. "I knew I had to be gentle

SNAPSHOT FROM
GERMANY

CLOCKWISE FROM RIGHT
Michael Schumacher's legacy
is clear by the fact that Ferrari
caps are still the ones of choice
in Germany; a Renault mechanic
prays for Nelson Piquet Jr to
hold on to second; Timo Glock
plays chauffeur; three-time World
Champion Niki Lauda loved racing
in a re-enactment of the BMW
Procar series that last raced in
1980; McLaren drivers old and
new – Mika Häkkinen and Lewis
Hamilton; Renault's Flavio Briatore
helps celebrate the July birthdays
of his drivers Nelson Piquet Jr and
Fernando Alonso; a pretty face in
the paddock

WEEKEND NEWS

■ Red Bull Racing followed up David Coulthard's retirement announcement at the British Grand Prix at
Silverstone with the not unexpected news that Sebastian Vettel would be promoted from Scuderia Toro
Rosso to Red Bull's 'senior' team for 2009, to partner Mark Webber.

■ Physiotherapist Balbir Singh returned to the Hockenheim paddock at the German Grand Prix in a new
role at Force India Formula One, working with Giancarlo Fisichella. Singh had been one of Michael
Schumacher's closest aides from the start of his Ferrari career at the end of 1995 until the end of 2005,
when he decided to quit in order to spend more time with his family in Germany.

■ The week after the German Grand Prix, Justice David Eady announced his verdict in Max Mosley's privacy
action against the *News of the World*, awarding the FIA president £60,000 in damages. Mosley quickly
announced that he was going to follow up with a libel action against the same newspaper.

■ KERS was in the news again after a battery explosion in the Red Bull Racing factory led to an evacuation
and the arrival of the emergency services at the team's Milton Keynes base. Two days after the German
Grand Prix, BMW Sauber ran a KERS-equipped F1.07 in public for the first time at the Jerez test, but the car
was put away after a mechanic suffered an electric shock.

■ BMW celebrated the 30th anniversary of its M1 sportscar model with a pair of Procar demonstrations on
Saturday and Sunday. Niki Lauda, Marc Surer and Christian Danner were among the contenders from the
original series in 1979/80 to participate in the demonstrations, while former BMW motorsport chief and
series founder Jochen Neerpasch drove the famous Andy Warhol-liveried car.

RACE RESULTS
GERMANY HOCKENHEIM

Official Results © [2008]
Formula One Administration Limited,
6 Princes Gate, London, SW7 1QJ.
No reproduction without permission.
All copyright and database rights reserved.

RACE DATE July 20th
CIRCUIT LENGTH 2.842 miles
NO. OF LAPS 67
RACE DISTANCE 190.414 miles
WEATHER Cloudy & dry, 24°C
TRACK TEMP 29°C
RACE DAY ATTENDANCE 115,000
LAP RECORD Kimi Räikkönen,
1m14.917s, 138.685mph, 2004

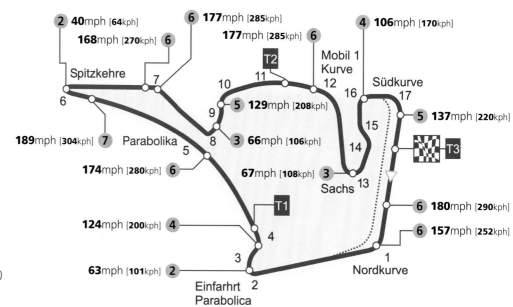

	PRACTICE 1				PRACTICE 2				PRACTICE 3				QUALIFYING 1			QUALIFYING 2	
	Driver	Time	Laps		Driver	Time	Laps		Driver	Time	Laps		Driver	Time		Driver	Time
1	L Hamilton	1m15.537s	22	1	L Hamilton	1m15.025s	37	1	H Kovalainen	1m15.621s	18	1	F Massa	1m14.921s	1	L Hamilton	1m14.603s
2	H Kovalainen	1m15.666s	19	2	F Massa	1m15.722s	31	2	F Massa	1m15.693s	21	2	K Räikkönen	1m15.201s	2	F Massa	1m14.747s
3	F Massa	1m15.796s	22	3	K Räikkönen	1m15.760s	34	3	L Hamilton	1m15.839s	21	3	L Hamilton	1m15.218s	3	H Kovalainen	1m14.855s
4	F Alonso	1m16.163s	22	4	H Kovalainen	1m15.990s	37	4	F Alonso	1m15.943s	18	4	H Kovalainen	1m15.476s	4	F Alonso	1m14.943s
5	K Räikkönen	1m16.327s	23	5	M Webber	1m16.017s	25	5	S Vettel	1m16.037s	24	5	S Vettel	1m15.532s	5	K Räikkönen	1m14.949s
6	N Rosberg	1m16.606s	27	6	F Alonso	1m16.230s	38	6	J Trulli	1m16.133s	25	6	J Trulli	1m15.560s	6	R Kubica	1m15.109s
7	S Vettel	1m16.618s	25	7	N Rosberg	1m16.355s	41	7	N Piquet Jr	1m16.161s	21	7	T Glock	1m15.560s	7	J Trulli	1m15.122s
8	N Heidfeld	1m16.719s	20	8	R Kubica	1m16.363s	36	8	M Webber	1m16.196s	19	8	N Heidfeld	1m15.596s	8	D Coulthard	1m15.338s
9	K Nakajima	1m16.821s	26	9	N Heidfeld	1m16.377s	40	9	K Räikkönen	1m16.380s	19	9	N Rosberg	1m15.863s	9	S Vettel	1m15.420s
10	N Piquet Jr	1m17.063s	26	10	D Coulthard	1m16.378s	35	10	N Rosberg	1m16.405s	20	10	M Webber	1m15.900s	10	M Webber	1m15.481s
11	D Coulthard	1m17.108s	18	11	S Vettel	1m16.422s	41	11	J Button	1m16.447s	22	11	F Alonso	1m15.917s	11	T Glock	1m15.508s
12	J Button	1m17.131s	28	12	J Trulli	1m16.530s	45	12	D Coulthard	1m16.515s	19	12	S Bourdais	1m15.927s	12	N Heidfeld	1m15.581s
13	T Glock	1m17.185s	28	13	J Button	1m16.542s	38	13	K Nakajima	1m16.530s	18	13	D Coulthard	1m15.975s	13	N Rosberg	1m15.633s
14	M Webber	1m17.268s	11	14	R Barrichello	1m16.677s	28	14	T Glock	1m16.636s	27	14	R Kubica	1m15.985s	14	J Button	1m15.701s
15	G Fisichella	1m17.471s	30	15	N Piquet Jr	1m16.734s	42	15	S Bourdais	1m16.808s	23	15	J Button	1m15.993s	15	S Bourdais	1m15.858s
16	R Barrichello	1m17.500s	24	16	T Glock	1m16.781s	44	16	N Heidfeld	1m16.906s	24	16	K Nakajima	1m16.083s			
17	J Trulli	1m17.556s	29	17	K Nakajima	1m16.829s	21	17	A Sutil	1m16.938s	20	17	N Piquet Jr	1m16.189s			
18	A Sutil	1m17.784s	29	18	S Bourdais	1m16.860s	14	18	R Barrichello	1m17.189s	20	18	R Barrichello	1m16.246s			
19	R Kubica	1m18.779s	8	19	A Sutil	1m17.008s	39	19	G Fisichella	1m17.312s	22	19	A Sutil	1m16.657s			
20	S Bourdais	1m21.506s	16	20	G Fisichella	1m17.047s	37	20	R Kubica	1m17.469s	15	20	G Fisichella	1m16.963s			

Best sectors – Practice			Speed trap – Practice			Best sectors – Qualifying			Speed trap – Qualifying		
Sec 1	L Hamilton	16.373s	1	F Massa	197.782mph	Sec 1	L Hamilton	16.276s	1	F Massa	198.341mph
Sec 2	L Hamilton	35.775s	2	K Räikkönen	196.974mph	Sec 2	L Hamilton	35.669s	2	K Räikkönen	197.968mph
Sec 3	L Hamilton	22.877s	3	K Nakajima	196.104mph	Sec 3	L Hamilton	22.615s	3	A Sutil	196.850mph

Kimi Räikkönen
"We have struggled all weekend. Usually, our race pace is good, but that was not the case, as I suffered with a lack of grip: only in the final stages did the situation improve."

Nick Heidfeld
"Not making the top 10 meant we were free to choose our fuel load, and so we went for a long first stint. That's why I was able to stay out during the safety-car period."

Fernando Alonso
"That was a difficult race for me. I had a bad start and lost several positions. Then I was on the pace, but it was difficult to recover. I think we were simply out of luck."

Nico Rosberg
"It was a bit difficult at the start, as I had a technical problem at the start which cost me a place. From then on I was able to push hard when I had free track."

David Coulthard
"Heidfeld put me wide at Turn 1, so people got by. Late on, Rubens got better traction. I came back on to my line to take the corner and he thought I wasn't going to."

Jarno Trulli
"It was looking good, but after our second stop, when we switched strategy because of the safety car, it became difficult. I was in eighth, holding off Vettel but I locked up."

Felipe Massa
"Hamilton's pace was unbeatable and I never had good grip. In the final stages, I had brake problems and wasn't able to attack Piquet, who I congratulate on his podium."

Robert Kubica
"I was able to match the pace of McLaren and Ferrari. Suddenly my car's pace was way too slow. My tyres lost lots of grip, perhaps because they cooled too much."

Nelson Piquet Jr
"I'm very happy! After qualifying, I thought my weekend was over, but we went for an aggressive strategy and we made great decisions when the safety car came out."

Kazuki Nakajima
"It would have helped if the safety car had stayed out a bit longer so I could have made my stop. Then, in the last stint, I picked up some debris and lost a place."

Mark Webber
"I had a good fight with Vettel on the first lap and, as the race unfolded, there wasn't much between the cars. It was my first mechanical retirement this year."

Timo Glock
"I was going well but ran a little wide at the last corner and felt the back of the car go. It was a really hard impact and my back hurt immediately after I got out."

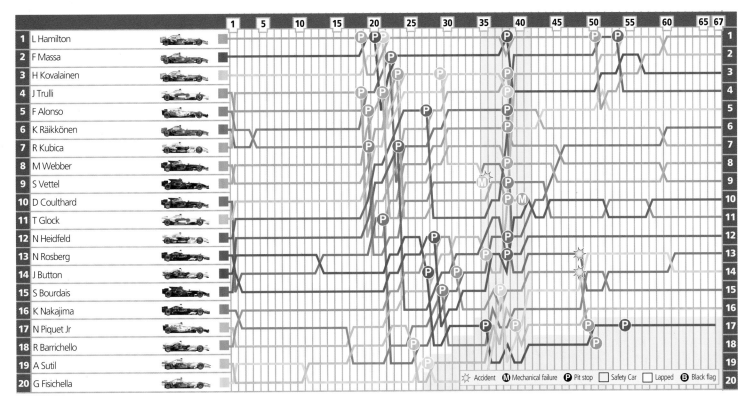

		1	5	10	15	20	25	30	35	40	45	50	55	60	65	67	
1	L Hamilton																1
2	F Massa																2
3	H Kovalainen																3
4	J Trulli																4
5	F Alonso																5
6	K Räikkönen																6
7	R Kubica																7
8	M Webber																8
9	S Vettel																9
10	D Coulthard																10
11	T Glock																11
12	N Heidfeld																12
13	N Rosberg																13
14	J Button																14
15	S Bourdais																15
16	K Nakajima																16
17	N Piquet Jr																17
18	R Barrichello																18
19	A Sutil																19
20	G Fisichella																20

☆ Accident   Ⓜ Mechanical failure   Ⓟ Pit stop   ☐ Safety Car   ☐ Lapped   Ⓑ Black flag

QUALIFYING 3

	Driver	Time
1	L Hamilton	1m15.666s
2	F Massa	1m15.859s
3	H Kovalainen	1m16.143s
4	J Trulli	1m16.191s
5	F Alonso	1m16.385s
6	K Räikkönen	1m16.389s
7	R Kubica	1m16.521s
8	M Webber	1m17.014s
9	S Vettel	1m17.244s
10	D Coulthard	1m17.503s

GRID

	Driver	Time
1	L Hamilton	1m15.666s
2	F Massa	1m15.859s
3	H Kovalainen	1m16.143s
4	J Trulli	1m16.191s
5	F Alonso	1m16.385s
6	K Räikkönen	1m16.389s
7	R Kubica	1m16.521s
8	M Webber	1m17.014s
9	S Vettel	1m17.244s
10	D Coulthard	1m17.503s
11	T Glock	1m15.508s
12	N Heidfeld	1m15.581s
13	N Rosberg	1m15.633s
14	J Button	1m15.701s
15	S Bourdais	1m15.858s
16	K Nakajima	1m16.083s
17	N Piquet Jr	1m16.189s
18	R Barrichello	1m16.246s
19	A Sutil	1m16.657s
20	G Fisichella	1m16.963s

RACE

	Driver	Car	Laps	Time	Avg. mph	Fastest	Stops
1	L Hamilton	McLaren-Mercedes MP4-23	67	1h31m20.874s	125.076	1m16.039s	2
2	N Piquet Jr	Renault R28	67	1h31m26.460s	124.948	1m16.910s	1
3	F Massa	Ferrari F2008	67	1h31m30.213s	124.863	1m16.502s	2
4	N Heidfeld	BMW Sauber F1.08	67	1h31m30.699s	124.852	1m15.987s	2
5	H Kovalainen	McLaren-Mercedes MP4-23	67	1h31m33.285s	124.793	1m16.495s	2
6	K Räikkönen	Ferrari F2008	67	1h31m35.357s	124.746	1m16.342s	2
7	R Kubica	BMW Sauber F1.08	67	1h31m43.477s	124.562	1m16.610s	2
8	S Vettel	Toro Rosso-Ferrari STR03	67	1h31m54.156s	124.321	1m16.772s	2
9	J Trulli	Toyota TF108	67	1h31m58.073s	124.232	1m17.023s	2
10	N Rosberg	Williams-Toyota FW30	67	1h31m58.532s	124.222	1m17.380s	2
11	F Alonso	Renault R28	67	1h31m59.499s	124.201	1m17.115s	2
12	S Bourdais	Toro Rosso-Ferrari STR03	67	1h31m59.985s	124.189	1m16m969s	2
13	D Coulthard	Red Bull-Renault RB4	67	1h32m15.845s	123.833	1m16.994s	2
14	K Nakajima	Williams-Toyota FW30	67	1h32m20.877s	123.721	1m17.691s	2
15	A Sutil	Force India-Ferrari VJM01	67	1h32m30.362s	123.510	1m17.889s	2
16*	G Fisichella	Force India-Ferrari VJM01	67	1h32m44.967s	123.186	1m18.208s	2
17	J Button	Honda RA108	66	1h32m01.303s	122.307	1m17.636s	3
R	R Barrichello	Honda RA108	50	Accident damage	-	1m17.986s	2
R	M Webber	Red Bull-Renault RB4	40	Oil cooler	-	1m17.206s	2
R	T Glock	Toyota TF108	35	Accident	-	1m16.712s	1

* INCLUDES A 25S PENALTY FOR UNLAPPING HIMSELF BEHIND THE SAFETY CAR BEFORE BEING SIGNALLED TO DO SO

CHAMPIONSHIP

	Driver	Pts
1	L Hamilton	58
2	F Massa	54
3	K Räikkönen	51
4	R Kubica	48
5	N Heidfeld	41
6	H Kovalainen	28
7	J Trulli	20
8	M Webber	18
9	F Alonso	13
10	R Barrichello	11
11	N Piquet Jr	10
12	N Rosberg	8
13	K Nakajima	8
14	D Coulthard	6
15	S Vettel	6
16	T Glock	5
17	J Button	3
18	S Bourdais	2

Fastest Lap
N Heidfeld 1m15.987s
(134.651mph) on lap 52

Fastest speed trap
F Massa 198.279mph
Slowest speed trap
N Piquet Jr 194.240mph

Fastest pit stop
1 N Heidfeld 22.263s
2 G Fisichella 22.850s
3 L Hamilton 22.952s

	Constructor	Pts
1	Ferrari	105
2	BMW Sauber	89
3	McLaren-Mercedes	86
4	Toyota	25
5	Red Bull-Renault	24
6	Renault	23
7	Williams-Toyota	16
8	Honda	14
9	Toro Rosso-Ferrari	8

 **Sebastien Bourdais**

"I was unlucky with the safety car, as it involved me queuing in the pits. I was able to keep up with Heidfeld in the first stint and the lap times were decent."

Jenson Button

"When the safety car came out, we switched back to the option tyre and sadly that meant that though I was a lap down, I wasn't able to overtake the leader."

 Adrian Sutil

"We lost time on the first stop, and then with the safety car we couldn't pit at the right moment, so I lost 10s or so. In my last stint, something didn't feel quite right in my car."

Lewis Hamilton

"When the team told me I had to build a 23s gap in seven laps, I knew I had to drive over the limit. It didn't quite work, but we had the pace in the car to keep pushing."

 **Sebastian Vettel**

"I was disappointed when I saw the safety car, but I fought on. Though I was quicker than Jarno I couldn't pass. Then he slipped, which put me back to eighth."

Rubens Barrichello

"I was trying to force Coulthard to take a wider line through Turn 9 so that on Turn 10 I'd be able to come up the inside, but he didn't see me on the inside and we touched."

 **Giancarlo Fisichella**

"I was struggling for grip, but it improved on the softer tyre. I made up some places and could have finished perhaps one place higher, but I locked up through Turn 8."

 **Heikki Kovalainen**

"I couldn't make the tyres work to their best. The safety car didn't help me, and I lost places during my stop. Then I lost time behind Kubica but managed to pass him."

FORMULA 1 MAGYAR NAGYDIJ 2008
BUDAPEST

HEIKKI'S BONUS

Felipe Massa muscled his way past Lewis Hamilton then drove away, before Hamilton had a puncture, but the Ferrari's engine failed at the close and Heikki Kovalainen took his first win

The 2008 F1 season had already seen its fair share of twists and turns in the battle between Ferrari and McLaren, but nothing quite prepared us for the rollercoaster ride of sheer emotion that we experienced in Hungary.

After McLaren dominated qualifying, Felipe Massa seized the initiative at the start, and then addressed any doubts about Ferrari's form by leaving Lewis Hamilton in his wake. When Hamilton dropped down the order with a puncture, it seemed that the balance of power had tipped in Ferrari's favour. Then, just three laps from home, Massa's engine failed and his pursuer, Heikki Kovalainen, strolled home for his first victory. Thus, despite finishing only fifth, Hamilton could allow himself a wry smile when the roulette wheel stopped spinning.

It looked as though McLaren would extend its recent advantage when Hamilton took pole position and Kovalainen qualified alongside him for the team's first front-row sweep of the year. Massa qualified third, but there was concern for Ferrari when Kimi Räikkönen could manage only sixth on the grid after making a mistake on his best lap. After his struggles in Germany, it was another sign that the World Champion's title defence had lost some momentum.

ABOVE **Lewis Hamilton expected to lead into Turn 1, from pole, but Felipe Massa had other ideas...**

OPPOSITE **The McLaren pit crew turns Heikki Kovalainen around at his first stop. He'd go on to win**

Robert Kubica qualified his BMW Sauber fourth, while Timo Glock – bouncing back after his huge crash at Hockenheim – was a surprise fifth for Toyota. As at Magny-Cours, where Jarno Trulli finished third, the TF108 seemed suited to this track. Indeed, Glock was second only to Hamilton in Q2, when the cars are running light and the definitive quick lap times are logged.

Despite being outpaced by both McLarens, Massa was confident that, come the race, he would be strong. The fact that in Hungary cars in even-numbered grid slots invariably get away poorly on the dirty line next to the pit wall gave him good reason to expect that he could jump into second place at the start.

In fact, he had loftier ambitions. Sure enough, he beat Kovalainen in the drag off the startline, and then, on the approach to Turn 1, he pulled alongside Hamilton. His front wheels locked and he performed an astonishing move around the outside, leaving Hamilton little choice but to cede the corner. After being embarrassed by Hamilton's aggressive pass in Germany, this was sweet revenge indeed for Massa.

"He was very, very fast and there wasn't very much I could do," said Hamilton. "I defended my line and he came around the outside."

Now we had an interesting race on our hands, as the assumption was that the McLarens would have

TALKING POINT
GOOD NEWS FOR HEIKKI

It was at Hungaroring a year ago where McLaren's 2007 season started to implode, where Lewis Hamilton had ignored that it was Fernando Alonso's turn to take priority in leading the 'fuel burn' qualifying laps and where Alonso had retaliated, pressing his claim to team leadership by threatening to let

the FIA have allegedly incriminating emails from his laptop in the midst of 'Stepneygate'.

In 2008, there is an altogether different karma at McLaren. Hamilton is established as team leader and championship contender with Heikki Kovalainen as the even-keeled back-up who has quickly become popular at Woking. The only nagging doubt was whether a single podium finish from his first 10 races was enough for Heikki to keep the seat.

That doubt was dispelled in Hungary when McLaren confirmed that Kovalainen had been retained for 2009, and the Finn celebrated by becoming the 100th World Championship race winner on Sunday afternoon. Truth told, it was a fortunate win, as Kovalainen had no answer to Felipe Massa or to

Hamilton, but the Ferrari's engine blew up with three laps to go and Lewis punctured a tyre. Heikki was happy to take it!

McLaren had refused to rise to some Alonso bait. "If I was racing for McLaren now, maybe I would be in the same position as I am now – without the possibility to win. But at least I have the full support of my team," Fernando had said at a press conference, with Heikki sitting alongside him...

All McLaren boss Ron Dennis would say in response was: "You could talk to any driver who has driven for McLaren and you will not find anyone – save for one – who will not verify that this team runs on the basis of equality."

Kovalainen confirmed: "I have the same car, the same opportunity

and am just working hard towards improving the results."

As far as McLaren was concerned, Kovalainen's sixth position in the championship coming to Hungary, 30 points behind Hamilton, was not a fair reflection of his performances. He'd been robbed by the unfortunate timing of a safety-car deployment in Australia and Germany, was hit by a grid penalty in France, was a potential winner in Turkey before puncturing after contact with Räikkönen, ditto Silverstone before the heavens opened, and suffered the heavy crash in Barcelona through no fault of his own.

"It took Mika Hakkinen 99 races to win and Heikki has won his 28th start, so he's got plenty of time," Dennis said, which was music to Kovalainen's ears, no doubt.

ABOVE Adrian Sutil's Force India was slowed by a brake problem that led to a puncture

BELOW The Hondas spent the early laps together, Jenson Button leading Rubens Barrichello

became academic on lap 41, when he suddenly slowed. Right at the start of the lap, he suffered a front left puncture, a result of debris apparently piercing the sidewall – possibly triggered by his press-on style creating flat spots that made the tyre more vulnerable to such damage.

Hamilton got back to the pits as quickly as he could, where the team effectively pulled off that second stop several laps earlier than scheduled, and fuelled him for the 29-lap run to the flag. The crawl back to the pits had cost him 40s, dropping him out of the points as he tumbled all the way down to 10th.

"I was going though Turn 1 and all of a sudden the car started bottoming," said Hamilton. "I was a bit cautious going into Turn 2, and then I realised I had a puncture. Trying to bring it home, I nearly went off a couple of times."

So, Kovalainen found himself in second position. He knew he was carrying McLaren's hopes, so there was a subtle change in emphasis as Massa now became his sole target, albeit with his attack starting from a deficit of around 23 seconds.

Massa knew that Hamilton was out of contention, and that took the pressure off, but Kovalainen also stepped up. Running four laps longer to his second stop, the Finn trimmed the gap to 17s. He now had 21 laps to run on the super-soft tyre. Not for the first time this year, McLaren found that on a rubbered-in track this tyre provided a useful gain for the last part of a race. The margin to Massa began to shrink. Massa was also being given instructions, and was taking just enough out of the car to stay ahead.

From 17s on lap 49 it came down to 14s by lap 55, and then 10s on lap 59s, with 10 laps to go. Now things were getting interesting. Over the next few laps, the gap went 9.8s, 9.6s, 9.6s, 7.9s, 7.5s, 7.2s, 6.7s. Then, as he came up to complete lap 67, with the gap down to 5.8s, Massa's engine failed.

the speed to push the Ferrari. In fact, at a track where passing is almost impossible, Hamilton soon dropped some 3s behind, and it looked as though Massa was well in control. He pitted on lap 18, and Hamilton came in just a lap later, and emerged still well behind.

Through the middle stint, the gap stabilised at around 4s, and now all depended on how far each driver would run until his second stop. Tyres are always a big concern in the Hungarian heat, so the issue was how each car would perform when they made their compulsory switch to the option – super-soft – tyre.

The question of whether a later pit stop would enable Hamilton to deal with the gap to Massa

It was hard not to feel sorry for the Brazilian, as he had done such a great job, and he could have let the gap drop to a second over those last three laps and still claimed victory on this track that offers so little opportunity for overtaking.

However, keeping your engine in one piece is a fundamental part of racing, as is maintaining pressure on someone in order to force them to push harder than they would like. We'll never know whether the Ferrari V8 would have lasted those extra three laps had Massa been able to back off to a greater degree, but the need to counter Kovalainen's charge wouldn't have helped. Furthermore, Massa would have had to

go even quicker for the last 29 laps if Hamilton had not had his puncture and thus still been in the frame.

Kovalainen could scarcely believe his good fortune. It took him 11 races at McLaren, but he finally did what everyone knew he was capable of, and won a grand prix. His turbulent season had seen a huge crash after wheel failure in Spain, a pitlane start after electronic problems in Monaco, a first-lap puncture in Turkey, and two questionable grid penalties for blocking in qualifying. This time, fortune fell in his favour, and he cruised home to take a popular maiden win.

"On the last stint, it felt particularly good on the

ABOVE Bouncing back from his shunt in Germany, Timo Glock kept Kimi Räikkönen back to claim second

INSIDE LINE
TIMO GLOCK
TOYOTA DRIVER

"From the stretcher at Hockenheim to the podium at Hungaroring – unbelievable! I almost had to pinch myself when I saw Felipe Massa's engine failing with three laps to go and I knew that I was in second position.

I had pressure from Kimi

Räikkönen in the other Ferrari over the closing laps and we knew from Friday practice that the soft tyres would be more difficult. I saw I was 9s ahead of Kimi, but then the team told me he was half-a-second a lap quicker. I just tried to push more while staying focused on not destroying the tyres. In the end, he was catching me big time, but I kept cool and made sure I didn't make any mistakes.

At Hockenheim, we had a good race pace before my crash, and we came to Budapest and just kept that speed. The car felt really good from Friday onwards and we didn't have to make any big changes. I qualified fifth, which was my best starting slot by three positions. It was just perfect until that last stint with super-soft tyres, which was a bit

tricky. Just half a season gone in F1 and I'm on the podium! It felt great – a perfect weekend.

It proved pretty important to beat Kubica off the grid, because Robert had a tough race. I've had to improve my starts because my reaction times were not perfect at the first couple of races. This time the start was really good and the performance stayed that way. I don't like an understeering car and that has been a problem sometimes this season, but at Hockenheim and Hungaroring the feel of the car was much more in my direction. I could just put the car where I wanted to.

I can recommend the podium as a better place to finish a race than the medical centre! After my Hockenheim crash I thought maybe I made a mistake and ran a bit too

wide over the kerb with a heavy-fuelled car. But the team told me the rear suspension collapsed. I must have breathed at the wrong moment as I was a bit winded. I was ready to leave hospital that night, but it was standard practice to keep me in overnight.

Answering all the same questions probably took more energy out of me than the shunt. I want to make the news for results, not for accidents, and this was a good way to put that right!"

soft tyres," he reported, "and I was able to increase the pace and try to put pressure on Felipe.

"I was hoping that something would happen, and I tried to put pressure on him in the last stint, and maybe he needed to go more aggressive on his engine settings or whatever. I caught him quite well, and to see him pull up of course was a surprise. After that, I backed off a bit to make sure we'd bring the car home.

"I saw it straight away, but it was a little bit difficult to believe. I had just lapped Bourdais's Toro Rosso and I thought maybe it could be the other, so I had to look which one it was, then I saw the yellow crash helmet and thought this is pretty good for us!"

His fellow countryman may be called the Ice Man, but equally Heikki is not the sort of guy to get overexcited. "The most important thing is to keep concentration and not to make mistakes," he continued. "I backed off a little with my engine, just no need to rush any more, and bring it home. Of course, I've thought about the moment when I would be leading in the last few laps and just to chill out, and perhaps I chilled out a little bit more. It's a very positive feeling, and to bring it home, it feels great."

Behind him, Glock had a strong run to take an unexpected second place. The GP2 champion passed Kubica for fourth at the start and, despite a delay with a fuel rig problem at his first pit stop, was able to take advantage of the problems for Hamilton and Massa to advance. He even had the pace to keep Räikkönen behind him in the closing laps, after the latter had got away poorly and been caught behind Fernando Alonso's Renault for the first two thirds of the race.

Any thoughts that Ferrari had of seizing second place were ended when the team detected a mechanical problem and asked their man to slow. Third place at least kept Räikkönen in the title hunt, as he moved a little closer to Hamilton.

"We had good pace with prime tyres," said Glock, "but we knew from the beginning that we would struggle with the soft tyres. In the end, I could keep the car on the track at reasonable pace and when Kimi had to back off, the last two laps were easy."

Alonso had a good run for Renault to take fourth, and in the final stint he was shadowed by his nemesis Hamilton. One year after their spectacular bust-up, the Spaniard was more than happy to head the British driver across the line. Hamilton was in turn relieved to at least salvage four points. That long last stint on the option tyre had not been an easy one.

"Fortunately, I managed to pull it off and score as many points as I could," said Hamilton. "It's nowhere near as bad as it could be, we could have Felipe and Kimi right at the front. Congratulations to Heikki, he did a fantastic job, I'm really happy for him, and also Glock was second, taking points away from everyone else, which was good for me."

Buoyed by his great result in Germany, Nelson Piquet Jr had another good run to sixth place for Renault, while the final points went to Trulli and Kubica, as BMW Sauber endured its most disappointing day of the season. From a lowly 15th on the grid, Nick Heidfeld could salvage only 10th.

SNAPSHOT FROM
HUGARY

CLOCKWISE FROM RIGHT The F1 transporters are things of beauty, even when shown in reflection on the face of McLaren's circuit headquarters; Red Bull's Christian Horner looks on as Renault's Flavio Briatore entertains Toro Rosso's Gerhard Berger; Felipe Massa walks back despondently after engine failure cost him victory; Timo Glock's second place triggered jubilation in the Toyota garage; Lewis Hamilton's punctured tyre is inspected after its failure dropped him from second to 10th; the Hungaroring was blessed with some of the prettiest faces...; and some of the rather less so...

WEEKEND NEWS

■ Michael Schumacher made the news in the UK when he was involved in a road accident in Kent. The seven-time World Champion was driving a Fiat Ducato van when he somehow struck a gate, fortunately without injuring the car dealer who was closing it. Schumacher had been attending a western-style horse show in Sussex.

■ A much-publicised auction of the assets of Super Aguri Racing fell flat when most of the lots – mainly tooling and car parts – were purchased in advance by German engineering company Formtec, which was associated previously with Midland/Spyker. However, a lone Super Aguri SA06 chassis remained available to the public, attracting £85,000.

■ Even prior to his superb victory in the Hungarian GP, McLaren had made it known that Heikki Kovalainen would be retained by the team for 2009. Although there was never any real doubt about the Finn staying on, his recent run of bad luck had fuelled rumours linking Nico Rosberg to the seat.

■ Several mechanics from the DPR GP2 team were lucky to escape with minor injuries after their minibus rolled off the motorway on Saturday morning. The ensuing traffic jam – exacerbated by the arrival of a medical helicopter – forced several delayed F1 drivers to hitch scooter rides into the track in order to make practice on time.

■ Dino Toso, the former director of aerodynamics at Renault F1, lost his long battle with cancer on 13 August. The Italian was just 39 years old. Toso left Renault only in June, having been with the Enstone-based team for eight years. Toso had previously been a race engineer at Jordan, and oversaw Damon Hill's famous 1998 Belgian GP victory.

RACE RESULTS
HUNGARY
HUNGARORING

Official Results © [2008]
Formula One Administration Limited,
6 Princes Gate, London, SW7 1QJ.
No reproduction without permission.
All copyright and database rights reserved.

RACE DATE August 3rd
CIRCUIT LENGTH 2.722 miles
NO. OF LAPS 70
RACE DISTANCE 190.540 miles
WEATHER Sunny & dry, 29°C
TRACK TEMP 44°C
RACE DAY ATTENDANCE 84,000
LAP RECORD M Schumacher
1m19.071s, 123.828mph, 2004

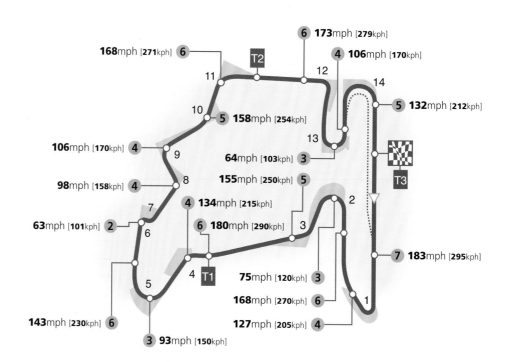

PRACTICE 1

	Driver	Time	Laps
1	F Massa	1m20.981s	19
2	K Räikkönen	1m21.345s	21
3	H Kovalainen	1m21.410s	17
4	L Hamilton	1m21.535s	18
5	F Alonso	1m21.802s	18
6	T Glock	1m21.931s	22
7	R Kubica	1m22.267s	18
8	N Piquet Jr	1m22.326s	19
9	N Heidfeld	1m22.370s	22
10	J Trulli	1m22.457s	25
11	M Webber	1m22.654s	23
12	D Coulthard	1m22.700s	16
13	S Bourdais	1m22.900s	26
14	J Button	1m22.917s	27
15	R Barrichello	1m23.093s	26
16	N Rosberg	1m23.147s	21
17	K Nakajima	1m23.274s	22
18	A Sutil	1m23.353s	25
19	G Fisichella	1m23.459s	28
20	S Vettel	1m23.923s	4

PRACTICE 2

	Driver	Time	Laps
1	L Hamilton	1m20.554s	35
2	N Piquet Jr	1m20.748s	38
3	H Kovalainen	1m20.760s	33
4	F Alonso	1m20.928s	35
5	K Räikkönen	1m21.009s	36
6	F Massa	1m21.010s	36
7	N Heidfeld	1m21.138s	46
8	R Kubica	1m21.363s	36
9	J Trulli	1m21.505s	42
10	N Rosberg	1m21.581s	34
11	T Glock	1m21.662s	39
12	M Webber	1m21.733s	43
13	D Coulthard	1m21.837s	34
14	K Nakajima	1m21.902s	33
15	S Bourdais	1m21.955s	41
16	J Button	1m22.150s	41
17	G Fisichella	1m22.197s	36
18	A Sutil	1m22.358s	37
19	R Barrichello	1m22.448s	33
20	S Vettel	1m22.945s	5

PRACTICE 3

	Driver	Time	Laps
1	L Hamilton	1m20.228s	14
2	F Massa	1m20.567s	14
3	T Glock	1m20.623s	21
4	H Kovalainen	1m20.657s	15
5	N Piquet Jr	1m20.917s	21
6	N Heidfeld	1m21.096s	15
7	S Bourdais	1m21.179s	21
8	S Vettel	1m21.184s	22
9	K Räikkönen	1m21.187s	18
10	N Rosberg	1m21.195s	19
11	F Alonso	1m21.228s	21
12	K Nakajima	1m21.357s	17
13	D Coulthard	1m21.489s	16
14	J Trulli	1m21.601s	18
15	R Barrichello	1m21.703s	20
16	M Webber	1m21.752s	17
17	J Button	1m21.772s	19
18	R Kubica	1m21.975s	18
19	G Fisichella	1m22.189s	22
20	A Sutil	1m22.550s	23

QUALIFYING 1

	Driver	Time
1	L Hamilton	1m19.376s
2	F Massa	1m19.578s
3	J Trulli	1m19.942s
4	H Kovalainen	1m19.945s
5	T Glock	1m19.980s
6	K Räikkönen	1m20.006s
7	R Kubica	1m20.053s
8	M Webber	1m20.073s
9	S Vettel	1m20.157s
10	F Alonso	1m20.229s
11	D Coulthard	1m20.505s
12	N Piquet Jr	1m20.583s
13	S Bourdais	1m20.640s
14	N Rosberg	1m20.748s
15	J Button	1m20.888s
16	N Heidfeld	1m21.045s
17	K Nakajima	1m21.085s
18	R Barrichello	1m21.332s
19	G Fisichella	1m21.670s
20	A Sutil	1m22.113s

QUALIFYING 2

	Driver	Time
1	F Massa	1m19.068s
2	T Glock	1m19.246s
3	L Hamilton	1m19.473s
4	H Kovalainen	1m19.480s
5	J Trulli	1m19.486s
6	K Räikkönen	1m19.546s
7	R Kubica	1m19.776s
8	F Alonso	1m19.816s
9	M Webber	1m20.046s
10	N Piquet Jr	1m20.131s
11	S Vettel	1m20.144s
12	J Button	1m20.332s
13	D Coulthard	1m20.502s
14	S Bourdais	1m20.963s
15	N Rosberg	No time

Best sectors – Practice
Sec 1	L Hamilton	28.996s
Sec 2	L Hamilton	28.399s
Sec 3	T Glock	22.543s

Speed trap – Practice
1	L Hamilton	184.982mph
2	H Kovalainen	183.180mph
3	K Räikkönen	183.056mph

Best sectors – Qualifying
Sec 1	L Hamilton	28.589s
Sec 2	F Massa	28.094s
Sec 3	T Glock	22.190s

Speed trap – Qualifying
1	S Bourdais	183.304mph
2	F Alonso	182.993mph
3	H Kovalainen	182.869mph

Kimi Räikkönen
"I spent a long time behind a slower car. When I could push, it was too late. I came up behind Glock, but I had to slow as I had a mechanical problem with the rear."

Nick Heidfeld
"I was able to pass three cars on lap 1. It then became harder to race. We went for a one-stopper, so my car was almost full of fuel and I had to take care of the tyres."

Fernando Alonso
"We were on the pace with a car that was working well. We scored some important points which is satisfying, even though we could have maybe been on the podium."

Nico Rosberg
"I lost a few places on lap 1. Then, during my first stop, something went wrong with the fuel rig which cost me a couple of seconds and put me behind Fisichella."

David Coulthard
"Unfortunately I got some traffic before my last stop, which allowed Nick to pass me; otherwise I could not do any more today. The car has a lot of oversteer and rear sliding."

Jarno Trulli
"I was quick today, but couldn't push, as I only had one lap all race that was clear of traffic. I gained one place early on, but passing here is practically impossible."

Felipe Massa
"I was managing the race, as I had an advantage over second place after Hamilton was delayed. I am frustrated, as we had a great car and had done everything perfectly."

Robert Kubica
"We were slow and I struggled for grip. I had huge oversteer and could not really push. I was trying hard to keep on the track. Anyway, one point is better than nothing."

Nelson Piquet Jr
"I scored valuable points which is promising for the rest of the year. I made a good start, but made a small mistake on lap 1, losing the two places that I had made up."

Kazuki Nakajima
"We converted to a one-stopper, which was the right thing to do, but I was heavy and struggled on the option tyres. I then made contact with Fisichella and lost a position."

Mark Webber
"We didn't do a good job in qualifying, which hurt us in the race. We struggled for pace, and it was hard to stay with the Toyotas and Renaults, our championship rivals."

Timo Glock
"I couldn't believe it when I saw Felipe's engine go. To get such a good result in my first year is fantastic. Everything went perfectly until the last stint on the soft tyres."

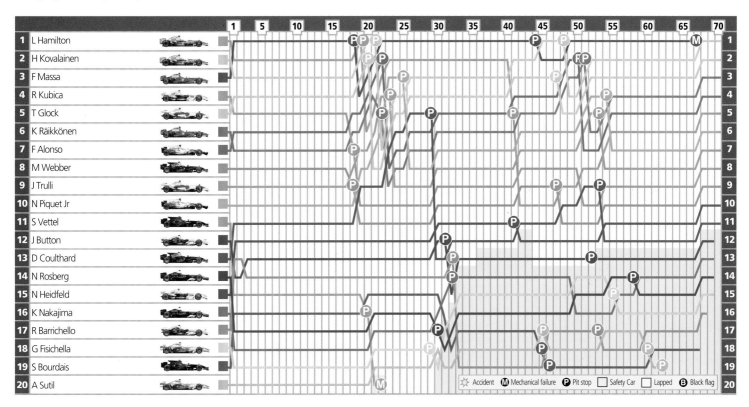

	1	5	10	15	20	25	30	35	40	45	50	55	60	65	70	
1	L Hamilton															1
2	H Kovalainen															2
3	F Massa															3
4	R Kubica															4
5	T Glock															5
6	K Räikkönen															6
7	F Alonso															7
8	M Webber															8
9	J Trulli															9
10	N Piquet Jr															10
11	S Vettel															11
12	J Button															12
13	D Coulthard															13
14	N Rosberg															14
15	N Heidfeld															15
16	K Nakajima															16
17	R Barrichello															17
18	G Fisichella															18
19	S Bourdais															19
20	A Sutil															20

☼ Accident Ⓜ Mechanical failure Ⓟ Pit stop ☐ Safety Car ☐ Lapped Ⓑ Black flag

QUALIFYING 3

	Driver	Time
1	L Hamilton	1m20.899s
2	H Kovalainen	1m21.140s
3	F Massa	1m21.191s
4	R Kubica	1m21.281s
5	T Glock	1m21.326s
6	K Räikkönen	1m21.516s
7	F Alonso	1m21.698s
8	M Webber	1m21.732s
9	J Trulli	1m21.767s
10	N Piquet Jr	1m22.371s

GRID

	Driver	Time
1	L Hamilton	1m20.899s
2	H Kovalainen	1m21.140s
3	F Massa	1m21.191s
4	R Kubica	1m21.281s
5	T Glock	1m21.326s
6	K Räikkönen	1m21.516s
7	F Alonso	1m21.698s
8	M Webber	1m21.732s
9	J Trulli	1m21.767s
10	N Piquet Jr	1m22.371s
11	S Vettel	1m20.144s
12	J Button	1m20.332s
13	D Coulthard	1m20.502s
14	N Rosberg	No time
15	N Heidfeld	1m21.045s
16	K Nakajima	1m21.085s
17	R Barrichello	1m21.332s
18	G Fisichella	1m21.670s
19*	S Bourdais	1m20.963s
20	A Sutil	1m22.113

* 5-PLACE PENALTY FOR IMPEDING HEIDFELD

RACE

	Driver	Car	Laps	Time	Avg. mph	Fastest	Stops
1	H Kovalainen	McLaren-Mercedes MP4-23	70	1h37m27.067s	117.333	1m21.753s	2
2	T Glock	Toyota TF108	70	1h37m38.128s	117.111	1m21.671s	2
3	K Räikkönen	Ferrari F2008	70	1h37m43.923s	116.996	1m21.195s	2
4	F Alonso	Renault R28	70	1h37m48.681s	116.900	1m21.793s	2
5	L Hamilton	McLaren-Mercedes MP4-23	70	1h37m50.115s	116.872	1m21.493s	2
6	N Piquet Jr	Renault R28	70	1h37m59.365s	116.688	1m21.537s	2
7	J Trulli	Toyota TF108	70	1h38m03.516s	116.606	1m21.638s	2
8	R Kubica	BMW Sauber F1.08	70	1h38m15.388s	116.371	1m21.941s	2
9	M Webber	Red Bull-Renault RB4	70	1h38m25.901s	116.164	1m22.125s	2
10	N Heidfeld	BMW Sauber F1.08	70	1h38m34.776s	115.989	1m22.183s	1
11	D Coulthard	Red Bull-Renault RB4	70	1h38m37.474s	115.936	1m22.732s	2
12	J Button	Honda RA108	69	1h37m44.160s	115.319	1m22.397s	2
13	K Nakajima	Williams-Toyota FW30	69	1h38m30.779s	114.409	1m23.307s	1
14	N Rosberg	Williams-Toyota FW30	69	1h38m31.269s	114.400	1m22.397s	2
15	G Fisichella	Force India-Ferrari VJM01	69	1h38m44.943s	114.136	1m22.641s	2
16	R Barrichello	Honda RA108	68	1h37m55.162s	113.435	1m22.436s	2
17	F Massa	Ferrari F2008	67	Engine	-	1m21.355s	2
18	S Bourdais	Toro Rosso-Ferrari STR03	67	1h37m48.266s	111.898	1m23.220s	3
R	A Sutil	Force India-Ferrari VJM01	62	Brakes	-	1m23.650s	3
R	S Vettel	Toro Rosso-Ferrari STR03	22	Engine	-	1m24.222s	1

CHAMPIONSHIP

	Driver	Pts
1	L Hamilton	62
2	K Räikkönen	57
3	F Massa	54
4	R Kubica	49
5	N Heidfeld	41
6	H Kovalainen	38
7	J Trulli	22
8	F Alonso	18
9	M Webber	18
10	T Glock	13
11	N Piquet Jr	13
12	R Barrichello	11
13	N Rosberg	8
14	K Nakajima	8
15	D Coulthard	6
16	S Vettel	6
17	J Button	3
18	S Bourdais	2

Fastest Lap
K Räikkönen 1m21.195s
(120.697mph) on lap 61

Fastest speed trap
N Piquet Jr 181.626mph
Slowest speed trap
J Trulli 176.718mph

Fastest pit stop
1 G Fisichella 25.126s
  N Rosberg 25.126s
3 J Trulli 25.132s

	Constructor	Pts
1	Ferrari	111
2	McLaren-Mercedes	100
3	BMW Sauber	90
4	Toyota	35
5	Renault	31
6	Red Bull-Renault	24
7	Williams-Toyota	16
8	Honda	14
9	Toro Rosso-Ferrari	8

 Sebastien Bourdais

"The race went to hell at the first stop, as the guys had to use the extinguisher and I got foam on my visor. It happened at the second stop too and I had to stop again."

Jenson Button

"I made a poor start, but passed Rubens on lap 3, which was fun. After that, I caught Heidfeld. He was very strong on the last two corners so I had no chance to pass."

Adrian Sutil

"I was on the outside into Turn 1, but had to go wide and lost a place. My brakes overheated on lap 3. From then on, I had lots of locking on the front then a puncture."

Lewis Hamilton

"My start was OK, but Felipe's was better and he passed me. I felt OK in the second stint, as I was going longer to the final stops, but the damaged tyre halted my progress."

 Sebastian Vettel

"I ran wide on lap 1 and lost places. I was stuck behind Barrichello, then didn't have a good stop and that caused the engine to overheat and I had no choice but to retire."

Rubens Barrichello

"After I made up four places on lap 1, it was a dull race. At my first stop we had the problem with the rig which resulted in a small fire and a delay while we got fuel into the car."

 **Giancarlo Fisichella**

"It was a tough race, as we were fighting a lot. We were quite heavy at the start, but the pace really wasn't too bad and I could keep up with those in front of me."

 **Heikki Kovalainen**

"Mid-race, I started pushing Felipe. I feel sorry for him as he drove a great race, but my car felt good and I knew I could push for victory. This is a great moment for me."

2008 FORMULA 1 GRAND PRIX OF EUROPE
VALENCIA

MASSA AT A CANTER

Apart from the hiccough of a near clash when leaving his second pit stop, Ferrari's Felipe Massa was in imperious form as F1 raced around Valencia's dockside for the first time

Felipe Massa gained revenge for his last-minute engine failure in Hungary by taking a dominant victory in the European GP at the spectacular new Valencia venue.

There were still smiles in the McLaren camp afterwards, though, as second place and eight points for Lewis Hamilton was a useful reward at the end of a meeting that many had regarded in advance as something of a lottery. Hamilton earned that result after a weekend when his physical condition had, if only for a few hours, put his participation in the race in doubt.

Despite being beaten by the Brazilian, Hamilton actually extended his lead in the championship. The only thing was, his closest pursuer was now Massa and not the non-scoring Kimi Räikkönen, a graphic illustration of the complex juggling act that the Scuderia faced as it tried to balance the interests of its two drivers.

Against expectations, the race passed with few incidents, and there were no safety-car interventions, which is quite an achievement on a street circuit. However, there was also very little overtaking as drivers struggled to run in the dirty air behind other cars. The general feeling afterwards was that it had been a great event, but a disappointing race.

Having run an F3/GT meeting a month earlier, the

organisers were still putting finishing touches to the venue when the teams arrived. Overall, the feeling was positive, although everyone noticed the curious lack of boats – and atmosphere of any kind – in the harbour.

It was in the early hours of Saturday morning that Lewis had a scare, waking up at 5am to find he had a problem with his neck.

"We were a little concerned yesterday morning," said McLaren boss Ron Dennis after the race. "Lewis had a neck spasm in the night. It gave him a very bad headache. At the beginning, he was really struggling, it was painful, it was pretty much locked up. Racing drivers build phenomenal neck muscles, and whenever they get some sort of spasm, it's not like you or I. It's such a powerful muscle that it undoubtedly puts pressure on one side of the spine."

The third practice session didn't start until 11am, so the team had a reasonable amount of time to try to get him into shape. Even then, Hamilton didn't go out until well into the session, in order to give him as much time as possible for his neck to recover.

"It was a bit iffy at first, but the guys did a good job, and Lewis handled it very well," said Dennis. "We cut down the programme on Saturday morning but, after

a couple of laps, he said he was fine, so we put the full programme back in place."

In the end, he qualified in second place, just behind Massa. People didn't know at the time about his problems, but in retrospect he was more than happy to have secured that result.

"What wasn't wrong is the question!" admitted Hamilton after the race. "Basically, I've had a bad fever most of the week, and I had a pretty bad case of a muscle that went into spasm yesterday, which caused a migraine, so I had to have acupuncture and injections in my neck. So during qualifying yesterday, was tough..."

From the less-favourable side of the grid, Hamilton was nearly beaten into the tight Turn 2 by Robert Kubica, but the Pole thought better of it and backed off. Massa emerged ahead of Hamilton, Kubica, Heikki Kovalainen and Räikkönen.

The entire field made it though intact, but there was drama later in the lap when Kazuki Nakajima ran into the back of Fernando Alonso's Renault. The local hero lost his rear wing, but made it back to the pits. However, to the obvious disappointment of the 115,000-strong crowd, he was forced to retire.

Massa was already 1.4s ahead at the end of the long

TALKING POINT
IMPRESSIONS OF VALENCIA

The eagerly anticipated Valencia circuit was the first of two new tracks on the year's F1 calendar.

City races have a different vibe from those held on permanent tracks that are sometimes far from major centres of population. When everyone has easy access to restaurants, especially beachside ones, a grand prix becomes much more of an 'event' than merely a race. The crowd is captive, the sponsors want to come and it becomes a fixture.

Hermann Tilke's circuit was constructed with its paddock set up around Valencia's historic port warehouses, with no alterations permitted, and if there were one or two teething problems with things such as drainage and sewers, there was universal praise for the job that the Valencians had done.

"I think you need a mix," said Toyota's John Howett. "You need some of the classic great racing circuits and then venues like Valencia."

Everyone agrees that the presence of sun, water and boats provides a compelling backdrop for a race, but there weren't as many boats as there might have been. Valencia is not Monte Carlo, but the 80,000 Euro mooring fees for the weekend were off-putting.

Many were predicting incident aplenty and multiple safety-car deployments. Valencia might be a street track, but it's not slow, as the average lap speed is about 30mph more than Monaco's. And, with low grip surfaces and bordering walls, nobody was anticipating a race to run from lights to flag without interruption. Yet, that's what we got.

Felipe Massa dominated it, which was a fine achievement after his disappointment in Hungary, and Lewis Hamilton, coping with neck spasms that at one stage threatened his further participation, had to settle for second, thereby guaranteeing that we still very much had a championship battle on our hands.

That was all positive, but the racing itself was something of a damp squib. "You have to build a track with what you have," admitted Tilke, as many voiced the opinion that perhaps some alterations could be made to assist overtaking.

Overall, the impression of Valencia was positive. "I think you'd start by saying that to create this and grow this out of this area is a fantastic achievement," said McLaren's Martin Whitmarsh. "The event ran without incident, so congratulations to Valencia. Looking at it here in the paddock, we can develop a little more atmosphere, but it's a very good start."

first lap, and after that Hamilton drifted inexorably back as the field became strung out and it became evident that we were not going to see much real racing.

Hamilton was 4.8s behind on lap 14. Then, at the end of the following lap, Massa came in for his first pit stop. It was earlier than McLaren had expected. Hamilton came in two laps later, revealing that he'd been carrying a two-lap disadvantage over the stint – a not insignificant amount at a track with a long lap, and where fuel consumption was high.

"We lost the race yesterday in qualifying," said Dennis. "If we had put two laps' less fuel in Lewis's car, he would have outqualified Massa. And this is a race that you had to win from the front. It was very clear that even if we'd caught Massa, it would have been very hard to get past. We felt we were running at least one lap longer, but we didn't think we were two laps longer. So maybe if we'd tried a bit harder…"

Hamilton was a little bit closer to Massa after the first round of pit stops, but again he was carrying that fuel disadvantage, and again the gap slowly drifted out.

"I thought at every stage that I could catch him, so I was pushing and pushing, even though the gap was increasing," said the McLaren driver. "I think also I was two laps heavier and [again] two laps heavier. So I was always heavier in the first two stints. It's difficult to say whether he was much quicker than me, but they were stronger. Maybe we even lost it in the second stint. Being two laps heavier then was not an advantage, it was a disadvantage."

The margin went out to over 10s before Massa came in for a second time on lap 37. Hamilton followed him in to the pits two laps later as McLaren responded to the Ferrari pit stop, and minimised the risks inherent in a possible safety-car intervention.

Of course, with all the pitstops of the leading contenders you can never be quite sure what they reveal, because those safety-car risks encourage the

leaders (those with most to lose) to pit with some sort of safety margin, that's to say fuel left in their tank. Dennis insisted that Hamilton still had some fuel left, but it can only have been enough for a lap or two.

"We did go longer [in the first pit stop]," said Dennis, "but then we covered Massa for the safety car. We could have gone quite a bit further. In the end, we didn't care about the safety car giving the race to anybody else, but we couldn't risk the safety car giving the race to Massa. So the moment he stopped, we covered him."

In fact, Massa lost time to Hamilton on both his in- and out-laps, and at least some of that was to do with the necessity to brake in avoidance as he left his pit, and follow Adrian Sutil's Force India out. Later, Massa was investigated for an 'unsafe release' by the team, but he escaped with a reprimand and the team with a 10,000 Euro fine rather than a time penalty that would have cost him victory.

Things were beginning to go wrong for Ferrari. Kovalainen had got past Räikkönen on the first lap, and the two Finns remained close together for much of the race, although neither was able to match the pace of his team-mate. The pair pitted together on lap 43 and, in his haste to depart, Räikkönen tried to leave before the fuel hose was disconnected, knocking over a mechanic. Fortunately, the mechanic was not seriously injured. Then, shortly after returning to the track, Kimi suffered a spectacular engine failure. The cause was not unexpected, as it was a con rod from the same batch that had triggered Massa's Hungarian GP retirement.

Remarkably, Massa's Hockenheim/Budapest engine and Räikkönen's Budapest/Valencia unit had run to within 10km of each other when they failed, taking into account both races, and all Saturday activity. The fact that both blow-ups happened on the pit straight was an unfortunate coincidence…

Meanwhile, Hamilton gained almost 4s after

BELOW Jarno Trulli demoted Sebastian Vettel at the first pit stops and raced on to finish fifth for his fifth helping of points in six races

OPPOSITE Nico Rosberg was back in the points for Williams for the first time since the Turkish GP in May, finishing in eighth place

INSIDE LINE
ROB
SMEDLEY
**FERRARI
RACE ENGINEER**

"After the Hungarian GP, Felipe was absolutely gutted. He'd come from third place on the grid, overtaken the two McLarens and had 10 points in the bag. It was all going absolutely fantastically and the poor lad was three laps from the end when the engine breaks...

We all had a few tears after that,

but you've got to pick yourself up again. When we fuel adjusted-qualifying, looked at Felipe's move on Hamilton at the first corner and then how he subsequently closed out the race, it was brilliant.

You look at it all, realise there are plenty of races left and say, alright, let's go forward. I talked to Felipe a lot on the telephone on Monday and by Tuesday he was really upbeat as we started looking ahead to coming here to Valencia.

In preparation, we went to the Fiat simulator in Turin. It gave Felipe an idea of which way the corners went on this new circuit and it gave us an idea of what to do with the car.

Because of this, we were able to travel to Valencia with a car that was more or less already set up. We only made two or three set-up changes to

the car on Friday and most of them we went back on. Felipe was really happy with the car, dead comfortable straight away, and that's part and parcel of what we try to do for him.

One of the biggest things for me and the lads who work on Felipe's car is that we must arrive at the track with a good car. I don't want to go to a circuit and start messing about trying to tune the car to it. We must have a good baseline and then tickle it from that point on.

We were able to do just that in Valencia and it stood us in good stead for the entire meeting. There's a great bunch of lads working on Felipe's car, we all pull together and I'm very fortunate from that point-of-view.

Felipe was quick straight away and just kept that momentum through the remainder of the meeting.

I warned him that the fast final corner was going to be a bit difficult with the car set up the way it was. In the first free practice, he jumped out and said that 'yes, there was a lot of oversteer and could we do something about it'. I said, 'Sorry son, you're going to have to live with it because that's how it is. If we concentrate on that corner, we are going to mess the rest of the circuit up.'

He just changed his driving style a little bit, then drove around the problem and dominated the whole weekend. He was great."

ABOVE Giancarlo Fisichella ran a one-stop tactic and delayed team-mate Adrian Sutil, who started with a light fuel load, in the early laps

BELOW The afternoon's work is done and Felipe Massa flashes past the chequered flag to become the first grand prix winner at Valencia

Massa's stop, bringing the gap down to 5.9s. It looked pretty interesting for a while but, despite Ferrari having obvious concerns about Massa's engine (although the team knew that it contained parts from a different batch), Massa began to extend his lead again. In fact, the gap was pegged at 7–8s, only coming down to 5.6s as Massa cruised across the line.

"We pretty much elected to come second halfway through the race," insisted Dennis. "Then, once Kimi was out, that was the deciding factor. We just said 'this is a race to be prudent about'..."

Massa had made it look easy, but he had worked hard for this win, and he deserved it.

"The first stint was very good, nothing special but very good," he said. "I was pulling away by a couple of tenths of a second every lap. I think we won the race in the second stint, as the car was just perfect and was improving lap by lap. It was amazing to see the gap increasing. Then, the last stint, with the grip on the track, the temperature, I was on the soft tyre and I was able to drive in a relaxing way, which can be a big problem. But I was doing similar lap times, so it is amazing how the car behaved on the last stint. It was just perfect."

Hamilton didn't blame his fitness scare. "It was nothing that distracted me from my race," he insisted. But, at the same time, he also hinted that he had felt less than 100%: "Fortunately today it was better, but doing a whole race with it... I think I'm just sweating more because of feverishness, but I'll be OK for the next race."

Kubica had his best run since his Montréal win, qualifying and finishing third. He had a minor worry early in the race when a plastic bag caught on the front of his car and disrupted the aerodynamics, but he later picked up his pace again and he finished a couple of seconds clear of Kovalainen, who had a low-key afternoon.

Jarno Trulli continued Toyota's good form with a strong run to fifth place, while his team-mate Timo Glock used a one-stop strategy to move up from 13th on the grid to seventh place at the flag. The Toyotas were split by Sebastian Vettel, the Scuderia Toro Rosso driver having backed up his excellent sixth place in qualifying with a consistent run in the race. The final point went to Nico Rosberg, who was well clear of a lacklustre Nick Heidfeld.

Aside from the Nakajima/Alonso collision, the only other significant contact came when David Coulthard tapped Adrian Sutil, and had a spin. Later in the race, Sutil slid his Force India into the tyre wall at the first corner. Incredibly, he was the only F1 driver to hit a barrier all weekend. And that is a statistic that few would have bet on before the action started...

SNAPSHOT FROM
EUROPE

CLOCKWISE FROM RIGHT
This aerial shot shows how the circuit runs around Valencia's docks, with the tricky Turn 8 and the Astilleros Bridge in the foreground; the drivers signed Bridgestone's commemorative tyres; local fans couldn't get enough of Formula One;... and Toyota attracted the prettiest one; Kimi Räikkönen's refueller Pietro Timpini is stretchered away after being knocked down, escaping with a broken toe and bruised ribs; seven-time World Champion Michael Schumacher was back with his old team, Ferrari, offering advice to Kimi Räikkönen on the grid; Nico Rosberg enjoys getting close to a finless porpoise on a visit to Europe's largest aquarium

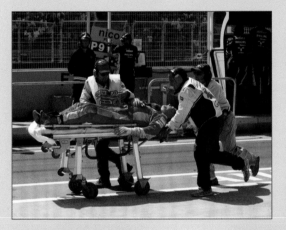

WEEKEND NEWS

■ In Valencia, Bridgestone celebrated its 200th grand prix since it entered the sport full time in 1997, and the current drivers signed a couple of golden coloured tyres to mark the occasion. The company chose not to count the two Japanese GPs of 1976 and 1977, in which it also participated.

■ The race weekend was overshadowed by a plane crash in Madrid on Wednesday afternoon that claimed the lives of more than 150 passengers. Drivers and other leading personalities joined in a silent tribute in the paddock on Friday, while at Fernando Alonso's request drivers also put Spanish flag stickers on their helmets.

■ Prior to the cars running on track on Friday, the drivers and Bridgestone expressed some concern about the surface transitions over the swing bridge. Fears that the narrow gaps might damage tyres proved to be unfounded, and drivers said that they barely even felt a bump as they crossed them.

■ Fernando Alonso landed himself in trouble on Friday when he made a late decision to enter the pitlane and cut across the white line at pit entry, at a point where cars staying on the track and those coming into the pits ran close to each other. The local hero earned himself a fine of €10,000 as well as a reprimand from the FIA stewards.

■ On August 28 came the sad news that 1961 World Champion Phil Hill had passed away in California at the age of 81, after fighting Parkinson's Disease for some time. Until recently, Hill had been a regular visitor to grands prix, usually as an ambassador for a travel company.

RACE RESULTS
EUROPE
VALENCIA

Official Results © [2008]
Formula One Administration Limited,
6 Princes Gate, London, SW7 1QJ.
No reproduction without permission.
All copyright and database rights reserved.

RACE DATE August 24th
CIRCUIT LENGTH 3.380 miles
NO. OF LAPS 57
RACE DISTANCE 191.919 miles
WEATHER Dry and bright, 30°C
TRACK TEMP 44°C
RACE DAY ATTENDANCE 115,000
LAP RECORD Felipe Massa, 1m38.708s, 122.806mph, 2008

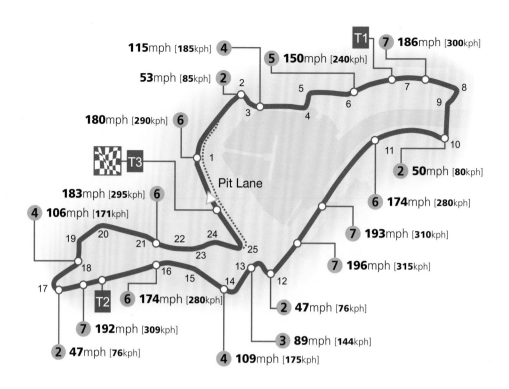

	PRACTICE 1		
	Driver	Time	Laps
1	S Vettel	1m40.496s	29
2	F Massa	1m40.654s	27
3	L Hamilton	1m40.822s	21
4	S Bourdais	1m41.099s	31
5	H Kovalainen	1m41.163s	23
6	R Kubica	1m41.281s	24
7	K Räikkönen	1m41.317s	27
8	K Nakajima	1m41.329s	26
9	F Alonso	1m41.385s	31
10	N Rosberg	1m41.706s	22
11	R Barrichello	1m41.830s	27
12	J Trulli	1m41.930s	27
13	A Sutil	1m41.951s	23
14	T Glock	1m42.036s	27
15	N Piquet Jr	1m42.107s	32
16	N Heidfeld	1m42.453s	23
17	J Button	1m42.460s	29
18	G Fisichella	1m43.075s	25
19	D Coulthard	1m43.312s	23
20	M Webber	1m43.524s	24

	PRACTICE 2		
	Driver	Time	Laps
1	K Räikkönen	1m39.477s	30
2	F Alonso	1m39.497s	39
3	J Button	1m39.546s	35
4	F Massa	1m39.678s	31
5	L Hamilton	1m39.712s	31
6	H Kovalainen	1m39.954s	30
7	T Glock	1m39.967s	32
8	R Kubica	1m40.149s	35
9	N Piquet Jr	1m40.439s	32
10	G Fisichella	1m40.500s	23
11	M Webber	1m40.585s	24
12	N Rosberg	1m40.607s	34
13	D Coulthard	1m40.696s	23
14	K Nakajima	1m40.742s	34
15	J Trulli	1m40.877s	32
16	S Vettel	1m40.982s	36
17	A Sutil	1m40.999s	32
18	N Heidfeld	1m41.084s	35
19	S Bourdais	1m41.246s	38
20	R Barrichello	1m41.377s	31

	PRACTICE 3		
	Driver	Time	Laps
1	R Kubica	1m38.754s	15
2	N Rosberg	1m38.877s	18
3	S Bourdais	1m39.009s	16
4	K Nakajima	1m39.270s	17
5	F Massa	1m39.276	18
6	S Vettel	1m39.300s	16
7	L Hamilton	1m39.314s	13
8	N Heidfeld	1m39.335s	18
9	D Coulthard	1m39.421s	16
10	N Piquet Jr	1m39.452s	20
11	M Webber	1m39.597s	17
12	J Button	1m39.628s	17
13	F Alonso	1m39.652s	17
14	H Kovalainen	1m39.802s	14
15	K Räikkönen	1m39.810s	20
16	T Glock	1m39.919s	22
17	A Sutil	1m40.019s	21
18	G Fisichella	1m40.059s	21
19	R Barrichello	1m40.512s	20
20	J Trulli	No time	2

	QUALIFYING 1	
	Driver	Time
1	J Trulli	1m37.948s
2	S Vettel	1m38.141s
3	F Massa	1m38.176s
4	F Alonso	1m38.268s
5	R Kubica	1m38.347s
6	L Hamilton	1m38.464s
7	T Glock	1m38.532s
8	M Webber	1m38.559s
9	N Rosberg	1m38.595s
10	S Bourdais	1m38.622s
11	H Kovalainen	1m38.656s
12	K Nakajima	1m38.667s
13	K Räikkönen	1m38.703s
14	N Heidfeld	1m38.738s
15	N Piquet Jr	1m38.787s
16	J Button	1m38.880s
17	D Coulthard	1m39.235s
18	G Fisichella	1m39.268s
19	R Barrichello	1m39.811s
20	A Sutil	1m39.943s

	QUALIFYING 2	
	Driver	Time
1	S Vettel	1m37.842s
2	F Massa	1m37.859s
3	N Heidfeld	1m37.859s
4	J Trulli	1m37.928s
5	L Hamilton	1m37.954s
6	R Kubica	1m38.050s
7	H Kovalainen	1m38.120s
8	K Räikkönen	1m38.229s
9	N Rosberg	1m38.336s
10	S Bourdais	1m38.417s
11	K Nakajima	1m38.428s
12	F Alonso	1m38.435s
13	T Glock	1m38.499s
14	M Webber	1m38.515s
15	N Piquet Jr	1m38.744s

	Best sectors – Practice	
Sec 1	N Rosberg	26.091s
Sec 2	S Bourdais	44.797s
Sec 3	R Kubica	27.618s

	Speed trap – Practice	
1	F Massa	196.539mph
2	S Bourdais	196.477mph
3	S Vettel	196.104mph

	Best sectors – Qualifying	
Sec 1	F Massa	25.827s
Sec 2	J Trulli	44.473s
Sec 3	R Kubica	27.210s

	Speed trap – Qualifying	
1	S Vettel	196.601mph
2	F Massa	196.415mph
3	K Räikkönen	196.353mph

Kimi Räikkönen

"I lost a place at the start and was stuck in traffic for the first stint. At the second stop, I left before I should have. Luckily, Pietro (Timpini) isn't too badly hurt. Then the engine broke."

Nick Heidfeld

"To finish ninth in a car good for third is a disaster. I had problems with the harder tyres in the first two stints, and it was only better at the end with the softer tyre."

Fernando Alonso

"At the start, I was touched by Nakajima and lost my rear wing. My mechanics did everything to try and allow me to continue, but my race was already compromised."

Nico Rosberg

"I'm happy as it's good to be going home with a point. The race went quite well and I was giving it my all, driving what felt like qualifying laps one after the other."

David Coulthard

"I was hit from behind on lap 1. Then I passed a few cars, but when I tried to pass Sutil's Force India, I clipped him, damaging my bargeboard and the side of the car."

Jarno Trulli

"That was good. I drove a strong race without attacking much, pushing hard when I needed to, while paying attention to taking care of my tyres and my brakes."

Felipe Massa

"It's fantastic having won after the disappointment of Budapest. I got a good start and pushed hard from the early laps. In the second part of the race, the car was exceptional."

Robert Kubica

"I was going to pass Lewis in Turn 2, but I saw Felipe braking early and I backed off. Then a bag went under the car and I couldn't steer for two corners, losing around 3s."

Nelson Piquet Jr

"Lap 1 was rough as I was in the middle of the pack and lost several positions. After that, I tried to fight back, but my front wing was bent and it was difficult to overtake."

Kazuki Nakajima

"On lap 1, going into Turns 4 and 5, I was just behind Alonso, but there was a battle going on in front and I couldn't avoid him. After that, I just tried to be consistent."

Mark Webber

"We just weren't quick enough. We were hoping for a few safety cars to come out in the race, so ran a one-stop strategy, but it didn't happen. We've got a lot of analysis to do."

Timo Glock

"I have had a bad cold for two days, but I had a good car and the right strategy and I think seventh was the best we could have achieved today, so I'm happy."

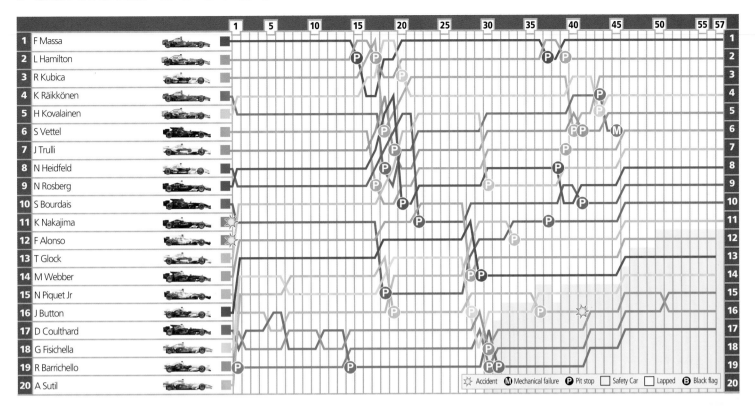

	Driver																								
1	F Massa																								
2	L Hamilton																								
3	R Kubica																								
4	K Räikkönen																								
5	H Kovalainen																								
6	S Vettel																								
7	J Trulli																								
8	N Heidfeld																								
9	N Rosberg																								
10	S Bourdais																								
11	K Nakajima																								
12	F Alonso																								
13	T Glock																								
14	M Webber																								
15	N Piquet Jr																								
16	J Button																								
17	D Coulthard																								
18	G Fisichella																								
19	R Barrichello																								
20	A Sutil																								

☆ Accident Ⓜ Mechanical failure Ⓟ Pit stop ☐ Safety Car ☐ Lapped Ⓑ Black flag

QUALIFYING 3

	Driver	Time
1	F Massa	1m38.989s
2	L Hamilton	1m39.199s
3	R Kubica	1m39.392s
4	K Räikkönen	1m39.488s
5	H Kovalainen	1m39.937s
6	S Vettel	1m40.142s
7	J Trulli	1m40.309s
8	N Heidfeld	1m40.631s
9	N Rosberg	1m40.721s
10	S Bourdais	1m40.750s

GRID

	Driver	Time
1	F Massa	1m38.989s
2	L Hamilton	1m39.199s
3	R Kubica	1m39.392s
4	K Räikkönen	1m39.488s
5	H Kovalainen	1m39.937s
6	S Vettel	1m40.142s
7	J Trulli	1m40.309s
8	N Heidfeld	1m40.631s
9	N Rosberg	1m40.721s
10	S Bourdais	1m40.750s
11	K Nakajima	1m38.428s
12	F Alonso	1m38.435s
13	T Glock	1m38.499s
14	M Webber	1m38.515s
15	N Piquet Jr	1m38.744s
16	J Button	1m38.880s
17	D Coulthard	1m39.235s
18	G Fisichella	1m39.268s
19*	R Barrichello	1m39.811s
20	A Sutil	1m39.943s

* STARTED FROM PITLANE

RACE

	Driver	Car	Laps	Time	Avg. mph	Fastest	Stops
1	F Massa	Ferrari F2008	57	1h35m32.339s	120.535	1m38.708s	2
2	L Hamilton	McLaren-Mercedes MP4-23	57	1h35m37.950s	120.417	1m38.884s	2
3	R Kubica	BMW Sauber F1.08	57	1h36m09.692s	119.755	1m39.330s	2
4	H Kovalainen	McLaren-Mercedes MP4-23	57	1h36m12.042s	119.706	1m39.112s	2
5	J Trulli	Toyota TF108	57	1h36m23.023s	119.479	1m39.657s	2
6	S Vettel	Toro Rosso-Ferrari STR03	57	1h36m24.964s	119.438	1m39.485s	2
7	T Glock	Toyota TF108	57	1h36m40.329s	119.122	1m39.535s	1
8	N Rosberg	Williams-Toyota FW30	57	1h36m43.796s	119.051	1m39.577s	2
9	N Heidfeld	BMW Sauber F1.08	57	1h36m54.516s	118.831	1m39.526s	2
10	S Bourdais	Toro Rosso-Ferrari STR03	57	1h37m02.133s	118.676	1m39.639s	2
11	N Piquet Jr	Renault R28	57	1h37m05.056s	118.616	1m39.544s	1
12	M Webber	Red Bull-Renault RB4	56	1h35m42.553s	118.210	1m40.264s	1
13	J Button	Honda RA108	56	1h35m53.740s	117.980	1m40.763s	1
14	G Fisichella	Force India-Ferrari VJM01	56	1h36m04.448s	117.761	1m40.353s	1
15	K Nakajima	Williams-Toyota FW30	56	1h36m19.117s	117.462	1m39.803s	2
16	R Barrichello	Honda RA108	56	1h36m29.660s	117.248	1m40.593s	1
17	D Coulthard	Red Bull-Renault RB4	56	1h37m07.559s	116.486	1m40.978s	2
R	K Räikkönen	Ferrari F2008	45	Engine	-	1m39.424s	2
R	A Sutil	Force India-Ferrari VJM01	41	Spun off	-	1m40.661s	2
R	F Alonso	Renault R28	0	Collision	-	-	0

CHAMPIONSHIP

	Driver	Pts
1	L Hamilton	70
2	F Massa	64
3	K Räikkönen	57
4	R Kubica	55
5	H Kovalainen	43
6	N Heidfeld	41
7	J Trulli	26
8	F Alonso	18
9	M Webber	18
10	T Glock	15
11	N Piquet Jr	13
12	R Barrichello	11
13	N Rosberg	9
14	S Vettel	9
15	K Nakajima	8
16	D Coulthard	6
17	J Button	3
18	S Bourdais	2

Fastest Lap
F Massa 1m38.708s
(122.806mph) on lap 36

Fastest speed trap
S Bourdais 194.986mph
Slowest speed trap
F Alonso 103.955mph

Fastest pit stop
1 N Heidfeld 20.440s
2 J Trulli 20.537s
3 L Hamilton 20.675s

	Constructor	Pts
1	Ferrari	121
2	McLaren-Mercedes	113
3	BMW Sauber	96
4	Toyota	41
5	Renault	31
6	Red Bull-Renault	24
7	Williams-Toyota	17
8	Honda	14
9	Toro Rosso-Ferrari	11

 Sebastien Bourdais

"That was a nice race, apart from the fact that I touched Heidfeld and broke my wing, losing 20s to the group I was in over 17 laps. The next two stints were good."

 Jenson Button

"I was running on a one-stopper, but was stuck behind Heidfeld after he had pitted. We ran the option for the second stint, which was fine but the rears went away."

 **Adrian Sutil**

"It was a shame that I couldn't pass Giancarlo quickly enough to take advantage of the two-stop strategy. I did pass him, but under braking I lost the rear and hit a barrier."

 **Lewis Hamilton**

"Despite my having a few problems health-wise, I maintained the gap and our lap times showed that our pace was good, which was encouraging."

 Sebastian Vettel

"My start wasn't so good on the dirty side. Going into Turn 1, I was on the limit and very close to Kimi, keeping Jarno back, but he stayed out an extra lap and got past."

Rubens Barrichello

"After qualifying, we chose to start from the pitlane. We changed the brakes completely so the car was very different to drive, but it did improve a bit during the race."

Giancarlo Fisichella

"We expected a safety car after seeing the support races, but it didn't come out. Our pace wasn't far off the others, and we made a step forward with the gearbox."

Heikki Kovalainen

"I was able to pass Kimi before Turn 1. However, I'm not really happy with how the race went for me after that, because I had grip problems with the prime tyres."

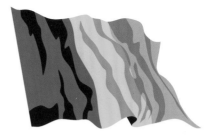

2008 FORMULA 1
ING BELGIAN GRAND PRIX
SPA-FRANCORCHAMPS

LEWIS LOSES OUT

This grand prix offered changing conditions, a great finish and, sadly, controversy. Hamilton had been first to the finish after a battle with Räikkönen, but a penalty gave victory to Massa

The Belgian GP provided one of the most sensational finishes of recent times, at the end of what, until then, had been a fairly mundane race. Rain fell on Spa-Francorchamps in the closing laps and allowed Lewis Hamilton to out-fumble Kimi Räikkönen as the pair slugged it out on dry tyres.

It was great stuff, but Hamilton lost what would have been his third wet win of the season on a classic track when he was docked 25 seconds. The Briton was deemed to have gained an unfair advantage while passing Räikkönen, even though the Finn himself crashed out within a lap. Victory was thus inherited by Felipe Massa, while Nick Heidfeld moved up to second place and Hamilton was demoted to third.

McLaren appealed the decision but, at a hearing in Paris on 22 September, the FIA Court of Appeal decided that the appeal was inadmissible.

Rain on Friday afternoon and a damp track on Saturday morning meant that teams didn't do as much homework as they had planned to, and prior to qualifying it wasn't clear who had got their sums right. In 2007, Ferrari thrashed McLaren, but McLaren had improved its form through the sweeping fast corners.

tyres. Nevertheless, the surface was very slippery in places, so everyone had to tread carefully through the first corner. Hamilton emerged from La Source in front, but team-mate Kovalainen was bundled down to 13th after a clash with Heidfeld, while further back Sebastien Bourdais hit Jarno Trulli under braking, and Giancarlo Fisichella struck a sideways Kazuki Nakajima on the exit.

Räikkönen dragged past Massa to claim second on the run out of Eau Rouge, giving his team-mate very little room. The Finn then had an unexpected bonus. First time into La Source at racing speed, Hamilton had a half spin and, while he lost very little time, Räikkönen had more momentum, and beat him in the rush down the hill.

Räikkönen then began to edge away, negating any doubts about his form, while Massa trailed around in third and was no threat to Hamilton.

The McLaren driver made his first stop a lap earlier than Räikkönen, and the gap grew to over 5s before both made their second stops on lap 24. On the harder tyre for the final stint, Hamilton was able to close the gap. Massa had dropped away from the leaders, but he picked up speed in his third stint and began to reel them in. Yet, with around eight laps to go, he dropped away again.

Everything began to change when rain fell in the final three laps. As we had seen at Monaco and Silverstone, Hamilton was much more comfortable in the wet than the Ferrari drivers, and in no time he was on Räikkönen's tail. Going into the chicane to start the penultimate lap, Räikkönen braked early, so Hamilton jerked left and attempted to go around the outside. Räikkönen didn't give him any room, so Hamilton steered hard left and jumped across the chicane run-off, emerging in front.

Mindful of his penalty at Magny-Cours, Hamilton realised that he would have to cede the position even

ABOVE Jenson Button had a weekend he'd like to forget, his Honda sometimes "undriveable"

BELOW This is not how Lewis Hamilton wanted to start lap 2, with a spin that let Kimi Räikkönen get by

Dark clouds hung over the track from the start of qualifying, but the rain held off. When the cars took their second and final runs in Q3, Massa briefly held top spot, but Hamilton was just behind him on the track, and snatched pole. "I did a perfect lap, but it was not enough," said the Brazilian. Heikki Kovalainen qualified third, ahead of Räikkönen as the Ferrari driver's disappointing qualifying form continued. The reigning World Champion's weekend wasn't helped by an accident on Friday afternoon.

Rain on Sunday lunchtime left the circuit very wet, but as the cars took to the grid it had dried sufficiently for everyone to take the start on regular

TALKING POINT
AND SO TO PARIS...

Lewis Hamilton's 25s penalty and demotion from first to third place, prompted considerable media reaction. For the first time, there was open talk about whether the sport was fixed and whether FIA really stood for Ferrari International Assistance.

Speaking on British national radio the following day, three-time world champion Niki Lauda called it the worst decision in the history of F1. The Austrian added that he would have denounced any suggestion of Ferrari bias before the event, but now he wasn't so sure. Strong stuff.

Looking at the evidence, though, it was easy to conclude that Hamilton had gained an advantage by missing out the final turn after trying to go around the outside of leader Kimi Räikkönen's Ferrari at Turn 18 two laps from home, even if he had briefly ceded the place back to Räikkönen.

At Suzuka in the epic 2005 Japanese Grand Prix, Fernando Alonso had done the self same thing while passing Christian Klien. Several laps later, the FIA decided that Alonso had not made enough of a concession and ordered him to slow down and let Klien re-pass. Alonso was running ahead of eventual race winner Räikkönen, and the decision ultimately cost him the race. So there was a precedent.

Several expressed the opinion that an intelligent non-application of the rules would have been the best PR option for F1 at Spa. After all, hadn't Räikkönen also used bits of the circuit that were not strictly speaking the main track, at both La Source and Pouhon? And had he not lost the race by crashing on his own, rather than through any action of Hamilton?

That was one view, but would it really have been correct not to look into the incident just because it involved Hamilton and McLaren and because of how it might look?

Hamilton could quite correctly claim that Räikkönen had forced him wide in Turn 18 but, as the leader of the race for the past 80 minutes, he was hardly going to allow Hamilton to pass him around the outside in a second-gear corner with two laps to go. Whether Hamilton had no option but to miss the final corner was debatable too.

However, where the sport did look a bit silly was when it announced that McLaren's appeal against Hamilton's penalty would be heard in Paris two weeks later. Why trail a number of McLaren and Ferrari witnesses, not to mention expensive lawyers, all the way to Paris, two days before most of them had to be in Singapore, just to decide that the 25s penalty was effectively a drive-through and therefore could not be appealed? Why not decide that on the Sunday evening at Spa? And what about Toro Rosso's appeal against Tonio Liuzzi's time penalty in the 2007 Japanese Grand Prix that was heard?

before the team got on the radio to him. He duly backed off and allowed Räikkönen to lead him across the start/finish line. Then, when they reached La Source, he dived down the inside into the hairpin, as Räikkönen was once again tentative on the brakes. As they turned in, the Finn actually tapped the rear of the McLaren, but both men continued on their way.

"I was getting closer and closer, but I was praying for some rain," Hamilton explained later. "Please, I need a little bit of rain just to make it more exciting, and it did! I was chasing him the whole time, just chasing, chasing, so I had time to plan where I'd go when I got close to him. I had to make sure when I did close enough there were no ifs, buts or maybes. I had to do the manoeuvre there and then. I pulled one off and then he pushed me wide, then I pulled another one off, and then we went off again. It was great.

"I was ahead in the corner, and he pushed me wide, which I thought was a little unfair. He literally pushed me beyond the white line. I was forced on the exit road. I had to lift to allow him back past. He was clearly past me and from then on I had to try and get back at him. The rules say you have to let him past, and I did."

ABOVE The run from La Source to Eau Rouge and then uphill to Raidillon is still one of the most impressive sights in F1

INSIDE LINE
NICK HEIDFELD
BMW SAUBER DRIVER

"Up to this point in the season, I'd been having problems with tyre warm-up, preventing me getting the best out of the car over a single lap in qualifying. Here at Spa, though, it was OK and I was the fastest non-Ferrari/McLaren and started fifth.

I had a pretty good getaway, at least better than the row in front of me, but Alonso was a bit better again. I decided to go for the outside at La Source because things were looking a bit congested on the inside and I had a feeling there would be contact. Unfortunately, Kovalainen drove into me. I thought I would spin, or that the race would be over because of car damage, and I was relieved when it felt alright and the steering was straight.

I lost a lot of positions and was 10th at the end of the first lap, but eighth again when Kovalainen and Webber tangled. I had to stop earlier than some, including Vettel and my team-mate at his second stop, but I had a pretty good out-lap and managed to pass Robert when he had a delay at his final stop. I then found myself stuck behind Vettel

and, although I was much quicker, I couldn't pass. The closer I got, the more I started to destroy the tyres. It was pretty much a hero or zero decision to make a third pit stop and switch to the wets. At first, it was just drizzle, but the next lap it was a bit heavier and I thought I would take the gamble: I was pretty sure that nobody else would have the balls to change tyres.

The team asked me again what I wanted to do and I think it was the perfect call. When I went back out again I asked how many laps to go and they said, 'this one and then another one'. I couldn't see anyone ahead of me and that's when I wondered whether I'd got it wrong.

But the rain got heavier, they all had to slow and I managed to overtake on the last lap. The last

one I overtook – it was either Alonso or a Toro Rosso – blocked pretty hard going into Turn 10 and I nearly went onto the grass which, in the wet, would have been tricky. I just managed to stay on the track by running wheel-to-wheel, but for a moment my wheels were inside his and nearly touching the sidepods, which wasn't very clever... But, it worked out, I got by and a podium was a fantastic result after achieving the maximum in qualifying too."

In the McLaren pit, there was clearly some concern that things should be done properly, so immediately after the incident Sporting Director Dave Ryan contacted FIA Race Director Charlie Whiting in race control, and twice asked if Hamilton had complied with the rules. Whiting gave a positive response. He'd seen only the live pictures, and his instant reaction was in Hamilton's favour. Later, McLaren made much of the fact that Hamilton had been 6.7km/h slower than the Ferrari across the start/finish line, supporting this claim with figures taken from the official timing.

Where things get complicated is that Whiting's rulings, which teams have to regard as sacrosanct in the heat of a race battle, can later be questioned by the three race stewards.

Meanwhile, there was much else happening. On that penultimate lap the rain came down harder. Hamilton and Räikkönen both ran wide across the run-off at Pouhon, and then Hamilton lost the lead when he went across the grass to avoid a spinning Nico Rosberg coming back across his path at the next corner, Fagnes. The surprised Räikkönen charged between them to regain the lead, only to spin seconds later, handing the advantage back to Hamilton. Then, a few hundred metres further on, Räikkönen went off again, this time hitting the tyre wall with some force.

Hamilton now had to do a further lap in intensifying rain, but with no pressure from behind, and with Massa a long way back in second – and going even more slowly – he made it to the flag without further dramas.

There was excitement further back, however. With two laps to go, Heidfeld dropped out of seventh place to pit for wet tyres. He fell to ninth, but found so much pace that he charged up to third over those closing laps, weaving in and out of rivals as they crawled around.

It was a truly amazing finish, but even before the flag fell the stewards announced that they would

investigate the Räikkönen/Hamilton chicane incident. Most observers felt that it had simply been good racing, but after a couple of hours a penalty was confirmed. Hamilton was to be docked 25s, the equivalent of a drive-through penalty, as that can't be given in the final five laps of a grand prix.

The FIA argument was that had Hamilton followed Räikkönen around the corner in the normal way, he would not have been close enough to attempt that second move at La Source. The stewards also considered the fact that at the point he made the decision to steer across the run-off area, his front wheels were aligned with the rears of the Ferrari.

OPPOSITE This was the pit stop of the race, as Nick Heidfeld changed to inters with two laps to go and rose from ninth to third on the track

ABOVE Fernando Alonso changed to inters right at the end and snatched fourth from Vettel

BELOW Sebastien Bourdais could have finished even higher in the other Toro Rosso, but dropped from fourth to seventh

The stewards concluded that he had an alternative course of action: to back off momentarily, slip back behind the Ferrari, and follow Räikkönen around the corner. Had he done that, thanks to being on a less favourable line, he would have probably had less momentum coming out of the chicane and so less chance of pulling a move on the run to La Source.

In fact, the behaviour of both cars on the run to the hairpin was a little unusual, as they jostled around. It could be argued that Räikkönen was distracted by having the McLaren much closer in his mirrors than it would normally have been, but that seemed to be taking the 'gaining an advantage' theme to an extreme.

Thus victory was gifted to Massa, who had at no stage been part of the lead battle, and finished his race with a lap of 2m45s – possibly the slowest non-pit stop, non-safety car race winner's lap since we last raced at the old Nürburgring back in 1976.

Even worse for Hamilton, he lost two extra points by dropping to third behind Heidfeld. It was pure chance that left the BMW driver 23.8s behind at the end, and thus within the 25s margin of Hamilton's penalty. It was also pure luck that Hamilton didn't go slower than he did. He finished the race with a 2m36s lap. Had he done as Massa did and really cruised in, four other cars could have crept into the 25s range and he would have tumbled to seventh in the final standings...

Fernando Alonso had perhaps Renault's most competitive run up to this point of the season, running fourth for most of the race. He lost a place to Heidfeld in the closing laps, but by making his own switch to wets – for just the final tour – he was able to salvage fourth, Räikkönen's late demise having also helped him.

Sebastian Vettel loved the damp conditions and claimed fifth position for Scuderia Toro Rosso, while Robert Kubica was sixth in the other BMW Sauber. Sebastien Bourdais had looked set for a great fifth place in the dry, but tumbled to seventh in the chaotic closing laps, suffering more than most in the wet.

Eighth place initially went to Toyota's Timo Glock, but he was penalised for overtaking under yellow flags that were being displayed for Räikkönen's crash, so Mark Webber gained the final point. Heikki Kovalainen should have scored, but stopped on the last lap with a gearbox problem after a nightmare race that included that troubled first lap and then a drive-through penalty for nudging Webber into a spin earlier in the race.

SNAPSHOT FROM
BELGIUM

CLOCKWISE FROM RIGHT

Red Bull Racing's Mark Webber has no time to check out this La Source landmark; watching at Eau Rouge can make even grown men blanch; "laundry for Senor Alonso"; this Toyota lollipop man makes his positioning clear for Timo Glock's late-race pit stop; another of Formula One's bashful fans...; Webber seldom misses a chance to get on his bike; some paperwork that McLaren didn't want to see, with notification of Lewis Hamilton's time penalty

WEEKEND NEWS

■ MotoGP World Champion Casey Stoner visited the Monza F1 test, held just before the Belgian GP. The Australian ace sat in a Red Bull RB4 and spent some time with his countryman Mark Webber, who repaid the compliment by dropping in to the San Marino GP at Misano at the end of the same week.

■ In a ceremony on Friday attended by Bernie Ecclestone, Stavelot corner was renamed Curve Paul Frère, in honour of the highly respected Belgian racer/journalist who died earlier in the year at the age of 91. Frère finished second in the 1956 Belgian GP and also had a fourth- and fifth-place finish in his home event.

■ Kimi Räikkönen's status as a national hero in Finland was confirmed when his local post office issued a pair of stamps to celebrate his 2007 World Championship victory, albeit a little behind schedule. One showed his maiden win for the Scuderia in Melbourne, and the other the prancing horse logo.

■ Meanwhile, despite his recent slump in form, Kimi Räikkönen was said to have spent a considerable chunk of his earnings on a new boat – a Sunseeker Predator 108, estimated to cost 10m Euro. He already owned a smaller Sunseeker 72 model that had been repaired after its captain had hit some rocks with it...

■ Charity football matches have been quite popular among the drivers for some years, with Michael Schumacher and Giancarlo Fisichella usually leading the VIP team. In a game on Wednesday, Force India test driver Vitantonio Liuzzi was carried off after a crunching challenge that left him hobbling around at Spa-Francorchamps. Henceforth, teams may be a bit wary about what their charges get up to...

RACE RESULTS
BELGIUM
SPA-FRANCORCHAMPS

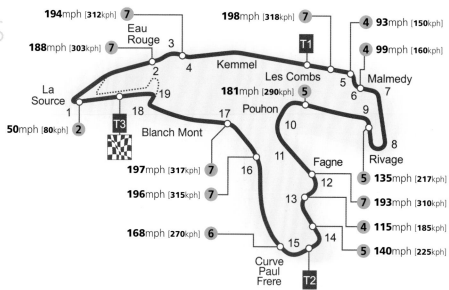

Official Results © [2008]
Formula One Administration Limited,
6 Princes Gate, London, SW7 1QJ.
No reproduction without permission.
All copyright and database rights reserved.

RACE DATE September 7th
CIRCUIT LENGTH 4.352 miles
NO. OF LAPS 44
RACE DISTANCE 191.491 miles
WEATHER Overcast, then rain, 15°C
TRACK TEMP 16°C
RACE DAY ATTENDANCE 65,000
LAP RECORD Felipe Massa 1m48.036s, 145.021mph, 2007

Track map labels:
- 194mph [312kph] — Eau Rouge
- 188mph [303kph]
- 50mph [80kph] — La Source
- 197mph [317kph]
- 196mph [315kph]
- 168mph [270kph] — Curve Paul Frere
- 198mph [318kph] — Kemmel
- 181mph [290kph] — Les Combs / Pouhon
- Blanch Mont
- Fagne
- 93mph [150kph] — Malmedy
- 99mph [160kph]
- Rivage
- 135mph [217kph]
- 193mph [310kph]
- 115mph [185kph]
- 140mph [225kph]

	PRACTICE 1				PRACTICE 2				PRACTICE 3				QUALIFYING 1			QUALIFYING 2	
	Driver	Time	Laps		Driver	Time	Laps		Driver	Time	Laps		Driver	Time		Driver	Time
1	F Massa	1m47.284s	26	1	F Alonso	1m48.454s	21	1	N Heidfeld	1m47.876s	19	1	S Bourdais	1m46.777s	1	H Kovalainen	1m46.037s
2	K Räikkönen	1m47.623s	26	2	F Massa	1m48.504s	16	2	H Kovalainen	1m48.165s	10	2	H Kovalainen	1m46.812s	2	L Hamilton	1m46.088s
3	L Hamilton	1m47.878s	27	3	H Kovalainen	1m48.740s	19	3	F Alonso	1m48.307s	19	3	F Massa	1m46.873s	3	K Räikkönen	1m46.298s
4	H Kovalainen	1m47.932s	24	4	L Hamilton	1m48.805s	17	4	L Hamilton	1m48.356s	10	4	L Hamilton	1m46.887s	4	N Heidfeld	1m46.311s
5	F Alonso	1m48.104s	26	5	K Räikkönen	1m49.328s	10	5	F Massa	1m48.692s	6	5	K Räikkönen	1m46.960s	5	F Massa	1m46.391s
6	M Webber	1m48.428s	29	6	N Rosberg	1m49.405s	17	6	S Vettel	1m48.768s	16	6	N Piquet Jr	1m47.052s	6	F Alonso	1m46.491s
7	S Bourdais	1m48.557s	31	7	S Vettel	1m49.427s	29	7	K Räikkönen	1m48.815s	10	7	R Kubica	1m47.093s	7	R Kubica	1m46.494s
8	S Vettel	1m48.958s	24	8	A Sutil	1m49.585s	22	8	N Rosberg	1m48.836s	13	8	D Coulthard	1m47.132s	8	S Bourdais	1m46.544s
9	T Glock	1m48.997s	26	9	J Trulli	1m49.715s	23	9	N Piquet Jr	1m48.946s	17	9	S Vettel	1m47.152s	9	S Vettel	1m46.804s
10	N Piquet Jr	1m49.068s	25	10	N Heidfeld	1m49.725s	22	10	M Webber	1m49.054s	14	10	F Alonso	1m47.154s	10	M Webber	1m46.814s
11	R Kubica	1m49.139s	25	11	R Kubica	1m49.875s	22	11	J Trulli	1m49.057s	16	11	M Webber	1m47.270s	11	J Trulli	1m46.949s
12	N Heidfeld	1m49.185s	26	12	D Coulthard	1m49.922s	20	12	D Coulthard	1m49.125s	16	12	T Glock	1m47.359s	12	N Piquet Jr	1m46.965s
13	N Rosberg	1m49.611s	30	13	S Bourdais	1m49.948s	20	13	R Kubica	1m49.250s	12	13	J Trulli	1m47.400s	13	T Glock	1m46.995s
14	J Trulli	1m49.625s	14	14	T Glock	1m50.281s	24	14	S Bourdais	1m49.256s	19	14	N Heidfeld	1m47.419s	14	D Coulthard	1m47.018s
15	D Coulthard	1m49.849s	18	15	K Nakajima	1m50.364s	20	15	T Glock	1m49.535s	18	15	N Rosberg	1m47.503s	15	N Rosberg	1m47.429s
16	G Fisichella	1m49.986s	27	16	G Fisichella	1m50.740s	11	16	K Nakajima	1m49.830s	12	16	R Barrichello	1m48.153s			
17	A Sutil	1m50.117s	19	17	J Button	1m50.925s	19	17	G Fisichella	1m49.949s	16	17	J Button	1m48.211s			
18	K Nakajima	1m50.125s	30	18	R Barrichello	1m51.238s	22	18	A Sutil	1m50.034s	16	18	A Sutil	1m48.226s			
19	J Button	1m50.464s	25	19	N Piquet Jr	1m51.334s	19	19	R Barrichello	1m50.061s	17	19	K Nakajima	1m48.268s			
20	R Barrichello	1m50.905s	25	20	M Webber	1m51.640s	7	20	J Button	No time	1	20	G Fisichella	1m48.447s			

Best sectors – Practice			Speed trap – Practice			Best sectors – Qualifying			Speed trap – Qualifying	
Sec 1	F Massa	31.267s	1	L Hamilton	192.065mph	Sec 1	L Hamilton	31.014s	1	L Hamilton	192.003mph
Sec 2	F Massa	46.796s	2	F Massa	192.003mph	Sec 2	K Räikkönen	46.178s	2	D Coulthard	191.879mph
Sec 3	N Rosberg	28.818s	3	K Räikkönen	191.817mph	Sec 3	H Kovalainen	28.612s	3	H Kovalainen	191.817mph

Kimi Räikkönen
"I passed Felipe, then Lewis when he spun. If you're in front in the rain, you have to be cautious. That's how Lewis caught me. Later, I ran wide, spun and ended up in the wall."

Nick Heidfeld
"I went for the outside at the start, but Heikki hit me. When drizzle set in, I changed to rain tyres. As I could not see any cars I thought this was the wrong choice, but it paid off."

Fernando Alonso
"We finished in fourth place after a difficult race with plenty of incidents. We missed out on a podium, but we have shown that we can be the third-strongest team."

Nico Rosberg
"I did the best I could from where I started and the performance we had in the car. We had to make the judgment to come in for the wet tyres, and it was a good decision."

David Coulthard
"I got held up behind the Hondas and it was hard to make up places. Changing conditions made things interesting and we should have changed to inters a lap earlier."

Jarno Trulli
"I was unlucky, as I had a great start and was in the top six, but was hit from the back. This also caused a gearbox problem, so my only target was to finish the race."

Felipe Massa
"I thought Eau Rouge might be wetter and was cautious. Kimi attacked and got by. When rain fell, I had a good margin and preferred not to take any risks."

Robert Kubica
"We had a problem in the second stop. I lost places, returning behind Nick. When it started raining, he pitted to change tyres. I couldn't do the same as I was right behind."

Nelson Piquet Jr
"The plan was to run a one-stop strategy, so my car was heavy. I made a good start and gained five places, but there were still damp patches and I made a mistake."

Kazuki Nakajima
"I had contact in the first corner and that cost me time. It was a tough call to see what the wets might do for us, but we didn't have enough time to make up any ground."

Mark Webber
"I was running short and when doing that it helps to have a clear track, but I didn't. I lost time behind Bourdais. Then I got hit by Heikki and lost time, hurting our strategy."

Timo Glock
"I saw Sebastien slide into Jarno at the first corner, so stayed out of the way. I changed to standard wets and it was the right thing to do, and I just got past Webber."

	Driver		
1	L Hamilton		
2	F Massa		
3	H Kovalainen		
4	K Räikkönen		
5	N Heidfeld		
6	F Alonso		
7	M Webber		
8	R Kubica		
9	S Bourdais		
10	S Vettel		
11	J Trulli		
12	N Piquet Jr		
13	T Glock		
14	D Coulthard		
15	N Rosberg		
16	R Barrichello		
17	J Button		
18	A Sutil		
19	K Nakajima		
20	G Fisichella		

☆ Accident　Ⓜ Mechanical failure　Ⓟ Pit stop　☐ Safety Car　☐ Lapped　Ⓑ Black flag

QUALIFYING 3

	Driver	Time
1	L Hamilton	1m47.338s
2	F Massa	1m47.678s
3	H Kovalainen	1m47.815s
4	K Räikkönen	1m47.992s
5	N Heidfeld	1m48.315s
6	F Alonso	1m48.504s
7	M Webber	1m48.736s
8	R Kubica	1m48.763s
9	S Bourdais	1m48.951s
10	S Vettel	1m50.319s

GRID

	Driver	Time
1	L Hamilton	1m47.338s
2	F Massa	1m47.678s
3	H Kovalainen	1m47.815s
4	K Räikkönen	1m47.992s
5	N Heidfeld	1m48.315s
6	F Alonso	1m48.504s
7	M Webber	1m48.736s
8	R Kubica	1m48.763s
9	S Bourdais	1m48.951s
10	S Vettel	1m50.319s
11	J Trulli	1m46.949s
12	N Piquet Jr	1m46.965s
13	T Glock	1m46.995s
14	D Coulthard	1m47.018s
15	N Rosberg	1m47.429s
16	R Barrichello	1m48.153s
17	J Button	1m48.211s
18	A Sutil	1m48.226s
19	K Nakajima	1m48.268s
20	G Fisichella	1m48.447s

RACE

	Driver	Car	Laps	Time	Avg. mph	Fastest	Stops
1	F Massa	Ferrari F2008	44	1h22m59.394s	138.417	1m48.222s	2
2	N Heidfeld	BMW F1.08	44	1h23m08.777s	138.157	1m49.067s	3
3*	L Hamilton	McLaren-Mercedes MP4-23	44	1h23m09.933s	138.125	1m48.135s	2
4	F Alonso	Renault R28	44	1h23m13.872s	138.016	1m49.238s	3
5	S Vettel	Toro Rosso-Ferrari STR03	44	1h23m13.970s	138.013	1m49.086s	2
6	R Kubica	BMW Sauber F1.08	44	1h23m14.431s	138.000	1m48.965s	2
7	S Bourdais	Toro Rosso-Ferrari STR03	44	1h23m16.129s	137.954	1m49.002s	2
8	M Webber	Red Bull-Renault RB4	44	1h23m42.170s	137.238	1m49.515s	2
9*	T Glock	Toyota TF108	44	1h24m06.439s	136.578	1m50.255s	2
10	H Kovalainen	McLaren-Mercedes MP4-23	43	Gearbox	-	1m48.223s	3
11	D Coulthard	Red Bull-Renault RB4	43	1h22m45.088s	135.660	1m50.177s	2
12	N Rosberg	Williams-Toyota FW30	43	1h22m47.042s	135.606	1m50.656s	2
13	A Sutil	Force India-Ferrari VJM01	43	1h22m49.057s	135.552	1m50.487s	2
14	K Nakajima	Williams-Toyota FW30	43	1h22m58.340s	135.299	1m50.970s	2
15	J Button	Honda RA108	43	1h22m59.886s	135.257	1m50.671s	2
16	J Trulli	Toyota TF108	43	1h23m40.609s	135.159	1m50.543s	2
17	G Fisichella	Force India-Ferrari VJM01	43	1h24m49.083s	132.355	1m51.701s	2
18	K Räikkönen	Ferrari F2008	42	Spun off	-	1m47.930s	2
R	R Barrichello	Honda RA108	19	Gearbox	-	1m52.072s	1
R	N Piquet Jr	Renault R28	13	Spun off	-	1m51.118s	0

* INCLUDES 25S TIME PENALTY ADDED

CHAMPIONSHIP

	Driver	Pts
1	L Hamilton	76
2	F Massa	74
3	R Kubica	58
4	K Räikkönen	57
5	N Heidfeld	49
6	H Kovalainen	43
7	J Trulli	26
8	F Alonso	23
9	M Webber	19
10	T Glock	15
11	N Piquet Jr	13
12	S Vettel	13
13	R Barrichello	11
14	N Rosberg	9
15	K Nakajima	8
16	D Coulthard	6
17	S Bourdais	4
18	J Button	3

	Constructor	Pts
1	Ferrari	131
2	McLaren-Mercedes	119
3	BMW Sauber	107
4	Toyota	41
5	Renault	36
6	Red Bull-Renault	25
7	Williams-Toyota	17
8	Toro Rosso-Ferrari	17
9	Honda	14

Fastest Lap
K Räikkönen 1m47.936s
(145.163mph) on lap 24

Fastest speed trap
H Kovalainen 195.980mph
Slowest speed trap
J Trulli 186.660mph

Fastest pit stop
1 T Glock 25.920s
2 S Vettel 26.000s
3 N Heidfeld 26.115s

Sebastien Bourdais
"It was a lottery on the last lap. It's a horrible situation, as everything had been under control until then. It was so close to being a great result I felt I could almost touch it."

Jenson Button
"I got boxed in at the start, then lost time in the train behind Rubens when he had his gearbox problem. Our rear tyre pressures were too low which made the car tricky."

Adrian Sutil
"We had a lot of fights and lots of overtaking. I caught Button and as there were two laps left and we were quick in the wet with dry tyres, we stayed out and I passed him."

Lewis Hamilton
"Kimi was cautious and I closed in. We almost clashed at the chicane and I needed to steer left to avoid him. I left him the space to get back ahead and got up the inside."

Sebastian Vettel
"Seb and I have reason to smile. The last lap was unbelievable and I was shocked as I got passed in the last 50m and then Heidfeld and Alonso drove past me on inters."

Rubens Barrichello
"The race was going well, but I lost sixth gear after I passed Trulli. The team thought it best to retire as this is my first race with this engine and I have to use it at Monza."

Giancarlo Fisichella
"Nakajima crossed in front of me and I broke my front wing. I lost time coming back to the pits. I came out just in front of the leaders and had blue flags 40 times."

Heikki Kovalainen
"I got squeezed at La Source, then later got alongside Webber. Maybe he didn't realise I was there and we hit, earning me a drive-through. Then my gearbox failed."

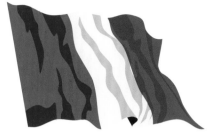

FORMULA 1 GRAN PREMIO SANTANDER D'ITALIA 2008
MONZA

VETTEL IS NEW STAR

Sebastian Vettel not only gave Scuderia Toro Rosso its first win, in horribly wet conditions, but became the youngest pole sitter and then the youngest winner in Formula 1 history

With rain throughout the weekend, the Monza win was there for the taking by anyone who took the trouble to get things just right. Against all the odds, Sebastian Vettel and Scuderia Toro Rosso simply did a better job than anyone else in the difficult circumstances, and won from the front in crushing style.

Pole position, 49 of 53 laps in the lead, victory by 12.5s over a healthy McLaren that ran a very similar pit-stop strategy – and yet Vettel registered only the 14th fastest lap as he became the youngest winner in F1 history at the age of 21 years and 73 days, almost a full year younger than Fernando Alonso had been when he won the Hungarian GP in 2003.

Scuderia Toro Rosso had high hopes for the Italian GP, especially when it became clear that it would be a wet weekend. However, Vettel wasn't particularly happy with the car initially, and it took changes for Saturday morning before he was really in the groove.

"I think the key was that I had very good confidence in the car," Vettel explained later. "On Friday, I didn't feel good in these conditions, but we did some changes, and in the morning it was much, much better. So I was pretty confident going into qualifying."

Vettel and the team that was once Minardi did an amazing job come qualifying, making all the right calls and getting out on track at just the right times. In Q1 he was third, behind only the two McLarens, while team-mate Sebastien Bourdais was sixth. Then in Q2 the blue and red cars were first and fifth fastest.

For Q1, Scuderia Toro Rosso thought about just one thing: how to be quickest. The race was to prove that Vettel was fuelled four laps lighter than anybody else. In fact, if there had been just one lap extra in his tank, or one less in Heikki Kovalainen's, the pole would almost certainly have been ceded to the Finn. But, even if he'd been fuelled as heavy as the rest of his closest opposition, Vettel probably would still have qualified second. On a great day for sponsor Red Bull, Mark Webber qualified third fastest and Bourdais fourth.

It was a mixed-up grid behind, with Felipe Massa sixth, Robert Kubica 11th, Kimi Räikkönen 14th and Lewis Hamilton 15th, the last-named compromised by an ill-judged gamble on intermediate tyres in Q2.

Scuderia Toro Rosso couldn't know for sure that the race would start behind the safety car but, when that was confirmed by the FIA just five minutes before

the start, it came as a massive bonus. Under normal circumstances, Vettel risked being swallowed up or maybe tapped from behind into the first chicane. With a safety car, he could just boot it when the track went green, knowing that Kovalainen and everyone else would be stuck in a cloud of spray behind him.

"It was a very, very difficult race, in very, very tricky conditions out there," admitted Vettel. "There was a lot of spray in the beginning. Being first is the easiest position you can be, as I've been behind before, done all that, where you go half-throttle down the straight without seeing anything..."

Vettel really went for it over those opening laps – the gap to Kovalainen opened out from 2.0s to 3.7s, 5.2s then 5.8s. By then, the McLaren driver was clear of the worst of the spray, but he obviously didn't have the supreme confidence that Vettel had.

"I knew that I would probably stop earlier than the others, so I knew that I had to pull out a gap as big as I could," said the 21-year-old. "I was pushing very, very hard every single lap, and sometimes I was close to losing it, but I think that's the way you have to do the race. I was pushing throughout the whole race."

Of course, Kovalainen wasn't the only man he was measuring himself against. The conditions also gave Vettel a huge advantage over the jokers in the pack, as quicker drivers found themselves trapped in traffic. After 10 laps, he was 18s clear of Massa in sixth place, and over 34s ahead of the Räikkönen/Hamilton battle. The lighter fuel load, which others had perhaps scoffed at, also contributed to his speed.

Vettel was 11s clear of Kovalainen by lap 17 and, most importantly, 33s ahead of fifth-placed Nico Rosberg, the man the team had surmised was the quickest of the one-stoppers. Crucially, that was more than enough to ensure that when he pitted a lap later, Vettel emerged still in front of the Williams.

Kovalainen, Webber and Massa all briefly moved

BELOW Toro Rosso's Sebastian Vettel kicked up the spray through which his rivals had to navigate

BOTTOM Heikki Kovalainen surprises Timo Glock by taking a trip across the first chicane on his way to second place

OPPOSITE Nico Rosberg ran second, but putting on a second set of full wets was the wrong choice just as the track started to dry

TALKING POINT
THE BIGGER PICTURE

Toro Rosso's victory was fantastic. Sebastian Vettel became the youngest driver ever to win a grand prix. It was a great story for F1, the media highlighting that the ex-Minardi crew had stuck it up the big guns.

There was congratulation aplenty for Gerhard Berger, for

Vettel, for Giorgio Ascanelli, racers all. But, in the background, the uncomfortable truth was that a 'customer car' had won a grand prix. And there were many with whom that did not sit well.

"First of all," said Williams CEO Adam Parr, "Toro Rosso is not a small team. The budget of Red Bull Technology to make chassis, is probably 70–80% more than Williams' budget. In fact, Toro Rosso's budget is more than our budget. So it's simply not true to say that a small team won. A two-team group with a 500 million Euro budget won a race.

"Second, let's take the scenario that McLaren had done its deal with David Richards and this year we had two silver

and red teams with the kind of performance they've got. Let's suppose that in Singapore, by going light with two of the four cars, they'd managed to block the first two rows of the grid. There would be total war. Ferrari would have to have a B-team too and the whole thing would be a nightmare. F1 would disintegrate."

BMW's Mario Theissen readily admitted. "We were approached by potential team owners. Basically they said give us the car free and we will do whatever you want all season…"

"I thought the position had been clarified last year," Toyota's John Howett commented. "There was a harmonisation period to become a full constructor and I'm

surprised the issue keeps coming back. Next year, we're faced with an all-new car. Technically, Red Bull could run four cars in winter testing and have a big advantage."

Some, it seems, are using the economic slump and a lack of teams wanting to enter F1 as constructors to once again champion the view that a mix of constructors and customer teams is the right way forward for F1. The issue was put back on the October FIA World Motor Sport Council agenda, until when the FIA was saying nothing. For the likes of Frank Williams, it remained imperative that pressure remained on Dietrich Mateschitz to take Toro Rosso forward to full constructor status.

ahead, and it was now a question of when they would call at the pits for their stops. All three came in together on lap 22, and Vettel reclaimed his lead. That put them out of the equation for the time being, but now there was the matter of the one-stoppers.

With considerably lighter fuel loads than Vettel was now carrying, and with their original sets of tyres seemingly well-suited to the conditions, Rosberg and Hamilton were closing. In fact, Hamilton had pulled off some aggressive passes as he charged up the order, and he was aiming for a single stop. By lap 26, Hamilton was just 1.1s behind Vettel and looking for a way by. However, at the end of the next lap, he came in.

Hamilton went back out still on extreme wets and, having been burned in qualifying by going too early to intermediates, he didn't want to make the same mistake again. However, the promised rain never returned, and he was only a lap or two off being able to make that choice without serious risk.

On lap 28, Rosberg went to extreme wets, but David Coulthard went for intermediates. Then, on lap 29, Nick Heidfeld went on to intermediates as well, followed by Fernando Alonso. Soon everyone was

coming back in for intermediates. For Heidfeld, Alonso and Kubica the timing was perfect, as the change coincided with their single stops, so they jumped up the order as a result.

It was a disaster for Hamilton and Rosberg, whose intended single stops had been just a shade too early, and who now needed an extra pit visit. Conversely, it was just about alright for Massa and Kovalainen, whose two-stop schedules dovetailed with the changing conditions.

As you can imagine, it was absolutely perfect for Vettel, who stayed out as long as possible, making use of his declining fuel load and covering what everyone else was doing before changing to inters on lap 36. Along with Hamilton and Nelson Piquet Jr, who came in that lap, he was the last to make the change.

"Every lap I was pushing harder and harder, fighting against myself, just trying to keep the gap as big as possible, and increase it," said Vettel. "It was never easy, especially when we were on extreme-wet tyres and there was less and less water. Everybody was looking for some water to cool the tyres down."

The team did its bit by not disturbing him, as team principal Franz Tost noted: "It was quiet because

BELOW LEFT Robert Kubica – wearing a special helmet for Monza – climbed from 11th place to third

BELOW RIGHT The tifosi let on as to which of the Ferrari drivers they favoured

BOTTOM Lewis Hamilton dives past Fernando Alonso at the first chicane on his climb from 15th on the grid

OPPOSITE Rubens Barrichello makes a splash in his Honda

INSIDE LINE
SEBASTIAN VETTEL
TORO ROSSO DRIVER

"Pole position. Incredible. I was joking with my engineers. We were saying if it's wet we have to go for pole! The conditions were so difficult that you never knew how much water to expect. Sometimes you were lucky not to lose the car because of the aquaplaning.

In wet practice on Friday, truthfully, I didn't feel very comfortable, but overnight we found just the right set-up. When you feel confident in these conditions it's a huge advantage. But in Q1 especially it was nearly impossible to see anything. In Q2, it was very difficult too, but I set the time early and was lucky to get a clean lap. With more and more rain, the people who waited had bad luck.

It's funny, as before the Belgian GP I did some karting. I hadn't driven one for a year and when we were building it up I said 'let's stay with slicks for the wet', because I had to run-in the engine. They thought I was mad, but I wanted the practice. A week later, all this Monza rain!

We did not expect to win and it was just unbelievable. We had no problems at all, I had a good strategy and crossing the finish line was just... For sure, it's the best day of my life. These pictures, these emotions, I will never forget. It's so much greater than you might even think.

We didn't go for more downforce in case it was dry and so on the straights we were bloody fast. The safety-car start helped and being first and having no visibility problems was key. I opened up a solid 6–7s gap to Heikki straight away. It got trickier mid-race looking for water to cool the tyres and it was very, very slippery. Then, before the last stint I was on the radio to my engineer and he said 'let's go for inters'. It was the right choice. What a perfect weekend. The youngest man to win a pole position and a grand prix. I don't really know what to say!

Compared to BMW, McLaren or Ferrari we haven't got that many staff. Obviously we get a lot of help from Red Bull Technology, but still we have only about 160 people working in Faenza and everyone can feel very special. To stand on the podium and see my team and my family going completely mad was great. And then to listen to the German national anthem… I nearly started to cry. Special thanks to Giorgio Ascanelli, I have to mention him! What he has done with that crew is unbelievable."

ABOVE Felipe Massa started sixth and finished sixth, but was able to cut the gap to Hamilton to a point

BELOW Starved of success when they raced as Minardi, it's no surprise that the Scuderia Toro Rosso crew went mad when Vettel won

Sebastian was driving well. He did very fast lap times, and you would disturb a driver just telling him to drive slow or drive different. Just let him go. He was experienced enough to bring it home."

Vettel never took his eye off the ball: "You are always on the edge, and that's just great. In the end, I didn't drink anything. I was so thrilled and enjoyed the race so much that I totally forgot to drink. So, in the last couple of laps I did try to drink something, but the taste wasn't as good anymore! Luckily, I only had some laps to go."

With the track drying by the lap, inevitably everyone set their fastest laps right at the end. Even

Vettel did his personal best on the final lap, although he was 12s clear and had no need to go too quickly. That left him 14th on the overall list of fastest laps, which was a strange statistical anomaly at the end of a perfect race.

Vettel's sheer joy afterwards was extremely refreshing: "Obviously, it was my first podium, so I have no other races to compare it to. But it was unbelievable, standing there and seeing the crowds, a lot of people running down the straight, everyone cheering and shouting. Winning here for an Italian team is probably the best that can happen to you as a driver."

Kovalainen ran a low-key second throughout, but he was never able to do anything about the car up ahead. Nevertheless, he was able to score eight vital constructors' points for McLaren.

"I was just struggling to find more time and trying to go faster," said the Finn. "We kept pushing, and towards the end it got a little bit better, but I think it was the maximum we could do today."

Kubica started with a very heavy fuel load and struggled early on, but his well-timed single pit stop and switch to intermediate tyres helped the BMW Sauber racer to claim third place, while similar strategies took Alonso to fourth and Heidfeld to fifth.

Hamilton caught sixth-placed Massa in the final stint when both were on intermediates, but the McLaren driver couldn't make a move, as his tyres went off. Nevertheless, by claiming seventh place he lost only one point in the fight with his main title rival. Had it continued to rain, Hamilton would have been the only driver who had any chance to topple Vettel.

"I was blindingly quick all the time," said Hamilton. "It's difficult once it gets drier and drier, as you overheat the tyres. Everyone was having the same problem. At the end of the race, the car was understeering in the high-speed corners and was very nervous on the rear. So I overcooked the rears and had no traction. I'm happy, because when it was wet I was demolishing the others. I was having a great time as I was able to brake 10 metres later than everyone else in certain places around the lap, and really find the grip."

The final point went to the Red Bull of Mark Webber. Kimi Räikkönen failed to score in ninth, but he was the quickest driver in the latter part of the race after finding his car much more competitive on intermediate tyres. But it was too little, too late.

Unluckiest man of the day was Vettel's team-mate Bourdais, who qualified fourth but had a steering wheel problem before the start, and then had trouble with its replacement on the grid. He started a lap down and showed his potential by setting second fastest lap on the way to 18th place in a race in which Giancarlo Fisichella was the only retirement.

It was a hugely popular result, but it was hard for McLaren and Ferrari to accept that they'd let this one slip away, harder still for such as Toyota, Heidfeld and Webber to take it in. A precious win still eluded each of them after so many years of trying. And yet Vettel had gone and made it all look so easy...

SNAPSHOT FROM
ITALY

CLOCKWISE FROM RIGHT Three days of rain meant that mechanics had to mop out the garages; style in the paddock; passion in the public areas; Force India's Colin Kolles and Michiel Mol share a joke with Virgin's Sir Richard Branson; a small gate that opens out into a magical park and a rather special circuit; double World Champion Emerson Fittipaldi dropped in; the team chiefs look happy enough before a FOTA (Formula One Teams' Association) meeting

WEEKEND NEWS

■ The big news at Monza was the announcement on Friday that Kimi Räikkönen had added 2010 to his existing Ferrari contract. With Felipe Massa already signed up for two more years, the deal put an end to any hopes Fernando Alonso might have harboured of going to Maranello any time soon.

■ Virgin boss Sir Richard Branson made a rare appearance at a grand prix as a guest of the Force India team. However, it was nothing to do with a shared passion with fellow airline owner, Kingfisher boss Vijay Mallya. In fact, he was present because the team's Dutch co-owner Michiel Mol had pre-booked a ticket on a Virgin space flight...

■ On race morning, a number of veteran Formula One personalities attended a ceremony at the start/finish line to mark the 30th anniversary of the death of the great Ronnie Peterson. Alas, although his contemporaries Jackie Stewart and Emerson Fittipaldi were both at Monza on Sunday, neither was able to make it on time for the ceremony.

■ McLaren confirmed at Monza that the veteran race engineer Steve Hallam was to leave the team at the end of the season, having been on board since the Ayrton Senna days in 1990, after a spell at Lotus. Hallam's surprise destination was a very different challenge in NASCAR's Sprint Cup.

■ Takuma Sato made his F1 comeback in a test at Jerez just after the Italian Grand Prix, driving for none other than Scuderia Toro Rosso. Out of the cockpit since the collapse of Super Aguri Racing in May, the Japanese driver was tipped as a possible Scuderia Toro Rosso candidate for 2009, thanks to the level of support he could potentially bring.

RACE RESULTS
ITALY
MONZA

RACE DATE September 14th
CIRCUIT LENGTH 3.600 miles
NO. OF LAPS 53
RACE DISTANCE 190.800 miles
WEATHER Raining then overcast, 16°C
TRACK TEMP 17°C
RACE DAY ATTENDANCE 90,000
LAP RECORD Rubens Barrichello
1m21.046s, 159.909mph, 2004

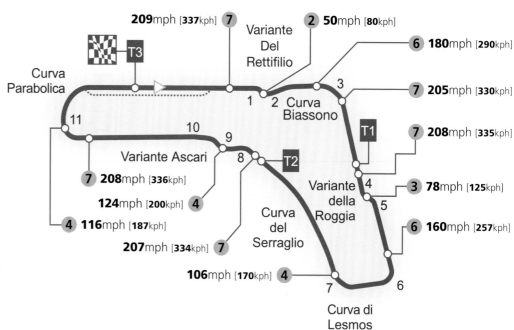

209mph [337kph] 7
Variante Del Rettifilio
2 50mph [80kph]
6 180mph [290kph]
Curva Parabolica T3
Curva Biassono
3
7 205mph [330kph]
1 2
11
T1
7 208mph [335kph]
10
9
Variante Ascari
8 T2
7 208mph [336kph]
4
4 78mph [125kph]
124mph [200kph] 4
Variante della Roggia
4
5
4 116mph [187kph]
Curva del Serraglio
6 160mph [257kph]
207mph [334kph] 7
106mph [170kph] 4
7
6
Curva di Lesmos

PRACTICE 1				PRACTICE 2				PRACTICE 3		
	Driver	Time	Laps		Driver	Time	Laps		Driver	Time	Laps
1	A Sutil	1m32.842s	18	1	K Räikkönen	1m23.861s	31	1	T Glock	1m35.464s	16
2	R Barrichello	1m33.428s	14	2	R Kubica	1m23.931s	26	2	S Vettel	1m36.129s	11
3	G Fisichella	1m33.695s	19	3	N Heidfeld	1m23.947s	29	3	N Rosberg	1m36.347s	13
4	T Glock	1m36.800s	13	4	L Hamilton	1m23.983s	25	4	J Trulli	1m36.686s	9
5	N Rosberg	1m36.900s	9	5	N Rosberg	1m24.110s	33	5	K Nakajima	1m36.706s	10
6	F Alonso	1m36.965s	10	6	F Massa	1m24.247s	34	6	N Heidfeld	1m36.972s	12
7	S Bourdais	1m37.142s	20	7	H Kovalainen	1m24.365s	29	7	D Coulthard	1m37.015s	7
8	J Trulli	1m37.214s	13	8	M Webber	1m24.521s	35	8	F Massa	1m37.263s	6
9	K Räikkönen	1m37.392s	5	9	A Sutil	1m24.669s	22	9	F Alonso	1m37.270s	10
10	S Vettel	1m37.754s	13	10	S Vettel	1m24.773s	35	10	G Fisichella	1m37.285s	9
11	N Piquet Jr	1m38.057s	11	11	D Coulthard	1m25.100s	25	11	A Sutil	1m37.504s	11
12	D Coulthard	1m38.303s	7	12	S Bourdais	1m25.192s	39	12	R Kubica	1m37.671s	7
13	J Button	1m39.062s	12	13	G Fisichella	1m25.204s	24	13	M Webber	1m37.778s	8
14	F Massa	1m40.233s	5	14	R Barrichello	1m25.296s	25	14	N Piquet Jr	1m37.833s	9
15	K Nakajima	No time	2	15	J Button	1m25.309s	34	15	J Button	1m37.882s	11
16	L Hamilton	No time	1	16	K Nakajima	1m25.330s	28	16	R Barrichello	1m38.689s	8
17	N Heidfeld	No time	1	17	T Glock	1m25.397s	28	17	S Bourdais	1m39.319s	8
18	H Kovalainen	No time	1	18	F Alonso	1m25.481s	22	18	K Räikkönen	1m41.164s	3
19	R Kubica	No time	1	19	J Trulli	1m25.753s	29	19	H Kovalainen	1m42.683s	6
20	M Webber	No time	1	20	N Piquet Jr	1m26.195s	23	20	L Hamilton	1m46.325s	8

QUALIFYING 1			QUALIFYING 2		
	Driver	Time		Driver	Time
1	H Kovalainen	1m35.214s	1	S Vettel	1m35.837s
2	L Hamilton	1m35.394s	2	H Kovalainen	1m35.843s
3	S Vettel	1m35.464s	3	N Rosberg	1m35.898s
4	N Rosberg	1m35.485s	4	J Trulli	1m36.008s
5	F Massa	1m35.536s	5	S Bourdais	1m36.175s
6	S Bourdais	1m35.543s	6	M Webber	1m36.306s
7	R Kubica	1m35.553s	7	F Alonso	1m36.518s
8	N Heidfeld	1m35.709s	8	T Glock	1m36.525s
9	T Glock	1m35.737s	9	N Heidfeld	1m36.626s
10	J Trulli	1m35.906s	10	F Massa	1m36.676s
11	K Räikkönen	1m35.965s	11	R Kubica	1m36.697s
12	M Webber	1m36.001s	12	G Fisichella	1m36.698s
13	G Fisichella	1m36.280s	13	D Coulthard	1m37.284s
14	F Alonso	1m36.297s	14	K Räikkönen	1m37.522s
15	D Coulthard	1m36.485s	15	L Hamilton	1m39.265s
16	R Barrichello	1m36.510s			
17	N Piquet Jr	1m36.630s			
18	K Nakajima	1m36.653s			
19	J Button	1m37.006s			
20	A Sutil	1m37.417s			

Best sectors – Practice			Speed trap – Practice		
Sec 1	R Kubica	27.125s	1	L Hamilton	215.491mph
Sec 2	K Räikkönen	28.462s	2	H Kovalainen	214.248mph
Sec 3	K Räikkönen	27.967s	3	R Kubica	213.813mph

Best sectors – Qualifying			Speed trap – Qualifying		
Sec 1	H Kovalainen	30.148s	1	M Webber	203.437mph
Sec 2	H Kovalainen	32.781s	2	S Vettel	203.250mph
Sec 3	J Trulli	31.789s	3	D Coulthard	202.567mph

Kimi Räikkönen
"In the conditions at the start, we couldn't keep our tyres up to temperature. When the conditions changed, unfortunately it was too late to aim for a points finish."

Nick Heidfeld
"Coming from 10th to fifth is OK. I left making the tyre choice to my race engineer, as they had more information about the weather. It was right to go for intermediates."

Fernando Alonso
"The result is very good as Monza was supposed to be the race that we were looking forward to the least. We made up the five points that we needed in our title fight."

Nico Rosberg
"Disappointing. Everyone else was staying on full wets, so we thought we'd do the same. There wasn't a dry line to see then, but it proved to be the wrong choice."

David Coulthard
"I had problems, as my brake balance bar jammed. Nakajima came around the outside at Parabolica, but there's an arc through there and I couldn't avoid him."

Jarno Trulli
"I was going well on the heavy wets, but the timings just didn't work out for us. My stop was four or five laps too soon for standard wets, so I had to pit again."

Felipe Massa
"When I passed Rosberg, the team told me to give back the place. That was decisive as after my first stop, I hit traffic. I tried to attack Heidfeld, but it wasn't worth taking risks."

Robert Kubica
"We went for one stop with a long first stint, but by the end I was having tyre problems. We were lucky with our stop, as it was just the right time to change to intermediates."

Nelson Piquet Jr
"I had a good fight through the pack and my pace was good considering the fuel load I started with. I finished outside the points, but it was decided in qualifying."

Kazuki Nakajima
"Starting from the pits to let me have some aero changes was not a penalty, as we started behind the safety car. We changed from extremes to wets at the right time."

Mark Webber
"We came out after the first stop behind Robert and Fernando and lost time on the fresh tyres. That's when Heikki got a good gap on me, so we did give some points away."

Timo Glock
"I made a good start, but I spun as I tried to pass Alonso. It was hard to attack, but I still managed to pull off some moves. The extra stop cost us the chance of points."

POSITIONS LAP BY LAP

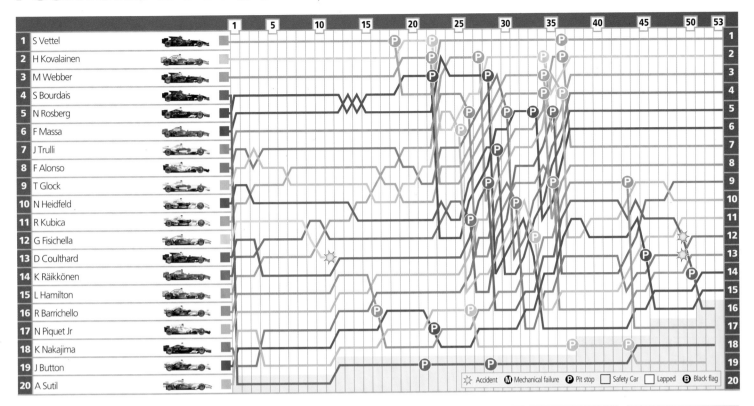

1	S Vettel							
2	H Kovalainen							
3	M Webber							
4	S Bourdais							
5	N Rosberg							
6	F Massa							
7	J Trulli							
8	F Alonso							
9	T Glock							
10	N Heidfeld							
11	R Kubica							
12	G Fisichella							
13	D Coulthard							
14	K Räikkönen							
15	L Hamilton							
16	R Barrichello							
17	N Piquet Jr							
18	K Nakajima							
19	J Button							
20	A Sutil							

☆ Accident Ⓜ Mechanical failure Ⓟ Pit stop ▢ Safety Car ▢ Lapped Ⓑ Black flag

QUALIFYING 3

	Driver	Time
1	S Vettel	1m37.555s
2	H Kovalainen	1m37.631s
3	M Webber	1m38.117s
4	S Bourdais	1m38.445s
5	N Rosberg	1m38.767s
6	F Massa	1m38.894s
7	J Trulli	1m39.152s
8	F Alonso	1m39.751s
9	T Glock	1m39.787s
10	N Heidfeld	1m39.906s

GRID

	Driver	Time
1	S Vettel	1m37.555s
2	H Kovalainen	1m37.631s
3	M Webber	1m38.117s
4	S Bourdais	1m38.445s
5	N Rosberg	1m38.767s
6	F Massa	1m38.894s
7	J Trulli	1m39.152s
8	F Alonso	1m39.751s
9	T Glock	1m39.787s
10	N Heidfeld	1m39.906s
11	R Kubica	1m36.697s
12	G Fisichella	1m36.698s
13	D Coulthard	1'm7.284s
14	K Räikkönen	1m37.522s
15	L Hamilton	1m39.265s
16	R Barrichello	1m36.510s
17	N Piquet Jr	1m36.630s
18*	K Nakajima	1m36.653s
19*	J Button	1m37.006s
20	A Sutil	1m37.417s

* STARTED FROM PITLANE

RACE

	Driver	Car	Laps	Time	Avg. mph	Fastest	Stops
1	S Vettel	Toro Rosso-Ferrari STR03	53	1h26m47.494s	131.755	1m30.510s	2
2	H Kovalainen	McLaren-Mercedes MP4-23	53	1h27m00.006s	131.466	1m30.300s	2
3	R Kubica	BMW Sauber F1.08	53	1h27m07.965s	131.266	1m30.298s	1
4	F Alonso	Renault R28	53	1h27m11.397s	131.180	1m29.961s	1
5	N Heidfeld	BMW Sauber F1.08	53	1h27m15.242s	131.084	1m29.807s	1
6	F Massa	Ferrari F2008	53	1h27m16.310s	131.057	1m29.696s	2
7	L Hamilton	McLaren-Mercedes MP4-23	53	1h27m17.406s	131.030	1m29.721s	2
8	M Webber	Red Bull-Renault RB4	53	1h27m19.542s	130.976	1m29.681s	2
9	K Räikkönen	Ferrari F2008	53	1h27m26.962s	130.791	1m28.047s	2
10	N Piquet Jr	Renault R28	53	1h27m41.939s	130.419	1m30.918s	1
11	T Glock	Toyota TF108	53	1h27m46.382s	130.309	1m29.948s	2
12	K Nakajima	Williams-Toyota FW30	53	1h27m49.509s	130.231	1m30.215s	1
13	J Trulli	Toyota TF108	53	1h27m53.448s	130.134	1m30.853s	2
14	N Rosberg	Williams-Toyota FW30	53	1h27m56.129s	130.068	1m30.019s	2
15	J Button	Honda RA108	53	1h28m00.864s	129.951	1m29.827s	2
16	D Coulthard	Red Bull-Renault RB4	52	1h27m09.395s	128.751	1m32.459s	2
17	R Barrichello	Honda RA108	52	1h27m37.452s	128.064	1m33.918s	2
18	S Bourdais	Toro Rosso-Ferrari STR03	52	1h27m57.260s	127.583	1m29.258s	2
19	A Sutil	Force India-Ferrari VJM01	51	1h27m45.015s	125.419	1m33.458s	3
R	G Fisichella	Force India-Ferrari VJM01	11	Accident	-	1m37.304s	0

CHAMPIONSHIP

	Driver	Pts
1	L Hamilton	78
2	F Massa	77
3	R Kubica	64
4	K Räikkönen	57
5	N Heidfeld	53
6	H Kovalainen	51
7	F Alonso	28
8	J Trulli	26
9	S Vettel	23
10	M Webber	20
11	T Glock	15
12	N Piquet Jr	13
13	R Barrichello	11
14	N Rosberg	9
15	K Nakajima	8
16	D Coulthard	6
17	S Bourdais	4
18	J Button	3

Fastest Lap
K Räikkönen 1m28.047s
(147.177mph) on lap 53

Fastest speed trap
L Hamilton 211.079mph
Slowest speed trap
G Fisichella 184.236mph

Fastest pit stop
1	J Button	27.666s
2	L Hamilton	28.460s
3	K Räikkönen	28.777s

	Constructor	Pts
1	Ferrari	134
2	McLaren-Mercedes	129
3	BMW Sauber	117
4	Toyota	41
5	Renault	41
6	Toro Rosso-Ferrari	27
7	Red Bull-Renault	26
8	Williams-Toyota	17
9	Honda	14

Sebastien Bourdais

"When I tried to get first I couldn't and let go of the flipper, and when the gear selected I stalled, when normally the anti-stall should come in. Then we couldn't get neutral."

Jenson Button

"I started from the pits, as it may have given us an advantage with tyre choice. But, when it started behind the safety car, it meant my tyres and brakes were cold."

Adrian Sutil

"I had no grip on the extreme wets. The second set was better, but it was drying out, so after 10 laps I lost even more grip. We then went over to the dry tyres, but it was too early."

Lewis Hamilton

"I was moving through the field when the circuit was at its wettest. I might have won but, as the circuit dried, my tyres cooked and I had to defend my position from Webber."

Sebastian Vettel

"We were fast in a straight line, as we didn't go for high downforce as we thought it might be dry. Being in front with no visibility problems was the key and I built a gap to Heikki."

Rubens Barrichello

"I pitted for the wet tyres as I felt it was starting to dry. Although my lap times fell, it interrupted our one-stop strategy. With 10 laps to go, the team put me on dry tyres."

Giancarlo Fisichella

"Coulthard passed me in the first chicane, but was slow in the corner, so I tapped him. That damaged the nose and it went under the car and I went off into the gravel."

Heikki Kovalainen

"I struggled to keep temperature in the brakes and had problems with my extreme wets. It didn't improve and only at the end was I able to match Vettel's pace."

2008 FORMULA 1 SINGTEL SINGAPORE GRAND PRIX
SINGAPORE

ALONSO'S NIGHT LIFE

Racing under floodlights was an instant hit, but this race produced an unexpected novelty. It turned Renault back into winners, albeit down to position when the safety car came out

Just across the river from Singapore's Marina Bay Grand Prix circuit a giant Sands casino complex is taking shape, and in a couple of years it will be a key part of the country's push to increase its profile as a tourist destination.

Fernando Alonso and Renault decided to roll the dice a little early, and their strategy gamble paid off spectacularly in a sensational first Singapore GP. After starting only 15th, the double World Champion had a break with a safety car and then rode his luck all the way to the chequered flag, giving the sport its second consecutive upset victory in a year that was supposed to be dominated by McLaren and Ferrari.

An unexpected winner was somehow appropriate as F1 embarked on this new showbiz era of night racing. Introduced so that rather than starting pre-dawn in the vital European market, the race could start in the afternoon for European viewers – thus guaranteeing a big international TV audience – the concept of racing under floodlights proved to be a huge success.

In addition to aligning the race timing with the key market, there was the bonus that the cars looked spectacular as drivers fought for control over a

TALKING POINT
WAS ALL AS IT SEEMED?

Although nobody wanted to be too outspoken on the record, many teams were deeply suspicious that Fernando Alonso's victory in Singapore, the first of the year for Renault, had been choreographed, with Nelson Piquet Jr crashing at an opportune moment to trigger the safety-car period that swung the race towards Alonso.

Alonso had been quick from Friday's first free practice and was deeply unhappy when a fuel-feed problem afflicted him early in Q2, before he'd had a chance to set a time. Starting only 15th on the bumpy Singapore street circuit, where overtaking was doubly difficult, his prospects were not promising. Piquet Jr had not made it out of Q1.

Normally, faced with Alonso's situation, a team will fuel up and run a long first stint one-stopper in an attempt to make up track position on some of the two-stopping cars and those one-stoppers with shorter stints. To go aggressive on strategy will only work on a circuit where overtaking is particularly easy and you have good top-end engine performance. Neither applied to Renault at Singapore's spectacular Marina Bay circuit and

Alonso said they did it because the brakes were running hot all weekend and would not cope with a heavy one-stop fuel load.

Alonso's first stop, on lap 12 of the 61, was very early. On the next lap, team-mate Piquet Jr, who had already spun on the warm-up lap, received a radio instruction: "Push, Nelson!" At the time, he was going nowhere fast, stuck down in 16th position behind Barrichello's Honda from the start. Was this a coded instruction? On the very next lap, Piquet Jr gyrated into the wall and brought out the safety car.

Rosberg and Kubica were forced to pit under the safety car, as they would otherwise have run out of fuel, attracting drive-through penalties as a result of this year's safety-car regulations. It proved that the first scheduled stints by anyone other than

Alonso had been to pit on laps 14 and 15. Most teams have a very good handle on when the opposition are going to stop, so Alonso's lap-12 stop was both as early as it legitimately could be and as late as possible if any 'plan' was to work.

"Looking at it from a purely statistical point-of-view," said a rival team strategist, "on a track like Singapore, stopping on lap 12 is not aggressive, it's stupid. It's something that cannot work. Your grandmother wouldn't do it... Then, it's true that stopping on lap 12 is the only way to open up a two-lap gap when the safety car will benefit only one car – the one that has stopped. And then, when you create this two-lap window and in it your team-mate crashes... If you add up the probability, you end up with a figure that is very close to zero."

Indeed, in Singapore, Jarno Trulli went for what turned into a marathon 33-lap first stint from 11th on the grid – four places ahead of Alonso.

Things are not always so clear-cut however, and there are always other factors to take into consideration. Alonso was obviously not happy with the performance of the supersoft tyres, despite setting quick times on them at the end of practice. He certainly wasn't keen to commit to them for half a race distance. The other major concern for Renault was that its brakes were marginal, as they had been in the past in Canada. It was that more than anything else that drove Renault towards an early first stop and a lighter fuel load.

The hope was that being lighter than most of those around him would help Alonso gain a few positions in the early laps. By then dropping out of the group at an early stage, he would potentially have a clear track ahead of him for a while, and be able to run at his optimum speed. If a safety car then popped up before most of his rivals had pitted, so much the better.

Massa led Hamilton away, and initially everything ran to plan as the Brazilian edged his Ferrari clear. Alonso gained a few places at the first corner, but became caught in a queue of cars and was over 50s behind the leader when he came in on lap 12. He was two laps early because he couldn't make progress, and he'd had enough of the supersoft tyres. Alonso dropped to the very back of the field, as much as 84s behind the leader. But just a couple of laps later, his own team-mate Piquet Jr crashed, triggering a safety car. It was perfect timing for Alonso.

Immediately after the accident, three drivers – Mark Webber, David Coulthard and Rubens Barrichello – managed to dive in for fuel just before the pitlane closed. That was a huge break, although Rubens retired almost immediately with an airbox fire.

The unfortunate Nico Rosberg came in next time

OPPOSITE Felipe Massa leads Lewis Hamilton into Turn 3 on the opening lap, with Kimi Räikkönen and Robert Kubica next in line

BELOW Nico Rosberg races across Anderson Bridge towards second position, even withstanding his drive-through penalty

bumpy, challenging street venue that wound between modern shopping malls and colonial buildings from an earlier era. Brake discs could be seen glowing, sparks flew as cars bottomed out over the bumps, and flames belched from red-hot exhaust pipes.

There were some concerns about safety, in particular with the pit entry and exit, both of which kept drivers taking the typical racing line on their toes. However, everything worked like clockwork and, to the obvious delight of Bernie Ecclestone, F1 provided a wonderful show.

The race itself should have been a battle between the World Championship contenders. With Felipe Massa and Lewis Hamilton securing the front row, and outsiders Kimi Räikkönen and Robert Kubica just behind, the stage was perfectly set. One man who looked to have no chance was Alonso. Quick in practice, he had a fuel line come adrift in second qualifying, and would start down in 15th.

The usual strategy for a driver in such circumstances is to fill the car up, go for a one-stop run, and hope that something like a safety car plays into your hands. That's what propelled Renault's Nelson Piquet Jr into second place at Hockenheim.

around because, like Alonso, he was due an early pit stop. He had to refuel with a closed pitlane, and then face a stop-and-go penalty. BMW Sauber hoped to avoid the same scenario with Kubica and kept him out on the assumption that the pitlane would open sooner rather than later, but he came in next time around as the entry remained closed.

When the pits finally opened, everyone else, except heavy one-stoppers Trulli and Giancarlo Fisichella, came barrelling down the pitlane. And that's where it went wrong for leader Massa. The mechanic controlling the team's overhead traffic light system – back to manual operation at busy, double-stacked safety-car stops – simply called for green too early. Massa accelerated away with the fuel hose still attached, knocking over several of his crewmen as he departed. He then had to wait at the end of the pitlane for team members to reach him and pull the fuel hose clear. Miraculously, there was no fire, and not even a single injury. Inevitably, in the confusion team-mate Kimi Räikkönen, queueing just behind him, also lost a lot of time.

When the track finally went green again, the order had a strange look about it. Rosberg was in front, but

a penalty was looming. Trulli and Fisichella were next, having not stopped, but they were not quick. Then came Kubica, also expecting to be penalised, and then Alonso, Webber and Coulthard, all of whom had lucked in. The first guy to have made a 'normal' stop, post pit-closure, was Hamilton in eighth. And he'd been running an easy second before it all kicked off.

Anyone following closely could see that Alonso was in fact in the driving seat, as he had the pace and the fuel load to deal with everyone else ahead. The joker in the pack was that it took the FIA an unusually long time to formally confirm the Rosberg/Kubica penalties, and then the drivers had the mandatory three laps in which to take them.

With a clear track ahead, Rosberg got his head down, piled on the laps and took advantage of a queue behind him to open up a big lead. When he finally took his 10s stop-and-go, he fell only to fourth. And when Trulli and Fisichella made their first and only stops, he moved back to second, behind Alonso.

Both men were fast enough to be under no threat from behind. The key was for Alonso to get his second pit stop done and dusted before a second safety car could pop up and influence the situation. In the end,

INSIDE LINE
FERNANDO ALONSO
RENAULT DRIVER

"The first podium of 2008 and it took a couple of days for it to sink in that we got a win this season. The only problem I had was the drinks bottle not working. I tried on lap 2 and it was disheartening to know I had no liquid all race at a place as hot as Singapore…

We were competitive Friday, fastest in Saturday practice and then really unlucky in qualifying, when I had a fuel-feed problem in Q2 and was forced to start 15th. But we made up for it by good luck with the safety car in the race. We chose to do a very aggressive first stint, as we knew that from 15th we would not be able to overtake. Normally you would think about a one-stop strategy and that's what our simulation said, but we had concerns about the brakes running too hot all weekend, as the straights weren't long enough to cool them. We thought a heavy one-stop fuel load was impossible for them and so decided to do something very different.

The car was also about 0.7s per lap quicker on the harder tyre, so I used the supersofts at the start of the race to try to make up some places and then the short 12-lap first stint we chose was to limit the number of laps I had to do on them. The safety car coming out three laps after my stop was a good break.

When the second safety car came after Sutil crashed, there were only 10 laps to go. I'd been comfortable, more than 18s ahead of Nico, but that was wiped out and I knew that Hamilton was behind the Williams. I had been running with low revs, but at the restart I switched the engine to maximum and was able to pull away from Nico.

I think it was a great weekend for Formula 1 as well as for me. The first night race was a new challenge and it was great to win a race that will be a landmark in F1 history. I think there'll be many more night races in the future because it was a great experience.

It has been a tough championship for Renault, but now we are ahead of Toyota and fighting for fourth place in the constructors' championship. The win is well deserved because the guys have worked really hard all year. At the start of the season, we were a long way behind, almost a second behind BMW, but now we are the same pace as them, or even better, and that's thanks to a great job by everyone."

the Spaniard came in on lap 41, immediately after Rosberg. It would have been silly to do anything except respond. Crucially he came out just in front of the third place Coulthard/Hamilton battle, so now it was clear cut – this was Alonso's race. The others in turn pitted in response.

"I was trying to understand which ones pitted under the safety-car conditions," said Alonso. "Then there was a moment when we were leading the race, but if there was a safety car in that moment, maybe we would have a problem. After the second stop, when I rejoined the track, it was 100% victory."

It wasn't a walk in the park, however, as Rosberg was still close enough to be a threat, and there was no margin whatsoever for a spin or trip up an escape road. But even a second late safety car after Adrian Sutil crashed did not give anyone behind a chance, although third-placed Hamilton gave Rosberg a hard time for a while, before settling for six points.

This was a superb team effort, as the Renault guys showed their World Champion credentials and took full advantage of an opportunity that fell into their laps. It was a curious outcome, as the winner had stopped so early that in normal circumstances he

BELOW This high shot sums up the magic of night racing in a city setting, showing Singapore at its best

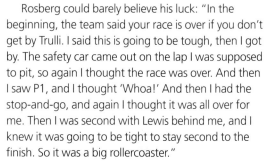

ABOVE Lewis Hamilton did well to work his way back to third after being caught out by the timing of the safety-car deployment

BELOW Fernando Alonso was overjoyed to have been in the right place at the right time to taste victory again after a barren season

would have been nowhere, while the runner-up had refuelled illegally, taken a penalty hit, and still beaten the World Championship leader...

"We've been on the podium twice this year," said Alonso. "Once in Hockenheim with Nelson and once here, and both times maybe thanks to the safety car, so we've been lucky in that aspect. We were thinking to do a one-stop strategy, we had no brakes to do it, so we found a very aggressive strategy with only 12 laps in the first stint. It worked at the end, so obviously we have no complaints with the strategy! It was a great race, I did no mistakes, and it was nearly a perfect weekend for us, apart from qualifying."

Rosberg could barely believe his luck: "In the beginning, the team said your race is over if you don't get by Trulli. I said this is going to be tough, then I got by. The safety car came out on the lap I was supposed to pit, so again I thought the race was over. And then I saw P1, and I thought 'Whoa!' And then I had the stop-and-go, and again I thought it was all over for me. Then I was second with Lewis behind me, and I knew it was going to be tight to stay second to the finish. So it was a big rollercoaster."

Behind Rosberg and Hamilton, Timo Glock took fourth for Toyota, while Sebastian Vettel had another great run to fifth for Toro Rosso. Penalised three places for allegedly impeding Barrichello in qualifying, Nick Heidfeld was stuck in traffic all day, and couldn't climb higher than sixth place.

The final points went to Coulthard, who would have been higher up but for a delay at his second stop that allowed Hamilton through, and Kazuki Nakajima. Webber would have finished on the podium had he not suffered a gearbox failure. Bizarrely, it was the result of electrical interference from an underground train line affecting the electronics at Turn 13.

Singapore turned into a disastrous race for Ferrari. Räikkönen looked set to at least salvage fifth place until he crashed heavily a few laps from home. After his earlier delay was compounded by a drive-through penalty for an unsafe release and then a late spin, Massa could manage only 13th. Hamilton thus gained six points, extending his lead on the Brazilian to seven.

"It was very tough to finish the race like that, especially after running a great first stint," said Massa. "But then I had a problem in the pit stop. The green light went away, and unfortunately the [fuel] hose was still in the car. It's really difficult to accept, but that's racing. We now need to focus on the last three races, but the title is still possible."

There was still everything to play for...

SNAPSHOT FROM
SINGAPORE

CLOCKWISE FROM RIGHT
Singapore's skyline looked magnificent, pitching F1 just where Bernie Ecclestone wanted it; Nico Rosberg and his Williams crew look more than a little pleased about his second place finish; east meets west; pedestrians get a sneak peek of the action on one of the giant screens; the heat and humidity made a supply of water essential for the crews; Timo Glock tries to work out what type of visor to wear for racing under floodlights; Renault team chief Flavio Briatore turns the tables on the photographers

WEEKEND NEWS

■ Singapore saw the biggest turnout of World Champions at a Grand Prix for some time with Fernando Alonso and Kimi Räikkönen joined by Sir Jackie Stewart, Niki Lauda, Jody Scheckter, Keke Rosberg, Damon Hill and Mika Häkkinen.

■ A few days after the race, Williams confirmed its line-up would remain unchanged into 2009. The team's arrangement with Toyota gave it access to any of the manufacturer's young drivers, but GP2 racer Kamui Kobayashi had done little to suggest that he was a better bet than Kazuki Nakajima.

■ The death of Hollywood star, amateur racer and Indycar team owner Paul Newman was announced on Saturday, after the 83-year-old legend lost his battle with cancer. Although rarely seen at F1 races – a visit to Montréal in 2000 as a guest of Jaguar was a rare exception – Newman kept a close eye on the sport.

■ Singapore featured stricter security controls than we are used to. Bags were searched at the public gates, and at the main turnstyle entrance to the paddock there was an airport-style X-ray machine for luggage, and a metal detector for personnel. Interestingly, there were no such precautions at the secondary turnstyle at the far end of the pits...

■ Honda tester Alex Wurz was seconded to drive the medical car, as regular Jacques Tropenat was indisposed. After Nelson Piquet Jr's crash, Wurz overtook both the safety car and Fernando Alonso and raced flat-out to the scene, egged on by F1 doctor Gary Hartstein. It was all too much for the local doctor in the back seat, who threw up...

RACE
RESULTS
SINGAPORE
MARINA BAY

Official Results © [2008]
Formula One Administration Limited,
6 Princes Gate, London, SW7 1QJ.
No reproduction without permission.
All copyright and database rights reserved.

RACE DATE June 8th
CIRCUIT LENGTH 3.148 miles
NO. OF LAPS 61
RACE DISTANCE 192.028 miles
WEATHER Hot and humid, 30°C
TRACK TEMP 33°C
RACE DAY ATTENDANCE 100,000
LAP RECORD Kimi Räikkönen,
1m45.599s, 107.358mph, 2008

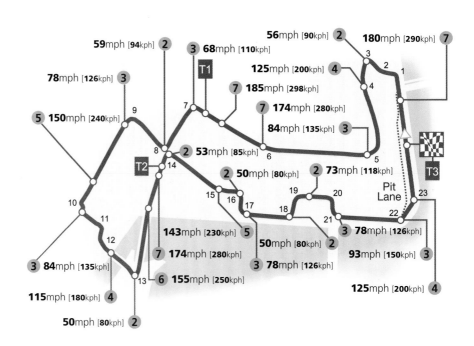

PRACTICE 1

	Driver	Time	Laps
1	L Hamilton	1m45.518s	20
2	F Massa	1m45.598s	23
3	K Räikkönen	1m45.961s	24
4	H Kovalainen	1m46.463s	20
5	R Kubica	1m46.618s	23
6	N Rosberg	1m46.710s	25
7	F Alonso	1m46.725s	29
8	N Heidfeld	1m46.964s	24
9	N Piquet Jr	1m47.175s	30
10	J Button	1m47.277s	30
11	S Vettel	1m47.570s	28
12	K Nakajima	1m47.662s	23
13	T Glock	1m47.706s	27
14	S Bourdais	1m48.097s	16
15	D Coulthard	1m48.517s	23
16	R Barrichello	1m48.725s	19
17	A Sutil	1m48.839s	24
18	G Fisichella	1m48.906s	25
19	J Trulli	1m49.064s	29
20	M Webber	1m53.703s	4

PRACTICE 2

	Driver	Time	Laps
1	F Alonso	1m45.654s	30
2	L Hamilton	1m45.752s	28
3	F Massa	1m45.793s	31
4	H Kovalainen	1m45.797s	31
5	N Rosberg	1m46.164s	34
6	R Kubica	1m46.384s	36
7	K Räikkönen	1m46.580s	25
8	J Button	1m46.901s	32
9	K Nakajima	1m47.013s	32
10	T Glock	1m47.046s	22
11	M Webber	1m47.137s	15
12	N Piquet Jr	1m47.145s	35
13	S Vettel	1m47.300s	33
14	S Bourdais	1m47.487s	24
15	D Coulthard	1m47.640s	31
16	N Heidfeld	1m47.760s	36
17	G Fisichella	1m47.965s	12
18	R Barrichello	1m48.009s	25
19	J Trulli	1m48.059s	28
20	A Sutil	1m48.311s	36

PRACTICE 3

	Driver	Time	Laps
1	F Alonso	1m44.506s	19
2	L Hamilton	1m45.119s	13
3	F Massa	1m45.246s	16
4	N Piquet Jr	1m45.249s	18
5	N Rosberg	1m45.386s	17
6	J Button	1m45.409s	20
7	R Kubica	1m45.425s	17
8	M Webber	1m45.450s	21
9	S Vettel	1m45.477s	19
10	S Bourdais	1m45.599s	18
11	N Heidfeld	1m45.689s	19
12	K Nakajima	1m45.982s	18
13	H Kovalainen	1m45.982s	13
14	R Barrichello	1m46.073s	21
15	T Glock	1m46.180s	23
16	J Trulli	1m46.221s	19
17	K Räikkönen	1m46.482s	10
18	D Coulthard	1m46.794s	6
19	G Fisichella	1m47.166s	14
20	A Sutil	1m47.727s	19

QUALIFYING 1

	Driver	Time
1	K Räikkönen	1m44.282s
2	H Kovalainen	1m44.311s
3	L Hamilton	1m44.501s
4	F Massa	1m44.519s
5	R Kubica	1m44.740s
6	F Alonso	1m44.971s
7	S Vettel	1m45.042s
8	N Rosberg	1m45.103s
9	K Nakajima	1m45.127s
10	T Glock	1m45.184s
11	M Webber	1m45.493s
12	N Heidfeld	1m45.548s
13	J Trulli	1m45.642s
14	J Button	1m45.660s
15	D Coulthard	1m46.028s
16	N Piquet Jr	1m46.037s
17	S Bourdais	1m46.389s
18	R Barrichello	1m46.583s
19	A Sutil	1m47.940s
20	G Fisichella	No time

QUALIFYING 2

	Driver	Time
1	F Massa	1m44.014s
2	H Kovalainen	1m44.207s
3	K Räikkönen	1m44.232s
4	S Vettel	1m44.261s
5	N Rosberg	1m44.429s
6	T Glock	1m44.441s
7	R Kubica	1m44.519s
8	N Heidfeld	1m44.520s
9	K Nakajima	1m44.826s
10	L Hamilton	1m44.932s
11	J Trulli	1m45.038s
12	J Button	1m45.133s
13	M Webber	1m45.212s
14	D Coulthard	1m45.298s
15	F Alonso	No time

Best sectors – Practice			Speed trap – Practice		
Sec 1	F Alonso	28.173s	1	N Piquet Jr	181.316mph
Sec 2	F Alonso	40.479s	2	L Hamilton	180.819mph
Sec 3	F Alonso	35.854s	3	S Vettel	180.508mph

Best sectors – Qualifying			Speed trap – Qualifying		
Sec 1	F Massa	27.977s	1	L Hamilton	180.881mph
Sec 2	N Heidfeld	40.315s	2	H Kovalainen	180.197mph
Sec 3	F Massa	35.512s	3	F Alonso	180.073mph

Kimi Räikkönen
"I was trying to attack Glock in case he made a mistake, but I went wide at the chicane, jumping over the kerb and when the car landed I lost control and hit the barriers."

Nick Heidfeld
"I shouldn't complain about coming sixth, from ninth, but I couldn't show my pace as I was stuck in traffic all the time. I had a good start during which I passed Nico."

Fernando Alonso
"Winning here seemed to be impossible, as we missed our chance in qualifying, but we chose a very aggressive strategy and we had a bit of luck today."

Nico Rosberg
"The safety car came out after I was called in for my stop. Before my stop-go, I pushed and was able to build enough of a gap to make my second stop and stay second."

David Coulthard
"That was my second points finish this year. As far as the second stop went, it's just one of those things. I go when the lollipop comes up, but thankfully we scored some points."

Jarno Trulli
"After the safety car, I led for a few laps, but had a hydraulic problem when I could have finished fifth; that would have been good from a weekend that has been hard."

Felipe Massa
"It's hard to deal with losing a race that was in our grasp. At the pit stop, one of the guys made a mistake. Then I got a drive-through and later I also picked up a puncture."

Robert Kubica
"The race was very physical. There are so many bumps. The decision not to pit on the first lap when the pitlane was closed because of the safety car cost me a good result."

Nelson Piquet Jr
"I had a lot of graining and the situation got ever worse. The team asked me to push, which I tried to do, but I lost the rear of my car. I hit the wall heavily, but I'm alright."

Kazuki Nakajima
"It was great for the team to return to form. The timing of the safety car was unfortunate for me, but I simply had to push my pace on regardless and overtake a few cars."

Mark Webber
"I lost seventh then fifth gear, which cost us a fantastic result, as I was due to make my second stop later than Alonso. It would have been nice to share the podium with him."

Timo Glock
"I made no mistakes and fourth is a good result. It was tough in the heat, and with such a bumpy track the car wasn't comfortable to drive; I'll feel the effects tomorrow."

	Driver			
1	F Massa			
2	L Hamilton			
3	K Räikkönen			
4	R Kubica			
5	H Kovalainen			
6	S Vettel			
7	T Glock			
8	N Rosberg			
9	N Heidfeld			
10	K Nakajima			
11	J Trulli			
12	J Button			
13	M Webber			
14	D Coulthard			
15	F Alonso			
16	N Piquet Jr			
17	S Bourdais			
18	R Barrichello			
19	A Sutil			
20	G Fisichella			

☆ Accident Ⓜ Mechanical failure Ⓟ Pit stop ☐ Safety Car ☐ Lapped Ⓑ Black flag

QUALIFYING 3

	Driver	Time
1	F Massa	1m44.801s
2	L Hamilton	1m45.465s
3	K Räikkönen	1m45.617s
4	R Kubica	1m45.779s
5	H Kovalainen	1m45.873s
6	N Heidfeld	1m45.964s
7	S Vettel	1m46.244s
8	T Glock	1m46.328s
9	N Rosberg	1m46.611s
10	K Nakajima	1m47.547s

GRID

	Driver	Time
1	F Massa	1m44.801s
2	L Hamilton	1m45.465s
3	K Räikkönen	1m45.617s
4	R Kubica	1m45.779s
5	H Kovalainen	1m45.873s
6	S Vettel	1m46.244s
7	T Glock	1m46.328s
8	N Rosberg	1m46.611s
9*	N Heidfeld	1m45.964s
10	K Nakajima	1m47.547s
11	J Trulli	1m45.038s
12	J Button	1m45.133s
13	M Webber	1m45.212s
14	D Coulthard	1m45.298s
15	F Alonso	No time
16	N Piquet Jr	1m46.037s
17	S Bourdais	1m46.389s
18	R Barrichello	1m46.583s
19	A Sutil	1m47.940s
20	G Fisichella	No time

* THREE-PLACE GRID PENALTY FOR OBSTRUCTING BARRICHELLO

RACE

	Driver	Car	Laps	Time	Avg. mph	Fastest	Stops
1	F Alonso	Renault R28	61	1h57m16.304s	98.219	1m45.768s	2
2	N Rosberg	Williams-Toyota FW30	61	1h57m19.261s	98.178	1m46.454s	3
3	L Hamilton	McLaren-Mercedes MP4-23	61	1h57m22.221s	98.137	1m46.072s	2
4	T Glock	Toyota TF108	61	1h57m24.459s	98.106	1m47.044s	2
5	S Vettel	Toro Rosso-Ferrari STR03	61	1h57m26.572s	98.076	1m47.271s	2
6	N Heidfeld	BMW Sauber F1.08	61	1h57m27.405s	98.065	1m47.306s	2
7	D Coulthard	Red Bull-Renault RB4	61	1h57m32.691s	97.991	1m47.562s	2
8	K Nakajima	Williams-Toyota FW30	61	1h57m34.793s	97.962	1m47.287s	2
9	J Button	Honda RA108	61	1h57m36.189s	97.942	1m48.128s	2
10	H Kovalainen	McLaren-Mercedes MP4-23	61	1h57m43.206s	97.845	1m47.337s	2
11	R Kubica	BMW Sauber F1.08	61	1h57m44.279s	97.830	1m46.899s	3
12	S Bourdais	Toro Rosso-Ferrari STR03	61	1h57m45.736s	97.810	1m47.820s	2
13	F Massa	Ferrari F2008	61	1h57m51.474s	97.731	1m45.757s	3
14	G Fisichella	Force India-Ferrari VJM01	61	1h57m59.875s	97.615	1m49.101s	1
15	K Räikkönen	Ferrari F2008	57	Accident	-	1m45.599s	2
R	J Trulli	Toyota TF108	50	Hydraulics	-	1m46.972s	1
R	A Sutil	Force India-Ferrari VJM01	49	Accident	-	1m49.270s	2
R	M Webber	Red Bull-Renault RB4	29	Gearbox	-	1m49.183s	1
R	R Barrichello	Honda RA108	14	Electrical	-	1m50.320s	1
R	N Piquet Jr	Renault R28	13	Accident	-	1m50.449s	0

CHAMPIONSHIP

	Driver	Pts
1	L Hamilton	84
2	F Massa	77
3	R Kubica	64
4	K Räikkönen	57
5	N Heidfeld	56
6	H Kovalainen	51
7	F Alonso	38
8	S Vettel	27
9	J Trulli	26
10	T Glock	20
11	M Webber	20
12	N Rosberg	17
13	N Piquet Jr	13
14	R Barrichello	11
15	K Nakajima	9
16	D Coulthard	8
17	S Bourdais	4
18	J Button	3

Fastest Lap
K Räikkönen 1m45.599s
(107.358mph) on lap 14

Fastest speed trap
H Kovalainen   179.949mph
Slowest speed trap
J Trulli   171.747mph

Fastest pit stop
1 T Glock   24.648s
2 K Räikkönen   24.974s
3 N Heidfeld   25.125s

Constructor	Pts
1 McLaren-Mercedes	135
2 Ferrari	134
3 BMW Sauber	120
4 Renault	51
5 Toyota	46
6 Toro Rosso-Ferrari	31
7 Red Bull-Renault	28
8 Williams-Toyota	26
9 Honda	14

Sebastien Bourdais

"Once I was in traffic, I kept losing the front end, even with the brake bias on the rear. I was running a heavy fuel load which meant my tyres were suffering near the end."

Jenson Button

"It was one of those races where the safety car could make or break your race. Luck was not on our side and the timing of the two safety cars hurt our two-stop strategy."

Adrian Sutil

"It was just so unlucky when Felipe spun in front of me and then suddenly pulled away. The way was blocked, but I avoided a crash with him only to hit the barrier myself."

Lewis Hamilton

"My rear tyres faded and I couldn't challenge Felipe. After my first pit stop, I was stuck behind David and although I was faster it was really difficult to overtake him."

Sebastian Vettel

"The hardest elements were dealing with the heat and not making mistakes. Fourth might have been possible if I hadn't lost a place when I missed a braking point."

Rubens Barrichello

"My race engineer made a brilliant call on lap 14 following Piquet's crash. I came into the pits just before the safety car was called, but infuriatingly the engine died."

Giancarlo Fisichella

"It was great to be racing again and we had a good strategy that let us move up a few places. In the final laps I had a problem, but I'm pleased we got to the finish."

Heikki Kovalainen

"I was going to pass Kubica round the outside, but he touched me and almost spun me around, damaging my floor. I lost momentum and two cars overtook me."

2008 FORMULA 1 FUJI TELEVISION JAPANESE GRAND PRIX
FUJI SPEEDWAY

ALONSO AGAIN

If his win in Singapore owed a great deal to the timing of the arrival of a safety car, Fernando Alonso had even more reason to smile in Japan, as he won fair and square. Sort of…

If after the Belgian GP someone had laid a bet that none of the next three grands prix would be won by a McLaren, Ferrari, or even BMW Sauber, the bookie would have rubbed his hands at the foolishness of his customer. However, he wouldn't be smiling after the Japanese GP, because the million-to-one shot came in.

Following Sebastian Vettel's rain-inspired victory at Monza, and Fernando Alonso's lucky break with the safety car in Singapore, there were no special circumstances to conspire against the top two teams at Fuji Speedway. Instead, McLaren and Ferrari self-destructed as the battle for the World Championship reached boiling point, and the top contenders conspired to ruin their own chances by making silly mistakes.

The man who stepped into the void was once again Alonso, making it two straight wins for the former World Champion and for Renault.

After 2007's atrociously wet weekend, things ran a lot more smoothly for the second grand prix to be held at the rebuilt circuit. Saturday morning's final practice session was damp but, other than that, the rain stayed away. Things ran relatively to plan in qualifying, as Lewis Hamilton claimed pole position with a very impressive lap. Indeed, after the race, Ron Dennis made it clear that

his British charge had been running a heavy fuel load.

Kimi Räikkönen showed better form than of late in claiming second on the grid, while Heikki Kovalainen gave McLaren more cheer with third, and Alonso was a surprising fourth. This meant Hamilton's main title rival, Felipe Massa, was down in fifth with three cars separating them. The Brazilian complained that he'd run out of grip towards the end of his flying lap.

Things certainly looked good for Hamilton and McLaren, but the balance of power changed at the start when he was easily beaten away by Räikkönen. At the end of the long run down to the tight Turn 1, Hamilton took the inside line and gambled on being

TALKING POINT
ROUGH JUSTICE?

Lewis Hamilton: pole position, beaten away by Räikkönen, late jink down the inside, huge lock-up, tyre down to the canvas, everyone forced wide to miss him, race-defining moment for Kubica and Alonso. Daft, certainly, but worthy of a penalty? Highly debatable. This, after all, was the first corner

of a grand prix and not the parking lot at your supermarket.

Whether or not Hamilton had taken leave of his senses in that his title rival was firmly behind him, is not the issue. He was racing, and that's what F1 is supposed to be about. If we want to encourage excitement, action and overtaking, it's probably not a good idea to penalise a driver every time he pulls a move. It was ill-judged, but there was no contact, so a drive-through penalty was harsh.

In hindsight, after plenty of video study, Kovalainen's Turn 1 actions looked more dubious. The Finn appeared to be following the expected trajectory to go for a Turn 1 apex, when suddenly he went left. Was this a bid to ensure that the Ferraris couldn't turn-in

cleanly? There was contact with Räikkönen this time. The Finn spent the rest of the afternoon with a bent steering arm that left him unable to overcome Alonso and Kubica. Arguably, this was a bigger case to answer.

A penalty for Felipe Massa for his Turn 11 removal of Lewis Hamilton? Hamilton, one tyre down to the canvas due to his Turn 1 exploits, knew he had to pit before he charged inside Massa. He was probably looking for trouble, looking to draw Massa in. Again though, it's irrelevant. If Lewis set the trap, Felipe didn't have to fall in. Contact with the McLaren could have been avoided and so Felipe's drive-through penalty looked fair.

A 25s penalty for Sebastien Bourdais for tangling with Massa as

he exited the pits? Hugely annoying for Ferrari, this. Massa had another pit stop to go and Toro Rosso could easily have informed Bourdais of the position and told him to let the Ferrari go. But that doesn't mean that Bourdais was obliged to back out of it. As far as he was concerned, he was racing Massa for position and had as much right to the apex as the Ferrari. If anything, you had to question Felipe's judgement. So, very harsh.

The three incidents once again focused attention on both the correctness and the consistency of stewards' decisions. More and more, the feeling is that these calls should be made by a respected, recently retired ex-F1 driver in the immediate aftermath of an incident and with no outside interference.

able to reclaim his lead. He had every opportunity to say to himself 'this isn't great, but Kimi is not the guy I'm racing,' take a more measured approach, and place himself so as to take advantage of any slip-up by the Finn. Instead, he blasted down the inside.

Hamilton locked up and slid wide, forcing Räikkönen to go off the edge of the track. Kovalainen also leaned on the Ferrari, having taken his braking to the extreme, while in the confusion Massa found himself trapped behind his team-mate. The upshot of it all was that from sixth on the grid Robert Kubica emerged in the lead ahead of Alonso and Hamilton.

Already, Hamilton had landed another penalty. It did look bad on the TV images as he lunged wide and Räikkönen was forced to adjust his line. The fact that a lot of other people didn't stop quite as well as they wanted to on cold tyres – and in the first flying start at this track – seemed to be disregarded. As did the fact that Kovalainen gave Räikkönen at least as much trouble, and certainly more of a touch, than did Lewis.

"We knew that the tyres and the brakes were a big factor in Turn 1," said Alonso. "So on the out-lap we tried to heat the tyres and brakes as much as possible. It wasn't enough. With these cold temperatures that we had today and the prime tyre, we arrived in Turn 1 on cold tyres and most went straight. We knew that before starting, but the title contenders, they need to push a little bit harder than us so they missed Turn 1."

The drama continued beyond the first corner. If Hamilton could be forgiven for a first-turn lock-up, what happened a few corners later was not very clever. Having come out of Turn 1 in relatively good shape in third place, and with other cars between himself and the Ferraris in his mirrors, he proceeded to slide off the road while trying to get back on terms with his nemesis, Alonso.

Before he could rejoin, four cars, including Massa's, had gone by. His tyres may have been damaged at Turn 1, but there really was no excuse for this second lapse, at which point he really should have got his emotions in check. It was reminiscent of Bahrain, where he not once but twice touched the back of Alonso. Even McLaren boss Ron Dennis admitted it was hard to completely exonerate his driver.

"It's all benefit of hindsight, isn't it?" said Dennis. "He's a racing driver. He could have been a bit more mindful of the situation, but I'm sure he was a bit frustrated with himself for screwing up the first corner.

OPPOSITE TOP How not to take Turn 1: Lewis Hamilton's slide wide pushed eveyone else wide, including Heikki Kovalainen and the Ferraris

OPPOSITE BOTTOM Lap 2, Turn 10 and Hamilton is facing the wrong way after a tap from Felipe Massa

BELOW Jenson Button and Rubens Barrichello were left to scrap with each other at the tail of the field, their Hondas both ending up lapped

INSIDE LINE
ROBERT KUBICA
BMW SAUBER DRIVER

"We had a lot of tyre-graining problems on Friday and unfortunately, in qualifying, when the weather was a bit cold, I was struggling to do one single lap without the graining. We did both Q1 runs on the harder tyre to save the soft tyres, and I only made it out of Q1 by 0.15s. In Q3 though, I did a really good lap to qualify sixth.

I was hoping for warmer temperatures and some sunshine in the race, but it didn't happen, so I was expecting quite a lot of problems with graining. In fact, the first stint, where you accommodate the tyre with the formation lap and with the initial pace not being so quick, you stress the tyres less and I survived that pretty well.

My start wasn't great, I had a slipping clutch, and Jarno Trulli went by. I decided to go for the inside at Turn 1 and I braked really too late. If anyone had managed to take the apex, I would have hit them for sure, but everyone went straight. I locked the front wheel quite a lot, but managed to stay on. I think I was the only one who did…

I was trying everything, but Fernando was staying with me and he went a lap further to his first pit stop and came out in front of me. I then had a graining problem that influenced the last sector, where I was very slow. Fernando had much better traction out of the low-speed turns and there was simply nothing I could do.

In the final stint, I had a great battle with Kimi for three or four laps while I had graining problems, but then the tyres cleaned up and I was alright. We were side-by-side in Turn 3 at one point, and there is no space for two cars to go through there. I was on the inside, but I wasn't going to back off, and he didn't for a long time. I managed to stay on the track but nearly went off, and he ran wide. I knew I had to stay ahead through that graining phase, and I did. After that, I managed to pull out a couple of seconds.

I think second place here is better than the Canada win with a car which, it is no secret, is not the one from the beginning of the season. We didn't improve a lot in the last two or three months, so to be able to finish on the podium, ahead of McLaren and Ferrari, is amazing. While you are still in the championship, you have to try."

That's what makes him the driver he is. He's going to fight for positions at every opportunity. You're not going to stop him doing that. Of course, it would have been nice if he had been just a little bit more prudent in the first corner."

Across the line first time around, Kubica led from Alonso, Kovalainen, Trulli, Massa, Hamilton and Räikkönen. Clearly rattled, Hamilton made an aggressive pass on Massa at the chicane on lap 2, and made it stick. But the Ferrari ran wide, hopped across the run-off, and rammed hard into the McLaren. Hamilton was spun around and had to let the entire field go by, before heading to the pits for new tyres and some extra fuel to give him a longer first stint.

"For me it was a racing incident," said Massa. "We braked very late into Turn 10. He tried to pass me, but then I was a little bit wide, and he put the car inside. I was outside, then he pushed me a little bit close to the gravel. Then I had two wheels on the gravel, and he closed and we touched. The next corner was already in my favour, but because I was on the gravel I couldn't do anything, and we touched. And that's it."

The stewards took a dim view of this and they gave Massa a drive-through penalty for his contact with Hamilton. More controversially, the Briton was also given one for his move on Räikkönen at Turn 1.

"We're still a bit mystified as to why Lewis got a penalty," said Dennis. "It's just a racing incident. I can remember lots of first corners like that, cars running wide on cold tyres. He flatspotted a tyre. He didn't do anything deliberately. He was just fighting.

"I think the thing that really got Lewis was the penalty. He was complaining about it bitterly in the car. He was just mystified about it, as were we. But you've just got to get on with the job."

When they took their drive-through penalties, around the time of the first scheduled pit stops, both title challengers dropped way out of contention. At the

same time, Kovalainen retired from third place with a rare Mercedes engine failure.

Meanwhile, Alonso pushed Kubica hard through the first stint. Renault felt he was quicker, and had to find a way to get him past. It helped when Kubica stopped one lap early and Alonso had one lap of clean air. Just to ensure that he could get out in front, Renault short-fuelled him relative to Kubica, to the tune of five laps, and he came out just in front of the BMW Sauber.

Now Alonso had to open up a clear lead in order that his earlier second pit stop would not leave him vulnerable, and he showed his World Championship class by doing exactly what he needed. In the end, it

OPPOSITE Robert Kubica led until the first round of stops, but Fernando Alonso emerged in front and stayed there to the finish

ABOVE Kovalainen was running third, set for a good result, when his engine failed and he was out

BELOW Jarno Trulli gave Toyota something to smile about on home ground, by racing to fifth place after gaining ground in the lap 1 mêlée

back. Second place left Kubica just 12 points off the World Championship lead.

An ultra-long first stint propelled Nelson Piquet Jr up the order, and indeed the Brazilian led briefly before his first pit stop. That was enough to allow him to claim fourth place as the race unfolded.

Trulli had a quiet run to fifth for Toyota, while sixth on the road went to Sebastien Bourdais, who also enjoyed a brief spell in the lead with a late first stop. But, as he emerged from his second stop, the Frenchman tapped Massa into a spin after the Ferrari cut across his bows at Turn 1. An investigation resulted in a 25s penalty that bounced Bourdais out of the points, upsetting many who thought Massa the culprit rather than victim.

The penalty boosted the other STR driver, Sebastian Vettel up to sixth, but more importantly gifted a priceless extra championship point to Massa, who had charged up to eighth place on the road.

"It could have been better," said Massa. "It could have been worse, looking at where we started, and looking at where Lewis started. But we can't leave saying that it was a disaster. It could have been for sure better in terms of points, but we at least finished in the points."

The other driver to benefit from the Bourdais situation was Red Bull's Mark Webber, who was promoted from ninth to eighth. Meanwhile, Hamilton finished 12th and was clearly not a happy man when he left the track, having seen his lead cut from seven points to five.

"I think my personal disappointment would be the start, and then my second disappointment would be the way I was treated," said Hamilton. "I got a bad start and I slipstreamed Kimi. I had an opportunity to go to the inside, so I went. Everyone brakes late there. If you watch the replay, everyone went wide. I just went a bit wider than everyone else, and for some reason I got a penalty for that. I can't honestly understand that. And then Felipe drove into me."

With two races to run, this was getting interesting...

ABOVE Sebastien Bourdais leads a recovering Felipe Massa, but a later clash would earn the STR driver a 25s penalty, dropping him to 10th

BELOW After his second win in a row, Alonso is more than happy to ham it up for the TV cameras

was a comfortable win, albeit one that even the team could not possibly have expected before the start.

"In Singapore, there was a luck factor that helped me a lot with the win," said Alonso, "but today was just the pure pace of the car. I think the title contenders were a little bit aggressive in Turn 1, so I took the benefit of that. Then, in the fight with Robert, thanks to the Renault car today, I was able to pull a gap."

In fact, Kubica fell into the clutches of Räikkönen, who tried hard to get past. Their battle got fraught, and at one point the Finn was sent over the run-off at full speed. It was great stuff, but tyres became an issue, and Räikkönen couldn't find the pace with which to fight

SNAPSHOT FROM
JAPAN

CLOCKWISE FROM RIGHT No circuit can offer a backdrop like Mount Fuji's; Jarno Trulli's helmet has changed from plain silver; David Coulthard was lucky to walk away from this with just a bruised foot; everyone at Red Bull smiled when the news came through that DC was fine; the green grooves represented Bridgestone's support of the 'Make Cars Green' campaign; there was a rumbling in the hills...; Heidfeld, Theissen and Kubica, BMW Sauber's line-up for 2008 and for 2009

WEEKEND NEWS

- A revised World Championship calendar for 2009 saw the unexpected absence of the Canadian GP and some reshuffling to create a break in August. Montréal's departure from the schedule came in the wake of a dispute over finances with Bernie Ecclestone. The city's mayor moved quickly in an attempt to secure the race's future.

- Just prior to the Japanese GP, BMW Sauber confirmed that Robert Kubica and Nick Heidfeld would be staying on in 2009. The news closed yet another door on Fernando Alonso, although Honda remained in the chase for his services. The Spaniard insisted that he'd made up his mind about which team he's drive for, but would not tell us until after the final race.

- Once again, the social highlight of the Japanese GP weekend was Tsukasa Shiga's Sunday-night party at Tokyo's famed New Lex nightclub, formerly known as Lexington Queen. Some 18 F1 race and test drivers (and three team bosses) let their hair down at the event, which ran until the early hours.

- Bridgestone joined forces with the FIA to promote the 'Make Cars Green' campaign, and even managed to get the four Ferrari and McLaren drivers to promote it at a press event in Tokyo. For the race weekend, all cars ran with green stripes painted in the grooves, which had the unexpected effect of highlighting tyre wear.

- After Alexander Wurz had stepped into the role for the Singapore GP, Red Bull test driver Sebastien Buemi was seconded to drive the FIA medical car at Fuji. The Swiss youngster spun it on one of his initial practice laps, but nevertheless retained the job for the balance of the meeting.

RACE RESULTS
JAPAN
FUJI SPEEDWAY

Official Results © [2008]
Formula One Administration Limited,
6 Princes Gate, London, SW7 1QJ.
No reproduction without permission.
All copyright and database rights reserved.

RACE DATE October 12th
CIRCUIT LENGTH 2.852 miles
NO. OF LAPS 67
RACE DISTANCE 191.084 miles
WEATHER Overcast and dry, 15°C
TRACK TEMP 17°C
RACE DAY ATTENDANCE 105,000
LAP RECORD Felipe Massa 1m18.426s, 130.150mph, 2008

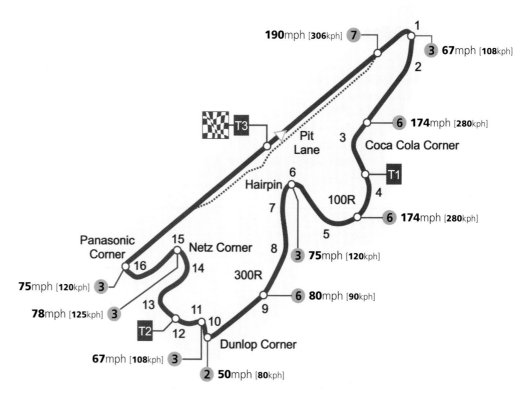

PRACTICE 1

	Driver	Time	Laps
1	L Hamilton	1m18.910s	23
2	F Massa	1m19.063s	24
3	H Kovalainen	1m19.279s	20
4	K Räikkönen	1m19.399s	31
5	F Alonso	1m19.473s	30
6	N Piquet Jr	1m19.743s	35
7	S Vettel	1m20.121s	30
8	R Kubica	1m20.160s	26
9	S Bourdais	1m20.182s	34
10	K Nakajima	1m20.217s	25
11	A Sutil	1m20.288s	26
12	N Rosberg	1m20.350s	28
13	M Webber	1m20.620s	24
14	N Heidfeld	1m20.628s	23
15	J Trulli	1m20.657s	33
16	R Barrichello	1m20.753s	32
17	J Button	1m20.769s	27
18	T Glock	1m20.823s	37
19	D Coulthard	1m20.905s	24
20	G Fisichella	1m21.014s	28

PRACTICE 2

	Driver	Time	Laps
1	T Glock	1m18.383s	44
2	F Alonso	1m18.426s	41
3	L Hamilton	1m18.463s	40
4	F Massa	1m18.491s	40
5	K Räikkönen	1m18.725s	39
6	M Webber	1m18.734s	39
7	K Nakajima	1m18.734s	36
8	S Vettel	1m18.761s	23
9	H Kovalainen	1m18.803s	32
10	J Trulli	1m18.863s	45
11	R Kubica	1m18.865s	39
12	N Piquet Jr	1m18.888s	43
13	N Rosberg	1m18.981s	41
14	S Bourdais	1m19.040s	41
15	R Barrichello	1m19.258s	42
16	A Sutil	1m19.287s	41
17	D Coulthard	1m19.327s	36
18	G Fisichella	1m19.482s	44
19	N Heidfeld	1m19.894s	37
20	J Button	1m19.999s	42

PRACTICE 3

	Driver	Time	Laps
1	R Kubica	1m25.087s	19
2	T Glock	1m25.171s	25
3	N Piquet Jr	1m25.415s	19
4	N Heidfeld	1m25.474s	24
5	K Nakajima	1m25.563s	23
6	D Coulthard	1m25.614s	20
7	F Massa	1m25.709s	15
8	M Webber	1m25.785s	20
9	F Alonso	1m25.799s	19
10	S Vettel	1m25.880s	24
11	L Hamilton	1m25.901s	8
12	S Bourdais	1m25.984s	22
13	J Trulli	1m26.013s	21
14	N Rosberg	1m26.213s	19
15	H Kovalainen	1m26.239s	10
16	K Räikkönen	1m26.277s	18
17	R Barrichello	1m26.662s	22
18	J Button	1m26.922s	26
19	A Sutil	1m27.357s	12
20	G Fisichella	1m27.918s	17

QUALIFYING 1

	Driver	Time
1	T Glock	1m17.945s
2	L Hamilton	1m18.071s
3	F Massa	1m18.110s
4	K Räikkönen	1m18.160s
5	H Kovalainen	1m18.220s
6	F Alonso	1m18.290s
7	N Piquet Jr	1m18.300s
8	D Coulthard	1m18.303s
9	M Webber	1m18.372s
10	J Trulli	1m18.501s
11	S Vettel	1m18.559s
12	S Bourdais	1m18.593s
13	K Nakajima	1m18.640s
14	R Kubica	1m18.684s
15	N Rosberg	1m18.740s
16	N Heidfeld	1m18.835s
17	R Barrichello	1m18.882s
18	J Button	1m19.100s
19	A Sutil	1m19.163s
20	G Fisichella	1m19.910s

QUALIFYING 2

	Driver	Time
1	F Massa	1m17.287s
2	H Kovalainen	1m17.360s
3	L Hamilton	1m17.462s
4	J Trulli	1m17.541s
5	T Glock	1m17.670s
6	S Vettel	1m17.714s
7	K Räikkönen	1m17.733s
8	F Alonso	1m17.871s
9	R Kubica	1m17.931s
10	S Bourdais	1m18.102s
11	D Coulthard	1m18.187s
12	N Piquet Jr	1m18.274s
13	M Webber	1m18.354s
14	K Nakajima	1m18.594s
15	N Rosberg	1m18.672s

Best sectors – Practice

Sec 1	K Räikkönen	21.466s
Sec 2	M Webber	27.509s
Sec 3	T Glock	28.149s

Speed trap – Practice

1	S Bourdais	199.273mph
2	D Coulthard	199.087mph
3	M Webber	198.466mph

Best sectors – Qualifying

Sec 1	F Massa	21.285s
Sec 2	S Bourdais	27.842s
Sec 3	H Kovalainen	27.862s

Speed trap – Qualifying

1	A Sutil	196.974mph
2	G Fisichella	196.104mph
3	D Coulthard	195.607mph

Kimi Räikkönen
"The McLarens arrived too fast at the first corner and stopped me from turning in. Before the second pit stop, I caught Kubica but couldn't pass him in the pit stop."

Nick Heidfeld
"The nicest moment for me was when I passed two cars at the same time on lap 4. I was on a one-stop strategy and it wasn't easy to handle the heavy car."

Fernando Alonso
"Winning in Singapore was not expected, but we benefited from special conditions. Today was even better as we won on a circuit that was not supposed to suit us."

Nico Rosberg
"Our start was poor due to a technical problem. I was also heavy with fuel, but could overtake in the first part of the race, driving one qualifying lap after another."

David Coulthard
"I went inside Bourdais into Turn 1. Piquet was in front of us and I found myself between them. As I accelerated out of Turn 2, whatever damage was done let go"

Jarno Trulli
"I was hoping we could make the podium. We've been competitive and the car was good, but the low temperatures didn't help. That made that the car unbalanced."

Felipe Massa
"I got away well, passing Alonso and Kovalainen. Then Hamilton braked too late and I was sandwiched. The duel with Hamilton that followed was hard but fair."

Robert Kubica
"My clutch slipped, so Trulli passed me. I took the inside and braked late, and after Turn 2 I was in front. After the stop, Alonso was in front of me and I couldn't match his pace."

Nelson Piquet Jr
"I am very happy with this great result for the team. I had a bit of luck at the start, but after that the car handled well, I was on the pace and I just had to keep pushing."

Kazuki Nakajima
"It was very disappointing to have an accident in the first corner, but I couldn't do anything about it. After the incident, I just tried to do my best for the remainder of the race."

Mark Webber
"After a poor start, I had a good first stint, but had a tricky time on the options in the second stint. Near the end, Felipe was faster, so I knew it would be hard to stay ahead."

Timo Glock
"After Coulthard's crash, I think I drove over debris and I lost the car out of Turn 6. I went over the grass and the car was launched. When I landed, it felt like something broke."

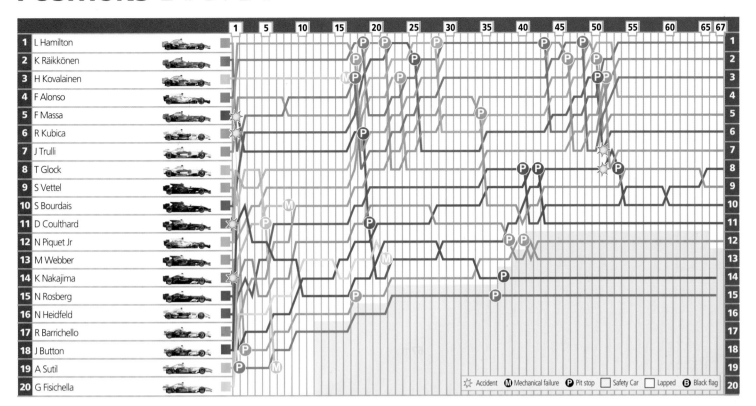

1	L Hamilton	
2	K Räikkönen	
3	H Kovalainen	
4	F Alonso	
5	F Massa	
6	R Kubica	
7	J Trulli	
8	T Glock	
9	S Vettel	
10	S Bourdais	
11	D Coulthard	
12	N Piquet Jr	
13	M Webber	
14	K Nakajima	
15	N Rosberg	
16	N Heidfeld	
17	R Barrichello	
18	J Button	
19	A Sutil	
20	G Fisichella	

☆ Accident Ⓜ Mechanical failure Ⓟ Pit stop ☐ Safety Car ☐ Lapped Ⓑ Black flag

QUALIFYING 3

	Driver	Time
1	L Hamilton	1m18.404s
2	K Räikkönen	1m18.644s
3	H Kovalainen	1m18.821s
4	F Alonso	1m18.852s
5	F Massa	1m18.874s
6	R Kubica	1m18.979s
7	J Trulli	1m19.026s
8	T Glock	1m19.118s
9	S Vettel	1m19.638s
10	S Bourdais	1m20.167s

GRID

	Driver	Time
1	L Hamilton	1m18.404s
2	K Räikkönen	1m18.644s
3	H Kovalainen	1m18.821s
4	F Alonso	1m18.852s
5	F Massa	1m18.874s
6	R Kubica	1m18.979s
7	J Trulli	1m19.026s
8	T Glock	1m19.118s
9	S Vettel	1m19.638s
10	S Bourdais	1m20.167s
11	D Coulthard	1m18.187s
12	N Piquet Jr	1m18.274s
13	M Webber	1m18.354s
14	K Nakajima	1m18.594s
15	N Rosberg	1m18.672s
16	N Heidfeld	1m18.835s
17	R Barrichello	1m18.882s
18	J Button	1m19.100s
19	A Sutil	1m19.163s
20	G Fisichella	1m19.910s

RACE

	Driver	Car	Laps	Time	Avg. mph	Fastest	Stops
1	F Alonso	Renault R28	67	1h30m21.892s	126.033	1m19.101s	2
2	R Kubica	BMW Sauber F1.08	67	1h30m27.175s	125.910	1m19.292s	2
3	K Räikkönen	Ferrari F2008	67	1h30m28.292s	125.884	1m18.995s	2
4	N Piquet Jr	Renault R28	67	1h30m42.462s	125.557	1m19.199s	2
5	J Trulli	Toyota TF108	67	1h30m45.659s	125.483	1m19.524s	2
6	S Vettel	Toro Rosso-Ferrari STR03	67	1h31m01.099s	125.128	1m19.617s	2
7	F Massa	Ferrari F2008	67	1h31m08.050s	124.969	1m18.426s	3
8	M Webber	Red Bull-Renault RB4	67	1h31m12.703s	124.862	1m19.820s	1
9	N Heidfeld	BMW Sauber F1.08	67	1h31m16.012s	124.787	1m19.461s	1
10*	S Bourdais	Toro Rosso-Ferrari STR03	67	1h31m20.977s	124.674	1m19.262s	2
11	N Rosberg	Williams-Toyota FW30	67	1h31m23.988s	124.606	1m19.531s	1
12	L Hamilton	McLaren-Mercedes MP4-23	67	1h31m40.792s	124.225	1m19.560s	3
13	R Barrichello	Honda RA108	66	1h30m54.306s	123.412	1m20.575s	1
14	J Button	Honda RA108	66	1h30m58.093s	123.326	1m20.849s	1
15	K Nakajima	Williams-Toyota FW30	66	1h31m09.438s	123.071	1m20.364s	2
R	G Fisichella	Force India-Ferrari VJM01	21	Gearbox	-	1m21.577s	0
R	H Kovalainen	McLaren-Mercedes MP4-23	16	Engine	-	1m19.258s	0
R	A Sutil	Force India-Ferrari VJM01	8	Tyre	-	1m21.189s	0
R	T Glock	Toyota TF108	6	Suspension	-	1m20.254s	1
R	D Coulthard	Red Bull-Renault RB4	0	Accident	-	-	0

*25S TIME PENALTY ADDED FOR COLLIDING WITH MASSA WHEN LEAVING PITS

CHAMPIONSHIP

	Driver	Pts
1	L Hamilton	84
2	F Massa	79
3	R Kubica	72
4	K Räikkönen	63
5	N Heidfeld	56
6	H Kovalainen	51
7	F Alonso	48
8	S Vettel	30
9	J Trulli	30
10	M Webber	21
11	T Glock	20
12	N Piquet Jr	18
13	N Rosberg	17
14	R Barrichello	11
15	K Nakajima	9
16	D Coulthard	8
17	S Bourdais	4
18	J Button	3

Fastest Lap
F Massa 1m18.426s
(130.150mph) on lap 55

Fastest speed trap
G Fisichella 200.143mph

Slowest speed trap
D Coulthard 161.370mph

Fastest pit stop
1	N Piquet Jr	32.581s
2	S Vettel	32.674s
3	F Massa	32.780s

Constructor

	Constructor	Pts
1	Ferrari	142
2	McLaren-Mercedes	135
3	BMW Sauber	128
4	Renault	66
5	Toyota	50
6	Toro Rosso-Ferrari	34
7	Red Bull-Renault	29
8	Williams-Toyota	26
9	Honda	14

 **Sebastien Bourdais**

"The incident with Massa? I was coming out of the pits. He turned in, but I was on the kerb and there was nowhere else I could go and I was racing him for position."

Jenson Button

"The race began well and I was in the top 10 at the first corner. Sadly going with the option tyre for my first stint didn't work well and I suffered from this in the early laps."

 **Adrian Sutil**

"I had a puncture on my right rear and suddenly on the straight it blew. It was a shame, as we were running 10th and it was feeling really good after a fantastic start."

Lewis Hamilton

"I went inside Kimi. A lot of cars went wide at Turn 1, and I just went a bit wider. On lap 2, Felipe ran wide and I went up the inside, but he tapped me into a spin."

 **Sebastian Vettel**

"At the first corner, I was forced to run wide as there was an incident on the inside. After that, it was hard to fight my way back, but it was great that both of us raced so well."

Rubens Barrichello

"I passed three or four cars on the way to the first corner, but I was then hit from behind by Fisichella, which damaged the rear end of my car and affected the balance."

 **Giancarlo Fisichella**

"The start was fantastic, but in the first corner, cars slowed a lot and I touched Barrichello and damaged my nose. I decided to stay out, but then I had a gearbox problem."

Heikki Kovalainen

"I made a good start and, though I ran wide, I managed to slot in behind Robert and Fernando. I was confident of catching them. Then, suddenly, the engine stopped."

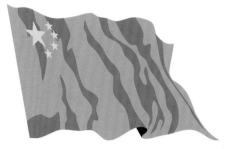

2008 FORMULA 1 SINOPEC CHINESE GRAND PRIX
SHANGHAI

TOTAL CONTROL

The critics were on his back for being too aggressive in Japan, but Lewis Hamilton answered in the best way possible by not putting a foot wrong and dominating

In Japan, Lewis Hamilton's first-lap antics had cost him any chance of scoring points, and subsequently he came under fire for his apparent inability to rein himself in and play a percentage game. Faintly bemused by such criticism, the McLaren driver insisted all weekend in China that his driving would do the talking.

It certainly did, for he dominated qualifying and then the race, leaving the Ferraris gasping for breath in his wake. His fifth victory of the year was the best possible answer, and it gave him a seven-point margin over Felipe Massa to take to the final round at Interlagos.

This truly was a masterful performance by Hamilton, who stated his intentions with his speed in both Friday practice sessions. It was clear that Ferrari didn't have the pace it expected to have in Shanghai. Indeed, Massa was nearly 0.4s off Hamilton in the morning and trailed by over 0.7s in the afternoon, when four other cars got between the Brazilian and the McLaren driver. Of course, there was the usual story of fuel loads and so on, but glum faces in the Ferrari camp told the story.

The team from Maranello bounced back in qualifying, after which Räikkönen and Massa lined up behind Hamilton, who put in a brilliant lap after messing up his first run with a mistake.

After the shenanigans in Japan, anything was possible through Shanghai's tight sequence of corners after the start, but it all passed off harmlessly as Hamilton slotted into the lead ahead of Räikkönen and Massa. And, immediately, the British driver began to edge away, ending any thoughts Ferrari might have entertained about stealing the lead back in the first round of pit stops. Indeed, Massa could not even keep pace with his own team-mate.

By the time Massa pitted on lap 14, Hamilton was over 4s clear of Räikkönen, and Massa was a similar margin behind the Finn. Hamilton and Räikkönen pitted a lap later. Then, through the middle stint, Hamilton continued to edge away, opening up around 9s on Räikkönen before the second round of pit stops.

They followed the same pattern as the first stops, with Massa coming in, then Hamilton and Räikkönen a lap later, McLaren in effect covering the Brazilian and ensuring that Hamilton wasn't exposed to any risks of a safety car coming out and the pitlane closing.

With the final round of pit stops done, it was a cruise to the finish for Hamilton, who went only as fast as he had to, mindful of the fact that, unlike the Ferrari drivers, he had to take his engine to Brazil.

"I was very happy with the balance," said Hamilton, "and I was able to look after my tyres very well and extract the most from them, but also to make them last. The track conditions were great and the car was great, so I just took my time, pushed where I needed to and really managed the gap. For sure, it was great to be able to pull away and open the gap as we did."

In the final stint, the only interest was focused on how long Räikkönen would go before letting Massa past for second place. Räikkönen duly did his duty, slowing down and making no attempt to disguise what he was doing, as Massa accepted his two-point bonus to maximise his title chances.

Massa admitted that the race had been harder than anticipated. "It was a little bit tougher," he reported. "We expected that we would have a slightly stronger pace in the race. I think Lewis showed a great performance Friday, Saturday and Sunday, so there was not much we could have done today. We tried, but he was quicker than us. I think the best position we could finish today was second and third, so we did the best we could achieve, and that's always important."

It was interesting that everyone at Ferrari was pretty open about the situation, and even complimentary. 'Hamilton was quicker on the day', 'he did a better job', that sort of thing. When asked what the main issue was, Massa's race engineer Rob Smedley had a straightforward answer.

"I think it's Lewis and his McLaren, to be honest," said the Brit. "I think he was quite fantastic here, and it was difficult for us to beat him. But, fair play to him, he's done a good job. We made good starts, but he did a better start than he did in Fuji. He got into the first corner first. He led from there and was just better than us. I don't think it was anything to do with the strategy.

"The strategy was always to get the car on pole position but, if the car's not quick enough, then you're never going to do it, are you? We've been to places

OPPOSITE TOP Nick Heidfeld had to overcome a grid penalty en route to fifth place for BMW Sauber

OPPOSITE BOTTOM Sebastien Bourdais speared Jarno Trulli's Toyota into a spin at the first corner

BELOW Timo Glock went for a one-stop strategy and this helped him climb from 12th to seventh

TALKING POINT
AN ENGINE BLOW-UP

The Shanghai paddock was busy.

"The FIA will today open the tender process for the appointment of a third-party supplier of engines and transmission systems to be used by competitors in the 2010, 2011 and 2012 FIA Formula One World Championship," read a brief FIA communiqué issued on Friday.

At Fuji a week earlier, Toyota's John Howett said: "I don't think there has been any discussion between the FIA and teams about a spec engine." He added that should they be introduced; "then we have to decide whether F1 is the right environment to remain in."

Honda's Nick Fry added: "Most of us are not happy with the idea of a standard engine. We are the largest manufacturer of internal combustion engines in the world... But, a prescriptive engine, tightly controlled, that we had the ability to put our brand identity on, would be a very different proposition."

The subject of standard engines and customer cars threatened the unity which the newly formed Formula One Teams Association was determined to maintain to best represent their wishes to the FIA. Such was the desire to maintain that solidarity that FOTA decided to send just its President, Ferrari's Luca di Montezemolo and its Vice President, Howett, to meet Mosley. Subsequently, Ferrari and Toyota put out statements threatening to withdraw from F1.

Many presupposed that Mosley was establishing a negotiating position for cost-cutting initiatives, but Williams co-owner Patrick Head said: "After years of dealing with teams and manufacturers, Max has developed the view that any mechanism of change is going to be painful. I think he's pretty serious.

"It's a hard one, but if you were on the board of a manufacturer and you read in the press the FIA saying that an engine must not be a performance differentiator, and talking about making all the engines level again, then an astute fellow might say 'well, if they are not a differentiator why should we be running engines costing as much as these V8s?' But, if you are a member of a manufacturer F1 team and are being told you have to run a standard-spec engine, you are going to say you don't want it.

"If it comes in, the people who commit the money to those manufacturers will have to decide whether F1 is important enough as a marketing tool. You don't get new races like Singapore often, but we've got Abu Dhabi next year, India in 2011, and it could be hard for a manufacturer to say they are not going to take part with the attention a race like Singapore had."

INSIDE LINE
PATRICK HEAD
**WILLIAMS
DIRECTOR OF ENGINEERING**

"At last year's Chinese GP we had a problem with what gets referred to as micro-graining on the tyres. It was judged for most of practice that we weren't getting enough heat in the tyres, so we were doing hard out-laps. And then it was noticed pretty quickly that our drivers Nico Rosberg and Alex Wurz were getting green (personal best) second- and third-sector times on their out-laps, not their timed laps.

It was realised therefore, that we couldn't be failing to get heat into the tyres, because they were bound to be hotter on the timed lap than they were on the out-lap. We started to twig that it was just the further you went, the more the tyres got into graining.

This year, we've spent a lot of time in testing understanding what it was that caused it, and in the debrief here Nico said that it was one of the few things we could pull out as a success. This year we have not been competitive in Shanghai again, but that's to do with the behaviour of our car in high-speed corners, not the tyres.

Looking at the championship battle, I'm very impressed with Felipe Massa. There has been the odd race, like Silverstone, where people have questioned him, but there's been intense focus and achievement in getting the best out of himself. Who would have said, a couple of years ago, that Massa would be the lead driver in terms of points achieved, when he was up against Kimi Räikkönen in the other car?

I'm not saying that I don't admire Lewis Hamilton. Someone asked how I would have dealt with the situation after Lewis's first corner in the Japanese GP, and I can only say that I'd have done so in the calmest possible manner! We've had somebody – Juan Pablo (Montoya) – who could be sublime or, in the heat of battle, could let the highest level of judgement slip. Lewis is a racer and his instinct is to be first and not to give way. Maybe he might better have accepted not being first out of the first corner. But Lewis will be his own strongest critic and he didn't do a lot wrong here in China!

We've had an up and down year and we're not feeling very pleased with ourselves so, in a way, I'd like to be in a position where I was dealing with a driver that was challenging for first place at the first corner. Williams have challenged for world championship titles on a number of occasions and it's a problem I'd love to have again!"

where we had the best car, we put it on pole position and we won quite easily. Today, we didn't have the best car, or we didn't have the best driver/car combination. If you look at McLaren, Kovalainen was really much slower compared to Lewis.

"Lewis is a very good driver, and you've got to take into account that he was 1s a lap faster than his team-mate on race pace. So, are we dealing with the car, or are we dealing with the driver?"

The other interesting story was Räikkönen's pace relative to Massa's. For the second successive race, Räikkönen outqualified his team-mate, and he did it driving a car with a heavier fuel load, albeit by just a lap. The Finn was much happier after Ferrari changed a few car parts and got it back closer to his liking.

"We were pushing all race," said Smedley. "In the first stint, Felipe wasn't very quick compared to Kimi. In the second stint, he was very good and he made a lot of the gap back. Especially in the pit stops and the out-laps, which are crucial, Felipe made a lot of the gap back. Then, with Kimi on the soft tyre at the end, it grained a little bit. Felipe was now on the hard tyre, and it just went a little bit better for him."

Massa confirmed this: "I had a bit of graining

sometimes during the race, and when the tyre came back it came back in a good way, and I was doing good lap times, reducing the gap. But, for sure, it was not easy in the beginning. The car was not 100% easy at any point all weekend."

In the end, the pace difference wasn't critical, because everyone knew that Räikkönen would eventually do his duty and let Massa by. He wasn't too subtle about it, dropping his lap time by some 2.5s on the lap that he moved over. The manoeuvre drew a chorus of sarcastic boos in the press room, although some people appeared genuinely affronted by the Ferrari strategy, seemingly oblivious to the fact that the FIA long ago made it clear that such tactics are fine when the world title is at stake.

After three crazy races where victory had escaped both McLaren and Ferrari, this was a much more straightforward affair, and frankly it was not the most exciting event of 2008. In fact, it was only the third time thus far that all three drivers on the podium were representatives of the two top teams, with no interlopers taking advantage of trouble ahead.

Fourth place in qualifying, and the race too, went to Fernando Alonso, who followed up his double win with

OPPOSITE It wasn't the greatest of races for Williams, as both Nico Rosberg and Kazuki Nakajima struggled with their tyres

BELOW Lewis Hamilton heads the Ferraris into the hairpin after making a clean getaway. He soon showed them his heels, controlling the race

another solid helping of points. The Spaniard lost out to Heikki Kovalainen at the start, but passed the McLaren driver with a bold move later in the lap. He then had a relatively lonely run to the flag, keeping the Ferraris in his sights. Kovalainen was set for fifth until he had to run almost a whole lap with a flat front tyre. Having dropped to the back of the field, he later retired with a hydraulic problem as his luckless season continued.

It was not a great weekend for BMW Sauber, and Robert Kubica saw his slim title hopes disappear after he managed to qualify only 12th, having struggled to find a balance. His team-mate, Nick Heidfeld, qualified sixth, but was docked three places for impeding David Coulthard in the first qualifying session. From ninth and 11th (Mark Webber went back 10 places for an engine change), the pair moved up to fifth and sixth places, at least earning some useful points.

Timo Glock ran an unusual one-stop strategy for Toyota. His car was a bit of a handful on a marathon 32-lap fuel load, but it paid off as it earned him seventh place and more useful points. Eighth place went to Nelson Piquet Jr, the Brazilian scoring again after a long first stint, and giving himself a better chance of retaining his Renault seat for 2009.

Sebastian Vettel should have been in the points again, but the Scuderia Toro Rosso man finished ninth after a problem in the pits. Meanwhile, his team-mate Sebastien Bourdais spoiled his race when he punted Jarno Trulli into a spin at Turn 1 and lost ground as he ran wide in what was the only incident of note all race. Trulli retired, while Bourdais finished down in 13th.

So, the Chinese GP was not a great spectacle and it reminded us of how spoiled we've been by recent dramas. However, to everyone's relief – with the obvious exception of Hamilton and McLaren – Massa ensured that the title battle went to Interlagos.

"It's never over until it's over," pondered Hamilton. "I'm going to approach Brazil the same as I did this weekend, and I think we'll be even more competitive. So I'm looking forward to driving there."

"Seven points is a difficult amount to claw back," said Massa, "but it's not impossible. That's the most important thing. We need to do what we can, thinking of winning the race. Maybe it's not enough, but I think that's the most important thing we have in our minds. We saw exactly this thing happen last year, and in many other sports, so we'll keep fighting.

"The spirit is to win the race and keep fighting for both championships. That's exactly what I want and what the team wants, to keep up our heads and do the maximum we can."

ABOVE LEFT Fernando Alonso did all he could to keep the Ferraris in his sights, as Renault's late-season charge continued. He finished fourth

LEFT Race winner Hamilton is greeted by his mother Carmen (right) and stepmother Linda after taking a step nearer the title

SNAPSHOT FROM
CHINA

CLOCKWISE FROM RIGHT The Shanghai circuit is state-of-the-art, but the neighbouring houses a little less so; Lewis Hamilton was buoyant all weekend, and with good reason; the race didn't catch everyone's attention; Kazuki Nakajima and David Coulthard meet and greet on the drivers' parade; 'ahem, eyes front'!; the float to transport the drivers on their parade was very conspicuously different to the plain and simple flatbed trucks used elsewhere; Felipe Massa's grid girl; some of the local fans jumped onto the Fernando Alonso bandwagon

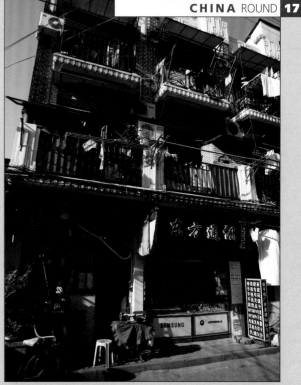

WEEKEND NEWS

■ Force India owner Vijay Mallya took the opportunity of an FIA press conference to confirm that Giancarlo Fisichella and Adrian Sutil would both be staying on at the Silverstone-based team for the 2009 World Championship. The news came as something of a surprise to other team members, not least because the Italian driver had yet to sign his new deal.

■ FIA President Max Mosley dropped a bombshell on the Chinese GP by announcing a tendering process for a standard F1 engine for 2010 onwards. The news gave extra focus to a series of meetings of FOTA team bosses prior to a summit with Mosley in Geneva on the Tuesday after the race.

■ Just before the Chinese GP, the Abu Dhabi GP organisers revealed plans for the new Yas Marina circuit, which had been substantially revised by new project boss Philippe Gurdjian. A large model of the venue was brought to Shanghai so that Formula 1 insiders could take a closer look at the sensational new venue, which is due to host the 2009 season finale.

■ Following the news that the Canadian GP had been dropped from the 2009 World Championship schedule, the FFSA made a surprise announcement that it would no longer be supporting a French GP at Magny-Cours. The news leant further urgency to efforts to find an alternative venue, with Disneyland Paris remaining top of the 'wish list.'

■ Martial arts movie star and local legend Jet Li was a guest of Ferrari in Shanghai, and spent some time in the team's garage. He was invited by his old pal and sometime co-star Michelle Yeoh, who is of course better known in racing circles as the partner of former Ferrari boss Jean Todt.

RACE RESULTS
CHINA
SHANGHAI

RACE DATE October 19th
CIRCUIT LENGTH 3.390 miles
NO. OF LAPS 56
RACE DISTANCE 189.680 miles
WEATHER Overcast and dry, 27°C
TRACK TEMP 30°C
RACE DAY ATTENDANCE 130,000
LAP RECORD Michael Schumacher
1m32.238s, 132.202mph, 2004

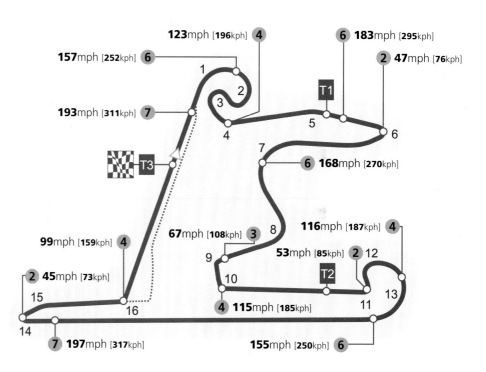

	PRACTICE 1		
	Driver	Time	Laps
1	L Hamilton	1m35.630s	23
2	F Massa	1m36.020s	24
3	K Räikkönen	1m36.052s	23
4	H Kovalainen	1m36.103s	21
5	R Kubica	1m36.507s	25
6	F Alonso	1m36.661s	25
7	N Heidfeld	1m37.040s	23
8	S Bourdais	1m37.070s	32
9	N Piquet Jr	1m37.180s	30
10	S Vettel	1m37.278s	25
11	M Webber	1m37.491s	26
12	J Button	1m37.619s	25
13	K Nakajima	1m37.630s	23
14	D Coulthard	1m37.638s	22
15	N Rosberg	1m37.638s	26
16	T Glock	1m37.664s	29
17	R Barrichello	1m37.827s	28
18	J Trulli	1m38.219s	24
19	A Sutil	1m38.285s	25
20	G Fisichella	1m38.479s	26

	PRACTICE 2		
	Driver	Time	Laps
1	L Hamilton	1m35.750s	33
2	F Alonso	1m36.024s	36
3	N Piquet Jr	1m36.094s	38
4	J Trulli	1m36.159s	32
5	M Webber	1m36.375s	38
6	F Massa	1m36.480s	31
7	S Bourdais	1m36.529s	32
8	K Räikkönen	1m36.542s	34
9	N Heidfeld	1m36.553s	38
10	N Rosberg	1m36.556s	33
11	T Glock	1m36.615s	33
12	R Kubica	1m36.775s	37
13	H Kovalainen	1m36.797s	33
14	D Coulthard	1m36.808s	36
15	S Vettel	1m36.925s	38
16	K Nakajima	1m36.975s	31
17	G Fisichella	1m37.473s	38
18	A Sutil	1m37.617s	33
19	J Button	1m37.800s	37
20	R Barrichello	1m37.904s	36

	PRACTICE 3		
	Driver	Time	Laps
1	N Heidfeld	1m36.061s	17
2	L Hamilton	1m36.135s	15
3	R Kubica	1m36.150s	18
4	H Kovalainen	1m36.324s	16
5	J Trulli	1m36.396s	22
6	N Rosberg	1m36.427s	20
7	S Bourdais	1m36.642s	20
8	D Coulthard	1m36.712s	18
9	K Nakajima	1m36.713s	20
10	N Piquet Jr	1m36.789s	20
11	R Barrichello	1m36.839s	19
12	F Massa	1m36.842s	16
13	K Räikkönen	1m36.901s	15
14	S Vettel	1m36.902s	18
15	J Button	1m36.958s	18
16	F Alonso	1m36.996s	18
17	T Glock	1m37.053s	22
18	M Webber	1m37.566s	22
19	A Sutil	1m37.648s	19
20	G Fisichella	1m37.964s	18

	QUALIFYING 1	
	Driver	Time
1	L Hamilton	1m35.566s
2	H Kovalainen	1m35.623s
3	S Vettel	1m35.752s
4	F Alonso	1m35.769s
5	F Massa	1m35.971s
6	K Räikkönen	1m35.983s
7	N Piquet Jr	1m36.029s
8	J Trulli	1m36.104s
9	T Glock	1m36.210s
10	N Heidfeld	1m36.224s
11	M Webber	1m36.238s
12	S Bourdais	1m36.239s
13	N Rosberg	1m36.434s
14	R Kubica	1m36.503s
15	R Barrichello	1m36.640s
16	D Coulthard	1m36.731s
17	K Nakajima	1m36.863s
18	J Button	1m37.053s
19	A Sutil	1m37.730s
20	G Fisichella	1m37.739s

	QUALIFYING 2	
	Driver	Time
1	L Hamilton	1m34.947s
2	F Massa	1m35.135s
3	H Kovalainen	1m35.216s
4	K Räikkönen	1m35.355s
5	S Vettel	1m35.386s
6	N Heidfeld	1m35.403s
7	F Alonso	1m35.461s
8	S Bourdais	1m35.478s
9	M Webber	1m35.686s
10	J Trulli	1m35.715s
11	N Piquet Jr	1m35.722s
12	R Kubica	1m35.814s
13	T Glock	1m35.937s
14	R Barrichello	1m36.079s
15	N Rosberg	1m36.210s

Best sectors – Practice			Speed trap – Practice			Best sectors – Qualifying			Speed trap – Qualifying	
Sec 1	L Hamilton	25.112s	1	S Vettel	196.726mph	Sec 1	L Hamilton	25.003s	1	S Bourdais	196.353mph
Sec 2	L Hamilton	28.277s	2	K Räikkönen	196.601mph	Sec 2	L Hamilton	28.063s	2	R Kubica	196.291mph
Sec 3	H Kovalainen	42.006s	3	F Massa	196..229mph	Sec 3	F Massa	41.805s	3	N Heidfeld	196.167mph

 Kimi Räikkönen

"At the start and after every tyre change, Hamilton managed to pull away, while when it got near to the pit stops I was able to go a bit quicker, but it was always too late."

Nick Heidfeld

"I gained places at the start and passed Vettel on the outside at Turn 2. He touched the rear of my car, but he told me it wasn't on purpose. Later on, I cut the revs."

 **Fernando Alonso**

"Fourth is the best result that we could have hoped for, so I am extremely satisfied. We had good pace, close to the Ferrari, which is another reason to be pleased."

Nico Rosberg

"My race wasn't good, but it wasn't for lack of trying. We ran a different strategy to Kazuki just to see if we could generate some advantage, but it didn't pay off."

 David Coulthard

"I had a fair start, then tried to keep out of racing too much with the two-stoppers so I wouldn't lose time, but there wasn't much more I could have done from 10th."

 Jarno Trulli

"I was side-by-side with Vettel, but had to give up, as he had the inside line. Then Bourdais hit the right side of my car at the rear and damaged it. He did the same at Spa too."

 Felipe Massa

"This is a great result for the team, less so for me. The race was hard: we were not quick enough to fight Hamilton. Losing two points does not mean that I have lost hope."

Robert Kubica

"After a difficult qualifying, I'm pleased with sixth. I made a place at the start then another two when Trulli and Bourdais touched. The balance was only good on the softs."

Nelson Piquet Jr

"I would have liked to have made more progress, but the result is satisfying and I have scored a point that has helped the team seal fourth in the constructors' series."

Kazuki Nakajima

"It was a good race considering where I started. It was hard work managing a heavy fuel load and hard in the last period when I had to keep quite a few cars behind me."

Mark Webber

"It was going OK until I got up to Nakajima, but it's so difficult to follow cars through the quick sections. The strategy was always going to be difficult with a 10-place penalty."

Timo Glock

"I struggled to warm up the tyres, but then on the car felt good. At the end of the first stint, I had a light car but couldn't make the most of it as I was stuck in traffic."

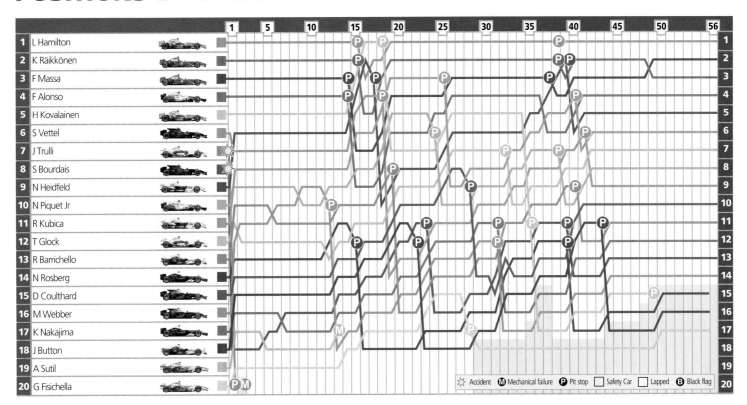

			1	5	10	15	20	25	30	35	40	45	50	56	
1	L Hamilton														1
2	K Räikkönen														2
3	F Massa														3
4	F Alonso														4
5	H Kovalainen														5
6	S Vettel														6
7	J Trulli														7
8	S Bourdais														8
9	N Heidfeld														9
10	N Piquet Jr														10
11	R Kubica														11
12	T Glock														12
13	R Barrichello														13
14	N Rosberg														14
15	D Coulthard														15
16	M Webber														16
17	K Nakajima														17
18	J Button														18
19	A Sutil														19
20	G Fisichella														20

☆ Accident Ⓜ Mechanical failure Ⓟ Pit stop ☐ Safety Car ☐ Lapped Ⓑ Black flag

QUALIFYING 3

	Driver	Time
1	L Hamilton	1m36.303s
2	K Räikkönen	1m36.645s
3	F Massa	1m36.889s
4	F Alonso	1m36.927s
5	H Kovalainen	1m36.930s
6	M Webber	1m37.083s
7	N Heidfeld	1m37.201s
8	S Vettel	1m37.685s
9	J Trulli	1m37.934s
10	S Bourdais	1m38.885s

GRID

	Driver	Time
1	L Hamilton	1m36.303s
2	K Räikkönen	1m36.645s
3	F Massa	1m36.889s
4	F Alonso	1m36.927s
5	H Kovalainen	1m36.930s
6	S Vettel	1m37.685s
7	J Trulli	1m37.934s
8	S Bourdais	1m38.885s
9*	N Heidfeld	1m37.201s
10	N Piquet Jr	1m35.722s
11	R Kubica	1m35.814s
12	T Glock	1m35.937s
13	R Barrichello	1m36.079s
14	N Rosberg	1m36.210s
15	D Coulthard	1m36.731s
16^	M Webber	1m37.083s
17	K Nakajima	1m36.863s
18	J Button	1m37.053s
19	A Sutil	1m37.730s
20	G Fisichella	1m37.739s

* 3-PLACE GRID PENALTY FOR OBSTRUCTION
^ 10-PLACE GRID PENALTY FOR ENGINE CHANGE

RACE

	Driver	Car	Laps	Time	Avg. mph	Fastest	Stops
1	L Hamilton	McLaren-Mercedes MP4-23	56	1h31m57.403s	123.683	1m36.325s	2
2	F Massa	Ferrari F2008	56	1h32m12.328s	123.349	1m36.591s	2
3	K Räikkönen	Ferrari F2008	56	1h32m13.848s	123.319	1m36.483s	2
4	F Alonso	Renault R28	56	1h32m15.773s	123.273	1m36.659s	2
5	N Heidfeld	BMW Sauber F1.08	56	1h32m26.326s	123.038	1m36.498s	2
6	R Kubica	BMW Sauber F1.08	56	1h32m30.622s	122.943	1m36.854s	2
7	T Glock	Toyota TF108	56	1h32m39.125s	122.755	1m36.727s	1
8	N Piquet Jr	Renault R28	56	1h32m54.048s	122.426	1m36.996s	2
9	S Vettel	Toro Rosso-Ferrari STR03	56	1h33m01.742s	122.258	1m37.212s	2
10	D Coulthard	Red Bull-Renault RB4	56	1h33m12.245s	122.028	1m37.753s	1
11	R Barrichello	Honda RA108	56	1h33m22.464s	121.805	1m37.845s	2
12	K Nakajima	Williams-Toyota FW30	56	1h33m28.250s	121.680	1m38.019s	1
13	S Bourdais	Toro Rosso-Ferrari STR03	56	1h33m28.860s	121.667	1m37.452s	2
14	M Webber	Red Bull-Renault RB4	56	1h33m29.825s	121.646	1m37.680s	2
15	N Rosberg	Williams-Toyota FW30	55	1h31m59.552s	121.426	1m37.246s	2
16	J Button	Honda RA108	55	1h32m02.481s	121.362	1m37.773s	2
17	G Fisichella	Force India-Ferrari VJM01	55	1h32m50.681s	120.312	1m38.372s	1
R	H Kovalainen	McLaren-Mercedes MP4-23	49	Hydraulics	-	1m37.302s	2
R	A Sutil	Force India-Ferrari VJM01	13	Gearbox	-	1m39.683s	0
R	J Trulli	Toyota TF108	2	Crash damage	-	2m39.612s	1

CHAMPIONSHIP

	Driver	Pts
1	L Hamilton	94
2	F Massa	87
3	R Kubica	75
4	K Räikkönen	69
5	N Heidfeld	60
6	F Alonso	53
7	H Kovalainen	51
8	S Vettel	30
9	J Trulli	30
10	T Glock	22
11	M Webber	21
12	N Piquet Jr	19
13	N Rosberg	17
14	R Barrichello	11
15	K Nakajima	9
16	D Coulthard	8
17	S Bourdais	4
18	J Button	3

Fastest Lap
L Hamilton 1m36.325s
(126.587mph) on lap 13

Fastest speed trap
H Kovalainen 197.968mph

Slowest speed trap
J Trulli 124.460mph

Fastest pit stop
1	R Kubica	25.730s
2	J Button	26.226s
3	S Bourdais	26.448s

	Constructor	Pts
1	Ferrari	156
2	McLaren-Mercedes	145
3	BMW Sauber	135
4	Renault	72
5	Toyota	52
6	Toro Rosso-Ferrari	34
7	Red Bull-Renault	29
8	Williams-Toyota	26
9	Honda	14

Sebastien Bourdais

"I'm not sure what happened at Turn 1. I guess Trulli didn't see me. I was halfway alongside and he turned in. We touched, he spun and I went really wide and fell to the back."

Jenson Button

"I had some fun overtaking Sutil and Nakajima into the hairpin at the start. From then, I really struggled with the car and from being stuck behind Coulthard."

Adrian Sutil

"Very early on I had a problem, I couldn't select gears anymore and had to pull off just before the main straight and park. It's disappointing not to finish yet again."

Lewis Hamilton

"I made one of my best-ever starts and had perfect balance during the race. I owe so much of that to the guys in the team – both at the track and back home."

 Sebastian Vettel

"I had a reasonably good start, but was surprised by Nick going down the outside. In my first stop, my front left wheel wouldn't come off. I think that cost me a points finish."

 Rubens Barrichello

"I had a great start and great first lap where I overtook three cars to move up to 10th and went flat-out. However, 11th is reflective of what the car is capable of."

Giancarlo Fisichella

"We knew our pace was not good enough, so we tried to find a different solution to gain places. We went for a one-stop strategy, but it was a fairly lonely race for me."

 **Heikki Kovalainen**

"I got past Fernando and almost alongside Felipe. Fernando got me before Turn 14. I had understeer and a puncture, then a problem with the pneumatic system."

FORMULA 1 GRANDE PRÊMIO DO BRASIL 2008
SÃO PAULO

LEWIS AT THE LAST

The 2008 finale could not have been closer. Massa had to win and did just that, but a late flurry of rain came close to derailing Hamilton who came good on the final lap

Just before the start of the Brazilian GP, Bernie Ecclestone was pacing around the Interlagos grid, clearly looking a little anxious. He was presumably hoping that F1 would serve us up a spectacular showdown, especially as we were in the prime-time Sunday evening television slot in Europe.

The F1 ringmaster had no reason to be worried. As, on cue, it rained heavily a few minutes before the start of the race and again a few minutes before the finish, and that contributed to one of the most sensational season climaxes ever seen.

In the end, it was Lewis Hamilton and McLaren who came out on top, but only by the slenderest of margins. If his rival Felipe Massa won, Hamilton had to finish fifth or better but, with just two laps to go, the British driver was demoted to sixth. He then failed to wrestle the place back from Sebastian Vettel, and it looked as though he had fallen at the final hurdle for the second year running. Then, on the entry to the very last corner, both men swept past the struggling dry-shod Toyota of Timo Glock, and Hamilton gained that vital place. It could not have been closer.

Hamilton came to Brazil with a seven-point lead, knowing that Massa had won at Interlagos in 2006

TALKING POINT
GLOCK'S LAST LAP

Timo Glock rubbished conspiracy theories suggesting that he pulled over on the final lap of the Brazilian GP, handing fifth position and the World Championship title to Lewis Hamilton.

The Toyotas of Glock and Jarno Trulli were the only point-scoring cars to remain on dry tyres as light rain started to fall near the end of the race and then, crucially, intensified on the last lap. The rain left Glock and Trulli grappling to keep their cars on the track as their pace dropped off and their lap times increased by more than 16s on that dramatic final lap.

"It was only the last lap where we lost the time," Glock reported. "I actually told the team I wanted to come into the pits to change onto wets, but the pits were blocked and there was no chance to get in. As it worked out, pitting would have made no sense because we would have lost even more time."

Glock was seen trying to talk to Hamilton to find out the outcome of the championship as he passed the McLaren in *parc fermé*, which fuelled some conspiracy theories, but Lewis was too preoccupied replacing his steering wheel.

Glock had been on course to finish fourth going into that final lap and admitted to disappointment at dropping to sixth place when passed by Sebastian Vettel and Hamilton.

"I had no chance to resist the guys on wets because they were just so much quicker," he explained. "I had to stay off the racing line because there was so much tyre rubber on it, which becomes incredibly slippery in the wet. I don't really know how anyone can think that I just pulled over. I was just driving my line where it was safest with dry tyres and if Lewis had not overtaken me in that corner he would have overtaken me on the following straight because there was no way I could go flat-out on the dry tyres.

"I had the car in fourth gear to minimise wheelspin and I was just concentrating on bringing it home. That's all I could do. In that situation, you cannot think about the championship. I was simply driving my own race and I wasn't looking out for Lewis or anybody else. I was too busy trying to keep my car on the track!"

As for the championship outcome, Glock added: "It was decided at the last corner of the last lap, and that's racing. But in reality it was decided by the points Lewis and Felipe scored over 18 races. In the end, both were a bit unlucky at different stages of the year and that, too, is racing. I don't think I decided the championship. It was a racing situation."

and handed victory to title-chasing team-mate Kimi Räikkönen at the same venue last year. This time, Hamilton didn't have to beat either of the Ferraris, as he knew that fifth would be enough, and the McLaren team approached the weekend on the basis that that was the target. It was all about how many other drivers, if any, could sneak between Hamilton and the two red machines. They would be the real opposition.

McLaren spared no effort in examining strategies and checking and rechecking every possible reliability concern. Since Hamilton had to carry his Chinese GP engine into this meeting, Mercedes built up an identical unit, using parts from the exact same batches, and ran it on a dyno to see how it looked. The prognosis was that there was no need to worry. "We're not going to have any sleepless nights," said team chief Ron Dennis. "There's not much that we haven't provided for."

For Massa, the target was simple. He had to win the race, or assume that if he was running second the only car ahead was likely to be his team-mate, and that they would be able to swap places before the chequered flag. What made life interesting for him was that this was his home race. Indeed, he was the first driver since the 1950 title was settled in Giuseppe Farina's favour at Monza to have a title showdown in his own country.

The burden of expectation on his shoulders was huge but, drawing on his experience of 2006 and 2007, Massa responded in superb style, soaking up the pressure and using it to turbocharge his performance. He took pole position by some margin, ahead of the surprise package of Toyota's Jarno Trulli and his own team-mate Räikkönen. Hamilton could manage only fourth on the grid after taking a more conservative approach than his rival and running a little heavier, although probably not by as much as McLaren insisted. Fourth was enough, of course, but it left him horribly exposed to a first-lap drama.

Such an incident became much more likely as dark

clouds gathered over the grid, although they failed to subdue the crowds chanting Massa's name. Rain had been predicted all week for Sunday, and it finally came some four minutes before the start. A brief, but heavy, shower soaked the circuit, forcing a 10-minute delay so that the teams could switch to wet-weather tyres.

It was a nervous time for all concerned, and when the start came everyone headed into the slippery Turn 1 with no idea of what to expect after a weekend of dry running. Thankfully, the leaders tip-toed through without problem and emerged in the same order, but further back David Coulthard was pushed off by Nico Rosberg into Turn 2, and then collected by

OPPOSITE Felipe Massa leads into Turn 2 from Jarno Trulli, Kimi Räikkönen and Lewis Hamilton in the damp, with just 70 laps to go

ABOVE Räikkönen, an inspired Fisichella, Hamilton, Glock and Bourdais crest Ferra Dura

BELOW Sadly, it was more a case of Wings For One Corner for David Coulthard, who was taken out of his final race by the two Williams racers

INSIDE LINE
DAVID COULTHARD
RED BULL DRIVER

"I was gutted. That's not how I wanted to end my F1 career: out on the first lap... I was cautious in Turn 1, but Rosberg hit me through Turn 2 which spun me, and then Nakajima took off my front corner. I had planned to get to the chequered flag and do some donuts for the crowd – something you normally get fined for! – but it wasn't to be.

The weekend was emotional. In qualifying, it wasn't lost on me that it was the last time I'd run a grand prix car on low fuel against the clock. I was really nervous before the session, like I've never been before. I was actually struggling to breathe and feeling a bit anxious. I so didn't want to go out in the first session, have to climb out and do the walk of shame! At least I got into Q2.

It does seem like yesterday that I started. It's just all over so quickly. People ask me about special moments. Well, there was the Magny-Cours race in 2000 and having to battle past Michael Schumacher. Giving him the finger and the wanker gesture was a bit ridiculous when I knew how small the mirrors were! But there was just so much emotion and passion that went into my drive that day. Then winning Monaco for the second time because it was a proper win, a first-corner-to-flag victory.

Back at Monza in 1994, I remember being told over the radio to move over for Damon Hill. I didn't understand the concept of team orders. No-one had told me about it, and I'm on the radio asking 'why?' Patrick [Head] came on and said firmly, you have to move over.... Well, no! He's not close enough. And of course you come to terms with the fact that there's not really an option. It wasn't the last time...

At McLaren, I had a fantastic opportunity with a good car, but it doesn't take away from the fact that with a little bit more support I think I could have delivered more. Michael [Schumacher] didn't achieve his success working against the team. You need them behind you. It's not bullshit, it's not Nigel Mansell-type complaining, it's a fact that I would be on pole, then Mika would take it and the pit wall would all be up cheering. You're like, well I'm not Ferrari, I'm the other side of your garage... It didn't happen the other way around, for a fact.

Driving apart, it's been fantastic. The travelling and the people I've met have been a real privilege. And I'd like to think I'm leaving with more friends than enemies."

BELOW Sebastian Vettel and Fernando Alonso fight hard over position through Turn 1

OPPOSITE TOP Räikkönen had little to worry about as he cruised to third, simply making sure that he finished ahead of Hamilton

OPPOSITE BOTTOM Lewis Hamilton's final pit stop as the rain returns, and the intermediates are on, but the drama was far from over

the other Williams of Satoru Nakajima. With Nelson Piquet Jr having his own accident as well, the safety car was called for. Coulthard, making the last start of a long and distinguished career, had no choice but to take a frustrated walk back to the pits.

Four laps of yellow-flag running meant that Massa couldn't do anything about extending his lead until the green flew. By then, the track was beginning to dry, and within a couple of laps drivers in the midfield with little to lose began to pit for grooved tyres.

Now the leading runners had to make a big decision, and Massa stayed out as long as possible to avoid any risks, coming in on lap 10. The three guys immediately behind him stayed out one lap too long, as those on dries began to lap quickly. Trulli, Räikkönen and Hamilton came in on lap 11 and emerged to find they'd lost ground, with their earlier stops propelling Sebastian Vettel and Fernando Alonso into second and third. The two men had already shown this year that they know how to take an opportunity, and clearly they were not fazed about getting mixed up with the title battle.

In fact, Hamilton briefly dropped out of magic fifth place he needed, falling to seventh. But Trulli struggled on the dry tyres, and Lewis soon passed the Force India of Giancarlo Fisichella, the Italian having

been the first driver to take dries, diving into the pits at the end of lap 1, just after the safety car picked up the leader and before the pitlane was closed.

Safely back in fifth place, Hamilton was where he wanted to be, but there was little margin for error, as one place lost would mean that it was all over.

The middle part of the race ran without drama, and it was stalemate as Massa held a secure lead. The only point of interest was Vettel dropping out of second place with an early second pit stop, making it clear that he alone was going for three rather than two stops. When he made his third pit stop, the Toro Rosso driver dropped out of the leading bunch, and Hamilton rose to fourth place.

As the finish drew near, the sky again turned grey, and their radar screens told the teams that rain would hit the track before the end of the race. It came around lap 64, with seven laps to go. Instantly, drivers began piling into the pits for rain tyres, and again the top runners had important decisions to make.

On lap 66, Massa stayed out but, behind him, Alonso, Räikkönen and Hamilton all pitted. Massa came in a lap later, but he had enough of a lead to stay well ahead of Alonso and the rest.

However, there was a joker in the pack. Running in seventh place, Glock decided not to pit and instead stayed out on dries. That moved him into fourth place, ahead of Hamilton, putting the McLaren driver 'on the bubble' again. Then the unthinkable happened. With just over two laps to go, Vettel stole that vital fifth place from Hamilton as he struggled with graining tyres on the slippery surface.

And that meant that the World Championship had fallen into Massa's lap. For two desperate laps, Hamilton followed Vettel with no apparent hope of getting by. Could it really go so wrong for him right at the death? But fate had another card to play. The rain

intensified once more with a lap to go, and suddenly Glock's dry tyres were useless. As Hamilton chased Vettel in vain, both men swept past the Toyota on the uphill run to the final turn, and that priceless extra place was in Lewis's hands.

When Massa powered across the finish line in first place, many in the Ferrari camp, including Felipe's family in the garage, thought he had done it, but the timing screens told the story as Hamilton popped back up in that crucial 'P5'. It was an unbelievable way to end a season of drama and intrigue that began in Melbourne way back in March.

"This was one of the toughest races of my life, if not the toughest," panted a drained and stunned Hamilton. "I was shouting 'Do I have it? Do I have it?' on the radio. It was only when I took the chequered flag and got to Turn 1 that the team told me I was World Champion. I was ecstatic."

"We knew Glock was on dry tyres," said McLaren chief Ron Dennis. "We saw the rain coming in on the radar. It came a little later than we anticipated. We just wanted to cover everybody. Glock was the enigma in the whole process, because we were playing a little bit with Vettel. With the two Ferraris and Alonso ahead we had to play with fourth and fifth all through the grand prix, turning the engine down, doing just what we had to do to win the World Championship. The weather could have played a key role. I was asking the weather forecaster 'where's the rain, where's the rain?' It came, and then we saw Glock lose so much time in the middle sector of the last lap, we knew we were going to get him, and we just did what we had to do…"

Almost unnoticed, Alonso took a fine second place, while Räikkönen was a rather low-key third on the day he gave up his world title. Behind Vettel and Hamilton, Glock held on to sixth, ahead of Heikki Kovalainen and Trulli. But all that was pretty academic as the McLaren celebrations kicked into full swing. After a nine-year wait since Mika Häkkinen's 1999 title, Hamilton's success meant a lot to Dennis: "If you look at the statistics, Lewis has scored more points in the past two years than any other driver. He's won more races than any other driver. He's had more podiums than any other driver. He's the youngest World Champion ever. He just keeps delivering. At the end of the day he's just two years into his career, so there's a long way to go."

The consensus was that Hamilton was indeed a worthy World Champion, especially taking his near miss last year into account, but most folk along the length of the pitlane had a lot of sympathy for Massa, who conducted himself with impressive dignity in the light of his crushing disappointment. But the real winner in 2008 was the sport of Formula One, with seven drivers and five teams winning races. Indeed, the only team not to score a podium was Force India, who of course should have been fourth in Monaco with Adrian Sutil.

In 2009, we will have KERS, slick tyres and huge aerodynamic changes to upset the status quo. Until things settle down, we are unlikely to see such a competitive season again.

SNAPSHOT FROM
BRAZIL

CLOCKWISE FROM RIGHT The São Paulo skyline is one of Formula One's most distinctive backdrops; the fans had eyes only for one driver – Felipe Massa; there were certainly other attractions at Interlagos, though; Jenson Button's Honda caught fire when it was parked at the end of the race; Nelson Piquet Jr changed his helmet design to remind the fans that there were other Brazilian drivers in the race, not just Massa; Sebastian Vettel showed he's pretty handy with a football, too; David Coulthard's Red Bull was given a special livery for the Scot's final race, and all the drivers offered their support to the Wings For Life spinal-cord charity

WEEKEND NEWS

- The Brazilian GP trophies were designed by the renowned architect Oscar Niemeyer, who at 100 years old is still active. Based on his designs for the Alvorada Presidential Palace, the trophies were made of renewable materials and the winner's version weighed in at 5kg. "What attracts me is the free and sensual curve," commented the centurion.

- To mark his final grand prix and the imminent birth of his first child, a son, David Coulthard received a small pedal car painted by his team in Red Bull Racing colours, along with a mini DC race suit, boots and helmet. At the drivers' briefing, the FIA race director Charlie Whiting presented David with a mounted traffic cone, reflecting his regular requests for such items to be placed at chicanes.

- Canadians are one of the few nationalities who require a visa to enter Brazil, so Red Bull made sure that the girl who won its Formula Una contest at the Canadian GP was told well in advance that she would need one in order to attend the Brazilian finale. Unfortunately, she arrived at the airport equipped only with a Visa, as in credit card, and thus failed to make it to São Paulo...

- Rubens Barrichello has always liked tinkering with his helmet design, and for his home race the Honda driver used a helmet painted in the orange and yellow colours of his old friend Ingo Hoffman, who raced briefly for the Fittipaldi team in the 1970s. Hoffman had recently retired after a long and successful career in Brazilian stock cars.

- Meanwhile, Barrichello was one of several drivers heading into the weekend not knowing whether they had a job for 2009, along with Nelson Piquet Jr and Sebastien Bourdais. Rubens insisted that he was not ready for retirement, but he was forced to wait for Honda to decide. GP2 star Bruno Senna had been lined up for a test with the team.

RACE RESULTS
BRAZIL
INTERLAGOS

Official Results © [2008]
Formula One Administration Limited,
6 Princes Gate, London, SW7 1QJ.
No reproduction without permission.
All copyright and database rights reserved.

RACE DATE November 2nd
CIRCUIT LENGTH 2.677 miles
NO. OF LAPS 71
RACE DISTANCE 190.067 miles
WEATHER Rain, dry, rain, 30°C
TRACK TEMP 33°C
ATTENDANCE 149,600
LAP RECORD Juan Pablo Montoya, 1m11.473s, 134.837mph, 2004

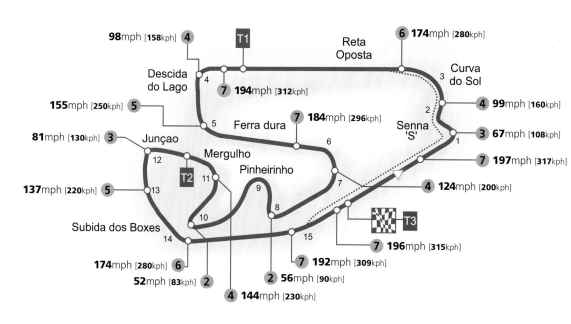

PRACTICE 1

	Driver	Time	Laps
1	F Massa	1m12.305s	24
2	L Hamilton	1m12.495s	23
3	K Räikkönen	1m12.507s	18
4	R Kubica	1m12.874s	24
5	H Kovalainen	1m12.925s	20
6	F Alonso	1m13.061s	25
7	M Webber	1m13.298s	24
8	N Piquet Jr	1m13.378s	39
9	N Heidfeld	1m13.426s	28
10	T Glock	1m13.466s	33
11	J Trulli	1m13.600s	24
12	N Rosberg	1m13.621s	23
13	S Bourdais	1m13.649s	30
14	R Barrichello	1m13.676s	28
15	J Button	1m13.766s	13
16	K Nakajima	1m13.806s	24
17	S Vettel	1m13.836s	30
18	D Coulthard	1m13.861s	19
19	A Sutil	1m14.704s	21
20	G Fisichella	1m14.821s	21

PRACTICE 2

	Driver	Time	Laps
1	F Alonso	1m12.296s	43
2	F Massa	1m12.353s	41
3	J Trulli	1m12.435s	44
4	K Räikkönen	1m12.600s	32
5	M Webber	1m12.650s	45
6	S Vettel	1m12.687s	47
7	N Piquet Jr	1m12.703s	44
8	N Rosberg	1m12.761s	42
9	L Hamilton	1m12.827s	33
10	K Nakajima	1m12.886s	42
11	D Coulthard	1m12.896s	38
12	R Kubica	1m12.971s	48
13	N Heidfeld	1m13.038s	49
14	T Glock	1m13.041s	39
15	H Kovalainen	1m13.213s	37
16	R Barrichello	1m13.221s	39
17	S Bourdais	1m13.273s	41
18	J Button	1m13.341s	49
19	A Sutil	1m13.428s	32
20	G Fisichella	1m13.691s	33

PRACTICE 3

	Driver	Time	Laps
1	F Alonso	1m12.141s	19
2	L Hamilton	1m12.212s	19
3	H Kovalainen	1m12.225s	18
4	F Massa	1m12.312s	17
5	S Vettel	1m12.389s	19
6	N Heidfeld	1m12.402s	19
7	S Bourdais	1m12.426s	18
8	M Webber	1m12.453s	18
9	N Piquet Jr	1m12.457s	24
10	J Trulli	1m12.457s	19
11	N Rosberg	1m12.625s	16
12	K Räikkönen	1m12.698s	18
13	T Glock	1m12.712s	22
14	R Kubica	1m12.971s	22
15	K Nakajima	1m13.054s	19
16	D Coulthard	1m13.058s	22
17	R Barrichello	1m13.135s	24
18	J Button	1m13.278s	23
19	G Fisichella	1m13.460s	22
20	A Sutil	1m13.680s	22

QUALIFYING 1

	Driver	Time
1	F Massa	1m11.830s
2	K Räikkönen	1m12.083s
3	L Hamilton	1m12.213s
4	F Alonso	1m12.214s
5	T Glock	1m12.223s
6	J Trulli	1m12.226s
7	N Piquet Jr	1m12.348s
8	H Kovalainen	1m12.366s
9	N Heidfeld	1m12.371s
10	R Kubica	1m12.381s
11	S Vettel	1m12.390s
12	M Webber	1m12.409s
13	S Bourdais	1m12.498s
14	R Barrichello	1m12.548s
15	D Coulthard	1m12.690s
16	K Nakajima	1m12.800s
17	J Button	1m12.810s
18	N Rosberg	1m13.002s
19	G Fisichella	1m13.426s
20	A Sutil	1m13.508s

QUALIFYING 2

	Driver	Time
1	H Kovalainen	1m11.768s
2	S Vettel	1m11.845s
3	L Hamilton	1m11.856s
4	F Massa	1m11.875s
5	T Glock	1m11.909s
6	K Räikkönen	1m11.950s
7	N Heidfeld	1m12.026s
8	S Bourdais	1m12.075s
9	F Alonso	1m12.090s
10	J Trulli	1m12.107s
11	N Piquet Jr	1m12.137s
12	M Webber	1m12.289s
13	R Kubica	1m12.300s
14	D Coulthard	1m12.717s
15	R Barrichello	1m13.139s

Best sectors – Practice

Sec 1	L Hamilton	18.162s
Sec 2	J Trulli	36.540s
Sec 3	L Hamilton	17.085s

Speed trap – Practice

1	L Hamilton	194.737mph
2	H Kovalainen	194.613mph
3	F Massa	193.557mph

Best sectors – Qualifying

Sec 1	H Kovalainen	18.061s
Sec 2	T Glock	36.311s
Sec 3	H Kovalainen	17.147s

Speed trap – Qualifying

1	H Kovalainen	194.737mph
2	K Räikkönen	192.003mph
3	L Hamilton	192.003mph

Kimi Räikkönen
"When we went onto wets, I got very close to Alonso, but the team told me to avoid taking risks as Felipe had a chance of winning the title and so I gave up attacking him."

Nick Heidfeld
"My biggest problem was the start. Then I had a few good overtaking moves. Later on, I was behind Webber and tried to fight him, which ruined my tyres."

Fernando Alonso
"I am very happy with second. We were able to take advantage of the conditions and the team made the right decisions, and I managed to keep Räikkönen behind me."

Nico Rosberg
"I am quite pleased with my race. Starting 18th and finishing 12th in such difficult conditions is OK. I drove a good race, had a great start and everything went well."

David Coulthard
"I'm gutted, it's not how I wanted to end my career. I was cautious into Turn 1 and left space, but Rosberg hit me, which spun me, then Nakajima hit my front corner."

Jarno Trulli
"It started to dry, and we went for dry tyres, but I got stuck behind Fisichella and lost a lot of time. When it rained we took the choice to stay on dries and got a point."

Felipe Massa
"We did everything to perfection and almost pulled it off. As I crossed the line, Rob told me that Hamilton had finished fifth and so took the title by one point. Sport is like this."

Robert Kubica
"Losing third in the championship is not great. Unluckily, I started on dry tyres, as we had the wrong data about track conditions. I was then stuck behind Sutil for too long."

Nelson Piquet Jr
"I don't know if I was touched or if I lost control, but I couldn't see that much and I lost the rear of my car in Turn 3. It's really frustrating not to complete my home race."

Kazuki Nakajima
"That was a very disappointing race and pretty much over for me in Turn 1. The car took a lot of damage to the bodywork and the suspension, which compromised my pace a lot."

Mark Webber
"The car was difficult to drive. We had a long middle stint, but the pace wasn't there. We knew some problems we had from practice and tried to cater for those in the race."

Timo Glock
"I was on drys at the end when it was raining and it was impossible on the last lap. I was fighting as hard as I could, but it was so hard to keep the car on the track."

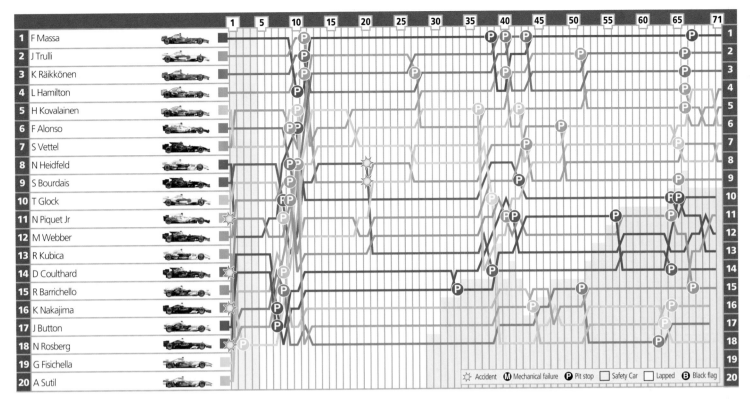

	Driver
1	F Massa
2	J Trulli
3	K Räikkönen
4	L Hamilton
5	H Kovalainen
6	F Alonso
7	S Vettel
8	N Heidfeld
9	S Bourdais
10	T Glock
11	N Piquet Jr
12	M Webber
13	R Kubica
14	D Coulthard
15	R Barrichello
16	K Nakajima
17	J Button
18	N Rosberg
19	G Fisichella
20	A Sutil

☆ Accident   Ⓜ Mechanical failure   Ⓟ Pit stop   ☐ Safety Car   ☐ Lapped   Ⓑ Black flag

QUALIFYING 3

	Driver	Time
1	F Massa	1m12.368s
2	J Trulli	1m12.737s
3	K Räikkönen	1m12.825s
4	L Hamilton	1m12.830s
5	H Kovalainen	1m12.917s
6	F Alonso	1m12.967s
7	S Vettel	1m13.082s
8	N Heidfeld	1m13.297s
9	S Bourdais	1m14.105s
10	T Glock	1m14.230s

GRID

	Driver	Time
1	F Massa	1m12.368s
2	J Trulli	1m12.737s
3	K Räikkönen	1m12.825s
4	L Hamilton	1m12.830s
5	H Kovalainen	1m12.917s
6	F Alonso	1m12.967s
7	S Vettel	1m13.082s
8	N Heidfeld	1m13.297s
9	S Bourdais	1m14.105s
10	T Glock	1m14.230s
11	N Piquet Jr	1m12.137s
12	M Webber	1m12.289s
13	R Kubica	1m12.300s
14	D Coulthard	1m12.717s
15	R Barrichello	1m13.139s
16	K Nakajima	1m12.800s
17	J Button	1m12.810s
18	N Rosberg	1m13.002s
19	G Fisichella	1m13.426s
20	A Sutil	1m13.508s

RACE

	Driver	Car	Laps	Time	Avg. mph	Fastest	Stops
1	F Massa	Ferrari F2008	71	1h34m11.435s	120.947	1m13.736s	3
2	F Alonso	Renault R28	71	1h34m24.733s	120.799	1m14.229s	3
3	K Räikkönen	Ferrari F2008	71	1h34m27.670s	120.737	1m14.117s	3
4	S Vettel	Toro Rosso-Ferrari STR03	71	1h34m49.446s	120.275	1m14.214s	4
5	L Hamilton	McLaren-Mercedes MP4-23	71	1h34m50.342s	120.256	1m14.159s	3
6	T Glock	Toyota TF108	71	1h34m55.803s	120.141	1m14.057s	2
7	H Kovalainen	McLaren-Mercedes MP4-23	71	1h35m06.509s	119.915	1m14.207s	3
8	J Trulli	Toyota TF108	71	1h35m19.898s	119.634	1m14.167s	2
9	M Webber	Red Bull-Renault RB4	71	1h35m31.101s	119.401	1m15.033s	3
10	N Heidfeld	BMW Sauber F1.08	70	1h34m22.761s	119.139	1m14.652s	3
11	R Kubica	BMW Sauber F1.08	70	1h34m48.549s	118.599	1m14.375s	3
12	N Rosberg	Williams-Toyota FW30	70	1h34m51.339s	118.523	1m14.934s	3
13	J Button	Honda RA108	70	1h35m01.806s	118.323	1m14.759s	4
14	S Bourdais	Toro Rosso-Ferrari STR03	70	1h35m05.349s	118.250	1m14.951s	3
15	R Barrichello	Honda RA108	70	1h35m20.589s	117.935	1m15.414s	4
16	A Sutil	Force India-Ferrari VJM01	69	1h34m31.247s	117.261	1m15.773s	3
17	K Nakajima	Williams-Toyota FW30	69	1h34m42.834s	117.022	1m15.865s	3
18	G Fisichella	Force India-Ferrari VJM01	69	1h35m09.395s	116.478	1m15.212s	3
R	N Piquet Jr	Renault R28	0	Collision	-	-	0
R	D Coulthard	Red Bull-Renault RB4	0	Collision	-	-	0

CHAMPIONSHIP

	Driver	Pts
1	L Hamilton	98
2	F Massa	97
3	K Räikkönen	75
4	R Kubica	75
5	F Alonso	61
6	N Heidfeld	60
7	H Kovalainen	53
8	S Vettel	35
9	J Trulli	31
10	T Glock	25
11	M Webber	21
12	N Piquet Jr	19
13	N Rosberg	17
14	R Barrichello	11
15	S Nakajima	9
16	D Coulthard	8
17	S Bourdais	4
18	J Button	3

Fastest Lap
F Massa 1m13.736s
(130.722mph) on lap 36

Fastest speed trap
L Hamilton 196.167mph

Slowest speed trap
D Coulthard 103.272mph

Fastest pit stop
1	S Vettel	26.102s
2	T Glock	26.160s
3	R Kubica	26.379s

	Constructor	Pts
1	Ferrari	172
2	McLaren-Mercedes	151
3	BMW Sauber	135
4	Renault	80
5	Toyota	56
6	Toro Rosso-Ferrari	39
7	Red Bull-Renault	29
8	Williams-Toyota	26
9	Honda	14

Sebastien Bourdais
"Timo and I caught Fisichella, but I couldn't get a good exit out of the final turn. Then Jarno outbraked himself and pushed me towards the grass, and I lost six places."

Jenson Button
"I had a good start, making up three places. We switched to a three-stop run to avoid traffic. We needed to stop again, but fitting extreme-wets didn't pay off for us."

Adrian Sutil
"We gambled at the end with the extreme-wet tyres, as it was very dark and looked as though it would rain very heavily, but the rain just did not arrive soon enough."

Lewis Hamilton
"When it started to drizzle, I didn't want to take risks, but Sebastian got past and I was told I had to get back in front. Then at the very last corner I managed to pass Timo."

Sebastian Vettel
"It was a difficult and chaotic race and it's great to end the season on a high with fourth place. It was great to be racing against Massa, Alonso and Hamilton. Great fun!"

Rubens Barrichello
"When the rain came right at the end, we took a gamble by fitting extreme-wets. That didn't work out for us and I dropped a few places when I was forced to stop again."

Giancarlo Fisichella
"It was a good decision to go to the drys after the safety car came out, even though Turns 1 and 2 were almost undriveable, but in the first stop I had a clutch problem."

Heikki Kovalainen
"The most important news is that Lewis pulled it off. I'll work even harder over the winter and hopefully next year's champion will be on the other side of our garage."

CHAMPIONSHIP RESULTS

DRIVER RESULTS

	Driver	Nationality	Car	ROUND 1 March 16 AUSTRALIAN GP	ROUND 2 March 23 MALAYSIAN GP	ROUND 3 April 6 BAHRAIN GP	ROUND 4 April 27 SPANISH GP	ROUND 5 May 11 TURKISH GP	ROUND 6 May 25 MONACO GP
1	Lewis Hamilton	GBR	McLaren-Mercedes MP4-23	1P	5	13	3	2	1
2	Felipe Massa	BRA	Ferrari F2008	R	RP	1	2	1P	3P
3	Kimi Räikkönen	FIN	Ferrari F2008	8	1	2	1PF	3F	9F
4	Robert Kubica	POL	BMW Sauber F1.08	R	2	3P	4	4	2
5	Fernando Alonso	SPA	Renault R28	4	8	10	R	6	10
6	Nick Heidfeld	GER	BMW Sauber F1.08	2	6F	4	9	5	14
7	Heikki Kovalainen	FIN	McLaren-Mercedes MP4-23	5F	3	5F	R	12	8
8	Sebastian Vettel	GER	Toro Rosso-Ferrari STR02B	R	R	R	R	17	
			Toro Rosso-Ferrari STR03						5
9	Jarno Trulli	ITA	Toyota TF108	R	4	6	8	10	13
10	Timo Glock	GER	Toyota TF108	R	R	9	11	13	12
11	Mark Webber	AUS	Red Bull-Renault RB4	R	7	7	5	7	4
12	Nelson Piquet Jr	BRA	Renault R28	R	11	R	R	15	R
13	Nico Rosberg	GER	Williams-Toyota FW30	3	14	8	R	8	R
14	Rubens Barrichello	BRA	Honda RA108	D	13	11	R	14	6
15	Kazuki Nakajima	JAP	Williams-Toyota FW30	6	17	14	7	R	7
16	David Coulthard	GBR	Red Bull-Renault RB4	R	9	18	12	9	R
17	Sebastien Bourdais	FRA	Toro Rosso-Ferrari STR02B	7	R	15	R	R	
			Toro Rosso-Ferrari STR03						R
18	Jenson Button	GBR	Honda RA108	R	10	R	6	11	11
19	Giancarlo Fisichella	ITA	Force India-Ferrari VJM01	R	12	12	10	R	R
	Adrian Sutil	GER	Force India-Ferrari VJM01	R	R	19	R	16	R
	Takuma Sato	JAP	Super Aguri-Honda SA08	R	16	17	13		
	Anthony Davidson	GBR	Super Aguri-Honda SA08	R	15	16	R		

RACE SCORING

1st	10	POINTS
2nd	8	POINTS
3rd	6	POINTS
4th	5	POINTS
5th	4	POINTS
6th	3	POINTS
7th	2	POINTS
8th	1	POINT

DATA KEY

D	DISQUALIFIED
F	FASTEST LAP
NC	NON-CLASSIFIED
NS	NON-STARTER
P	POLE POSITION
R	RETIRED
W	WITHDRAWN

QUALIFYING HEAD-TO-HEAD

Ferrari
Massa–Räikkönen **12–6**

McLaren-Mercedes
Hamilton–Kovalainen **14–4**

BMW Sauber
Kubica–Heidfeld **13–5**

Renault
Alonso–Piquet Jr **18–0**

Toyota
Trulli–Glock **14–4**

Toro Rosso-Ferrari
Vettel–Bourdais **13–5**

Red Bull-Renault
Webber–Coulthard **16–2**

Williams-Toyota
Rosberg–Nakajima **14–4**

Honda
Barrichello–Button **10–8**

Force India-Ferrari
Fisichella–Sutil **10–8**

Super Aguri-Honda
Davidson–Sato **2–2**

Race results for both drivers, ie. first and second listed as 1/2 with team's best result listed first.

CONSTRUCTOR RESULTS

1	Ferrari
2	McLaren-Mercedes
3	BMW Sauber
4	Renault
5	Toyota
6	Toro Rosso-Ferrari
7	Red Bull-Renault
8	Williams-Toyota
9	Honda
10	Force India-Ferrari
11	Super Aguri-Honda

ROUND 7 June 8 CANADIAN GP	ROUND 8 June 22 FRENCH GP	ROUND 9 July 6 BRITISH GP	ROUND 10 July 20 GERMAN GP	ROUND 11 August 3 HUNGARIAN GP	ROUND 12 August 24 EUROPEAN GP	ROUND 13 September 7 BELGIAN GP	ROUND 14 September 14 ITALIAN GP	ROUND 15 September 28 SINGAPORE GP	ROUND 16 October 12 JAPANESE GP	ROUND 17 October 19 CHINESE GP	ROUND 18 November 2 BRAZILIAN GP	TOTAL POINTS
RP	10	1	1P	5P	2	3P	7	3	12P	1PF	5	98
5	1	13	3	17	1PF	1	6	13P	7F	2	1PF	97
RF	2F	4F	4	3F	R	18F	9F	15F	3	3	3	75
1	5	R	7	8	3	6	3	11	2	6	11	75
R	8	6	11	4	R	4	4	1	1	4	2	61
2	13	2	4F	10	9	2	5	6	9	5	10	60
9	4	5P	5	1	4	10	2	10	R	R	7	53
8	12	R	8	R	6	5	1P	5	6	9	4	35
6	3	7	9	7	5	16	13	R	5	R	8	31
4	11	12	R	2	7	9	11	4	R	7	6	25
12	6	10	R	9	12	8	8	R	8	14	9	21
R	7	R	2	6	11	R	10	R	4	8	R	19
10	16	9	10	14	8	12	14	2	11	15	12	17
7	14	3	R	16	16	R	17	R	13	11	15	11
R	15	8	14	13	15	14	12	8	15	12	17	9
3	9	R	13	11	17	11	16	7	R	10	R	8
13	17	11	12	18	10	7	18	12	10	13	14	4
11	R	R	17	12	13	15	15	9	14	16	13	3
R	18	R	16	15	14	17	R	14	R	17	18	
R	19	R	15	R	R	13	19	R	R	R	16	

ROUND 1 March 16 AUSTRALIAN GP	ROUND 2 March 23 MALAYSIAN GP	ROUND 3 April 6 BAHRAIN GP	ROUND 4 April 27 SPANISH GP	ROUND 5 May 11 TURKISH GP	ROUND 6 May 25 MONACO GP	ROUND 7 June 8 CANADIAN GP	ROUND 8 June 22 FRENCH GP	ROUND 9 July 6 BRITISH GP	ROUND 10 July 20 GERMAN GP	ROUND 11 August 3 HUNGARIAN GP	ROUND 12 August 24 EUROPEAN GP	ROUND 13 September 7 BELGIAN GP	ROUND 14 September 14 ITALIAN GP	ROUND 15 September 28 SINGAPORE GP	ROUND 16 October 12 JAPANESE GP	ROUND 17 October 19 CHINESE GP	ROUND 18 November 2 BRAZILIAN GP	TOTAL POINTS
8/R	1/R	1/2	1/2	1/3	3/9	5/R	1/2	4/13	3/6	3/17	1/R	1/18	6/9	13/15	3/7	2/3	1/3	172
1/5	3/5	5/13	3/R	2/12	1/8	9/R	4/10	1/5	1/5	1/5	2/4	3/10	2/7	3/10	12/R	1/R	5/7	151
2/R	2/6	3/4	4/9	4/5	2/14	1/2	5/13	2/R	4/7	8/10	3/9	2/6	3/5	6/11	2/9	5/6	10/11	135
4/R	8/11	10/R	R/R	6/15	10/R	R/R	7/8	6/R	2/11	4/6	11/R	4/R	4/10	1/R	1/4	4/8	2/R	80
R/R	4/R	6/9	8/11	10/13	12/13	4/6	3/11	7/12	9/R	2/7	5/7	9/16	11/13	4/R	5/R	7/R	6/8	56
7/R	R/R	15/R	R/R	17/R	5/R	8/13	12/17	11/R	8/12	18/R	6/10	5/7	1/18	5/12	6/10	9/13	4/14	39
R/R	7/9	7/18	5/12	7/9	4/R	3/12	6/9	10/R	13/R	9/11	12/17	8/11	8/16	7/R	8/R	10/14	9/R	29
3/6	14/17	8/14	7/R	8/R	7/R	10/R	15/16	8/9	10/14	13/14	8/15	12/14	12/14	2/8	11/15	12/15	12/17	26
D/R	10/13	11/R	6/R	11/14	6/11	7/11	14/R	3/R	17/R	12/16	13/16	15/R	15/17	9/R	13/14	11/16	13/15	14
R/R	12/R	12/19	10/R	16/R	R/R	R/R	18/19	R/R	15/16	15/R	14/R	13/17	19/R	14/R	R/R	17/R	16/18	0
R/R	15/16	16/17	13/R															0

FORMULA ONE STATISTICS

STARTS

269	Rubens Barrichello
256	Riccardo Patrese
250	Michael Schumacher
247	David Coulthard
213	Giancarlo Fisichella
210	Gerhard Berger
208	Andrea de Cesaris
204	Nelson Piquet
201	Jean Alesi
	Jarno Trulli
199	Alain Prost
194	Michele Alboreto
187	Nigel Mansell
180	Ralf Schumacher
176	Graham Hill
175	Jacques Laffite
171	Niki Lauda
165	Jacques Villeneuve
163	Thierry Boutsen
162	Mika Häkkinen
	Johnny Herbert
161	Ayrton Senna
159	Heinz-Harald Frentzen
158	Martin Brundle
	Olivier Panis
154	Jenson Button
152	Nick Heidfeld
	John Watson
149	René Arnoux
147	Eddie Irvine
	Derek Warwick
146	Carlos Reutemann
144	Emerson Fittipaldi
140	Kimi Räikkönen
135	Jean-Pierre Jarier
132	Eddie Cheever
	Clay Regazzoni
128	Mario Andretti
126	Jack Brabham
123	Fernando Alonso
	Ronnie Peterson
122	Mark Webber
119	Pierluigi Martini
116	Damon Hill
	Jacky Ickx
	Alan Jones
114	Keke Rosberg
	Patrick Tambay
112	Denny Hulme
	Jody Scheckter

OTHERS

106	Felipe Massa
93	Takuma Sato
53	Nico Rosberg
40	Robert Kubica
35	Lewis Hamilton
	Heikki Kovalainen
	Adrian Sutil
26	Sebastian Vettel
24	Anthony Davidson
22	Timo Glock
19	Kazuki Nakajima
18	Sébastien Bourdais
	Nelson Piquet Jr

CONSTRUCTORS

776	Ferrari
649	McLaren
568	Williams
490	Lotus
418	Tyrrell
409	Prost (+ Ligier)
394	Brabham
	Toro Rosso (+ Minardi)
383	Arrows
317	Benetton (+ Toleman)
303	Force India (+ Jordan/Midland/Spyker)
270	BMW Sauber
246	Renault
230	March
206	Red Bull (+ Stewart/Jaguar)
197	BRM

OTHERS

123	Toyota
88	Honda
39	Super Aguri

WINS

91	Michael Schumacher
51	Alain Prost
41	Ayrton Senna
31	Nigel Mansell
27	Jackie Stewart
25	Jim Clark
	Niki Lauda
24	Juan Manuel Fangio
23	Nelson Piquet
22	Damon Hill
21	Fernando Alonso
20	Mika Häkkinen
17	Kimi Räikkönen
16	Stirling Moss
14	Jack Brabham
	Emerson Fittipaldi
	Graham Hill
13	Alberto Ascari
	David Coulthard
12	Mario Andretti
	Alan Jones
	Carlos Reutemann
11	Felipe Massa
	Jacques Villeneuve
10	Gerhard Berger
	James Hunt
	Ronnie Peterson
	Jody Scheckter

OTHERS

9	Rubens Barrichello
	Lewis Hamilton
3	Giancarlo Fisichella
1	Jenson Button
	Heikki Kovalainen
	Robert Kubica
	Jarno Trulli
	Sebastian Vettel

CONSTRUCTORS

209	Ferrari
162	McLaren
113	Williams
79	Lotus
35	Brabham
	Renault
27	Benetton
23	Tyrrell
17	BRM
16	Cooper
10	Alfa Romeo
9	Ligier
	Maserati
	Matra
	Mercedes
	Vanwall
4	Jordan
3	Honda
	March
	Wolf
1	BMW Sauber
	Eagle
	Hesketh
	Penske
	Porsche
	Toro Rosso
	Shadow
	Stewart

IN 2008

6	Felipe Massa
5	Lewis Hamilton
2	Fernando Alonso
	Kimi Räikkönen
1	Heikki Kovalainen
	Robert Kubica
	Sebastian Vettel

CONSTRUCTORS

8	Ferrari
6	McLaren
2	Renault
1	BMW Sauber
	Toro Rosso

WINS IN ONE SEASON

13	Michael Schumacher	2004
11	Michael Schumacher	2002
9	Nigel Mansell	1992
	Michael Schumacher	1995
	Michael Schumacher	2000
	Michael Schumacher	2001
8	Mika Häkkinen	1998
	Damon Hill	1996
	Michael Schumacher	1994
	Ayrton Senna	1988
7	Fernando Alonso	2005
	Fernando Alonso	2006
	Jim Clark	1963
	Alain Prost	1984
	Alain Prost	1988
	Alain Prost	1993
	Kimi Räikkönen	2005
	Michael Schumacher	2006
	Ayrton Senna	1991
	Jacques Villeneuve	1997

CONSTRUCTORS

15	Ferrari	2002
	Ferrari	2004
	McLaren	1988
12	McLaren	1984
	Williams	1996
11	Benetton	1995
10	Ferrari	2000
	McLaren	1989
	McLaren	2005
	Williams	1992
	Williams	1993

POLE POSITIONS

68	Michael Schumacher
65	Ayrton Senna
33	Jim Clark
	Alain Prost
32	Nigel Mansell
29	Juan Manuel Fangio
26	Mika Häkkinen
24	Niki Lauda
	Nelson Piquet
20	Damon Hill
18	Mario Andretti
	René Arnoux
17	Jackie Stewart
16	Fernando Alonso
	Stirling Moss
	Kimi Räikkönen
15	Felipe Massa
14	Alberto Ascari
	Lewis Hamilton
	James Hunt
	Ronnie Peterson
13	Rubens Barrichello
	Jack Brabham
	Graham Hill
	Jacky Ickx
	Juan Pablo Montoya
	Jacques Villeneuve
12	Gerhard Berger
	David Coulthard

OTHERS

3	Jenson Button
	Giancarlo Fisichella
	Jarno Trulli
1	Nick Heidfeld
	Heikki Kovlainen
	Robert Kubica
	Sebastian Vettel

CONSTRUCTORS

203	Ferrari
141	McLaren
125	Williams
107	Lotus
50	Renault
39	Brabham
16	Benetton
14	Tyrrell
12	Alfa Romeo
11	BRM
	Cooper
10	Maserati
9	Prost (+ Ligier)
8	Mercedes
7	Vanwall
5	March
4	Matra
3	Shadow
2	Honda
	Jordan
	Lancia
	Toyota
1	BAR
	BMW Sauber
	Jaguar
	Toro Rosso

IN 2008

7	Lewis Hamilton
5	Felipe Massa
2	Kimi Räikkönen
1	Heikki Kovalainen
	Robert Kubica
	Sebastian Vettel

	CONSTRUCTORS
8	Ferrari
	McLaren
1	BMW Sauber
	Toro Rosso

FASTEST LAPS

75	Michael Schumacher
41	Alain Prost
35	Kimi Räikkönen
30	Nigel Mansell
28	Jim Clark
25	Mika Häkkinen
24	Niki Lauda
23	Juan Manuel Fangio
	Nelson Piquet
21	Gerhard Berger
19	Damon Hill
	Stirling Moss
	Ayrton Senna
18	David Coulthard
15	Rubens Barrichello
	Clay Regazzoni
	Jackie Stewart
14	Jacky Ickx
13	Alberto Ascari
	Alan Jones
	Riccardo Patrese
12	René Arnoux
	Jack Brabham
	Juan Pablo Montoya
11	Fernando Alonso
	Felipe Massa
	John Surtees

	OTHERS
3	Lewis Hamilton
2	Giancarlo Fisichella
	Nick Heidfeld
	Heikki Kovalainen
1	Nico Rosberg

	CONSTRUCTORS
217	Ferrari
137	McLaren
129	Williams
71	Lotus
40	Brabham
35	Benetton

	OTHERS
27	Renault
2	BMW Sauber
	Honda

	IN 2008
10	Kimi Räikkönen
2	Nick Heidfeld
	Heikki Kovalainen
	Felipe Massa
1	Lewis Hamilton

	CONSTRUCTORS
13	Ferrari
3	McLaren
2	BMW Sauber

POINTS

(Figures given are for gross tally – ie, including scores that were later dropped.)

1369	Michael Schumacher
798.5	Alain Prost
614	Ayrton Senna
541	Fernando Alonso
535	David Coulthard
531	Kimi Räikkönen
530	Rubens Barrichello
485.5	Nelson Piquet
482	Nigel Mansell
420.5	Niki Lauda
420	Mika Häkkinen
385	Gerhard Berger
360	Damon Hill
	Jackie Stewart

	OTHERS
298	Felipe Massa
267	Giancarlo Fisichella
231	Jenson Button
213	Jarno Trulli
207	Lewis Hamilton
201	Nick Heidfeld
120	Robert Kubica
100	Mark Webber
83	Heikki Kovalainen
44	Takuma Sato
41	Nico Rosberg
	Sebastian Vettel
27	Timo Glock
19	Nelson Piquet Jr
9	Kazuki Nakajima
4	Sebastien Bourdais
1	Adrian Sutil

	CONSTRUCTORS
4021.5	Ferrari
3301.5	McLaren
2571.5	Williams
1352	Lotus
1056	Renault
877.5	Benetton
854	Brabham
617	Tyrrell
468	BMW Sauber
439	BRM
424	Prost (+ Ligier)
333	Cooper
288	Force India (+ Jordan/Midland/Spyker)
219	Toyota
191	Red Bull (+ Stewart/Jaguar)

	OTHERS
154	Honda
86	Toro Rosso (+Minardi)
4	Super Aguri

LAPS LED

5108	Michael Schumacher
2931	Ayrton Senna
2683	Alain Prost
2058	Nigel Mansell
1940	Jim Clark
1918	Jackie Stewart
1633	Nelson Piquet
1590	Niki Lauda
1490	Mika Häkkinen
1363	Damon Hill
1347	Juan Manuel Fangio
1222	Fernando Alonso

	OTHERS
997	Kimi Räikkönen
897	David Coulthard
819	Felipe Massa
729	Rubens Barrichello
616	Lewis Hamilton
209	Giancarlo Fisichella
160	Jarno Trulli
104	Jenson Button
74	Robert Kubica
52	Sebastian Vettel
40	Heikki Kovalainen
24	Nick Heidfeld
13	Nelson Piquet Jr
11	Nico Rosberg
10	Mark Webber
3	Sebastien Bourdais
	Timo Glock

	IN 2008
363	Felipe Massa
294	Lewis Hamilton
178	Kimi Räikkönen
66	Robert Kubica
62	Fernando Alonso
49	Sebastian Vettel
31	Heikki Kovalainen
21	Nick Heidfeld
13	Nelson Piquet Jr
	Jarno Trulli
11	Nico Rosberg
7	Rubens Barrichello
3	Sebastien Bourdais
	Timo Glock
1	David Coulthard

	CONSTRUCTORS
541	Ferrari
325	McLaren
89	BMW Sauber
75	Renault
52	Toro Rosso
16	Toyota
11	Williams
7	Honda
1	Red Bull

MILES LED

14992	Michael Schumacher
8345	Ayrton Senna
7751	Alain Prost
6282	Jim Clark
5905	Nigel Mansell
5789	Juan Manuel Fangio
5692	Jackie Stewart
4820	Nelson Piquet
4475	Mika Häkkinen
4386	Niki Lauda
3958	Stirling Moss
3939	Damon Hill
3667	Alberto Ascari
3631	Fernando Alonso
3191	Kimi Räikkönen

	OTHERS
2617	David Coulthard
2455	Felipe Massa
2185	Rubens Barrichello
1784	Lewis Hamilton
676	Giancarlo Fisichella
413	Jarno Trulli
324	Jenson Button
209	Robert Kubica
185	Sebastian Vettel
123	Heikki Kovalainen
73	Nick Heidfeld
40	Nelson Piquet Jr
35	Nico Rosberg
28	Mark Webber
9	Sebastien Bourdais
8	Timo Glock
6	Takuma Sato

	IN 2008
1090	Felipe Massa
884	Lewis Hamilton
576	Kimi Räikkönen
188	Robert Kubica
181	Fernando Alonso
176	Sebastian Vettel
98	Heikki Kovalainen
60	Nick Heidfeld
40	Nelson Piquet Jr
38	Jarno Trulli
35	Nico Rosberg
18	Rubens Barrichello
9	Sebastien Bourdais
8	Timo Glock
3	David Coulthard

DRIVERS' TITLES

7	Michael Schumacher
5	Juan Manuel Fangio
4	Alain Prost
3	Jack Brabham
	Niki Lauda
	Nelson Piquet
	Ayrton Senna
	Jackie Stewart
2	Fernando Alonso
	Alberto Ascari
	Jim Clark
	Emerson Fittipaldi
	Mika Häkkinen
	Graham Hill
1	Mario Andretti
	Giuseppe Farina
	Lewis Hamilton
	Mike Hawthorn
	Damon Hill
	Phil Hill
	Denny Hulme
	James Hunt
	Alan Jones
	Nigel Mansell
	Kimi Räikkönen
	Jochen Rindt
	Keke Rosberg
	Jody Scheckter
	John Surtees
	Jacques Villeneuve

CONSTRUCTORS' TITLES

16	Ferrari
9	Williams
8	McLaren
7	Lotus
2	Brabham
	Cooper
	Renault
1	Benetton
	BRM
	Matra
	Tyrrell
	Vanwall

NB: Renault stats are based on the team that evolved from Benetton in 2002, and include the stats that have happened since plus those from Renault's first F1 spell from 1977– 85. Likewise, Honda stats from the 1960s are combined with those from the 21st century team that evolved from BAR from the start of 2006.